Great Aircraft Collections of the World

Spirit of St. Louis
N-X-211
RYAN

Great AIRCRAFT COLLECTIONS of the World

Bob Ogden

GALLERY BOOKS
An imprint of W H Smith Publishers Inc
112 Madison Avenue, New York City 10016

This book was devised and produced by
Multimedia Publications (UK) Ltd

Editors: Valerie Passmore and Edward Bunting
Production: Karen Bromley
Design: John and Orna Design

First published in the United States of America 1986 by
Gallery Books, an imprint of W H Smith Publishers Inc.,
112 Madison Avenue, New York, NY 10016

ISBN 0 8317-4066-3

Typeset by Rapidset and Design Limited
Origination by Inline Studios, London
Printed by Cayfosa, Barcelona, Spain

Above: **A North American Valkyrie bomber stands outside the US Air Force Museum in Ohio**

Endpapers: **Sopwith Dolphin replica at Old Rhinebeck Aerodrome, New York. This British fighter first flew in 1917**

Half Title Page: **The Ryan X-13, a vertical-take-off-and-land (VTOL) fighter of 1955, at San Diego Aerospace Museum in California**

Facing Title Page:
Of a number of replicas of the "Spirit of St Louis," in which Charles Lindbergh made the first solo transatlantic flight, this one is based at the Experimental Aircraft Association in Wisconsin. The original is in the National Air and Space Museum in Washington, DC.

Contents

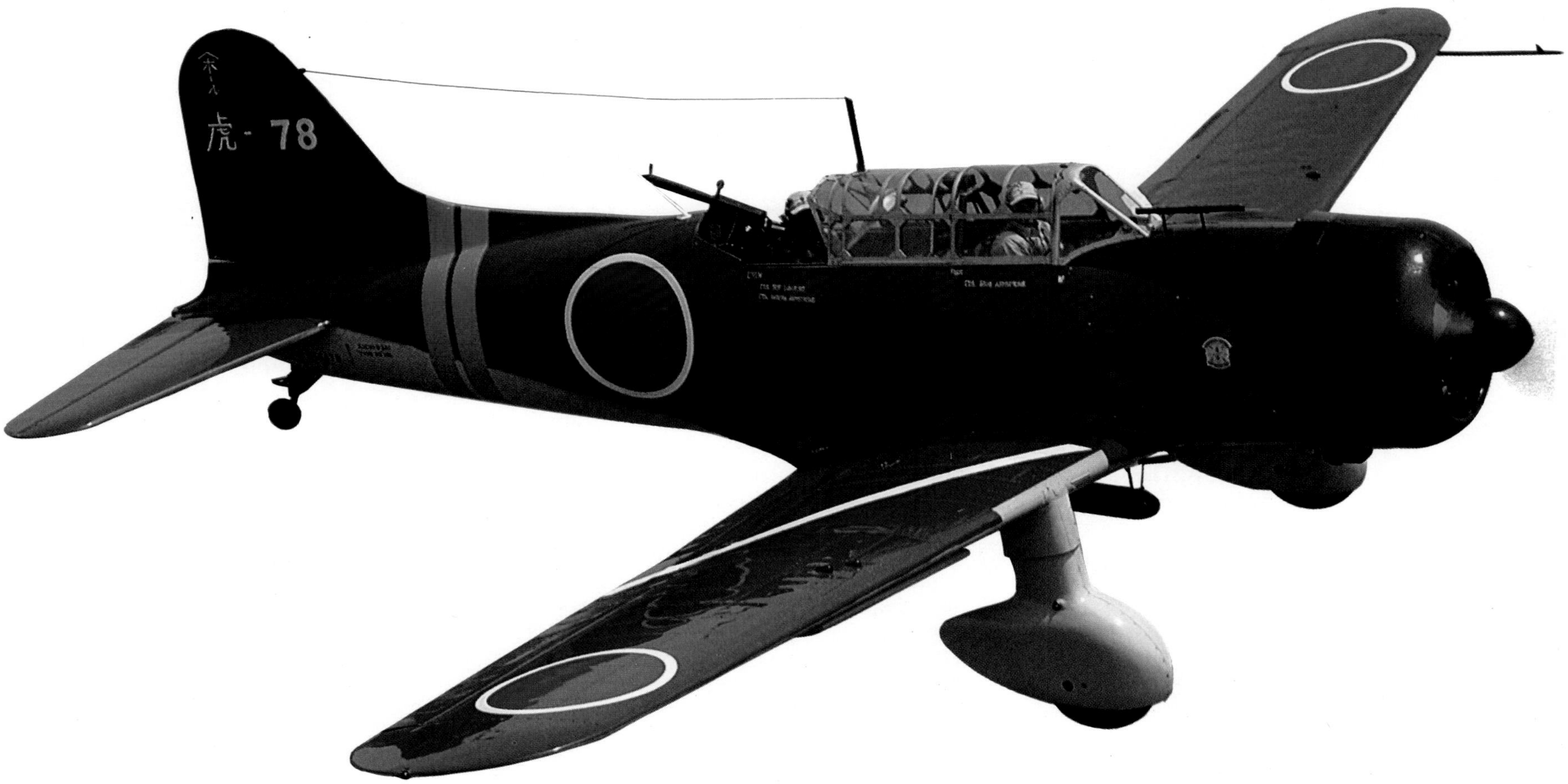

A Vultee Valiant, transformed to look like a Japanese Aichi 'Val' dive bomber for the film 'Tora, Tora, Tora': the aircraft now serves with the Confederate Air Force in Texas

Picture credits

Covers and preliminary pages
Stuart Howe this page, **Jim Koepnick** Facing title page, **Frank B Mormillo** Front cover, **Bob Ogden** Back cover (Both), Copyright/credit page, **John Wegg** Half title page.

Gregory Alegi/GAVS 62 bottom, 63 bottom **Sue Bushell** 98, 99, 169, 170, 171 bottom, 172 **Champlin Fighter Museum** 118, 119 bottom **Dansk Veteranflysamlung** 33 top **Experimental Aircraft Association** 197, 198 top, middle, 199 bottom **FlyPast Magazine** 89-91, 102 (bottom), 103, 111 bottom, 113 **Karl-Fredrik Geust** 85-7, **Marco Gueli/GAVS** 58, 59 bottom, 62 top, 63 top **Peter Hambrook** 13 **Stuart Howe** 20-21, 31, 64, 65, 106, 114, 117, 142, 143, 145, 146, 182-4, **Bernard King** 10, 11, 68, 69 **Kozlekedesi Muzeum, Budapest** 57 bottom **Barry Lewis** 76, 77, 102 (top) **Militaire Luchtvaart Museum** 66, 67 **Frank B Mormillo** 2, 125-7, **Musée de l'air** 44, **Museu Aerospacial, Rio de Janeiro** 19 **Museum of Flight** 193, 194 **NASM** 138 top, bottom, 139 bottom, 141 top **Naval Aviation Museum** 144, **Bob Ogden** 14-15, 22-24, 28-9, 33 bottom, 40-42, 45, 46, 49-55, 70, 71, 73, 75, 79 top and middle, 80, 81, 92-7, 100, 103-5, 107-110, 111 top, 112, 115, 119 top, 121-3, 134-6, 138 middle, 139 top, 140, 141 bottom, 148-65, 167 top, 171 bottom, 173, 186-91, 198 bottom, 199 top **Old Rhinebeck** endpapers, 166-7 bottom **George Pick** 128, 129-131 **Alberto Priori/GAVS** 61 **Robin Ridley** 59 top **Eino Ritaranta** 34-8, 79 bottom **Starliner Aviation Press** 47, 48 **John Wegg** 82, 83, 133 **Western Canada Aviation Museum** 26-7 **Chris Wills** 56, 57 top

Introduction

Only 30 years ago it would have been a simple task to include all the aircraft museums in the world in a book of this size. Since then, interest in the collection and display of aircraft and aeronautical artifacts has increased so greatly that there are now about 700 public museums and collections in the world, of which only about a tenth are covered in this book. Also there are many private collections, not normally available to the public, which hold significant items. The majority of air forces have, if belatedly, realized the importance of their heritage, and their collections are expanding as, despite many restrictions, aircraft are being gathered from all possible sources. The scene is constantly changing and I am sure that between the writing and the publishing of these words, a number of new museums will have opened and others disappeared.

The choice of collections to feature has been a very difficult task and the final selection is my own responsibility. The number of aircraft in the collection is obviously a major factor, and on this criterion alone a number of museums were certain of inclusion. The three greatest aviation museums are generally acknowledged to be the Musée de l'Air in France, the National Air and Space Museum in the US and the United States Air Force Museum. However, other collections are beginning to close the gap.

A recent development has been the establishing of collections of flyable vintage aircraft. The trend was set by the Shuttleworth Collection in England, which was founded in the 1930s, but now there are collections in many countries, notably in the US.

The USAF Museum Program has been of great assistance to many collections, supplying aircraft to base museums and private organizations, mainly in the US but also in other countries. Aircraft are allocated from central stocks and are maintained by the museum or group. Thus a number of relatively modern aircraft which survive open storage are on view. The problem of space for exhibiting the aircraft is another major problem. The size of the aircraft in most cases necessitates a large building if they are to be shown fully assembled, and many museums have raised or are raising vast sums for hangars and exhibition halls.

In the 1960s in the UK a number of preservation societies were formed, many of which now have fairly large collections of aircraft thanks to the dedication of individuals. This development has spread to other countries, both in Europe and the US.

For those who wish to know about all the other museums, I would refer them to my books in the FlyPast Reference Series (Key Publishing, 1 Wothorpe Road, Stamford, Lincolnshire PE9 2JR, England). These books are *British Aviation Museums* (1983 and 1986); *European Aviation Museums* (1985); *US and Canadian Aviation Museums* (1986). In these, all known museums are listed, together with fuller details on their aircraft.

Finally, two points of qualification apply to the data listed throughout this book:

1. The opening times are the latest known and the author and the publishers are not responsible for any errors.
2. The dates given for each aircraft are in many cases approximate. Some types have had long production runs and the actual date of each aircraft may not be available. In USAF aircraft the serial number tells the fiscal year in which the order was placed and this is not necessarily the completion date. This information is included only as a guide to the era in which the aircraft first appeared.

Australia

DRAGE'S AIRWORLD

Wangaratta Airfield, Wangaratta, Victoria
Tel: 57-218-788

Opening times: 10am–5pm daily
Location: about 120 miles (190 km) northeast of Melbourne

Auster J/5G Autocar (1951)
Avro 643 Cadet (1935)
British Aircraft Eagle (1935)
Beech F17D (1939)
Cessna 195 (1948)
Chrislea CH.3 Super Ace (1950)
de Havilland DH 60M Moth (1929), **DH 82A Tiger Moth** (1942), **DH 84 Dragon** (1943), **DH 85 Leopard Moth** (1935), **DH 89A Dragon Rapide** (1942), **DHA 3 Drover** (1950)
Edgar Percival EP.9 (1957)
General Aircraft Genairco (1929)
Klemm L 25 (1931)
Percival D.3 Gull Six (1934)
Rearwin 9000L Sportster (1937)
Stinson SR.8C Reliant (1938)

Joe Drage started an earth-clearing business after World War II with tanks from which the turrets had been removed. With the profits from these ventures he began collecting vintage aircraft. The numbers steadily grew and in 1972 Drage's Historical Aircraft Museum was opened at Wodonga. The collection consisted mainly of classic aircraft but there were a few more modern types and engines, steam engines, tractors and one of the original tanks also on view. In the early 1980s the collection was put up for sale as a going concern, and was bought by the city of Wangaratta as a tourist attraction, with Joe Drage as manager.

The vast majority of the aircraft are maintained in flying condition and in the summer of 1984/85 made the journey by air to their new home. The City Council bought more aircraft to increase the range of the exhibition and a collection of warbirds was planned.

Possibly the rarest aircraft on show is the Genairco biplane which was built at Mascot Airport, Sydney in the early 1930s. Two versions, a three-seat open cockpit model and a four-seat cabin model with the pilot in an open cockpit aft, were produced. The aircraft on show is of the former version and is believed to be the only one left; one of the cabin Genaircos is in the USA.

As there was little action in Australia during World War II a number of vintage aircraft survived. The British Aircraft Eagle, of which none survive in the UK, is one of two left in Australia. The prototype of this low-wing monoplane first flew in 1934 and its clean lines gave it an assured future in air racing and long-distance work. Forty-three were built and the Eagle on show was delivered new to Australia. This rare machine has been rebuilt in Queensland by Greg and Nick Challinor. The Avro Cadet is another type which is rare in Europe with one in the UK, two in Ireland and one in Portugal. The Royal Australian Air Force (RAAF) ordered 34 in 1935, of which a number survived to be sold on the civil market.

De Havilland aircraft have always been popular in Australia and the museum has an interesting selection of types on view. The oldest is a Metal Moth which was delivered to the Civil Aircraft Board in 1930 after more than a year with the de Havilland company in Australia. After a number of owners it was withdrawn from use in 1971 in Bendigo, Victoria. Joe Drage bought the Moth soon afterwards and restored it to flying condition. Two Australian-built Tiger Moths are on view along with a Leopard Moth. The Leopard is one of three complete surviving examples in Australia of the 10 which were delivered to the country in the 1930s. An aircraft which has been on show is the Puss Moth which owner Tim Williams and Henry Labouchere flew from England to Australia in October/November 1984 to celebrate the 50th anniversary of the famous McRobertson Air Race.

In addition to the Moth line de Havilland produced a range of highly successful light transports, which are represented in the collection. The twin-engined Dragon was first flown in late 1932 and a number imported into Australia. The RAAF needed a navigation trainer at the start of World War II so the Dragon was put back into production at Bankstown near Sydney. Eighty-seven were made in Australia, of which 53 survived the rigors of service life to be sold as civil machines. The Dragon Rapide, with sleeker lines and more powerful engines, was a development of the Dragon; over 700 were built between 1934 and 1945. The aircraft at Drage's was used by the RNZAF after the RAF and flew as a civil machine in New Zealand before arriving in Australia in the early 1970s. In the 1940s the Australian de Havilland company designed a Dragon replacement, the three-engined Drover. Twenty were built and the museum's aircraft is one of six survivors.

The remaining aircraft include some American classics such as the Beech Staggerwing, a Rearwin Sportster and a Stinson Reliant. A couple of post-1945 British designs are

VH-UTI

Above
This colorful de Havilland DH 60M Moth was delivered to Australia in 1929; it has been in Joe Drage's collection since 1971

Top Left
The Australian-designed Genairco was built in very small numbers. This is an open-cockpit version which seated three

Bottom Left
The British-built BA Eagle now survives only in Australia and the example at Wangaratta is one of two left

the Chrislea Super Ace and the Edgar Percival EP.9 and one of Australian designers' pre-1939 'greats', a Gull Six, is also on show.

With its future assured Drage's should develop into one of the major collections of flyable vintage civil aircraft in the southern hemisphere.

ROYAL AUSTRALIAN AIR FORCE MUSEUM

RAAF Base, Point Cook, Victoria 3029
Tel: 03-368-1373 or 1443
Opening times: 10am–4pm Wednesday and Sunday
Location: about six miles (10 km) south of Laverton off Pacific Highway 1

Avro 652A Anson V (1942)
Bell 47G (1960)
Bristol 152 Beaufort V (1941)
Commonwealth CA-6 Wackett Trainer (1940), **CA-16 Wirraway** (1942), **CA-22 Winjeel** (1951), **CA-25 Winjeel** (1955)
de Havilland DH 60G Gipsy Moth (1929), **DH 82A Tiger Moth** (1942), **DH 100 Vampire FB.31** (1950), **DH 115 Vampire T.35** (1955)
Douglas DC-3 (C-47B) (1944)
English Electric Canberra B.20 (1954)
Farman MF.11 (1913)
Fokker Dr I (R) (197?)
Gloster Meteor T.7 (1951), **Meteor F.8** (1953)
Government Aircraft Factory Pika (1951)
Hawker Demon (1935)
Hunting-Percival P.84 Jet Provost T.2 (1960)
Lockheed 237 Ventura (PV-1) (1943), **414 Hudson** (1941), **P2V-7 Neptune** (1961)
North American AT-6D Texan (1942), **P-51 Mustang (CAC 17/18 Mk 21)** (1946) **and (Mk 23)** (1947), **F-86F Sabre (CAC 26)** (1954) **and (CAC 27 Mk 31)** (1955)
Percival P.28B Proctor I (1941)
Sikorsky S-51 Dragonfly (1951)
Sopwith Pup (R) (197?)
Supermarine 236 Walrus (1939), **Spitfire** (composite)(?)
Tachikawa Ki-54 (1942)

Military aviation in Australia dates back to 1909 when the government offered a prize of £5000 for a suitable aircraft. No suitable designs were submitted but in 1912 two army officers were sent to England to learn to fly. They returned home in 1913 with five aircraft. The Defence Department purchased 734 acres (297 ha) of land at Point Cook and on March 1, 1914 Lt Eric Harrison made the first flight from the airfield in a Bristol Boxkite. Later the same day Lt H Petre crashed a Deperdussin monoplane on landing, so military flying in Australia got off to a varied start. Since these early days Point Cook has been to the forefront of firstly the Australian Flying Corps and since 1921 the Royal Australian Air Force (RAAF). Today Point Cook houses the RAAF Academy, an officer training school and a flying training school among its units.

An RAAF museum was proposed in July 1949 by the then Chief of Air Staff, Air Marshal George Jones. The first exhibition opened in a hut at Point Cook in 1952 with documents, memorabilia and uniforms. Items were steadily acquired and a second hut added in 1957, a full-time curator being appointed in 1966; in 1971 the collection moved into the old RAAF College headquarters building and in 1975 four more huts were renovated as display galleries. In 1971 it was decided to add aircraft to the museum inventory, since when a varied collection has been assembled from RAAF stocks and other sources. A number of aircraft are on loan from private owners, some in flying condition.

The aircraft collected represent most of the types which have been used by the RAAF since the mid-1950s, including many built in Australia under license, such as an English Electric Canberra built by the Government Aircraft Factory (GAF), de Havilland Vampires built by the local branch and North American Mustangs and Sabres constructed by the Commonwealth Aircraft Corporation (CAC). A rare GAF aircraft is one of the two Pika research monoplanes

Right
A Wackett Trainer, restored to original condition by the manufacturers, on display at Point Cook

Opposite Top
The Commonwealth Winjeel trainer was designed in the late 1940s, and 62 production aircraft were used by the RAAF

Opposite Bottom
A Douglas DC-3, which was one of 124 operated by the RAAF, being held at Point Cook for the proposed National Aviation Museum

built in 1950 as part of a program which led to the Jindivik pilotless target aircraft.

The CAC factory also produced a number of original designs: the CA-1 Wirraway trainer which first flew in 1939 was a development of the North American NA.32 and NA.33, and the Wackett intermediate trainer was designed by Sir Lawrence Wackett. Both these types gave outstanding service in World War II. The firm designed the Winjeel as a Wirraway replacement in the late 1940s and it was used until the mid-1970s.

Probably the rarest aircraft in the collection is a Hawker Demon. In all the RAAF used 64 of the famous Sydney Camm biplane from 1934 to 1942. The type was thought to be extinct but in 1977 the remains of one which had crashed in Tasmania was recovered. Soon after another Demon was found in South Australia and the rebuilds at Point Cook have provided one static and one flyable Demon at the museum.

The museum provides a comprehensive exhibition of the RAAF's aircraft in peace and war.

Belgium

ROYAL ARMY MUSEUM
Musée royale de l'armée
Koninklijk Legermuseum

Parc du Cinquantenaire/Jubelpark 3, B1040 Brussels
Tel: 734-21-57
Opening times: 9–11.45am, 1–4.30pm Tuesday–Sunday
Location: about one mile (2.5km) east of the city center on Route N3 to Louvain, close to the outer ring road

Airspeed AS.40 Oxford (c.1942)
Auster J/1 Autocrat (1946), **AOP.6** (1947)
Aviatik C I (1916)
Avro-Canada CF-100 Canuck Mk 5 (?)
Bataille Triplane (1911)
Blériot XI (1911)
Boeing 707-329 (1959)
Bréguet 905 Fauvette (1961)
Bristol 149 Bolingbroke IVT (1942)
Bücker Bü 181B Bestmann (1942/47)
Caudron G.3 (1914), **C.800** (1945)
Cessna 310 (1958)
Chandellon Helicopter (?)
Dassault MD.450 Ouragan (1951)
de Havilland DH 82A Tiger Moth (1934-44), **DH 89A Dragon Rapide** (1945), **DH 98 Mosquito NF30** (1944), **DH 115 Vampire T11** (1955), **DHC 1 Chipmunk T20** (1952), **DHC 3 Otter (UC-1)** (1959)
DFS 108-14 Schulgleiter SG-38 (c.1942), **Weihe 50** (194?)
Dornier Do 27J-1 (1961)
Douglas DC-3 (1943), **A-26C Invader** (1945)
Fairchild F.24R Argus (UC-61K) (1943/44), **C-119G** (1953)
Farman F.11A-2 (1914)
Farman-Voisin (c.1911)
Fiat G.91R-3 (?)
Fieseler Fi 103 (1944), **Fi 156C-3 Storch** (c.1942)
Fokker Dr I (R) (?)
Fouga CM.170 Magister (1961)
Gloster Meteor F.8 (1951), **Meteor TT.20 (NF.11)** (1952)
Goppingen Go IV Govier (c.1942)
Halberstadt C V (1918)
Hanriot-Dupont HD-1 (1918)
Hawker Hurricane IIC (1942), **Hunter F4** (1956)
Jodel D.9 (196?)
Junkers Ju 52/3m (c.1935)
Kassel 12 (1931)
Kreit & Lambrickx KL-2 (1934)
Livingstone BO-2 Hang-glider (?)
Lockheed T-33A (1955), **F-104G Starfighter** (1963)
LVG C VI (1918)
Mignet HM-290 (c.1948), **HM-293 Pou-du-Ciel** (?)
Miles M.14A Magister (1940), **M.38 Messenger 2A** (1947)
Morane-Saulnier MS.230 (1948), **MS.315** (1946), **MS.500 (Fi 156)** (1946), **MS.880B Rallye** (1970)
Nieuport 17C1 (1917)
Nord N.1002 Pingouin (1948)
North American AT-6D Texan (1941/42), **F-86F Sabre** (1952)
Percival D.2 Gull 4 (1932), **P.31C Proctor 4** (1944), **P.40 Prentice** (1950), **P.44 Proctor 5** (1946), **P.66 Pembroke C.51** (1954), **Piper J-3 Cub (L-4H)** (1943), **J-3 Cub (L-4J)** (1944), **PA-18 Super Cub (L-18C)** (1953)
Republic F-84F Thunderstreak (1952), **RF-84F Thunderflash** (1951), **F-84G Thunderjet** (1951)
Royal Aircraft Factory RE.8 (1917)
RRG Zogling (?)
Rumpler C IV (1917)
SAAB J-35A Draken (c.1959)
SABCA Junior (?), **Poncelet Vivette** (1925)
SAI KZ.III (1947)
Schneider Grunau Baby II (DFS 108-49) (?), **Baby III (DFS 108-66)** (?)
Schreck FBA Type H (1914)
Schleicher Ka-2 Rhonschwalbe (1952)
Sikorsky S.58 (c.1958)
Sopwith F1 Camel (1917), **1½ Strutter** (1916)
SPAD XIII C.1 (1918)
Stampe SV.4B (1940/48), **SV.4C** (1947), **SV.4D** (1959)
Stampe-Renard SR.7B (1954)
Sud Aviation SE.210 Caravelle (1961)
Supermarine 361 Spitfire LF.IXC (1943), **379 Spitfire F.XIV** (1944)
Tipsy S.2 (1938)
Voisin LA5-B (1915)
Westland Lysander III (c.1942)

This trainer is the SR.7B, designed as a replacement for the SV.4, but never put into production

The vast Palais du Cinquantenaire, built in 1881 to celebrate the 50th anniversary of Belgium's independence, now houses a number of museums including the Royal Army Museum. In order to reach the aeronautical section the visitor has to pass through a section of the military history exhibition which is virtually a museum within a museum. Until the early 1970s some 15 aircraft hung from the ceiling of the military exhibition, the majority being World War I types which had been suspended for almost 50 years. In the jousting hall of the palace a similar number of aircraft from the 1940s and 1950s were stored and could be seen only by appointment.

Although there was potential for a major aeronautical museum the setting up of the collection came about almost by chance. In the late 1960s Colonel Mike Terlinden and WO Jean Booten were in a military hospital recovering from air crashes and after many hours of discussions they decided to approach the military authorities who ran the Army Museum. The Chief of Staff of the Belgian Air Force supported the idea and Jean Booten was allocated to the museum to organize and develop the section.

The Hanriot HD.1, designed by Pierre Dupont, was used by the Belgian Air Force in World War I. This example carries the colors of 9 Squadron

The aircraft were to be displayed in the great jousting hall which has a raised gallery round all four sides. Work on the restoration and alteration of the hall began in 1969. The aircraft in the main building, which were all in need of restoration, were steadily moved to the hall and now the museum has one of the finest collections of 1914-18 aircraft in the world.

A volunteer group, the AELR, was set up and became responsible for all aspects of the museum with Jean Booten directing. The air force has helped in the transport of aircraft, technical aspects and the supply of parts, and seconding serving personnel to the museum to assist with specific tasks. Fund-raising is by the AELR sales desk which sells books and photographs to aid the restoration program.

Soon after the setting up of the aeronautical section a large number of aircraft were acquired from all over Belgium, as all rumors of derelict aircraft were followed up and the hall became full. Acquisition slowed down as there is obviously a limit to the number of available machines and the museum entered a period of consolidation, with many duplicate aircraft moved to storage and a number of significant exchanges made with museums in other countries. The collection today numbers about 140 aircraft, with about 80 in the main hall. The restored machines have been finished to a high standard and much research has gone in to presenting them in authentic color schemes and markings.

There are a few relics from before 1914, including the fuselage and tail surfaces of the triplane built by César Bataille in 1908 and the wings from Jan Olieslager's Blériot XI plus a number of small items from other aircraft.

The World War I aircraft from three countries exhibited in one of the upper galleries present a fascinating insight into the development of the fighting machine over a short period. An excellent Caudron G.3 was exchanged with the French Musée de l'Air and the spindly structure of this biplane is in contrast to the later aircraft of World War I. The G.3 first flew in 1913 and over 3000 were built: they were among the initial equipment of many of the embryo air forces of Europe and South America. The type was built under license in Belgium and served with the air force in the early 1920s. The airframe making the journey to Paris was a German LVG CVI which had been found along with the

The true identity of this Halberstadt C V is not known, since it has carried two different serials in recent years

fuselage of a SPAD XIII in a basement at Charleroi University. Since the museum already had one of the two LVG CVIs known at the time the exchange benefited both collections. The complete LVG was one of several German aircraft which had been captured in World War I and later used for training at the flying school at Asch – the Halberstadt C V came from this source and both aircraft were presented to the military museum in the early 1920s. In addition to these two German aircraft the museum has one of the two remaining Rumpler C IVs and the sole Aviatik CI. Both these priceless relics were found in very poor condition and restored.

The Belgian Air Corps in its early days used almost entirely French and British equipment and the rest of the collection of this period are from the two countries. The names of Farman, Hanriot, Nieuport, SPAD and Voisin were synonymous with the excellent French aircraft which served with many forces. The Belgian Army acquired models from all these famous designers, all of which are represented in the collection. Three British types show aircraft used in this formative period: the RE.8 is believed to be from a batch built at the Coventry Ordnance Works, the Sopwith Camel was built by Clayton and Shuttleworth at Lincoln and the Sopwith 1½ Strutter is probably French-constructed.

In the 1920s there was little development of military aircraft but some interesting civil types were designed and flown. At the airfield of Evere the SABCA firm was established. The head of its woodworking section, Paul Poncelet, in 1923 built a powered glider, the Castar, which won the trials at Verville. For the 1925 'World Championship' light plane trials Poncelet was again first with the Vivette, which was flown until 1931 before going to the Army Museum. The 1934 Kreit KL-2 built at Diest by a Belgian Air Force pilot and powered by a 35 hp Anzani was presented to the museum after the death of the designer in a crash in 1937.

The names that are perhaps most associated with Belgian designs are those of Jean Stampe and Ernest Oscar Tips. Stampe formed a flying school at Antwerp in 1922 in conjunction with Maurice Vertongen and they employed Alfred Renard as designer. Over 100 of four main types were produced before Renard left to form his own company. His place was taken by George Ivanow and soon one of the classic biplane trainers of all times, the Stampe SV.4, appeared. A small number were produced before the outbreak of World War II, including some of the SV.4B model with swept wings with rounded tips. When Germany invaded Belgium the third production SV.4B was hidden but on July 5, 1941 it was used by two air force pilots, Michel Donnet and Leon Divoy, for a daring escape to England. After an initial period of exhibition in England the Stampe was used by the RAF until the end of the conflict. A similar aircraft is on display in the museum.

The SV.4 was built in considerable numbers in France in World War II and others were constructed in Algeria. Renard rejoined Stampe in 1947 and the SV.4 was put back into production for the air force. On show are a number of variants of this design plus a low-wing SR.7 Monitor. Tips was the chief of Avions Fairey, set up at Gosselies to produce the Fox and Firefly under license. The new company joined with SEGA, of which Tips was one of the founders. Tips also produced aircraft to his own designs: the first, the single-seat S, flew in 1936 and later in the year the improved S.2 appeared. Twenty were constructed in Belgium and another nine made by Aero Engines near Bristol. Three of the Belgian S.2s came to England and the aircraft on show, which was stored during the war, was presented by the Fairey Company to the museum in 1949 and painted in the markings of the prototype S.

One interesting civil aircraft of the 1930s is a rare Percival D.2 Gull. Built by the Parnall company, it crashed in December 1934 according to British records. The aircraft was obtained by the museum in 1975 following a letter from a man in Waterloo in Belgium who said that he had what he believed to be a Percival Proctor in store but which turned out to be the oldest surviving Gull. According to the man at Waterloo it had been there for about 30 years so did it crash in Belgium?

After the end of World War II the Belgian air force was equipped with mainly British types, a number of which were given to the Army Museum in the 1950s as they were withdrawn from service. Such classics as two Spitfires, a Hurricane, a Mosquito, a Magister, an Oxford and a number of Tiger Moths are from this period. When the air force turned to jet fighters the Gloster Meteor and later the Hawker Hunter were produced under license in Belgium and the Netherlands. Both these famous types are represented in the museum. With the advent of NATO US aircraft dominated many European air forces and naturally the collection features a number of these.

Civil aircraft which have reached the end of their useful lives have been collected from a number of airfields and exchanges have added to the range of exhibits. The museum obtained many Tiger Moths from the state gliding schools and SABENA, some of which have been exchanged for classic French designs such as Morane-Saulnier MS.315s. Some Stampe SV.4s were exchanged in the US for a Bristol Bolingbroke and a Westland Lysander. A Junkers Ju 52 has been obtained from the Portuguese Air Force Museum.

This collection with its wide range of aircraft covering the whole period of powered flight is one of the most significant exhibitions in the world and is a credit to a mostly volunteer force with military backing.

Twenty-two RE.8s were supplied to Belgium and modified to take the 180 hp Hispano-Suiza engine. This aircraft carries the markings of 6 Squadron

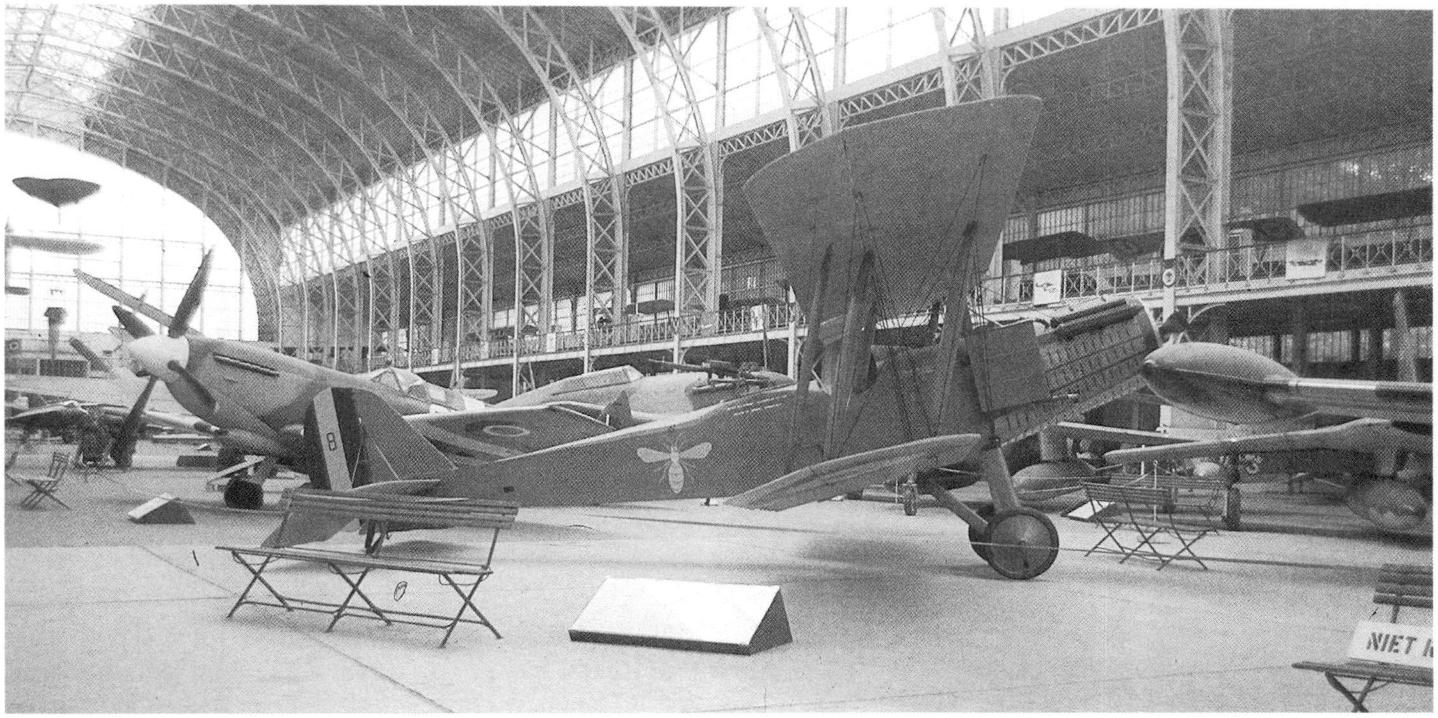

Brazil

AEROSPACE MUSEUM
Museu Aeroespacial

Avenue Mal Fontenelle, Campo dos Afonsos, Rio de Janeiro 21740
Tel: 21-359-8880
Opening times: 9am–3pm Tuesday–Friday, 10am–4pm Saturday–Sunday
Location: about 18 miles (27km) west of the city center

Aerotec T-23 (1965)
Beech D17S (UC-43) (1944), **B18S Kansas (AT-11)** (1942), **D18S** (1948)
Bell 47J (H-13J) (1958)
Boeing 299 Fortress (B-17G) (1944)
Boeing-Stearman A75 Kaydet (1940), **A76** (1937)
Bücker Bü 131B Jungmann (1938)
Caudron G3 (1916)
Cessna 318 (T-37C) (1967)
Consolidated 28 Canso (PBY-5A) (1943)
Curtiss 51 Fledgling (1929), **87 Warhawk (P-40N)** (1944)
Douglas A-20K Havoc (1944), **A-26C Invader** (1941), **DC-3 (C-47B)** (1943)
de Havilland DH 82A Tiger Moth (1935)
EAY CAP-4 (1941)
Embraer EMB-100 Bandeirante (1968), **EMB-200** (197?), **EMB-312 Tucano** (1983)
Fairchild C-82A Packet (1945), **C-119G Flying Boxcar** (1951), **F.24R6** (1941), **M.62 Cornell (PT-19B)** (1942)
Focke-Wulf Fw 44J Stieglitz (1936), **Fw 58 Weihe** (1941)
Fokker S.11 Instructor (1957), **S.12** (1960)
Gloster Meteor T.7 (1953), **Meteor F.8** (1960)
Grumman G.44 Widgeon (J4F-2) (1942), **G.64 Albatross (SA-16A)** (1949), **G.89 Tracker (S2F-1)** (1954)
Lippisch Hols-der-Teufel (1942)
Lockheed 18 Lodestar (C-60A) (1942), **F-80C Shooting Star** (1949), **T-33A** (1953), **P2V-5 Neptune** (1951)
Morane-Saulnier MS.760 Paris (1958)
Muniz M-7 (1938)
Neiva L-6 (1954), **YT-25** (1966), **L-42** (1967)
Nieuport 21 (R) (?)
Niess 5FG (195?)
North American B-25J Mitchell (1944), **AT-6D Texan** (1942, 1954), **T-28A Trojan** (1950)
Pilatus P.3-03 (1957)
Republic P-47D Thunderbolt (1945)
Santos-Dumont 14bis (R) (1973), **20 Demoiselle (R)** (1973)
Stinson SR.10D Reliant (1941)
Vickers V.789D Viscount (1957)
Vultee BT-15 Valiant (1941)
Waco CSO (1932), **CJC** (1934), **CPF-5** (1935)

As in other South American nations, the aeronautical history of Brazil is varied, reflecting the turbulent political state of the continent. The Museu Aeroespacial at the airfield of Campo dos Afonsos some 18 miles (27 km) outside the capital city, Rio de Janeiro, has become one of the major collections in the last decade and exhibits aircraft from a number of countries.

The Brazilian pioneer Alberto Santos Dumont became famous in the first decade of the 20th century and put the name of his country firmly on the aviation map although most of his work was done in France. He arrived in Europe in 1898 and initially devoted his energies to the construction of airships before turning his attention to aircraft. His first machine was the 14bis, which was so named because it carried out its initial tests suspended under his balloon, No. 14. The 14bis made a series of hops at Bagatelle in late 1906 and these were the first powered flights in Europe with the aircraft taking off under its own power. The Demoiselle, which was the first really ultralight aircraft, appeared in November 1907 and by 1909 there were ambitious plans to construct large numbers, but only around 30 were actually completed. The museum staff have built replicas of these two types as they were a significant step in the development of interest in aviation in the country.

With this inspiration it was only a short time before aviation came to Brazil and a naval seaplane school was set up in 1913 with the army following the next year. One of the earliest military bases in the country was Campo dos Afonsos which became the site of the Air Academy in 1914 and is thus an appropriate site for the museum. The museum was officially set up in 1974 and opened for the first time on October 18, 1976. Located in the southwestern corner of the base, the collection is housed in a two-story building and five hangars.

In the exhibition building are shown the nine oldest aircraft in the collection along with other displays. There are rooms devoted to civil aviation, naval aviation, armaments and engines on the ground floor with one aircraft on show in the first two exhibitions. The second floor has an art gallery and four rooms with displays relating to Brazilian aviation with special reference to the aviation pioneers of the country. The aircraft on show in the five hangars are arranged chronologically with the exception of Hangar 1 which has a display of Brazilian-designed machines.

Many important relics have been donated to the museum including a propeller from the Graf Zeppelin. This was removed from the airship in Rio when an engine vibration developed, and was spirited away by one of the German engineers, who subsequently took up residence in the country. There is also a propeller from one of the twelve Savoia-Marchetti S.55X twin-hulled flying boats which took part in the famous formation flights of the early 1930s. In the latter part of World War II the 1st Fighter Group of the Brazilian Air Force fought in Northern Italy using

P-47D Thunderbolts, and there is an exhibition devoted to their exploits in the hangar area.

The earliest aircraft on show is a Curtiss Fledgling painted to represent the machine which inaugurated the Army Air Mail service in 1931. The prototype of this biplane design flew in 1928 and over 200 were built for the US forces and the civil market. The aircraft on show is one of the 109 examples built for the Curtiss Flying Service. Purchased in the US, the Fledgling was completely rebuilt to the Brazilian army configuration and flew into the museum after rebuild.

The mail services were taken over in 1932 by Waco CPF-5s and fortunately one of these has survived and is exhibited in original configuration. Most of the collection's biplanes are in the main hall: a comparatively new addition is a Caudron G.3 built in 1916, one of a pair which were restored in France in the 1960s by Jean Salis. This aircraft was a familiar sight at air shows in Europe before its move across the Atlantic. Another French type which was used in Brazil between 1921 and 1930 for training was the Nieuport 21E1 and a replica is on show. The museum has in fact constructed a number of replica aircraft to fill gaps in their collection.

Two Stearman aircraft are in the main hall: the 75 is a well-known type, vast numbers having served with the US and other forces and many survivors still flying. The A76C-3, which was used for armament training by the Brazilian Air Force, and which has a gun mounted in the rear cockpit and bomb racks under the center section, is the only survivor of its type. Brazil has always used aircraft from a number of countries, and the UK is represented by a Tiger Moth. The British army and navy ordered 40 DH 60T Moth Trainers in 1932 after the type had won a competition against six other aircraft. It was only natural that Brazil should order the Tiger Moth when it became available.

In recent years Brazil has made a name for itself in aviation with the Embraer company, but the country has a long history of aircraft manufacture, producing types of indigenous design and foreign models under license. The first Brazilian design to enter production was the Muniz M-7 biplane constructed at Afonsos in the late 1930s. Only 11 were delivered to the army, and the type used a Gipsy Major engine.

In the hangar devoted to the Brazilian industry, other types include the CAP-4 of which almost 800 were built, the first prototype Bandeirante, a type which has achieved notable success on the world markets, two Neiva prototypes and a production L-6. A tour through the other hangars will show the visitor training, fighting, communications, bombing and transport aircraft from six countries spanning over four decades.

One of the aircraft on show, the Douglas A-20K Havoc, which is in pristine condition, is the result of a four-year rebuild. The aircraft was found in derelict condition in a children's playground, and is now in the state in which it was flown by the 1st/10th Grupo de Aviacão in 1952. One current occupant of the workshops is the sole remaining Focke-Wulf Weihe. Considerable numbers of this light twin were built in Germany in the late 1930s and early 1940s, with license production in Brazil and Hungary. The survivor is one of a batch of 15 built in Brazil by the Oficinas Gerais da Aviacão Naval for the naval air arm. When the Força Aerea Brasileira was formed in 1940 by combining the army and navy air elements the Weihe transferred to the new force.

The Waco CPF-5, restored and painted in the colors it wore in the late 1930s

Far Left

This Curtiss Fledgling has been restored to represent the aircraft which flew the first Army Air Mail Service in 1931

Left

The Embraer Bandeirante has been a great success for the Brazilian firm. This is the first prototype, photographed in 1974 before going into the museum

Canada

CANADIAN WARPLANE HERITAGE

PO Box 35, Hamilton Civic Airport, Mount Hope, Ontario LOR 1WO
Tel: 416-679-4141
Opening times: 10am–4pm daily
Location: the airport is about 8 miles (12 km) south of Hamilton off Route 6

Auster K AOP.6 (1948)
Avro 652A Anson V (1943), **683 Lancaster BX** (1944)
Beech D18S (1952), **D18S (3NM)** (1952), **45 Mentor (T-34)** (1953)
Bristol 149 Bolingbroke IVT (1942)
Cessna T-50 Bobcat (Crane 1) (1942)
de Havilland DH 82C Tiger Moth (1942), **DH 100 Vampire F.3** (1949), **DHC 1 Chipmunk 2** (1948)
Douglas DC-3 (C-47B) (1944)
Fairchild F.24R Argus (1946), **M.62A Cornell** (1942)
Fairey Firefly AS.5 (1948)
Fleet 7C Fawn II (1936) **16B Finch** (1940) **60K Fort** (1941)
Grumman G.40 Avenger (TBM-3) (1944)
Hawker Hurricane XII (1942)
North American NA.64 Yale (1939), **T-6G Texan** (1949), **T-6J Texan (Harvard IV)** (1951), **B-25J Mitchell** (1945)
Piper J-2 Cub (1938)
Stinson 105 (1940)
Supermarine 377 Seafire XV (1944)
Travel Air E-4000 (1927)
Vought FG1D Corsair (1945)
Waco ZQC-6 (1936)
Westland Lysander III (1942)

Below
A Canadian-built Avro Anson V, seen flying over the Ontario countryside close to its base at Hamilton

Opposite Top
This Hawker Hurricane was built in Canada and starred in the 1969 British film, 'Battle of Britain'. At that time it belonged to the Strathallan Collection in Scotland

In 1971 a group of Canadian enthusiasts bought a derelict ex-Royal Australian Navy Fairey Firefly in Georgia in the USA. The aircraft was restored and first flown in Canada in 1972. This single aircraft led to the formation of the Canadian Warplane Heritage (CWH) in 1973. The main objective of the organization was to acquire as many as possible of the training, transport and combat aircraft that were flown by Canadians in World War II. The collection was to restore these to flying condition and establish a museum dedicated to the airmen of the country. The group grew steadily and obtained a hangar at Mount Hope Airport near Hamilton. As time passed, the number of aircraft increased greatly and a second hangar was taken over in 1984. The CWH can now claim to have one of the best fleets of flyable military aircraft in North America and the situation should improve still further as many aircraft are nearing the end of their restoration programs. One of the highlights of the aviation calendar in Canada is the annual air show held each summer when these superbly restored warbirds are shown in their natural habitat. The show has achieved international status and many US owners bring their prized possessions to the airport.

The CWH suffered a major setback at their 1977 show when one of the founders, Alan Ness, was killed in the original Firefly. He apparently stalled and span into Lake Ontario. This tragic event did not halt the progress of the organization, and no doubt had he survived Alan Ness would have been proud to see his dream grow into such a major collection. A replacement Firefly was sought and this was delivered by sea from Australia in 1978. A major restoration was then undertaken. Another major rebuild was initiated in 1977 when an Avro Lancaster, which had spent many years exposed to the elements at Goderich on the shores of Lake Huron, was donated to the CWH by the Sulley Foundation. The four-engined bomber was transported to Mount Hope under a Canadian Armed Forces Chinook helicopter on November 5, 1979. The outer wings and engines were removed for this trip of about 100 miles (160 km). Help with was provided by the forces and Air Canada.

The historic significance of this acquisition was underlined when, in June 1984, the aircraft was dedicated to the memory of Pilot Officer Andrew Mynarski of 419 Squadron RCAF. On the night of June 12, 1944, Mynarski was aboard the Lancaster KB726 which flew from the English airfield of Middleton St George to attack railway yards at Cambrai in France. The aircraft was attacked by a Junkers Ju 88 and fire broke out. Mynarski, who was the mid-upper gunner, tried to save the rear gunner who was trapped by the fire. He failed in this task, and was severely burned and died soon after landing by parachute. He was posthumously awarded the Victoria Cross. The Lancaster at Mount Hope has been given the markings of KB726, and a similar policy of painting aircraft in the colors of machines which have performed heroic tasks in the history of Canadian service has been applied elsewhere in the CWH collection.

A Canadian-built Hurricane that had starred in the 1969 British film 'Battle of Britain' was later bought by Sir William Roberts for his Strathallan Collection. With no example of the type airworthy in Canada, it was appropriate that the Hurricane should return to the CWH. The organization was unable to raise the purchase price but with the help of a donation from the Canadian Government, the Molson Company and individuals, the aircraft was acquired and arrived at Mount Hope in May 1984. Now it is resplendent in the colors of No. 1 Squadron which was the only RCAF unit to fly in the Battle of Britain.

The Hurricane should soon be joined in the air by a Supermarine Seafire. This is being completely rebuilt in the US, and when completed it will be the only airworthy example of the naval Spitfire.

A recent policy change has seen a few historic civil aircraft join the collection. These include a Waco ZQC-6 which was used in a 1942 film starring James Cagney, and a Travel Air E-4000. Some civil types which had seen military service were already with the CWH, including a Stinson HW-75 and a Piper J-2 Cub.

Wings of the CWH have been set up in other parts of Canada and these have aircraft in their care. The Western Canada Wing has a few aircraft at Vancouver.

The Fleet Finch trainer was used in large numbers in the Commonwealth Air Training Plan

NATIONAL AVIATION MUSEUM

Principal site: Rockcliffe Airport, Ottawa, Ontario K1A OM8
Tel: 613-998-4566
Subsidiary sites:
Canadian War Museum, 330 Sussex Drive, Ottawa
Tel: 613-992-2774
National Museum of Science and Technology, 1867 St Laurent Boulevard, Ottawa
Tel: 613-998-4566

Opening times: Rockcliffe: 10am–8pm daily May–mid-September; 10am–6pm Tuesday–Sunday mid-September–April
CWM: 10am–5pm daily closed Monday mid September–April; closes 9pm Tuesdays in summer period
NMST: same hours as Rockcliffe
Location: Rockcliffe Airport is in the northeastern suburbs of the city off St Laurent Boulevard
CWM is close to the government buildings in the city center
NMST is about 5 miles (8 km) south of Rockcliffe

Aerial Experiment Association Silver Dart No.2 (R) (1959), **Silver Dart No.3 (R)** (1959)
Allgemeine Electrizitäts (AEG) G IV (1918)
Aeronca C-2 (1929)
Aichi D3A2 (1943)
Airspeed AS.65 Consul (AS.40 Oxford) (1944)
Auster K AOP.6 (1948)
Avro 504K (1917, 1918), **504K (R)** (1967), **616 Avian IVM** (1930), **652A Anson V** (1944), **683 Lancaster B.X** (1944), **683 Lancaster B.X** (nose only) (1944)
Avro-Canada CF-100 Canuck 5 (1958), **CF-100 Canuck 5D** (1958), **C-102 Jetliner** (nose only) (1949), **CF-105 Arrow** (nose only) (1958)
Bell 47G (HTL-6) (1955)
Bellanca CH-300 Pacemaker (1930)
Blériot XI (R) (1911?)
Boeing 247D (1933)
Bristol 149 Bolingbroke IVT (1942), **156 Beaufighter TT.10** (1943)
Canadair CL-28 Argus 2 (1960), **CL-84** (1970)
Cessna T-50 Bobcat (Crane 1) (1942)
Consolidated 28 Canso (PBY-5A) (1944), **32 Liberator (B-246)** (1944)
Curtiss JN-4C Canuck (1918), **HS-2L** (1918), **25 Seagull** (1920), **87 Kittyhawk (P-40E)** (1942)
Czerwinski-Shenstone Harbinger (1975)
de Havilland DH 60X Moth (1928), **DH 80A Puss Moth** (1931), **DH 82C Tiger Moth** (1941), **DH 98 Mosquito B.20** (1944), **DH 100 Vampire F.1** (1945), **DH 100 Vampire F.3** (1947), **DHC 1 Chipmunk** (1956), **DHC 2 Beaver** (1947), **DHC 3 Otter** (1960), **DHC 6 Twin Otter** (1965)
Douglas DC-3 (1943), **DC-3 (C-47B)** (1945), **DC-4M (Canadair 4)** (1948), **DC-4M (Canadair 4)** (nose only) (1948)
Fairchild FC-2W2 (1928), **82A** (1937), **M.62A Cornell (PT-26A)** (1943)
Fairey Swordfish (1942), **Battle 1T** (1939)
Farman S.11 Shorthorn (1914)
Fieseler Fi 103 (1943)
Fleet 2 (1930), **16B Finch** (1940), **50K** (1939), **80 Canuck** (1946)
Fokker D VII (1918)
Found FBA-2C (1962)
Gibson Twinplane (R) (?)
Hawker Hind (1937), **Hurricane XII** (1942), **Sea Fury FB.11** (1948)
Heinkel He 162A-1 (1945)
Hispano HA-1112K (Bf 109) (1954)
Junkers J 1 (Ju 4) (1918), **W 34f/fi** (1932)
Lockheed 10A Electra (1937), **12A** (1937), **T-33AN** (1957), **CF-104 Starfighter (F-104A)** (1962)
McDonnell F2H-3 Banshee (1953), **F-101B Voodoo** (1957)
McDowall Monoplane (1915)
Messerschmitt Me 163B-1 Komet (1945)
Nieuport 12 (1915), **17 (R)** (1962)
Noorduyn Norseman VI (1943)
North American AT-6A Texan (Harvard II) (1940, 1941), **T-6J Texan (Harvard IV)** (1952), **B-25J Mitchell** (1944), **P-51D Mustang** (1944), **F-86 Sabre (CL-13B VI)** (1955, 1956)
Northrop Delta (1937)
Piasecki PV.18 Retriever (HUP-3) (1951)
Pitcairn PCA-2 (1932)
Royal Aircraft Factory BE.2c (1915)
Sikorsky VS-316 Hoverfly (R-4B) (1943), **S-51 Dragonfly (R-5)** (1947), **S-55 (H04S-3)** (1953)
Sopwith Pup (R) (1967), **2F.1 Camel** (1917), **7F.1 Snipe** (1918), **7F.1 Snipe (fuselage only)** (1918), **Triplane (R)** (1966)
SPAD VII (1917)
Stearman 4EM Junior Speedmail (1930)
Stinson SR.10J Reliant (1940)
Stits SA-3A Playboy (1955)
Supermarine 329 Spitfire IIB (1940), **361 Spitfire IX** (1944), **361 Spitfire XVI** (1945)
Taylor E-2 Cub (1934)
Travel Air 2000 (1929)
Vickers Vedette (1929), **757 Viscount** (1957)
Westland Lysander III (1942)
Wills Wing XC-185 Hang-glider (1977)
Zenair CH-300 Tri-Zenith (c.1978)

The only surviving German twin-engined bomber of World War I is this AEG G IV which was shipped to Canada in 1919

Before the opening of its new premises, due for 1987, Canada's National Aviation Museum had been evolving, under that name and various others, for the best part of 70 years. One of the earliest collectors in the country was Dr Alexander Graham Bell, who preserved some artifacts from his experiments, and items were also saved by W R Turnbull who built the first wind tunnel in Canada. Just after the end of World War I the Dominion archivist, Lt Col Arthur Doughty, had a number of aircraft transported to Canada along with other war trophies.

Canadian pilots had fought with distinction in the conflict and among the aircraft Doughty acquired was the BE.2c used by Lt F Sowrey when he shot down Zeppelin L 32 on September 24, 1916. Another famous relic was the fuselage of the Sopwith Snipe used by Major William Barker in a famous fight with up to 60 German machines on October 27, 1918. In spite of the overwhelming odds Barker shot down four before crashing behind British lines. For this amazing piece of valor he was awarded the Victoria Cross. Fortunately these two priceless aircraft which are so significant for Canada have survived.

Along with the British aircraft, Doughty obtained at least 30 German machines, some of which were exhibited in

Above
A replica Sopwith Pup, built by the former de Havilland test pilot George Neal. Its setting is one of Rockliffe's historic hangars

Left
The restoration of this Curtiss HS-2L flying boat, recovered from Foss Lake in 1968-69 after almost 50 years under water, was a major task for the museum team

The Curtiss Kittyhawk was used in considerable numbers by the RCAF in World War II

Toronto in 1919. The German aircraft were then moved to storage at Camp Borden near the city. In 1920 some were dispatched around the country for display, while the air force issued orders for the remainder to be scrapped. Two relics somehow survived this tragedy and joined the Canadian War Museum, which was set up in Ottawa in the 1920s. These are a Junkers Ju 4 armored biplane and the only remaining example of a German twin-engined aircraft of the period, an AEG G IV.

The War Museum was the only organization preserving aircraft in Canada until in 1937 an aeronautical museum was set up in the premises of the National Research Council in Ottawa. The only aircraft on show was a Sopwith Camel but there were items from the Bell Collection and the engine of Canada's first aircraft, the AEA Silver Dart. Little progress was made until 1959 when the RCAF constructed two Silver Dart replicas, one of which was flyable. This machine flew at Baddeck, Nova Scotia, on February 23, 1959, on the 50th anniversary of the flight by the original aircraft. After its celebration flight the replica became the sole complete aircraft on show in a new museum, the first in Canada to be called the National Aviation Museum, which opened on October 25 in the new terminal building at Ottawa airport. 1959 also saw Wing Commander C R V Manning taking over as historian for the RCAF.

The National Aviation Museum set about acquiring examples of aircraft which had been important in the development of aviation in Canada. The first type to be produced in large quantities in the country was the Canadian version of the famous Curtiss Jenny. The JN-4 Canuck, as it was known, was the first military aircraft in Canada and also was the first type to cross the Rockies. Many were exported to the US and in 1962 one was bought from E Faulkner in New York State and refurbished in the markings of an 85 Squadron aircraft. One of the most significant developments in the opening up of the country was the advent of the bush aircraft. Rugged machines from a number of countries performed sterling tasks in transporting men and equipment to lakes and hastily prepared airstrips in the north. A number of aircraft were obtained from both Canada and the US, and now some have been restored and are an important part of the exhibition.

In parallel with these developments in the civil field, Manning was active within the RCAF. The service had stored some World War II types in western Canada and these were moved to Ottawa. Restoration work on some of these began, and others including a Bristol Bolingbroke and an Avro Lancaster were added. The National War Museum, too, started to acquire military aircraft including a Sopwith Snipe which had been built by Ruston and Proctor in Lincoln, England. The aircraft had gone to the US in 1926 and had been flown in several films before being on show in two museums. Jack Canary, the well known rebuilder, had restored it in the 1950s and it was in full flying order. This superb biplane came to Canada in 1963 and was flown at Rockcliffe, near Ottawa, up to 1967.

Rockcliffe had been an air force base for over 40 years when in 1964 the force decided to cease flying there, as the site was now too close to the built-up area of the city and its runways were too short for modern aircraft. Manning obtained three wooden two-bay hangars for museum use and the War Museum, the National Aviation Museum and the RCAF all moved some of their exhibits to Rockcliffe.

The War Museum took over the day-to-day running of Rockcliffe, with assistance from the NAM. Since then, the exhibition has became known as the National Aeronautical Collection. In 1967 the War Museum obtained more exhibition space and about six aircraft were placed on show. In the same year the National Museum of Science and Technology was formed, and took over the NAM. The exhibition at the airport remained until 1981, but a new museum was opened in the southern outskirts of Ottawa, where new aircraft were placed. The RCAF handed over its responsibilities for the collection to the NMST. The wooden hangars at Rockcliffe are to continue in service but constitute a serious fire risk, and new buildings are due for opening in late 1987.

A prime exhibit due for 1987 is a Curtiss HS-2L flying boat. The type was the first aircraft to be used in bush flying, for which many ex-US Navy aircraft were used. One of these boats crashed in Lake Foss in Ontario in 1922, and the wreck was located and raised in 1968-69. The wings and tail surfaces of another, found in California in 1965, were acquired a few years afterwards. A further wrecked HS-2L was located in 1976 on a joint expedition with the Western Canada Aviation Museum, and the parts were transported to Rockcliffe for rebuilding.

So remote is northern Canada that any derelict aircraft have tended to be left where they crashed or went out of use, while on the other hand any that remained serviceable were kept flying for years after their types became obsolete in more accessible regions. Thus there were plenty of rare aircraft for the museum to obtain. A Junkers W 34 was flown into Rockcliffe from British Columbia in 1962, and this is believed to be the last flight made by a member of the classic range of single-engined monoplanes produced by the Dessau firm. A Fairchild FC-2W2 was bought in the US, and a Bellanca Pacemaker made the long journey from Alaska to Ottawa.

The museum now has a wide range of types from the early days illustrating both world wars, private and transport flying, and modern military and civil aircraft. Canada has not been the sole source of exhibits. Other than in the US, the museum has searched far and wide. In an exchange deal with the Indian Air Force, a Liberator bomber was flown to Canada in 1968, while in the previous year a Canadian-built Westland Lysander was shipped to Delhi. A Curtiss Seagull was acquired from the Science Museum in London in 1968, and a Hawker Hind came from Afghanistan in 1975.

The collection of aircraft is one of the most significant and comprehensive in North America and its new premises are long overdue. As well as the aircraft, the large number of engines, photographs and documents, along with components and memorabilia, in a country whose development has been crucially influenced by aviation, needs a proper, purpose-built museum.

WESTERN CANADA AVIATION MUSEUM

Hangar T-2, 958 Ferry Road, Winnipeg, Manitoba R3H OY8
Tel: 204-775-8447
Opening times: 10am–4pm Monday–Saturday; 1pm–4pm Sunday and Holidays
Location: at the airport which is in the western suburbs of the city

Avro 504K (R) (1967), **652A Anson II** (1942), **652A Anson V** (1944)
Avro-Canada CF-100 Canuck 5 (1958)
Beech D18S (1951)
Bellanca 31-55A Skyrocket (1946), **66-75 Aircruiser** (1935, 1948), **14-13 Crusair** (1948)
Bensen B-8 (?)
Bristol 149 Bolingbroke IVT (1942), **170 Freighter 31** (1955)
Canadair CL-28 Argus 1 (1958)
Cessna T-50 Bobcat (Crane) (1942)
de Havilland DH 82C Tiger Moth (1941), **DH 83C Fox Moth** (1947), **DH 89A Dragon Rapide** (1939), **DHC 2 Beaver** (1953)
Douglas DC-3 (C-47A) (1942)
Fairchild FC2W2 (1928), **FC-2** (1928), **71C** (1928), **Super 71** (1934), **Super 71P** (1934), **F.24W** (1946), **F-11 Husky** (1946, 1947)
Fairey Battle 1 (1942)
Fleet 60K Fort (1942)
Fokker Super Universal (1929), **F.XIA (B.IVA)** (1930)
Found 100 Centennial (1967)
Froebe Helicopter (1938)
Howard DGA-15P (1939)
Junkers F 13 (1930), **W 34** (1933), **Ju 52/1m** (1951)
Lockheed T-33AN (1953)
McDonnell F-101B Voodoo (1955)
Noorduyn Norseman IV (1937), **Norseman VI** (1943), **Norseman** (?), (c.1943)
North American NA-64 Yale (1940), **AT-6A Texan (Harvard II)** (1940), **T-6J Texan (Harvard 4)** (1952), **F-86J Sabre (CL-13 3)** (1954)
Republic RC-3 Seabee (1941)
Saunders ST-28 (1975)
Schneider Grunau Baby II (DFS 108-49) (c.1942)
Stearman 4EM Junior Speedmail (1930)
Stinson SR.8 Reliant (1936)
Vickers Vedette V (1928, 1929), **757 Viscount** (1953)
Vultee BT-13A Valiant (1941)
Waco YKC-S (1934), **CG-4A Hadrian** (1944)

The Western Canada Aviation Museum (WCAM), which opened a major display at Winnipeg International Airport in October 1984, owes its origins to a small group of enthusiasts. In the early 1970s the Manitoba Aircraft Restoration Group formed to collect and preserve aircraft which had served in their region. The terrain of Manitoba had resulted in many aircraft crashes over the years and remains were often still at these sites. Their first expedition was to Cormorant Lake to look for a Vickers Vedette and this was followed by a trip to Pickle Crow, Ontario, where they located a Bellanca Aircruiser in 1973. In 1973 a workshop was rented and restoration of the aircraft and engines commenced.

From these modest beginnings it was decided to set up a museum in which aircraft and artifacts could be displayed. Thus the WCAM came into being in 1974. Among its first exploits was to show three aircraft in Winnipeg at the Highlander Curling Club, and in 1975 a small exhibition was staged at the Manitoba Museum of Man and Nature. Industry has helped the museum in these tasks.

In 1979 an exhibition was opened at Lily Street in Winnipeg, and in the larger area available here the work of the museum really came to public notice. The WCAM then became one of Canada's major museums when it obtained hangarage at Winnipeg International Airport in September 1983, instantly acquiring 10 times the exhibition space of Lily Street. The status of the collection was enhanced with the official opening by Her Majesty the Queen on October 7, 1984.

The fleet of over 70 aircraft contains several unique or rare types. Canada's first helicopter was designed by the three Froebe brothers (Douglas, Nicholas and Theodore) at

Many examples of the Fairchild F.24 have seen use in Canada. Their rugged construction was specially suited to the harsh climate

Excellent craftsmanship turned this Spanish-built Junkers Ju 52/3m into a replica of the single-engine version operated by Canadian Airways

Homewood, Manitoba, and made its first brief flight in November 1938. Bush aircraft have played an important role in Manitoba and the museum has acquired a number of types, many from crash sites. The Bellanca Aircruiser from Ontario is nearing the end of its restoration, and a Fokker Super Universal is in the workshops. Representing the post-World War II period is a Fairchild Husky, built at Vancouver in the late 1940s. Financial problems with the company resulted in only 12 examples being completed. One restored aircraft is on show, and the parts from three other wrecks are in store.

The preservation of airliners is always a problem because of their size, but the museum now has space for examples of passenger and freight types. Air Canada was a major user of the Vickers Viscount, its predecessor Trans Canadian Airlines having ordered 15 in 1954. The fleet eventually numbered 51 and the Viscount was a common sight all over the country. The museum bought one in 1975 but five years later this was damaged by a cabin fire. A second example was acquired soon after this setback and is now on show in the red and white livery of the airline.

Another British aircraft on show is a Bristol Freighter. This rugged aircraft was ideally suited to outback work and a dozen saw Canadian use. The aircraft on show was built for the RCAF's flight at Langar in the UK, and was used in this military transport role from 1955 to 1967. It was then converted to civil standards and its last Canadian operator was North Canada Air, who used it for supplying remote Arctic settlements, often landing on hastily prepared strips on frozen lakes.

A spectacular addition to the museum took place in April 1985 when a replica of the single-engined Junkers 52 was completed. Five single-engined examples of this design, which afterwards became famous in its three-engined version, were constructed and the last of these was delivered to Canadian Airways at Winnipeg in 1931, continuing in service until 1942. In 1982 the museum bought, in Florida, a Spanish-built CASA 352L, which was a license-built version of the Junkers three-engined classic. The aircraft was flown to Manitoba, and Bristol Aerospace undertook the task of transforming this aircraft into a replica of the original single-engined Canadian Airways machine.

With military and sporting aircraft joining the collection at a steady rate this museum is developing rapidly, and future plans envisage more expansion of the premises at Winnipeg International Airport.

This Bristol Freighter, delivered to the RCAF in 1955, became a civil aircraft in 1967, spending over a dozen years operating in Canada's northern territories

Czechoslovakia

MILITARY MUSEUM – AIR AND SPACE SECTION
Vojenske Muzeum – Exposice Letectva a Kosmonautiky

Kbely, Praha 9, 19706
Tel: 422-27-29-65
Opening times: 9am–5pm Saturday–Thursday, 2.30pm–5pm Friday
Location: on Route 10 (E14) about 5 miles (8 km) northeast of Prague

Aero A-10 (1922), **A-11 (R)** (?), **A-12 (R)** (?), **A-18c** (1924), **Ap-32** (1930), **45** (1947), **145** (1959), **XL-29 Delfin** (1959), **L-29 Delfin** (1959), **L-29A Akrobat** (1967), **L-39 Albatros** (1968), **L-60 Brigadyr** (1956), **XL-160 Brigadyr** (1958)
Antonov An-2 (c.1944)
Arado Ar 96B (Aero C-2) (1946)
Avia B-534 (1938), **BH-10** (1924), **BH-11B** (1929), **BH-11C** (1926), **BH-11K** (1927), **CS-199 (Bf 109** modified**)** (1946), **S-199 (Bf 109** modified**)** (1947)
Benes-Mraz M-1C Sokol (1947), **M-1D Sokol** (1947)
Bücker Bü 131 Jungmann (Aero C-104) (1946), **Bü 181 Bestmann (Zlin Z-381)** (1946)
C-02 (?)
CS VTS Autogyro (c.1965), **VTS Gyroglider** (c.1965)
Dobias Gyroglider (?)
Douglas DC-3 (Lisunov Li-2D) (c.1942)
Dvoracek BDv-2 (?)
Elsnic EL-2M Sedy Vik (c.1925)
Fieseler Fi 156 Storch (Mraz K-65) (1946)
Focke-Wulf Fw 190 (1944)
Henschel Hs 293A-1 (1942)
Hutter H17 (1942)
Ikarus 522 (1958)
Ilyushin Il-2m3 (1942), **Il-10 (Avia B-33)** (1953), **Il-10U (Avia CB-33)** (1953), **Il-14 (Avia Av 14/32)** (1957), **Il-14FG** (1955), **Il-18** (c.1960), **Il-28B** (1952), **Il-28RT** (1952), **Il-28RTR** (1956), **Il-28U** (?)
Jirasek Ornithopthera (?)
Junkers Ju 52/3m (1941)
Kabele Homebuilt (?)
Kratochvil KLZ-VII (?), **KLZ-VIII** (?), **Gyroglider** (?)
Lavochkin La-7 (1944)
LET L-13 Blanik (1958), **L-21 Spartak** (1956), **L-200A Morava** (1960), **L-200D Morava** (1962), **L-410 Turbolet** (1969), **XZ-37 Cmelak** (1963), **Z-37 Cmelak** (1964)
Letov KT-04 (?), **S-2** (1921), **S-20** (1925), **S-20J** (1926), **S-218** (1930), **SK-38 Komar (SG-38** modified**)** (1947), **LF-107 Lunak** (1950), **LF-109 Pionyr** (1950), **MK-1 Kocour** (1969)
Messerschmitt Me 262A (Avia S-92) (1946), **Me 262B (Avia CS-92)** (1946)
Mignet HM-14 Pou-du-Ciel (1935)
Mikoyan-Gurevich MiG-15 (1951), **MiG-15bis (K)** (1951), **MiG-15bis R** (1950), **MiG-15UTI** (1953), **MiG-15UTI-P** (1954), **MiG-15SB** (1953), **MiG-17F** (1954), **MiG-17PF** (1954), **MiG-19S** (1955), **MiG-19P** (1956), **MiG-19PM** (1957), **MiG-21F** (1961)
Mil Mi-1 (1949), **Mi-4** (1950)
Motor-Balloon (?)
Orlican L-40 Meta Sokol (1956)
Piper J-3 Cub (L-4H) (1944)
Polikarpov Po-2 (CSS-13) (1949)
Praga E-114M Air Baby (1947)
Rapac Glider (?)
Rogallo Standard (?)
Saunders-Roe A.19 Cloud (1933)
Schneider Grunau Baby IIb (DFS 108-49) (1946)
Siebel Si 204D (Aero C-3A) (1947), **Si 204D (Aero C-3AF)** (1947)
SPAD VII (1918)
Stakr Homebuilt (?)
Supermarine 361 Spitfire LF.IXE (1944)
Taylor E-2 Cub (1934)
Trajbal-Prasil Glider (?)
Tupolev Tu-104A (1958)
Vaculik-Sidi Motor-glider (?)
Vega VSB-66 Orlice (1970), **VSM-40 Demant** (1958)
VOSLM BAK-01 (?)
VZLU HC-2 Heli Baby (1953), **HC-3** (1960), **TOM-8 (L-8)** (1956)
VZLU-Orlican HC-4 (1962)
WSK SM-2 (c.1960)
Yakovlev Yak-11 (LET C-11) (1953), **Yak-12R** (1951), **Yak-17** (1947), **Yak-23** (1948)
Zlin XII (1935), **XIII** (1937), **Z-22 Junak** (1946), **Z-23 Honja** (1947), **Z-24 Krajanek** (1945), **Z-25 Sohaj** (1947), **Z-26 Trener** (1947), **Z-26/126 Trener** (1953), **Z-42** (1967), **Z-43** (1968), **Z-123 Honza** (1948), **Z-124 Galanka** (1949), **Z-125 Sohaj 2** (1950), **Z-130 Kmotr** (1950), **Z-135 Heli Trainer** (1965), **HC-102 Heli Baby** (1960), **VT-425 Sohaj 3** (1955)

One of the largest European military collections is held by the Czechoslovak Military Museum (Vojenske Muzeum) in Prague. The Historical Exhibition, housed in the Schwarzenburg Palace, traces the development of armed forces and weapons from the earliest times. Side by side with this exhibition in Central Prague, the Institute of Military History houses another military exhibition. A few aircraft have been displayed here, but the Military Museum possessed no aircraft until the air and space section was opened in the late 1960s at the airfield of Kbely just northeast of Prague.

The site was the first Czechoslovak Air Force airfield and in the inter-war period staged some of the finest air shows in Europe. Kbely was also the scene of many developments in civil aviation, including the first scheduled flight by Czechoslovak Airlines, to Bratislava in October 1923. In the mid-1960s the Military Museum set up a task force to recover and preserve historic aircraft, many of which were still scattered about the country. These were stored at Kbely airfield.

In 1968 the 50th anniversary of Czechoslovak aviation was marked by a flying display at Kbely. The stored aircraft were presented in an exhibition which later that year became the air and space section of the Military Museum. The collection developed rapidly: by 1972 there were 86 aircraft, and by 1986 there were over 170. In common with many museums, however, there is a distinct lack of exhibition space and only about 60 are on show.

The highlight of the display is a superbly restored partial replica of the Aero A-10 airliner of 1923. The type is a biplane with an enclosed cabin for the passengers and the pilot seated in an open cockpit to the rear of this. The cabin shows the elegance of the era with wicker seats, curtains and other trimmings. The Aero company is just one of the Czechoslovak firms represented, and other exhibits representing this name are an Aero A-32 light bomber and the 45/145 series of light twins which were produced by the state industry in the communist period of rule.

The museum also is anxious to fill in gaps in the exhibition, and replicas are being constructed of many types including the Aero A-11 (a license-built Brandenburg C I) and the A-12. The Avia company showed its first aircraft, the BH-1, at the 1920 Prague Exhibition and this low-wing monoplane was victorious at the first flying meeting held in the country. The type was developed steadily and achieved notable success when the BH-5 won the King of the Belgians' Prize in 1924.

The museum has a replica of the BH-10 and three variants of the BH-11, the most interesting of which is the BH-11C. This aircraft won the Coppa d'Italia in 1926 when flown by Bican and Kinsky and survived in a dilapidated state in store at the West Bohemia Museum at Plzen. In July 1965 it was taken to Kbely for restoration. Other famous Czech designs of the inter-war period include a Praga E-114 Air Baby, a type which was license-produced in the UK, and many products of the Zlin company.

The Soviet influence in Czechoslovakia is evident in the modern section in the collection, which includes one of the largest ranges of Mikoyan and Gurevich jet fighters in the world. Over 20 examples of these swept-wing interceptors are held but only five are on show. Even though the combat aircraft since 1948 have all been supplied by the Soviet Union the local industry has been allowed to develop its own designs, and several of these have found substantial export markets. The museum has been able to acquire examples of almost all Czech-designed types since 1948.

During World War II many Czechoslovak nationals fought with the Royal Air Force and their efforts are honoured by a superbly restored Spitfire which is on loan from the National Technical Museum. In the immediate post-World War II period the US and the UK supplied aircraft to the country, but only one Piper Cub survives.

One of the most interesting aircraft in the collection for western eyes is the fuselage of a Saunders-Roe Cloud amphibian. This aircraft undertook a sales tour of Europe in 1933 and at the completion of the promotion it was purchased by the national airline and re-engined with Walter Pollux radials. The company used it on its Adriatic services until 1939 when it was put in store, but during World War II the wings were lost. The shortened fuselage was used as a motor launch until the mid-1960s, but this now unique aircraft is being rebuilt to its former glory.

In two decades this enterprising museum has acquired one of the major European aircraft collections from virtually nothing, and it is to be hoped that finances will allow the construction of a major new museum building.

Top
This Aero A-10 airliner was constructed from the remains of an original aircraft. Its cabin was furnished to the lavish standards of a long gone era

Above
The Letov S-218, seen during an engine run after its restoration for the museum. Although not flown, many of the aircraft are restored to flying condition

NATIONAL TECHNICAL MUSEUM
Narodni Technicke Muzeum

Kostelni 42, 170 00 Praha 7
Tel: 373-651-9
Opening times: 9am–5pm Tuesday–Sunday
Location: in the center of the city just north of the river

Aero A-18L (1923, wings only, out on loan to Air and Space section of Military Museum (q.v.)), **L-29 Delfin** (1959)
Anatra DS Ansalja (1917)
Avia BH-9 (1924), **BH-10** (1925), **BH-11C** (1924)
Benes-Mraz M-1C Sokol (1947)
Bensen B-8W (1968)
Bohemia B-5 (1919)
Bücker Bü 131 Jungmann (Aero C-104) (1947), **Bü 181 Bestmann (Zlin Z-381 C-106)** (1949)
Deltaplane Hang-glider (1977)
DFS Weihe (1943)
Etrich 1905 Motorglider (1905), **Limusina** (1928)
Fieseler Fi 156 Storch (Mraz K-65) (1949)
Hansa-Brandenburg D-1 (1915)
Kaspar Monoplane (1910)
Knoller C II (1915)
Lavochkin La-7 (1944)
Letov S-2 (1921), **LF-107 Lunak** (1950)
Mignet HM-14 Pou-du-Ciel (1935)
Morse LWF Scout (1918)
Mrkev Racek III (1937)
Piper J-3 Cub (L-4H) (1944)
Praga E-114M Air Baby (1947)
Praha Zenith Balloon (1904), **Glider** (1932)
Ressel Balloon (1893)
Shimunek VBS-1 Kunkadlo (1925)
Silimon IS-3D (1958)
Smrcek VT-225 Medak (1952)
Supermarine 361 Spitfire LF.IXE (1944)
VZLU HC-2 Heli Baby (1955)
Zlin XIII (1937), **Z-25 Sohaj** (1947), **Z-125 Sohaj 2** (1950), **Z-130 Kmotr** (1950)

The National Technical Museum in Prague is one of the oldest in Europe. The origins of the collection go back to 1799 although there were some private collections prior to this. The present museum was established as the Technical Museum of the Kingdom of Bohemia in 1908. The first location of the collection was at the Schwarzenburg Palace at Prague Castle and even at this time there was a fairly large aeronautical section. One of the co-founders of the museum was Gustav Finger, a renowned expert on aviation. When the Czechoslovak Republic was founded in 1918 the museum had so many exhibits that its halls were overcrowded. New premises were ready in 1941, but were requisitioned and the museum did not take possession until 1945. The collection was nationalized in 1951 and became the central technical museum in the country. The museum has seven main departments and an excellent library and archive section.

The Transport section, which includes the aircraft, is housed in the large central hall with three galleries around the sides. Around 1968, when the Air and Space section of the Military Museum was being set up, there was considerable interchange of both aircraft and engines between the two organizations. The earliest machines on show are balloons, together with a 1905 attempt by Igo Etrich to produce a powered glider. A prized exhibit is the Kaspar Monoplane in which the first Czech pilot Jan Kaspar flew from Pardubice to Prague, a distance of some 60 miles (96 km) in 1911. The design was influenced by the Blériot XI: Kaspar had seen drawings of the Blériot but did not know the actual dimensions of the French machine, so although very similar in appearance, the Kaspar has a different span and length.

World War I is represented by three aircraft which are believed to be the only survivors of their types. These are a

In the foreground is the Russian-built Anatra DS Ansalja, with the American Thomas Morse LWF to its right. Both are the sole survivors of their types

The Knoller CII, painted with the markings of the Austro-Hungarian air force. Above it is the Avia BH-9

Russian Anatra DS trainer wearing post-World War I Czech colors, an Austrian Knoller C II in Austro-Hungarian Air Force markings and an American Morse LWF.

Before World War I a group of constructors at Plzen had started on a two-seat biplane with a 32 hp NAG engine. In 1918 they resumed the project and the Bohemia B-5 flew in April 1919. This was the first aircraft to fly in the new state, and parts of this historic machine are in store. Sporting flying of the inter-war period is represented by several gliders and light aircraft. From the Czechoslovak industry are the Avia BH-9 and BH-10 low wing monoplanes. These aircraft, designed by Benes and Hajn, were derived from the BH-1 of 1920 and the range achieved international recognition when the BH-5 won the 1924 King of the Belgians' Prize Race. Benes went on to design the Sokol, which was developed further during the German occupation and flew in 1945. One interesting variation on the Mignet HM-14 Pou-du-Ciel theme is shown: a Czech-built machine in which both front and rear wings are adjustable. Whether this eliminated the control problems experienced by most HM-14s is unknown.

A unique aircraft which has recently been restored is the Etrich Limusina of 1927. Etrich, who became famous for his Taube aircraft before World War I, is known to have built a high-wing cabin monoplane in 1929 called the Sporttaube. This aircraft was supposed to have been ordered to be burned by the Czech authorities as it was faster than any of their fighters. They were worried that it might be used for smuggling. The Limusina may possibly prove to be the same aircraft.

In one of the galleries there is a most comprehensive display of models tracing the history of flight and on the ground floor almost all the Walter engines are represented. The NTM is an excellent museum of the old school of European technical museums, and compares with the Deutsches Museum in Munich and the Technical Museum in Vienna.

Denmark

DANISH VINTAGE AIRCRAFT COLLECTION
Dansk Veteranflysamlung

Stauning Lufthavn, Skjern 6900
Tel: 07-369044
Opening times: 3pm–5.30pm Tuesday–Friday; 1pm–5pm Saturday–Sunday or on request
Location: the airport is on the western side of Jutland between Ringköbing and Skern about 45 miles (72 km) north of Esbjerg

Aero Super 45 (1955)
Auster J/1 Autocrat (1942)
de Havilland DH 82A Tiger Moth (1942), **DH 87B Hornet Moth** (1935), **DHC 1 Chipmunk T.22** (1950)
Druine D.31 Turbulent (1962)
Gumpert G2 (?)
Hollschmidt 222 (1955)
Jurca MJ.2A Tempete (1975)
Lockheed T-33A (1951)
Mignet HM-14 Pou-du-Ciel (c.1935)
Miles M.28 Mercufy VI (1946)
North American AT-16 Texan (1942)
Piper J-3F Cub (1939), **J-4A Cub Coupe** (1940)
Raab Doppelraab IV (c.1978)
Rearwin 9000L Sportster (1937)
Republic F-84G Thunderjet (1951)
SAI KZ IIK (1937), **KZ IIT** (1946), **KZ IV** (1943), **KZ VII** (1946), **KZ G1** (1943), **KZ I (R)** (c. 1975)
Scheibe Spatz B (?), **Mu 13 Bergfalke II** (?)
Schneider Grunau Baby II (DFS 108-49) (c.1950)
Taylorcraft Plus D (Auster 1) (1942)

The airfield of Stauning on the west coast of Jutland is host each June to one of the largest gatherings of vintage and classic aircraft in Europe. Organized by the KZ Veteranfly Klubben this rally attracts enthusiasts from all over Europe. In the early 1970s members of the club began formulating the idea of a flying museum of vintage aircraft. Thus on April 19, 1975 the Dansk Veteranflysamlung (DV) came into being. Progress was initially rapid and by 1977 a large hangar with workshop facilities had been constructed on land close to the approach road to the airport.

Aircraft from the Kramme and Zeuthen (KZ) firm naturally feature prominently in the exhibition. Many of those on view are privately owned and on long term loan to the collection. The earliest KZ type on show is Hans Roy's KZ II Kupe. Only one KZ I single-seater was built before the company produced the two-seat side by side Kupe. Only 13 examples were built before the German occupation in World War II and the aircraft on show is one of three survivors. During the occupation a sole G I primary glider was built; this was flown in 1943, and now hangs from the roof of the museum along with other gliders.

The high-wing KZ III, which first flew in 1944, was the most numerous of all KZ aircraft, with 64 examples built. For the first flight the prototype was painted in the colours of the Danish Air Ambulance Service so as to obtain permission from the Germans, although they did not notice that it was not equipped for stretcher carrying. The restoration of a KZ III in ambulance configuration has just been completed.

Two KZ IV twin-engined aircraft were built for ambulance work, and both survive: the first of these, which flew on May 4, 1944, is at Stauning. The DV acquired it in 1977 but it was severely damaged in an accident at Stauning in May 1979. A fund has been started for the rebuild of this historic aircraft.

The KZ II Trainer was developed from the KZ II Sport of the 1930s, and 15 production aircraft were supplied to the Danish Air Force in 1947. Three examples in varying stages of restoration are normally housed in the museum. A damaged KZ VII has recently been obtained from Germany, and this four-seat development of the KZ III will be restored. Denmark has not had a large aviation industry and it is fitting that such an important collection should be on Danish soil.

Among the British aircraft at Stauning is the sole surviving Miles Mercury. Six slightly differing examples of this low-wing retractable undercarriage monoplane were built between 1941 and 1946. The museum aircraft is the last of the breed, and was for a time the personal aircraft of the Chairman of British European Airways. The Mercury went to Germany in 1956 and finally to Denmark in 1978. Two Tiger Moths and a Hornet Moth represent the de Havilland line.

Under restoration is the prototype Auster J/1 Autocrat. Built as the prototype Plus D in 1939, it was retained by the manufacturers but crashed in 1942. For the post-war market Auster modified it to J/1 Autocrat form. Chairman of the KZ Club Magnus Pedersen's Plus D is also on show and can be compared with the J/1.

The most interesting American aircraft on view is the Rearwin 9000L. This particular aircraft was imported into Sweden in the late 1930s to serve as a pattern aircraft for the license-built GV-38. In the 1970s it was in store at the Malmö Technical Museum, whose interest was in having a

high-wing monoplane on show. Jens Toft and others built up an Auster Autocrat from the non-airworthy parts they had and exchanged this hybrid for the Rearwin.

The museum contains an interesting variety of vintage and homebuilt aircraft, which are complemented by some ex-air force jets.

Top
Hans Roy's delightful KZ II Kupe, airborne over the flat Jutland countryside

Above
The sole surviving Miles Mercury, owned by Hans Koldby Hansen, is on loan to the collection

Finland

Opposite Top

Flying over the countryside near Halli, this Gloster Gauntlet is the last surviving example of its kind. Restored by Kalevi Eskonmaa, the aircraft has been fitted with a non-original engine

Opposite Bottom

Six Morane-Saulnier MS.50Cs were used by the Finnish air force from 1925-32. The restoration of the sole survivor was carried out at Utti AFB

FINNISH NATIONAL COLLECTION

Developments in Finland since the mid-1970s include the establishment of a number of new museums and the formation of a preservation policy. The country has always had a good record of saving historic aircraft, and of the roughly 150 types used by the air force around 50 have survived. Vintage and historic aircraft are now held at five centers, which are scattered throughout the country. Although their total holdings are impressive, some of them are quite small and technically they are all subdivisions of the national collection.

AVIATION MUSEUM OF CENTRAL FINLAND
Keski-Suomen Ilmailumuseo

PL 1, 41161 Tikkakoski
Tel: 941-752-125
Opening times: June 1–August 20: 10am–8pm daily. August 21–May 31: 5pm–7pm Monday–Friday, midday–7pm Saturday–Sunday
Location: about 12 miles (20km) north of Jyvaskyla just off Route E4 on the west (military) side of the airfield

Avro 504K (1917)
Bell P-39Q Airacobra (1944)
Bristol 142 Blenheim I (1942), **142 Blenheim IV** (1944)
Cessna F.172H Skyhawk (1967)
de Havilland DH 60X Moth (1929), **DH 100 Vampire FB.52** (1953), **DH 115 Vampire T.55** (1956)
DFS 108-70 Meise (1915), **Weihe** (1939)
Douglas DC-2 (1935), **DC-3 (C-47A)** (1943)
Fokker C.X (1943), **D.XXI** (1939)
Folland Fo.141 Gnat F.1 (1958)
Gourdou-Leseurre GL-21C1 (1923)
Hawker Hurricane I (1939)
Ilyushin Il-28R (1950)
Martinsyde F.4 Buzzard (1918)
Messerschmitt Bf 109G-10 (1944)
Mignet HM-14 Pou-du-Ciel (1936)
Mikoyan-Gurevich MiG-15UTI (1950), **MiG-21UTI** (1965)
Mil Mi-1 (1955), **Mi-4** (1951)
Morane-Saulnier MS.50C (1925)
Paatalo Tiira (1977)
Percival P.66 Pembroke C.53 (1956)
PIK 3B (1959), **5b** (1956)
Polikarpov Po-2 (1937)
Schneider Grunau Baby II (DFS 108-49) (1936)
SAAB 91D Safir (1959)
SZD-10bis Czapla (1959)
Thulin D (1918)
Valmet Vihuri II (1951), **Myrsky II** (1944), **Humu** (1944), **Pyorremyrsky** (1945), **Pyry II** (1941)

Below

The Gourdou-Leseurre GL-21 equipped the first Finnish fighter squadron in 1924. The sole survivor was restored in 1970

A volunteer team of servicemen at the Finnish Air Force Headquarters has achieved a considerable amount of aircraft restoration work. The team's work was formally recognized when the Aviation Museum of Central Finland (Keski-Suomen Ilmailumuseo) opened on June 1, 1979. Emphasis is naturally on military aircraft and the first Finnish Air Force machine, a Swedish-built Thulin D, is under restoration. This aircraft was presented to Finland by Count von Rosen and his personal emblem, the blue Swastika, was the symbol of the Finnish Air Force for many years.

The museum holds no less than eight British types, including the only remaining product of the famous Martinsyde firm which was founded in 1906 and closed in 1921. The Buzzard was one of the fastest British aircraft in production at the end of World War I and 15 were used in Finland. The Hispano-Suiza engine of this biplane is in running order and the aircraft could fly if allowed. Another classic British biplane is an early Avro 504K built by Harland and Wolff, and this served in Finland for four years from 1926.

France is represented by two sole survivors, both parasol-wing monoplanes. These are the Gourdou-Leseurre GL-21, which equipped the first Finnish Fighter squadron in 1924,

and a Morane-Saulnier MS.50 of 1925.

The museum is well-endowed with unique machines, as it also possesses two from Finland's own State Aircraft Factory. The Pyorremyrsky fighter, using mainly wooden construction and a Daimler-Benz engine, was flown in 1945 but was never put into production, as it was by that time outdated. Finland used 44 Brewster Buffalo fighters in the Continuation War, and the Humu was a development of this, using wooden construction and a Russian M-63 engine. Both these aircraft were restored by a team at Tampere in the late 1970s under the leadership of Seppo Uolamo.

The predominantly Soviet influence in modern combat aircraft used in Finland is becoming increasingly evident in the collection as more types are withdrawn for preservation. In general, display reflects the wide range of countries that have supplied aircraft to Finland over the years, and gives the visitor an unusual opportunity to see both eastern and western European aircraft at one site.

HALLI AVIATION MUSEUM
Hallinportti Ilmailumuseo

35600 Halli
Tel: 942-82112 ext 272
Opening times: May–August: 6pm–7pm Monday–Friday, 2pm–7pm Saturday–Sunday; admission during September–April is by prior permission only, to be arranged by telephoning the above number
Location: about 44 miles (70 km) northeast of Tampere, about 6 miles (10km) north of Route E4

Bristol 105A Bulldog IV (1934)
Caudron G.3 (1920)
de Havilland DH 100 Vampire FB.52 (1953)
Folland Fo.141 Gnat F.1 (1958)
Focke-Wulf Fw 44J Stieglitz (1940)
Gloster Gauntlet (1936)
Ilmailuvoimien C.24 (1924), **D.27 Haukka II** (1927)
Karhumaki Karhu 48 (1948)
Mikoyan-Gurevich MiG-15UTI (1950)
Mil Mi-1 (WSK SM-1/600Sz) (1960)
Rumpler 6B (1919)
SAAB 91D Safir (1959)
Valtion Saaski II (1929), **Viima I** (1935)

The Halli Aviation Museum is located at the Finnish Air Force Test Center at Halli, and is run by the Aviation Technical Guild (an association of past and present air force personnel). The guild opened a small museum in a wooden hut in the late 1960s, after which they steadily acquired material and funds, establishing a larger exhibition which opened in August 1980. The large display, tracing the whole history of aviation in Finland, provides the visitor with an insight into the varied political and technical developments influencing Finland's air force. Some of the rarest photographs, for instance, show de Havilland DH 9s in Estonian and Latvian markings, from the days before Finland gained her independence.

The outstanding aircraft at Halli are two British biplanes, and it is a sad reflection that a journey of such distance has to be made in order to see two aircraft which were a backbone of the Royal Air Force in the golden era. Finland purchased 17 Bristol Bulldogs in 1934 and later acquired two more from Sweden. These veterans served with great distinction in the Winter and Continuation Wars, and the Halli example, restored by former Bulldog fitter Sauli Valkeiskangas, was the last to be withdrawn in 1944.

An even more ambitious restoration project, which

involved over 7000 hours of spare time in five years by Kalevi Eskonmaa, resulted in a Gloster Gauntlet flying in 1982. Finland was presented with 24 Gauntlets in 1939 and all were withdrawn in 1950 and sold for scrap. The remains of one example were discovered in the mid-1970s and Kalevi Eskonmaa was alone among Finnish aviation experts in believing it was possible to restore the aircraft to flying condition. The Aviation Technical Guild purchased the Gauntlet in late 1976 and Eskonmaa proceeded to rebuild it. Although he was forced to fit a modern engine – an Alvis Leonides – this beautiful biplane is otherwise authentic in appearance, and is now a regular performer at shows when conditions permit. This small museum contains several other interesting aircraft and is a must for tourists to Central Finland.

NATIONAL AVIATION MUSEUM
Suomen Ilmailumuseo

PL 42, 01531 Helsinki-Vantaa-Lento
Tel: 90-821-870
Opening times: midday–6pm daily
Location: just off the approach road to the airport which is about 12 miles (20 km) north of Helsinki

Adaridi (1923)
Bell 47D (1953)
Convair CV-340/440 (1953)
de Havilland DH 115 Vampire T.55 (1956)
DFS 108-14 Schulgleiter SG-38 (1944), **Weihe** (c.1952)
Eklund TE-1 (1949)
Fibera KK.1e UTU (1968)
Fieseler Fi 156K-1 Storch (1939)
Folland Fo.141 Gnat F.1 (1958)
Harakka II (1952)
Heinonen HK-1 Keltiainen (1954)
Ilmailuvoimien A.22 Hansa (1922)
Junkers A 50ce Junior (1931)
Karhumaki Karhu 48B (1948)
Kokkola KO-04 Super Upstart (1968)
Lockheed 18 Lodestar (1940)
Messerschmitt Bf 109G-6 (1944)
Nyborg and Blomqvist Monoplane (?)
PIK 3a (1950), **5b** (1950), **10 Moottoribaby** (1949), **11 Tumppu** (1953)
Polikarpov I-16UTI (UTI-4) (1940)
Schneider Grunau 9 (1939), **Baby II (DFS 108-49)** (1943)
SAAB 91D Safir (1959)
SZD-9 Bocian (?)
Valtion Saaski II (1931), **Tuisku** (1937), **Viima II** (?), **Pyry II** (1941)
WWS-1 Salamandra (1939)

The Finnish Aviation Museum Society was formed in 1969 specifically in order to create the National Aviation Museum (Suomen Ilmailumuseo). Three years later this society set up a permanent exhibition in a basement area of the terminal building at Vantaa airport just outside Helsinki. The room was long and narrow and the few aircraft on show had to be exhibited minus their wings. Despite these restrictions a comprehensive display of models, photographs and memorabilia traced the history of both civil and military aviation in the country. Land for the definitive, purpose-built museum was acquired just off the main approach road to the airport, construction of the building commenced in 1979, and the exhibition was ready to open on September 24, 1981. The National Aviation Museum concentrates mainly on civil aircraft, which is in marked contrast to the predominantly military displays in other parts of the country. One aircraft from the collection has been mounted in the main terminal building for over a decade, and this is the Junkers Junior used by the pilot Waino Bremer on many record-breaking flights. The Junior was bought in 1931 and was powered by an Armstrong-Siddeley Genet radial of 80 hp. The Junior made a number of long-distance flights including a round the world journey in 1933. Bremer used the aircraft up to 1966 when this historic machine was retired for preservation.

The design of the museum building has resulted in aircraft displays at two levels with lighter aircraft and gliders suspended from the ceiling and others shown on the floor. In addition there is a large yard outside the building for the exhibition of larger aircraft.

One of the first locally-designed aircraft was the Adaridi monoplane powered by a 12 hp Salmson engine. This ultralight machine was tested by the air force in 1923–24 and operated for a short time on skis. No production was undertaken but the aircraft survived and was restored in the early 1970s for show in the original basement exhibition. There has always been a strong gliding movement in Finland and as early as 1910 gliders were successfully flown, but the sport really gained strength in the 1930s. The ceiling display shows a Finnish Harakka from 1952, a Polish Salamandra built in 1939, a German Grunau 9 primary from the same year, a Grunau Baby II built at Jami in 1943 and a Finnish design from 1968 known as the Fibera KK-1 Utu. This exhibition shows clearly some of the significant developments in glider construction over the years and also shows that the clubs have turned to designs from several countries.

The highlight of the Vantaa show is the last surviving IVL Hansa twin-float seaplane. Two Hansa-Brandenburg W 33s were purchased in a dismantled condition from Germany in 1922 and assembled as a prelude to license production of the design at the newly set up Air Force Aircraft Factory near Helsinki. The Hansa was the first model to be made by the factory and eventually 120 examples were built, including two exported to Latvia. Powered by a 300 Fiat A.12 bis engine, the type gave outstanding service until 1936. The survivor is one of the two pattern aircraft and was restored by the Aviation Institute of Finnair in 1964–66 before being placed on view in the cramped surroundings of the Tampere Technical Museum. In 1980 it was moved to Vantaa and can now be seen in all its splendor.

Some interesting Finnish types are also on view and show the talent of amateur designers in the country. Juhani Heinonen designed the HK-1 single-seat monoplane in the early 1950s and the sole example flew at Jami in 1954. The power unit is a Czechoslovak Walter Mikron engine of 62 hp and the HK-1 achieved fame with a flight on July 20,

1957. The aircraft took off from Madrid and landed later in the day in Turku to establish a distance record of 1778 miles (2844km) for machines weighing less than 1100 lb (500 Kg). The aircraft was withdrawn in 1970 but a development, the two-seat HK-2, was flown in 1963 and is still in use. Torulf Eklund of Vaasa designed the TÈ-1 single-seat amphibian which was constructed by the State Aircraft Factory at Halli in 1949. The initial engine was a 28 hp Poinsard, but the aircraft was underpowered and a 40 hp Continental A-40 was fitted. This diminutive aircraft was in regular use until 1969, when it was dismantled and put in the owner's garage until 1982, when it was moved to the museum.

As in many countries, the light autogyro has enjoyed a resurgence in Finland, and Seppo Kokkola built a gyroglider, the KO-1, in 1959. Unfortunately it crashed on its first flight, but was rebuilt as the KO-2 with a 28 hp Poinsard engine; however, this was only in use for a short time before it once again was involved in an accident. The designer was not to be deterred and an extensively modified version, the KO-3 took to the air in 1961 to be followed by the KO-4, which is on show, in 1969.

Students and staff of the Finnish Institute of Technology Flying Club have been involved in the design of gliders and light aircraft for over half a century. Their first venture was the construction of a German Zogling primary glider in 1934, and others were built before World War II. Four examples of their work can be seen in the Vantaa exhibition. Two are gliders: the PIK-3a prototype glider of 1950, and the PIK-5b developed from the Polish Salamandra in the early 1950s; the others are the PIK-10 Moottoribaby, which is a powered version of the Grunau Baby, and the PIK-11 Tumppu low-wing monoplane. The PIK-10 was the first powered aircraft to be produced by the team, and used initially a 17 hp French Aubier and Dunne engine, probably from a Mignet Pou-du-Ciel, but this was replaced by the ubiquitous Poinsard. The first true powered aircraft to be constructed was the PIK-11 which flew in 1953 and two later examples were built. In 1966 the prototype was placed in the small private museum of the Institute, and when this closed it was acquired by the Finnish Aviation Museum Society for Vantaa. Three Finnish military aircraft – a Pyry, the sole remaining Tuisku biplane and a Saaski biplane – all products of the State Aircraft Factory, and a Polikarpov I-16UTI from the USSR constitute the service side of the display, along with two British jets, a Vampire Trainer and a Gnat. The outside yard is for the showing of airliners in particular, and on view are a Convair 340/440 used by Finnair for 28 years, a Lodestar used by Karhumaki Airways for geological survey work and one of the oldest DC-3s surviving. This enterprising museum is a just reward for a group of dedicated and enthusiastic volunteers.

This rare two-seat Polikarpov UTI-4 was captured by the Finns in 1941 and flown for a short time. Now in the Vantaa museum, it is depicted in a typically Finnish scene

TAMPERE TECHNICAL MUSEUM
Tampereen Teknillinen Museo

Itsenaisyydenkatu 21, 33500 Tampere 50
Tel: 931-32-000
Opening hours: midday–6pm Tuesday–Sunday
Location: in the center of the town just east of the main railway station

de Havilland DH 60X Moth (1927)
Fokker D.10 (1923)
Gyroglider (?)
Mignet HM-14 Pou-du-Ciel (1935)
Mil Mi-1 (WSK-SM-1/600Sz) (1960)
Valtion Saaski II (1929), **Pyry II (I)** (1939)

In the early 1970s, the Tampere Technical Museum was the only one in Finland with aircraft on show, and these were (and still are) confined to one floor of the rather small building. The star of this show is the de Havilland Moth 'Ilmatar', the first light plane in the country, which was flown to Finland in October 1927 by Hubert Broad for use by Aero O/Y. The aircraft was used until 1931 when it crashed, but after a two-year rebuild it flew until 1937 when it was put in store.

Another prize exhibit is the first prototype of the locally-designed Pyry advanced trainer, which first flew in March 1939 and was followed by 40 production examples. The display also includes a number of components, engines, photographs and other items.

VESIVEHMAA COLLECTION
Vesivehmaan Varastohalli

Contact Matti Vahvaselka, Kariniemenkatu 28 B 65, Lahti 14 for information and admission
Location: about 12 miles (20km) northeast of Lahti just off Route 313

Aero A-11 (1927), **A-32** (1929)
Blackburn Ripon IIF (1937)
Bréguet 14A2 (1919)
Caudron C.59 (1923), **C.60** (1927), **C.714** (1939)
Fokker C.VE (1934)
Folland Fo.141 Gnat F.1 (1958)
Gloster Gamecock (1929)
Harakka I (1946)
Ilmailuvoimien D.26 Haukka I (1927), **K.1 Kurki** (1927)
Kassel 12A (1935)
Mikoyan-Gurevich MiG-15UTI (1950)
Valtion E.30 Kotka II (1931)

After the end of World War II a large hangar at the former air force base of Vesivehmaa, north of Lahti, was the site for storing most of the preserved aircraft in Finland. Initially this large earth-floored building was crammed with aircraft, the majority of which were in reasonable condition although several were without engines. Over the years, the number has been greatly reduced as aircraft have been taken to air force bases and schools to be restored and allocated to other museums. Known as the Vesivehmaa Collection (Vesivehmaan Varastohalli), the store is run by volunteer members of the Finnish Aviation Museum Society and is usually open to visitors at weekends.

Now hanging in the terminal at Helsinki Airport, this Junkers Junior was flown by Vaino Bremer on his many long distance flights

The group has put on a small exhibition of memorabilia and cleaned up several of the airframes and assembled others. In addition two fairly modern aircraft, a Folland Gnat and a MiG-15UTI two-seat trainer, have been added from air force stocks. One of the assembled aircraft is the sole surviving Blackburn Ripon. Finland bought one of the type in 1928, and subsequently another 25 were built under license in Tampere. The Ripon at Vesivehmaa was the last to be used in the country and was withdrawn from use in December 1944: it is the only remaining example of the Yorkshire company's large biplanes. This aircraft was due to move to Tikkakoski for restoration in the late 1980s.

When Finland gained its independence in 1918 a French aviation mission visited the country, and soon afterwards the Air Force Aircraft Factory was set up. The mission led to the purchase of a number of French types, three of which are at Vesivehmaa. The Bréguet 14 was one of the most widely used military aircraft of the 1920s, and a great number were manufactured and exported to many countries in a number of variants. Finland acquired 38 between 1919 and 1922, and the last example was withdrawn in 1927. Also awaiting rebuild are two Caudron biplanes which are the only survivors of their types in the world. The Hispano-Suiza-powered C.59 is one of three bought in 1923, and the C.60 using a Clerget engine is one of a batch of 34 built under license by the state factory following on from 30 purchased from the manufacturer in France. A fourth French aircraft is one of six Caudron C.714 low-wing fighters which were given to Finland by France in 1940 to help the country in the Winter War against the Soviet Union.

In the early inter-war period Finland adopted a policy of purchasing small numbers of many types from abroad for competitive evaluation against each other and against designs from the State Aircraft Factory, and it was not really until the 1930s that equipment became standardized.

In the late 1920s Finland ordered aircraft from Czechoslovakia and two products of the Aero company have survived, these being one of the eight A-11s (license-built Brandenburg C I) acquired in 1927 and withdrawn in 1939, and one of the 16 A-32s which were in use from 1929 to 1945.

France

AIR AND SPACE MUSEUM
Musée de l'Air et de l'Espace

Aéroport du Bourget, 93
Tel: 837-01-73
Opening times: 10am–6pm Monday–Friday (closes at 5pm October–April), 10am–midday and 2pm–6pm Saturday–Sunday

Location: Le Bourget is about 6 miles (10 km) northeast of Paris on Routes A1 and N2. Chalais–Meudon is about 7 miles (12 km) southwest of Paris off Route N306A. Villacoublay is about 10 miles (16 km) southwest of Paris on Route N186.

Ader Avion III (R) (1969)
Aero 45 (1954)
Aérospatiale SA.3210 Super Frélon (1962)
Aérospatiale/BAC Concorde (1969)
Amiot Monoplane (?), 351 (1940)
Arado Ar 96B (1939)
Arsenal Air 100 (1945), 102 (1950)
Avia 15P (1932), 40P (1937)
Beech B18S (JRB-4) (1944), B18S (C-45) (1945), E18S (c.1957)
Bell 47G (1954)
Bernard 191 Grand Raid (1929)
Biot Planeur (1879)
Blériot IX (1908, 1909), XI-2 (1913), XXXVI (c.1919)
Bloch MB-152 (1939)
Boeing 299 Fortress (B-17G) (1944), 707-328B (1966)
Boeing-Stearman A75NI (1941)
Boisavia B.601L Mercurey (1959)
Bréguet 14A2 (1917), 19 Grand Raid (1926), 19 Super Bidon (1929), 111 Gyroplane (1946), 900 (1957), 901 (1958), 904S (1959), 941S (1967), 1001 Taon (1958), 1050 Alize (1959)
Bréguet/BAC Jaguar (1969)
Bristol 149 Bolingbroke IVT (1942)
Brochet MB.50 (MB.30) (1955), MB.83 (MB.80) (1950), MB.85 (MB.81) (1950)
Bruel, Duhamel, Molinari Helicopter (c.1950)
Bücker Bü 181B Bestmann (1938)
Castel C.25S (c.1946), C.242 (1942), C.301S (1945), C.310P (1946), C.311P (1950)
Castel-Mauboussin CM.8/13 (1949)
Caudron G.3 (1913), G.4 (1915), C.60 (1921), C.109 (1925), C.277 Luciole (1935), C.282 Phalène (1933), C.366 Atalante (1933), C.510 Pelican (?), C.600 Aiglon (c.1935), C.635 Simoun (1935), C.714 (1938), C.714R (1939), C.800 (1945), C.801 (1952)
Chanute Glider (1921)
Charles et Robert Balloon (?)
Cierva C.8L (Avro 611) (1928), C.30 (LeO 402) (1936)
Colomban MC-10 Cri-Cri (1974)
Croses Mini Criquet (1975)
Curtiss-Wright CW.1 Junior (1930)
Dassault MD-311 Flamant (1952), MD-312 Flamant (1953), MD-315R Flamant (1952), MD-450 Ouragan (1950), Mirage IIIA (1965), Mirage IIIC (1961), Mirage IIIV (1965), Mirage IVA (1960), Mirage F.1 (R) (?), Mirage G.8 (c.1965), Mystère IIC (1952), Mystère IVA (1954, 1955), Super Mystère B2 (1957, 1958, 1959), Mystère 20 (1965)
de Havilland DH 9 (1918), DH 80A Puss Moth (1935), DH 82A Tiger Moth (1940), DH 89A Dragon Rapide (1944), DH 100 Vampire (SE.535) (1951), DH 115 Vampire T.55 (1955)
Deperdussin B (1911), Monocoque (1913)
Dewoitine D.VII (1923), D.520 (1939), D.530 (1937)
DFS 108-14 Schulgleiter SG-38 (?), 108-30 Kranich (1939), 108-53 Habicht II (1937), 108-70 Meise (1938), Weihe (VMA 200 Milan) (1950), 230B-2 (1941), 230C-1 (1941)
Donnet Leveque A (1912)
Dornier Do 28B-1 (?)
Douglas A-26B Invader (1941, 1944), DC-3 (C-47A) (1941), DC-3 (C-47B) (1942), DC-7C/AMOR (1956), AD-4N Skyraider (1952)
Dumolard Autoplan Pou du-Ciel (1962)
English Electric Canberra B.6 (1954)
Fabre Hydravion (1910)
Farman F.60 Goliath (1919), F.192 (1929), F.455 Moustique (1936), HF.20 (1912), MF.7 (1911)
Fauvel AV.22S (1959), AV.36 (1955), AV.45 (1963)
Ferber 6 (R) (?)
Fieseler Fi 103 (1944)
Focke-Achgelis Fa 330A-1 Bachstelze (1942)
Focke-Wulf Fw 190A-8 (NC.900) (1942)
Fokker D VII (1918)
Fouga CM.170R Magister (c.1956, c.1962)
Fournier RF.2 (1962)
Gambetta Balloon (?)
Gary GR.1 Autogyro (1978)
Gloster Meteor T.7 (1951), Meteor NF.11 (1948, 1951), Meteor NF.13 (1953), Meteor NF.14 (1954)
Gourdou-Leseurre B.7 (1937)
Grassi Planeur (1938)
Guerchais-Roche SA.103 Emouchet (1946), SA.104 Emouchet (1950)
Hanriot HD-14 (1924)
Hawker Hunter F.4 (1956)
Heinkel He 46D (1934), He 111 (CASA 2.111) (1955), He 162A (1944)
Hirsch H.100 (1954)
Hurel Aviette MPA (1974)
Hurel-Dubois HD.10 (1947), HD.34 (1957)
Jodel D.9 Bébé (1947), D.119 (1958)
Junkers J 9 (D-1) (1918), F 13 (1924), Ju 52/3m (AAC.1) (1946)
Kellner-Bechereau E.60 (1940)
Leduc 010 (1946), 022 (1956)
Levavasseur Antoinette (1909)
Lilienthal Glider (R) (c.1927)
Lockheed T-33A (1951, 1953, 1955), T-33AN (Canadair) (1954), RT-33A (1954), L-749A Constellation (1947), SP-2H Neptune (P2V-7) (1956)
LVG C VI (1918)
Martin B-26 Marauder (1942)
Matra-Cantiniau MC.101 (1952)
Mauboussin M.121 Corsaire (1931)
Max Holste MH.1521M Broussard (1955, 1957, 1958), MH.260 (1959)
Messerschmitt Bf 109E (1942), Bf 109 (HA.1112K) (1953)
Mignet HM-8 (1932), HM-14 Pou-du-Ciel (1934, 1935), HM-280 Pou-du-Ciel (1944)
Montgolfière Balloon (R) (?)
Morane-Saulnier G (1913), MS.29 (1917), MS.30 (A1) (1921), MS.149 (1929), MS.230 (?), MS.315 (1946), MS.317 (1947), MS.406 (D-3801) (1938), MS.472 Vanneau (1947), MS.500 (Fi 156) (1944), MS.505 (Fi 156) (1944, 1945), MS.733 Alcyon (1952), MS.880 Rallye (1959), MS.1500 Epervier (c.1966)
Moynet M.360 Jupiter (1963)
Nieuport 2N (1910), 11 (R) (c.1972)
Nieuport-Delage XI (1915), 29C.1 (1918)
Nord NC.701 (Si 204) (1945), NC.702 (Si 204) (1947), NC.856N Norvigie (1954), N.1002 Pingouin (Bf 108) (1946), N.1101 Noralpha (1946), N.1203 Norécrin VI (1947), N.1300 (1945), N.1500 Griffon (1957), N.2000 (1947), N.2200 (1949), N.2501 Noratlas (1952), N.3202 (1961), N.3400 (1959)
North American T-6G Texan (1951), T-6J Texan (1953), T-28A (Sud Fennec) (1951), B-25J Mitchell (1944), P-51D Mustang (1944), F-86K Sabre (1955), F-100D Super Sabre (1955)
Oemichen Helicopter 1 (1920), Helicopter 2 (1923), Helicopter 3 (1927), Helicopter 6 (1935), Helicopter 7 (1937)
Packard Lepère C2 (1918)
Paumier Biplane (1912)
Payen PA.49b (1954)
Perrin Helicopter (1924)
Pescara F.3 (1923)
Pfalz D XII (1918)
Piel CP.1310 Super Emeraude (c.1963)
Piper PA-18 Super Cub (L-18C) (1953)
Polikarpov I-153 (1938)
Potez 36/13 (1929), 43/7 (1931), 53 (1933), 58/2 (1935), 842 (1965), 94A (Fouga CM.173) (1964)
REP D (1910), K (1913)
Renard Helicopter (R) (?)
Renard and Krebs Airship (?)
Republic P-47D Thunderbolt (1944), F-84E Thunderjet (1950), F-84F Thunderstreak (1952)
Royal Aircraft Factory Be.2C (1915)
RRG Zogling (?)
SAAB 29B (J-29B) (1954), 35 Draken (J-35) (?)
Saconney Cerf Volant (c.1910?)
Santos-Dumont 14bis (R) (1973), Demoiselle (1908), Demoiselle (R) (?)
Schleicher Ka-2 Rhonschwalbe (1952), Ka-6 Rhonsegler (1956)
Schmitt PS.1 (c.1918)
Schneider Grunau Baby II (DFS 108-49) (1942)
Schreck FBA, 17HT4 (1930)
Short S.25 Sandringham 7 (Sunderland III) (1943)
Sikorsky S.55 (H-19D) (1955), S-58 (H-34) (c.1958), S.58 (HSS-1) (c.1958)
Siren C.30S (1965), C.34 Edelweiss (1967)
SNECMA C.400P2 Atar Volant (1957)
SNIAS Pegase (T-33AN modified) (?), Sustentateur Ludion (?)
Sopwith 1½ Strutter (1917)
SPAD VII (c.1916), XIII.C1 (1917), XIII.C2 (1917), 52 (1921), 54 (1922)
Stampe SV.4C (1947)
Sud-Est SE.210 Caravelle (1956, 1960, 1963), SE-212 Durandal (?), SE-3101 (1948), SE-3130 Alouette (1955), SE-5000 Baroudeur (1953)
Sud-Ouest SO-30P Bretagne (1951), SO-1110 Ariel II (1949), SO-1220 Djinn (1953), SO-1221S Djinn (1955), SO-4050 Vautour IIB (1957), SO-4050 Vautour IIN (1957), SO-6000 Triton (1949), SO-9000 Trident (1953)
Supermarine 361 Spitfire IX (1942), 361 Spitfire XVI (1944)
SZD-24 Foka (1960)
Vertol V.43 CH-21C1 (1952)
Voisin 1907 (1907), 10 (1911), L-A5B2 (1915)
Vuia 1 (1906)
Wassmer WA.21 Javelot (1958), WA.22A Super Javelot (1961), WA.51 Pacific (1969)
Westland Lysander III (1942)
Wright Flyer (R) (?), Baby (1910)
Yakovlev YAK-3 (1943)
Zeppelin C IV (1918)
Zlin Z-326 Trener Master (1967)
Zodiac Moto-Balloon 31 (?)

France's major aviation museum is generally accepted as being one of the three most important collections in the world along with the NASM in Washington and the USAFM at Dayton, although some other US museums may soon be rivaling the three in terms of numbers of aircraft on the inventory. The museum, which was founded in 1919, was the first truly aeronautical museum in the world. The originator of the collection was Gen Caquot, an engineer, and initially the exhibits were stored at Issy-les-Moulineaux. The museum was officially opened at Chalais-Meudon on November 23, 1921.

The exhibition hall was an 1878 building constructed for the Paris Exhibition and moved to Meudon to serve as a hangar for the airship 'La France'. The site was rather inconvenient for visitors, so a new building on the Boulevard Victor was constructed in 1933 and part of the collection was on show there from 1936. The new halls were damaged in 1940 and the aircraft returned to Meudon for storage. During World War II and in the period immediately afterwards a limited amount of restoration took place, and the museum hangar at Meudon reopened in 1950.

Aircraft mainly from a bygone era were everywhere – resting on the floor, mounted on pedestals and suspended from the ceiling. Cabinets containing models, photographs, documents, posters, instruments, medals and other items seemed to be in every gap. On a visit three years later, the writer was taken to 'Y' hangar where even more material was crammed into another vast building – here no attempt had been made to present a display and aircraft, components and engines were everywhere. The next fifteen or so years saw little change except that a hangar in which some flyable aircraft were housed was sited at St Cyr l'Ecole airfield and other storage premises were obtained at Villacoublay.

The 1970s saw the next major developments which led to the main exhibition moving north of the city to Le Bourget. The airfield at Le Bourget was opened in World War I and in 1919 became the civil airport for the city. A number of historic events either started or finished from this airfield. Many of the famous French long-distance flights commenced from Le Bourget, and on May 21, 1927 Charles Lindbergh landed there after his solo crossing of the Atlantic. The opening of Orly Airport after World War II caused a decline in the importance of Le Bourget but many short-haul services still used the field. An increase in executive

The Sud-Ouest Trident was designed as a fighter but was used for research. The aircraft was powered by two tip-mounted jets, and had three rocket motors in the rear fuselage

flying and a military base on the west side still meant that the airfield was busy. In 1951 the famous Salon de l'Aéronautique moved from its traditional home in the Grand Palais, and exhibition halls were erected at Le Bourget. The construction of the new Charles de Gaulle Airport at Roissy-en-France meant that hangars were being vacated at Le Bourget, and the museum, under its then dynamic leader Gen Pierre Lissarague, was quick to take advantage. The first hall was ready for the 1975 Paris Air Show, with a second opening the following May.

The Meudon collection was at this stage reorganized to present aircraft and items from the pre-1918 period. For the first time there was space to show the aircraft in an ordered way and the whole exhibition proved a unique presentation of the history of the early days of flight. As more space was acquired at Le Bourget, the plans for Meudon were changed and the display closed in 1983. The terminal building at Le Bourget was acquired by the museum in 1982 and has undergone a massive refurbishment, enabling it to house the pre-1918 collection. The vast Eiffel building at Meudon is likely to become an exhibition of balloons and airships. The museum has several lighter-than-air craft in store, a number of them from the famous balloonist Charles Dollfus, who was curator of the museum for many years.

By 1981 five halls were open at Le Bourget, and including those in the outside aircraft park almost 150 machines were on show. The museum also has workshops at Meudon and there are three stores, at Meudon, at Dugny on the west side of Le Bourget, and at Villacoublay. Even with the largest exhibition space in Europe only about half of the collection can be seen at the present time, and it is hoped that further expansion into the remaining Le Bourget hangars is not too far away.

The display in the terminal building traces the story of flight from the early hang-gliding pioneers and the earliest example is the aircraft of Biot. Constructed in 1879, this frail glider flew at Clamart and is the oldest left in the world. The museum acquired the Biot in 1925 and it was completely restored in 1960. Other hang-gliders include an 1895 Lilienthal monoplane replica, built in 1927, and an original 1896 Chanute biplane.

There is a French school of thought which would have the first powered flight accredited to Clément Ader, whose steam-powered Eole bounced briefly into the air in 1890. In 1897 Ader constructed the Avion III, which was again not a success, but the museum has a replica of this (built in 1969

The Farman Moustique of 1936 was an attempt to produce an ultra-light sporting aircraft

The Bréguet Super Bidon used by Costes and Bellonte on their 1930 Paris-New York flight

for a film) and they have the original in their workshops. The first real powered flight in Europe was carried out in the Parc du Bagatelle on September 13, 1906. The museum has a replica of this unconventional machine.

The French were among the leaders in aviation in the pre-1914 period and the museum collection from this period is probably the best in the world. Highlights include the first seaplane in the world, in which Henri Fabre took off from the Etang de Berre on March 28, 1910, the Blériot in which Adolphe Pégoud carried out some of the first aerobatics, and the Deperdussin monocoque in which Maurice Prévost won the Gordon Bennett Trophy and set a speed record of over 120 mph (200 km/h). On September 21, 1913 at the airfield of Buc just south of Paris a crowd gathered to see Pégoud perform in public a loop, a roll and a tail slide. At Meudon the famous Blériot was mounted upside down to acclaim the feat. An interesting biplane is the one constructed in 1912 by Emile Paumier, stored for over 60 years before being presented to the museum.

The collection includes a significant number of World War I aeroplanes from France, the UK, Germany and the US. From America is the sole surviving Packard Lepère C2. This two-seat biplane was designed by the French engineer Lepère but by the time of the Armistice only 55 of the 5500 ordered by the US Army had been completed. Three of the type saw active service and the C2 set altitude records in 1921 and 1922.

At Le Bourget, Hall A covers the inter-war period with 25 aircraft on view. All are originals and 10 have made significant contributions to the history of aviation. In this era French aviators made many long-distance flights, and three famous aircraft can be seen. The Bréguet 19 Grand Raid in which Costes and Le Brix made the first crossing of the South Atlantic from Dakar in Senegal to Natal in Brazil on October 10, 1927 is the oldest of the trio. Derived from the 19 is the Super Bidon of 1929 which was used in a number of flights. On September 2, 1930, with Costes and Bellonte as crew, it made the first direct Paris–New York flight followed by a tour of the world which finished in Paris on October 10. The famous aerobatic pilots of the time are honored, with their brightly-painted machines mounted in flying postures. These are the Morane A 1 of Fronval which appeared at many meetings in the 1920s, the SPAD 52 of Casale, the Gourdou- Leseurre B.7 of Malinvaud and the famous Dewoitine D.530 of Marcel Doret. Doret, who had in 1927 performed 1111 consecutive loops in just under five hours in a Morane A 1 at Munich, was one of the foremost aerobatic pilots of his day. He was chief pilot for the Dewoitine company, and in 1937, following the crash of his D.272, he developed from the D.27 the D.530. This high-wing monoplane with a 500 hp Hispano-Suiza 12-cylinder engine delighted air show crowds until May 1955, when the combination made their last appearance at Reims.

The French were also to the fore in the air racing field and three of their famous machines can be seen. The Potez 53, with which Dêtre won the 1933 Coupe Deutsch at Etampes at a speed of over 200 mph (322 km/h) for the 1250 mile (2000 km) course, is shown alongside the Caudron C.366, which was designed for the same contest but crashed before it could take part. However, in January 1934 it set a speed record of 222.5 mph (358 km/h) over a 625 mile (1000 km) course with Louis Masotte in command and the same duo was second in the 1934 Coupe Deutsch race. The final member of the trio is the Caudron C.714R, a special version of the C.714 fighter.

Other aircraft in the hall show the transport and private flying of the era. An interesting relic is the sole surviving fuselage of a giant Farman Goliath airliner which made some of the first passenger flights between Paris, London and Brussels. The decor and seating is in stark contrast with

A view of the large Hall E, where a Dragon Rapide is portrayed dropping parachutists; sporting aircraft and gliders may also be seen

modern airliners. No display of French aircraft of the period would be complete without an example of Henri Mignet's tandem-wing HM-14 Pou-du-Ciel which almost revolutionized home building in the mid 1930s. Inspired by his book *Le Sport de l'Air* thousands of enthusiasts in many countries rushed into constructing Poux. Unfortunately for a number of reasons there were many fatalities, and the tandem-wing formula was forgotten except in France where many developments of the basic concept are still being constructed.

Hall B is devoted to World War II and aircraft from four of the participants are on view. Classic fighters such as the Spitfire, Mustang, Thunderbolt, Focke-Wulf 190, Morane-Saulnier 406 and Dewoitine 520 show the ideas in force at the time. The display is unusual in that two Russian aircraft are on view. These are the stubby biplane Polikarpov I-153, a type which was used in the Spanish Civil War, and the monoplane Yakovlev Yak-3 in the markings of the 'Normandie-Niemen' regiment. Some of the larger World War II aircraft are on view in the outside park.

Hall C traces the development of the French aviation industry in the post-1945 period. As in earlier days the

This Dewoitine D.520 fighter is maintained in airworthy condition, and is normally based at Brétigny

designers in the country have again shown great inventiveness and some unusual configurations are on view. France's first jet, the SO 6000 Triton, which first flew in November 1946, is alongside two of the Leduc ram jet research aircraft. Experiments in this form of propulsion started in 1929 and the first aircraft, the 010, was commenced in 1937 and made its first powered flight on April 21, 1949, achieving a speed of 450 mph (720 km/h) at half power. The 010 on show is modified from the later 016 and the later 022 can also be seen. There are examples of the famous Dassault range of jets including prototypes of the Mystère IV, Mirage IIIA and Mirage IIIV, with a Mirage IVA outside. This display is a fitting memorial to a vibrant industry and there are also galleries showing the French engine industry.

Hall D has a display of 10 aircraft used by the Armée de l'Air from 1945, with many other types on view outside.

The largest hall in this line is Hall E with a spectacular arrangement of sporting aircraft and gliders. Around 40 machines are on view, shown at different levels in order to create the impression of a flying display. Suspended close to the ceiling is a de Havilland Dragon Rapide from which a string of parachutists are falling, and this classic biplane is surrounded by examples of gliders which have been used at many clubs around the country. Over 60 years of sporting flying are portrayed in all aspects: there are helicopters and autogyros, man-powered aircraft and home built machines in this impressive exhibition.

Coupled with the large modern types such as Concorde in the outside display, the exhibition at Le Bourget provides a comprehensive record of the history of flight this century.

CHAMPAGNE AERONAUTICAL MUSEUM
Musée Aéronautique de Champagne

Aérodrome de Brienne-le-Château, 10
Tel: 3325-9284-11
Opening times: variable
Location: the airfield is about 3 miles (5 km) northwest of the town on Route N60 and about 22 miles (30 km) northeast of Troyes

Adam RA.14 Loisirs (1954, 1959)
Bréguet 904S (1959)
Brochet MB-50 Pipistrelle (c.1950)
Castel C.25S (1946), **C.310P** (1946)
Caudron C.282 Phalène (1932), **C.800** (1945)
Centre Aviation GA-620 Gaucho (1963)
Chanute Glider (R) (?)
Chapeau EC.19 Planeum (?)
Denize RD-105 Raid Driver (1963)
DFS 108-14 Schulgleiter SG-38 (c.1942)
Drezair Hang-Glider (?)
Druine D.31 Turbulent (1965)
Dassault Mystère IVA (1953)
Fauvel AV.36 (1954)
Fleury Vedette (c.1954)
Fouga CM.170 Magister (1956)
Gardan GY-201 Minicab (1961), **GY-80 Horizon** (1966)
Guerchais-Roche SA.103 Emouchet (1946), **SA.104 Emouchet** (1950)
Jodel D.112 (1955)
Lachassagne AL.07 (1958)
Leduc RL-19 (1952)
Lemaire RL-1 (1970)
Léopoldoff L-55 (1956)
Lockheed T-33A (1951), **P2V-7 Neptune (SP-2H)** (c.1959)
Max Holste MH.1521M Broussard (1957)
Mignet HM-14 Pou-du-Ciel (1935), **HM-360 Pou-du-Ciel** (1963), **HM-3?? Pou-du-Ciel** (?)
Miroue Dodier MD Pou-du-Ciel (1973)
Mirouze AM.01 Pulsar (c.1968)
Nord N.2000 (1947), **N.2501 Noratlas** (1953), **NC.856N Norvigie** (1953)
Nuville JN-2 Gyrocopter (1970)
Piel CP.80 (1974)
Pottier P.170S (c.1980)
SFAN4 (BAC Drone) (c.1936)
Schleicher ASK-16 (1974)
SIPA S.903(901) (1951)
Siren C-30 Edelweiss (1957), **C-34** (1967)
Taylor Monoplane (c.1975)
Tresy Monoplane (c.1978)
Van Lith VI (1958)
Williams Motorfly (1953)

The French have always been innovative in the design and construction of home-built aircraft and many original designs have been most successful. One of the earliest to achieve fame was Henri Mignet with his 14th design, the infamous Pou-du-Ciel. The Réseau du Sport de l'Air was founded by Pierre Lacour to organize and administer the movement in the post World War II years. The RSA held an annual rally at different locations throughout the country from the late 1940s. In the 1970s one of these gatherings was held at the airfield of Brienne-le-Château which was built as a US military base but never used operationally. The field with its lengthy runway housed a gliding club in one of its vast hangars. For a time the rally was held in alternate years at Brienne, but now this site has become the permanent venue for the national fly-in, with smaller ones held around the country.

In the late 1970s a collection of vintage and homebuilt aircraft began appearing in the hangar, and these were put on show at the rally. The numbers began to grow and the RSA set up an official museum. Variety to the exhibits was obtained when ex-French military aircraft began arriving. As the collection was no longer solely concerned with homebuilt aircraft, the museum took up its present title in 1984 and widened its scope to cover the aeronautical history of the region.

In honor of Henri Mignet two original HM-14s are present, and comparison of these aircraft with later versions of the tandem-wing formula show significant differences in

The SFAN 2 was a license-built British Aircraft Company Drone; this two-seat development, the SFAN 4, was constructed after World War II from prewar components

The Fleury Vedette was built in the early 1950s when the home building movement was taking off again in France

both design and engineering. Also from the 1930s is a SFAN 4 two-seater. The design was developed from the British BAC Drone powered glider. Examples of both the single-seater and the two-seater, a French innovation, were built before World War II. A number of components were discovered after the end of the war and these were assembled in the late 1940s. A postwar development of a pre-war design is the delightful Léopoldoff L-55 biplane.

One question that arises in connection with museums of homebuilt aircraft is why should a designer donate a successful flying aircraft to a museum? Fortunately, there are some individuals who wish to see their work preserved. Charles Gasse constructed the Leduc RL.19 in 1952 and René Leduc had achieved fame with his RL.16 which set an altitude record for light planes in 1949. Roger Adam is another designer whose RA.14 high-wing monoplane was adopted by many amateur constructors. The design work commenced in 1945 and it flew at the end of the year, to become the first European postwar type to be available for amateur construction.

Many of the French designers are not content with just one design and over a span of years their fertile minds produce a variety of machines. Jean Van Lith has been active in both pre- and post-World War II France and his high-wing twin- ruddered VI flew in 1959.

One of the most successful European designs ever flew at Beaune in 1948. The single seat Jodel D.9 flew in the January of that year and a two-seat version the D.11 followed in May 1950. These low-wing monoplanes with the distinctive cranked shape were an instant success and were taken up by firms in several countries. Thousands of both basic designs and their developments, which have included four-seaters and models with nose wheel undercarriages, have been produced.

The design and construction of any aircraft requires both time and money, so naturally some projects fall by the wayside. The museum has been able to acquire some in this category and the visitor can see the methods of construction involved in their incomplete airframes. Others have ambitious plans for their projects and a stand at the 1963 Paris Air Show extolled the virtues of the Centre Aviation Gaucho low-wing monoplane. Four versions of the basic design were proposed, which could be used for touring and aerobatics. The type then faded into obscurity and the writer remembers, while touring France by air in the early 1970s, calling at the airfield at which their factory was supposedly located. The premises turned out to be little more than a large shed in which the Gaucho was sitting forlornly on flat tyres. This unique aircraft is now preserved as a reminder to those who see a golden future for their design, while even though it is a good aircraft, financial backing is required to turn it into a commercial venture.

The museum contains what many consider to be one of the most hideous designs in any collection. The Mirouze Pulsar is constructed with a fiberglass skin and this delta with a pusher engine has a rough surface, with the two wings of apparently different section if viewed from the front. There appears to be little provision for an undercarriage but photos exist in which the aircraft appears to be flying. One wonders if the photo is faked.

This collection is a memorial to the many individuals who have helped the French homebuilt movement become one of the most respected. In rooms at the rear of the hangar can be seen engines, photos and other items which trace the history of amateur aviation in the country.

JEAN-BAPTISTE SALIS ASSOCIATION
L'Amicale Jean-Baptiste Salis

Aérodrome de la Ferté-Alais, 91
Tel: 331-6457-5289

Opening times: whenever the airfield is open, but obtain permission at Control
Location: off Route N449 about 1 mile (2 km) north of the town, which is about 25 miles (40 km) south of Paris

Abraham 2 Iris (c.1932)
Agusta-Bell 47G (c.1958)
Albatros C II (R) (1978)
Arsenal Air 100 (1945), **102** (1950)
Auster J/1 Autocrat (1947)
Beech A-35 Bonanza (1949), **D18S** (1951), **E18S** (1952)
Bell 47G (1956)
Blériot XI (R) (1955)
Boeing-Stearman A75N1 (1941, 1942)
Bréguet XIVP (R) (1980), **904S** (1959)
Brochet MB.72 (1950)
Bücker Bü 131 Jungmann (Doflug) (1936), **Bü 131 Jungmann (CASA 1131E)** (1939), **Bü 133C Jungmeister (Doflug)** (1936), **Bü 181 Bestmann** (1947)
CAP.10AJBS (1981), **20LS** (1983)
Caudron C-69 (1931), **C-275 Luciole** (1932), **C-282 Phalène** (1932), **C-601 Aiglon** (1935), **C-800** (1945)
Cessna 305 Bird Dog (0-1A) (1951)
Dassault MD-311 Flamant (c.1950)
Deperdussin Monocoque (R) (1980)
de Havilland DH 82A Tiger Moth (1942–44), **DH 89A Dragon Rapide** (194?,1945), **DH 94 Moth Minor** (1939), **DH C1 Chipmunk T.22** (1953)
Dewoitine D-26 (1931), **D-520DC** (1945)
Douglas AD-4N Skyraider (1951), **DC-3 (C-47B)** (1942)
Fairchild F.24W Argus (UC-61A) (1943-44)
Farman F.400 (c.1936)
Fauvel AV.36 (1955)
Fokker Dr I (R) (1980)
Fouga CM.8/15 (1954)
Great Lakes 2T (?)
Hatry-Opel RAK.1(R) (1982)
Jodel D.120 (1956)
Latécoère 17P (R) (1980)
Léopoldoff L-3 (1935), **L-55** (1956), **L-6** (1954)
Mauboussin M.120 (1932), **M.127** (1947), **M.130** (1948)
Max Holste MH.1521M Broussard (1956, 1958)
Mignet HM-8 (1934)
Miles M.14A Magister (1939)
Morane-Saulnier A1 (R) (1980), **MS.130Et2** (1927), **MS.138** (1928), **MS.181** (1930), **MS.185** (1931), **MS.230** (c.1932), **MS.315** (1946), **MS.317 (MS.315)** (1946), **MS.341/3** (1933), **MS.505 (Fi 156)** (1946), **MS.733 Alcyon** (1952)
Navion Rangemaster G (1962)
Nieuport 11 (R) (1980)
Noorduyn UC-64A Norseman (1944)
Nord N.1002 Pingouin (1946), **N.1101 Noralpha** (1946), **N.1203 Norécrin VI** (194?), **N.1203 Norécrin II** (1948), **N.2000** (1947), **N.3202** (1960), **N.3400** (1959), **NC.856A** (1953), **NC.702** (1949)
North American AT-6C Texan (1941), **T-6G Texan** (1949/51), **T-28A** (1950)
Piel CP.1310 Super Emeraude (1963)
Pilatus P.2-05 (1947), **P.2-06** (1949)
Piper J-3 Cub (L-4J) (1944, 1945)
Pitts S-2A (1977), **S-1S** (1978)
Polikarpov Po-2 (c.1937)
Poullin PJ.5B (1949)
Republic P-47D Thunderbolt (1944)
Royal Aircraft Factory SE.5A (R) (1984)
Ryan Navion B (1950)
Salmson 2A2 (R) (1980), **D.6** (1949), **D.6/3** (1947), **D.7** (1949)
Scintex ML.250 Rubis (1963)
SFAN 2 (BAC Drone) (1937)
SFCA-Govin Taupin (1936)
SIPA S.903 (1949, 1951), **S.121** (1948)
Soko 522 (c.1952)
SPAD XIII (1918)
Stampe SV.4A (1946), **SV.4C** (1946-49)
Stinson SR.10C Reliant (1940), **108 Voyager** (1947)
Taylor J-2 Cub (R) (1944)
Yakovlev Yak-11 (c.1948), **Yak-18P** (c.1959)
Zlin XII (1937), **Z-326 Trener Master** (1967)

The classic lines of the de Havilland Dragon Rapide: this is one of the two examples kept at La Ferté-Alais

Jean-Baptiste Salis was born in 1896 at Montmorin in the Puy-de-Dôme region of the country and at the age of 16 he started a flying course at Aulnat. After a distinguished career as an instructor in World War I he spent the rest of his life serving aviation in a number of ways. Among his achievements were the establishment of the first airfields in the Alps, the first flight over Mont Blanc and participating in the setting up of the airfield at Toussus-le- Noble outside Paris. In 1938 he was asked to set up a training school for air force mechanics at Villacoublay and this establishment for 1200 students was open in 1939, but when France was invaded all the equipment was sabotaged.

In 1937 Salis bought a farm on a plateau at Ardenay above the town of La Ferté-Alais, some 30 miles (45 km) south of Paris. He had acquired a number of vintage aircraft over the previous 20 years, some of which were purchased with his war service gratuity in 1918. He cleared the land to produce an airfield with two grass runways, and started work on the construction of hangars, workshops and a house. At the outbreak of World War II around 30 aircraft were at the field but when the Germans invaded France they confiscated most of these and destroyed them. However, before the invasion a number had been moved to other

Two replicas of the Bréguet XIVP were built in the 1970s for film work

sites and well hidden, so that some survived the conflict.

After World War II the field became the site for one of the national gliding schools, but in his main workshops through some woods Jean-Baptiste carried on his vintage activity. He was involved in the restoration of aircraft for the Musée de l'Air but also he restarted his own collection and many historic remnants arrived at the airfield. A Blériot XI was found in the early 1950s and restored to retrace the cross-Channel flight of Louis Blériot in both 1954 and 1959 – the latter being the 50th anniversary of the historic event. Since the 1950s many aircraft have been acquired and many replicas have been created. The founder died in December 1967, and since then the running of the establishment has been carried out by his widow and his son Jean. The gliding school left in 1972, as the site was now too close to the airports of the region, and the collection was able to move into the vacated hangars. Jean realized that he would need assistance to develop the collection and in 1972 the 'Amicale Aéronautique de la Ferté-Alais' was founded. In 1976 the group was renamed 'Amicale Jean-Baptiste Salis' in honor of the founder.

Within a short time of the founding of the association the number of aircraft began to grow and at most times in the week members could be found working on the restoration of aircraft and engines. By 1980 some 40 flyable aircraft were present and this number has by now almost doubled. Hangarage was once again at a premium and in the early 1980s construction of a museum hangar commenced. This U shaped exhibition hall was constructed in three stages and now has considerable floor space.

The Blériot XI which really started the post World War II collection is still in flyable order and when conditions permit it is a performer at the annual air show at Whitsun and at other events in the country. Some aircraft were sold to the US in the late 1960s, but soon after that moves were made by the authorities to prevent other historic aircraft leaving the country unless there was justification for the sale. In the early 1960s the remains of two Caudron G.3s were found and both were faithfully restored to flying condition. One was soon sold to the US, while the other was flown regularly until a recent sale to South America which brought an ex-Venezuelan Air Force Republic Thunderbolt to France for the collection.

Other deals have included the supply of a Nieuport 11 replica to Yugoslavia and in return one of the few Polikarpov Po-2s to leave Eastern Europe now flies at the field. In

1984 some of the hangars were filled with ex-Egyptian Air Force Yakovlev 11 trainers. Jean Salis had heard that some of these exciting aircraft were available in Egypt but when he inquired about buying a few he was told that he had to purchase the whole batch or none at all. Undaunted, all were acquired and the fleet of around 42 were shipped to La Ferté-Alais. Other collections have shown interest in these Russian-designed aircraft and some have moved on to locations in France, Switzerland and the US.

While the original fleet consisted mainly of light aircraft, a number of warbirds have joined the collection (such as the Thunderbolt) and these should be in great demand for film and TV work which greatly helps the finances of the organization. In 1984 Salis bought four Douglas Skyraiders which had been the complete fleet of the Presidential Guard of Gabon. These aircraft arrived at Rouen in August 1984 and were taken to the local airfield of Boos for preparation for the ferry flight to La Ferté-Alais and St Rambert D'Albon (home of Aéro Rétro). With such a large organization it is inevitable that splinter groups emerge and leave and some of these can now be found at Etampes, a little way from La Ferté-Alais. While the hangarage at La Ferté-Alais was in short supply a large number of the collection's aircraft were stored at this historic ex-military airfield. On the positive side, the Amicale Jean-Baptiste Salis has close links with many of the other collections in France, and the four Skyraiders were purchased in conjunction with Christian Martin's Aéro Rétro.

Replica building has been a major part of the work of the collection in the 1970s and 1980s and some of these have involved starting from scratch while others have shown some inspired conversions of existing airframes. Some of the first to be built were World War I fighters for a French TV series. Two Tiger Moths were converted into Albatros C II scouts, and two Salmson 2A2 biplanes were conjured out of some derelict Caudron Luciole airframes. 'New' aircraft built include two Nieuport 11s, two Nieuport 17s, a Fokker Dr I triplane and three Morane A 1 parasols.

Another production required early airliners and postal aircraft for the story of the famous pioneer pilot Antoine St Exupéry. The Bréguet 14, which had started life as a reconnaissance and bomber in World War I, with over 8000 examples made, had been converted for postal work in the 1920s. Two replicas of this type were made using some components of other aircraft, and also a Latécoère 17 was reworked from a Noorduyn Norseman transport of the 1940s. Only the basic wing and fuselage structure of the Norseman remained. The wing was moved into the parasol position on a new system of cabane and wing struts and the front fuselage was completely altered, even though the 600 hp Pratt and Whitney engine was retained. New tail surfaces and undercarriage were built and the finished article bears little resemblance to the rugged Canadian bush plane from which it was evolved. The first Bréguet and the Latécoère were completed in 1979, and the second Bréguet was ready the following year. Although plans for the Bréguet did not exist, Roland Payen, who had designed a number of small delta-wing jet aircraft, was able to supervise the construction using dimensions and sketches he obtained from the example owned by the Musée de l'Air.

Acquired from Yugoslavia, this Polikarpov Po-2 is the only example flying in Western Europe

Two Albatros C II replicas were constructed from Tiger Moth airframes. One is seen here at the airshow at Bex in Switzerland.

The French aviation industry has been a major force in world aviation since the pioneer days and the collection includes many classic light aircraft from some of the famous firms. Morane-Saulnier was established at Puteaux in 1911 by the brothers Léon and Robert Saulnier along with Raymond Saulnier. They became well known for a series of parasol-wing monoplanes starting with the 1913 Type L. Mention has already been made of the A 1 replicas and the collection contains several other sporting and training parasols. Two have unfortunately been damaged in flying accidents, but examples of five different models are on the inventory.

The ingenuity of French aeronautical engineers has resulted over the years in some rather weird designs taking to the air. The tandem-wing formula highlighted by Henri Mignet with his Pou-du-Ciel has been taken up by several others. Louis Peyret built his Scorpion prototype in 1935 and in association with Lignel's company SFCA the design was developed into the Taupin. A small series was constructed and in the early 1960s some components were stored at Caen. These were taken to La Ferté-Alais in 1970 and nine years later the sole survivor of the breed took to the air.

Federal Republic of Germany (West Germany)

GERMAN MUSEUM OF ACHIEVEMENT IN SCIENCE AND TECHNOLOGY
Deutsches Museum von Meisterwerken der Naturwissenschaft und Technik

Museumsinsel 1, 8000 München 22
Tel: (089) 2179
Opening times: 9am–5pm daily
Location: on the Isarinsel in the center of the city

Agusta-Bell 47G-2 (c.1958)
Airbus-Industrie A.300B (1973)
Akaflieg Hannover Vampyr (1921)
Akaflieg München Mü 10 Milan (1934), **Mü 13E Bergfalke** (1951)
Akaflieg Stuttgart Fs 24 Phönix (1957)
Arado Ar 66D (1935)
Bachem Ba 349 Natter (BP 20) (1945)
Blériot XI (1909)
Bohne Homebuilt (1960s)
Buding Ornithopter (1957)
de Havilland DH 104 Dove 6 (2B) (1953)
DFS 108-?? Schulgleiter SG-36 (1936), **108-14 Schulgleiter SG-38** (1938, 1956), **108-30 Kranich II** (c.1956), **108-70 Meise** (1959)
Dittmar Condor IV (1951)
Dornier A Libelle II (1930), **Do 27B-1** (1959), **Do 31E-3** (1967), **Do 32E** (1964), **Do 335A-02 Pfeil** (1945)
Douglas DC-3 (C-47B) (1944)
EWR-Sud VJ-101C (1965)
Fauvel AV-36 (1956)
Fieseler Fi 103 (1944), **Fi 156C Storch** (1939)
Focke-Achgelis Fa 330A-1 Bachstelze (1942)
Focke-Wulf Fw 44J Stieglitz (1940)
Fokker Dr I (R) (1975), **D VII** (1918)
Goppingen Go IV Govier (1952), **Go IV Govier III** (1953)
Gosslich Pedalcopter (1958)
Grade A Libelle (1909)
Haase, Kensche, Schmetz HKS 3 (1955)
Hamburger Flugzeugbau HFB 320 Hansa (1964)
Hatry-Opel RAK 1 (R) (?)
Heinkel He 111 (CASA 2111) (1949)
Horten Ho IV (1942)
Hutter H 17A (1942)
Junkers F 13 (1928), **A 50ci Junior** (1931), **Ju 52/3m (AAC.1)** (1945)
Klemm L 25e (1935)
Lilienthal Type II (1895), **Type 15** (1896)
Lockheed T-33A (1953), **F-104F Starfighter** (1959), **F-104G Starfighter** (1961)
Messerschmitt M 17 (1925), **Bf 108 (Nord N.1002)** (1945), **Bf 109E-3** (1938), **Me 163B-1a Komet** (1944), **Me 262A-1** (1944)
MBB Bo 105 (1969)
North American F-86 Sabre (Canadair CL-13B Sabre 6) (1957)
Panavia Tornado (?)
Pelzner Glider (R) (1977)
Putzer Motorraab (1955)
Quickie Aircraft Quickie 1 (1981)
Raab Doppelraab (1954)
Republic RF-84F Thunderflash (1952)
Rumpler Taube (1910), **C IV** (1917)
SAAB J-35A Draken (c.1959)
Scheibe L-Spatz 55 (1958), **L-Spatz 55M** (1961)
Schleicher Ka-6 (1958)
Schneider Grunau Baby IIB (DFS 108-49) (1944, 1957), **Baby III (DFS 108-66)** (1952)
Schulz FS 3 Besenstiel (?)
Sikorsky S-55 (H-19B) (1953), **S-58 (H-34G)** (1958)
Solair 1 (?)
Sud-Est SE-3130 Alouette II (1960)
VFW-Fokker VAK 191B (1972)
Vollmoeller Monoplane (1909)
Wolfmüller Glider (1907)
Wright Standard Type A (1908)

A contrast in size and methods of construction. The famous Junkers Ju 52/3m with its corrugated metal skin towers over the composite Rutan-designed Quickie

Designed by students at Hannover University, the Vampyr was one of the first really successful gliders

One of the outstanding fighters of World War I was the Fokker D VII

At the turn of the century many European countries began setting up major museums which would portray the rapid advances in science and technology which were then underway. Oskar von Miller put forward the idea of such a museum in the Bavarian capital of Munich. Work started in 1906, three years after the plan was formulated, but progress was slow and the buildings were not completed until 1914. The outbreak of World War I was a further hindrance, and the opening did not take place until 1925. The interwar period saw a steady expansion in the number of exhibits and the number of exhibition halls, but in the latter stages of World War II the museum was 80 per cent destroyed and a number of valuable exhibits were lost. Reconstruction, to as near as possible the prewar configuration, started in 1948 and over the next decade galleries were opened as they were completed.

The aeronautical section until 1984 normally had around 20 aircraft on show but a new three-story extension at the end of this gallery has almost doubled the types on view. The opening ceremony of this magnificent new hall took place on May 6, 1984, when plans were announced for the development of Oberschlessheim airfield. On the north side of the airfield, which is to the north of the city, are hangars and other buildings dating back to World War I when the base was a major training establishment. Plans envisage the restoration of the historic buildings and the establishment of an exhibition so that the many aircraft and gliders which are currently stored at the airfield can be viewed by the public. Also, flyable vintage aircraft are to be based at Oberschlessheim.

A feature of the old exhibition hall in Munich was the series of beautifully restored early aircraft hanging from the ceiling. Many of these were badly damaged in the 1944 raids, but prior to the reopening they were rebuilt to original condition. They have not moved with the completion of the new gallery, and they remain as one of the best exhibitions of the period anywhere in the world. One of the earliest German pioneers was Hans Grade, whose model A with an engine of his own design won the Lanz Prize at Johannisthal near Berlin on October 30, 1909. He gained the sum of 40,000 Marks for a figure-of-eight flight of 1¼ mile (2.5 km) in which a height of 3281 feet (1000 meters) was attained. The company did not really develop its designs, and when World War I started it faded from the scene. The model A on show was presented to the museum by Hans Grade in November 1917. Prior to Grade, Otto Lilienthal had revolutionized gliding in the 1890s and his 15th aircraft from 1896 was given to the collection by Reichau and Schilling of Berlin in 1904.

The classic shape of a Taube wing is seen to advantage from the floor of the gallery. The term Taube was first used by the Austrian engineer Igo Etrich for an aircraft he built in 1909/10. The wing shape was based on the seed of the *Zanonia* plant which is native to Java. Many others copied the wing form of this successful aircraft, which set a number of Austrian records (Etrich's second Taube may be seen in the Technical Museum in Vienna). The Taube success was such that between 1910 and 1914 over 50 manufacturers produced over 500 aircraft of around 140 designs. Although dated by 1914, the Taube saw military use. The aircraft on show is a monoplane manufactured by Edmund Rumpler at Johannisthal, and when flown by Hellmuth Hirth it set many records including a 438 mile (705 km) flight from Munich to Berlin in 1911, after which Rumpler presented the Taube to the museum.

A rare aircraft is the last surviving Wright A biplane. About seven of this model were built by the brothers in 1908/9, and others were constructed under license in France, Germany and Britain. The model A on view was built in 1908 and donated by August Scherl. (A Danish museum claims to have a French-built A but there is considerable controversy among experts as to whether it is an original or a faithful replica constructed by the late Jean Salis.)

Other pioneer aircraft are in store, including a monoplane built by Hans Vollmoeller of Stuttgart in 1909. Powered by a three-cylinder Anzani engine, the craft was successfully flown and was then exhibited in a museum in Boblingen before going to the family home for storage prior to World War II. Vollmoeller died in 1917, but it was not until 1950 that his sister wrote to the museum asking if they would be interested in the aircraft, which was bought for the nominal sum of 100 Marks.

World War I is represented by two genuine aircraft and one replica and these make up for the destruction of a Fokker D VII and a Rumpler C IV in the 1944 raids. Both types have been replaced with genuine machines – the 'new' Fokker was obtained from the Bavarian military authorities, and it now carries the serial of the aircraft destroyed and the original engine from this aircraft. The Rumpler came from a Berlin collection which closed in the early 1970s and when it arrived in Munich it was in poor condition. Craftsmen and apprentices at the Messerschmitt-Bölkow-Blohm factory at Ottobrun outside the city started the reconstruction in 1977 and it is now in an authentic World War I scheme with lozenge camouflage on the wings.

Products from many of the German manufacturers which became household names in the thirties and forties are an important feature of the collection. Hugo Junkers did not produce his first aircraft until 1915 when he was 56 years old. Prior to this he had been a major industrialist and academic. The J I was the first all-metal aircraft in the world but was rather underpowered and this pioneer monoplane was destined to be used for experimental work. At the end of its use it was donated to the Deutsches Museum but was completely destroyed in 1944. In 1917 the J 7 appeared and this low-wing monoplane was fitted with corrugated duralumin skinning, which was to be the trademark of many of the successful types to emerge from the Dessau design office.

One of the aircraft which ensured the development of safe and reliable air transport was the F 13 which first flew on June 25, 1919. Seating four passengers in a cabin in which each seat had safety belts, and operated by a crew of two, the F 13 remained virtually unaltered during its long production run, which resulted in over 300 being constructed. The museum searched for a long time for an example of the F 13 to replace the one lost and in early 1969 the remains of two were found in a hangar at Kabul in

Parked in the yard of the museum is the Dornier Do 31E-3, which remains the only VTOL transport aircraft ever produced

Afghanistan. The Royal Flight of King Amanullah had used the aircraft in 1928, but by luck they had survived years in the harsh climate. Both examples were acquired and air-freighted to Erding Air Base near Munich for reconstruction into the single example on show. The corrugated skin can also be seen on a Junior touring aircraft from 1931 and a classic French-built Ju 52/3m which was presented to the museum by the French Air Force in 1958.

Willi Messerschmitt first became interested in aviation when he met the pioneer glider constructor Friedrich Harth. The young man was inspired to emulate Harth and his first powered glider, the S 15, appeared in 1923, although it was two years before he achieved any real success. 1925 saw the arrival of the M 17 high-wing two-seater with a 32 hp Bristol Cherub engine. About six M 17s were built and one achieved fame with a flight over the Alps from Bamberg to Rome. The first was stored by Messerschmitt for many years, and was restored in the 1950s, to be seen at open days at the Augsburg factory of his new company.

The Bf 108 tourer, from which the famous Bf 109 fighter was developed, was of advanced design with a fully retractable undercarriage and an enclosed cabin for four. The 108 set many records in the 1930s and many were acquired by the Luftwaffe for communications. When the German government, in defiance of Allied agreements, decided to produce military aircraft, it was a comparatively easy design task to evolve the Bf 109, of which over 34,000 had been made when production ceased in Spain in the 1950s. The Bf 108 on show is a French-built example (Nord 1002) while the Erla built Bf 109E is believed to have flown in the Spanish Civil War. Two aircraft which show rapid technical developments in Germany in World War II are the Me 163 rocket-powered interceptor designed by Alexander Lippisch, and the first jet to be used in combat, the Me 262.

Claude Dornier, who had joined the Zeppelin company in 1910, moved into aircraft design in 1914 and became famous for large all-metal monoplanes. One of the most exciting aircraft to return to Europe in recent years is a Dornier Libelle. This small flying boat was delivered to Fiji in 1930 and flew for only a few months before being put in store. After protracted negotiations Dornier bought the Libelle in 1978 and it was completely rebuilt and presented to Professor Cladius Dornier (son of the founder) on his 65th birthday. This delightful little aircraft is on loan to the Deutsches Museum. The inventiveness of Dornier is well illustrated with a 'push-pull' Do 335 fighter (this aircraft is on loan from the NASM in the USA and was expected to return in late 1986), a Do 31 from 1967 which remains the only VTOL transport aircraft constructed, and other of his post World War II designs.

The museum is steadily gathering examples of aircraft and gliders used by the reborn Luftwaffe and civilian operators so that a comprehensive picture of German aviation can be presented when the Oberschlessheim project comes to fruition.

HELICOPTER MUSEUM
Hubschrauber Museum

Postfach 1310, Sableplatz, Bückeburg 3062
Tel: 057-22-5533
Opening times: 9am–5pm daily
Location: in the center of the town, which is about 31 miles (50 km) west of Hannover on route 65

Air and Space A18A (1962)
Bell 47G-2 (H-13H) (1958)
Bölkow Bo 46 (1963), **Bo 102 Helitrainer** (1959), **Bo 103** (1960), **Bo 105** (1965), **Flying Jeep** (1961)
Bristol 171 Sycamore HR.52 (1958)
Dornier Do 32K Kiebitz (1971)
Focke Achgelis Fa 330A-1 Bachstelze (1942)
Focke-Wulf Fw 61 (R) (1961)
Focke-Borgward BFK 1 Kolibri (1960)
Georges G 1 Papillon (1971), **G 2** (1974)
Gosslich Pedalcopter (1958)
Havertz HZ 5 (1963)
Heimbaecher 4 (1951)
Hiller UH12C (H-23C) (1955)
Kaman HH-43B Husky (1962)
Merckle SM 67 (1958)
Mil Mi-1 (1959)
Müller WG-21 (c.1969)
Nagler-Rolz NR 54 (1941)
Saunders-Roe Skeeter AOP.12 (1958)
Schilling HSX-3 Cierva (1975)
Siemetzki Asro 4 (1964)
Sikorsky S-58 (H-34G) (1958)
Sud-Est SE-3130 Alouette II (1961), **SO-1221 Djinn** (1958)
Vertol V.43 (Weserflug H-21C) (1958)
VFW H2 (1968), **H3** (1970)
Wagner Rotocar 3 (1962)
Westland-Sikorsky WS.55 Whirlwind HAR.3 (?)
Zierath Z 1 (1981)

A 16th-century house in the middle of a small German town may seem to be an unlikely setting for an aviation museum. However, due to the enthusiasm and dedication of one man it is the site of one of the most comprehensive exhibitions of one form of flight. Just outside Bückeburg is a large German army air base which in recent years has become the weapons school of the force operating a wide range of helicopters. Werner Noltemeyer was stationed at the base and he began collecting photographs, documents and models relating to rotary-wing flight. His ultimate aim was the creation of a museum devoted entirely to this form of flight, which has gained steadily in importance in the last 40 years. His dream became a reality in 1971, when the local town donated the former residence of Baron von Münchausen to

The Mil Mi-1 was the first product of the Soviet design bureau, and flew in 1948. This example is one of two in museums outside Eastern Europe

The Bölkow Bo 105 first flew in 1967; it will probably be the first German post-1945 type to achieve a production run of over 1000. The third prototype is shown here

the new collection. Work started on the building in the spring, and the museum was ready to open by September. Most of the rooms were small and the complete aircraft had to be shown in the yard at the rear of the building. Nevertheless, the displays traced the origins of rotary-wing flight from the Chinese toys of many centuries ago.

The museum steadily gained in stature and became noted as one of the foremost research centers. Helicopters and autogyros were collected steadily, while the lack of exhibition space meant that storage facilities were used at both the airfield and at barracks in the town. Plans were submitted for the construction of an extension to the building but careful consideration had to be given to the architecture so that the medieval character of the square was not lost. The brick and glass extension was ready for the 1980 season and does not seem out of place.

The first part of the exhibition in the old house gives the visitor a vivid insight into the early days of rotary-wing flight, when the principles were not fully understood and fanciful machines were designed, of which some were constructed and tested. The early pioneers of helicopter design were all in Europe, and the first to leave the ground was a gyroplane designed by Louis Bréguet, which hovered at a height of 5 feet (1.5 meters) in 1907. Others who became interested in the problem at this stage included Ellehammer in Denmark, Oemichen in France and Pescara in Spain, and examples of their craft have survived and are in other European museums.

The new hall of the museum houses around 30 helicopters and autogyros from many countries, which show the range of ideas which have filled the minds of the designers. One of the first persons to really tackle the engineering problems of the helicopter was Heinrich Focke who constructed the Fw 61 which was flown by Ewald Rohlfs in June 1936. Several records fell to the Fw 61, which is regarded as the first truly successful helicopter, and the spectacular flights by Hanna Reitsch in the Deutschlandhalle in Berlin in 1938 brought the general public to realize the potential of this form of flight. For three weeks she gave flights every evening which showed the control of the machine. The museum constructed a faithful static replica of the Fw 61, which now occupies a place of pride overlooking the town square.

German inventors have produced several unusual helicopters since World War II, and fortunately many have survived. Ludwig Bölkow founded his company in 1956, and in addition to fixed-wing aircraft he initiated a program of rotary-wing machines. Almost all the rotary-wing products of Bölkow are represented at Bückeburg. Three prototypes of the Bo 46 were built to test the Derschmidt high-speed lead-leg rotor system, in which the outer portion of the five blades could swivel about drag hinges so that the advancing blades were swept back relative to the airstream. The Bo 102 was a non-flying trainer designed to act as a flight simulator, and this was developed into the Bo 103. The Bo 105, which first flew in 1967, has now become a great success and is almost certain to become the first post World War II German type to achieve a production run of over 1000. A Bölkow experimental vehicle on view is the Flying Jeep of 1962, built to the plans of Dr Götz of Heidelberg. A series of adjustable vanes deflected the thrust from its two propellers and a height of some 4 feet (1.2 meter) was attained.

With another 12 German models and helicopters from America, Great Britain, France and the Soviet Union on show and yet more promised, this superb museum should be visited by anyone with an interest in the helicopter, whether it be technical or historical. Werner Noltemeyer is a great enthusiast, and will welcome any genuine fellow enthusiast to what has developed from a small private collection into one of the most authoritative exhibitions in the world.

Hungary

TRANSPORT MUSEUM
Kozlekedesi Muzeum

Varosligeti Korut 11, Budapest XIV
Tel: 420-565
Opening times: 10am–6pm Tuesday–Sunday
Location: in the northeast of the city near the ring road

Aero Super 45 (1954), **L.60 Brigadyr** (1958)
Alag A-08 Siraly (1958), **A-08b Siraly II** (1958)
Benes-Mraz M.1C Sokol (1947)
Beniczky M-30/c.1 Fergeteg (1955), **M-30 Super Fergeteg** (1956), **E-31 Esztergom** (1957)
Brandenburg B I (1926)
Douglas DC-3 (Lisunov Li-2) (1946)
Fabian Levente (1941)
Janka Gyongyos 33 (1933)
Junkers F 13 (1921)
Lampich L-2 Roma (1925)
Lloyd 40.01 (1914)
Mil Mi-1M (?)
Polikarpov Po-2 (194?)
PZL-101 Gawron (1959)
Rubik R 07b Vocsok (1940), **R 08 Pilis** (1942), **R 15 Koma** (1950), **R 15b Koma** (1952), **R 16B Lepke** (1949), **R 18C Kanya** (1949, 1954), **R.22S Junius 18** (1956), **R.22 Super Futar B** (1958), **R.25 Mokany** (1959)
Samu-Geonczy SG-2 Kek-Madar (1948)
Zlin Z-326 Trener Master (1958)
Zsabo-Bohn Z.03b Ifjusag (1952)
Zselyi-Aladar 2 (R) (1965)
Hang-glider of unknown type

One of the oldest established transport museums, the Kozlekedesi was set up in Budapest in 1896. With exhibitions on a variety of themes, the museum became recognized as one of the most important in Central Europe. The aeronautical collection was started in the pioneer days and two early Hungarian aircraft were soon on view. These were the 1910 Zselyi-Aladar 2 and the 1911 Horvath II or III. The Zselyi appeared first at Rakosmezon airfield near Budapest in February 1910, and incorporated several original ideas for the time, including a wooden fuselage braced by piano wires, steel bracing rods for the wings and a novel suspension for the undercarriage. After a crash, the aircraft was modified into the 2. Erno Horvath was a teacher of mathematics and physics, and with the help of his students he built his first aircraft in 1910, with the II and II appearing the following year. These two early machines were completely destroyed in an air raid in 1944, and only the engine of the Zselyi was salvaged; this now reposes in a

The Russian Polikarpov Po-2 was in production from 1927 to 1953 and was probably built in greater numbers than any other aircraft

Designed by Erno Rubik, the Junius 18 glider is suspended over the Czechoslovak-built Zlin Trener Master

The Lloyd company built 13 prototypes for the Austro-Hungarian air force. In 1917 the aircraft set an altitude record, and it was presented to the museum in the same year

faithful replica of the original. Two other aircraft were also completely lost in this raid, a Fiat Br. 3 bomber and a fighter aircraft of now unknown type, since many records were destroyed.

The museum did not open again to the public until 1966, and the restricted space meant that the aviation section was small. This situation has recently been remedied with the opening of a bigger, new hall, in which a large proportion of the aircraft can be exhibited. In addition to the aircraft, the museum has a world famous collection of 1/16th scale model railway engines as used by Hungarian Railways, and models of all the Danube bridges along with many road vehicles.

On show in the museum is one of the earliest indigenous military aircraft. The Hungarian Lloyd Aircraft and Engine Factory was set up at Aszoldon in 1914, and initially produced German DFW types under license. The chief engineer was Tibor Melczer, who was responsible for 13 prototypes and five production models, all of the latter serving with the Austro-Hungarian Air Force. The first prototype was a biplane powered by a 185 hp Austro-Daimler engine, and with Henrik Bier at the controls it set an altitude record. This graceful design was completely restored in its original red, white and blue scheme in 1970.

One of the most interesting exhibits is one of the few Junkers F 13 airliners left out of the 300 produced. The aircraft was one of a small fleet owned by the Swiss airline Ad Astra, and in October 1921 it was leased by two Hungarian officers Ors Fekete and Andras Alexat who were part of a conspiracy which was trying to restore the Hapsburg dynasty to the Hungarian throne. The aircraft, which was damaged just before the lease, was fitted with the wings of another of the fleet, and the two conspirators flew the Junkers from Dubendorf ostensibly to Geneva, but landed near Sopron at the end of a devious route. The plot was unsuccessful and the aircraft was seized and used in Hungary by Regent Horthy in the 1920s.

The Junkers survived the raid of 1944 and was restored to its original Ad Astra markings in the late 1960s. The writer saw the aircraft in the MALEV hangar at Ferihegy Airport in 1968, where the person in charge of the rebuild was Erno Rubik, whose son later achieved notoriety with the 'dreaded cube'.

Erno Rubik is a former student of the Budapest Technical University, and while there he built his first glider. He founded the Aero Ever company at Esztergom in 1938, and this firm has over the years produced a range of Rubik-designed gliders and light aircraft, a number of which are in the collection. While at the university Rubik was taught by Arpad Lampich and Antal Banhidi. In 1924, while still an undergraduate, Lampich designed and built the L 1 Mama, a shoulder-wing monoplane powered by a 12 hp engine designed by another student, Peter Thorotzkai. In the following year the L 2 appeared with a three-cylinder Thorotzkai motor, and this aircraft first flew on September 4. As a reward for their efforts, Lampich and Banhidi were trained as pilots.

The L 2 was a feature of almost every Hungarian meeting for many years, and it subsequently set many records. With Karoly Kaszala at the controls it flew back and forth between Matyasfold and Monor, staying aloft for almost 10 hours in 1927, and the next year the same pilot took it from Budapest to Rome. A more spectacular flight occurred in 1929 when Banhidi flew it from Budapest via Austria, Czechoslovakia, Germany and Denmark to Sweden, returning via the Netherlands. A final record was established in 1931 when a closed-circuit flight of 642 miles (1033 km) was set. The L 2 was damaged in 1944 but was restored in the early 1970s by a team led by Banhidi, and was placed on show on September 4, 1975, the 50th anniversary of its first flight.

The museum contains several other unique aircraft, and the new gallery has given the visitor a chance to see some of these for the first time.

Italy

CAPRONI AERONAUTICAL MUSEUM
Museo Aeronautico Caproni di Taliedo

Via Durini 24, Milano 20122
Tel: 78-19-15
Opening times: Vizzola Ticino is open on summer Sunday afternoons, otherwise by prior permission only; Venegono Superiore by prior permission only

Location: Venegono Superiore is a village about 25 miles (40 km) northwest of Milan just off Route No. 233 to Varese: the museum is in the Caproni villa in the center of the village. Vizzola Ticino is an airfield about 25 miles (40 km) northwest of Milan on Route No. 336 to the west of Malpensa Airport

Aerolombarda GP.2 Asiago (1938)
Ansaldo SVA 5 (1918), **A1 Balilla** (1918)
Avia FL.3 (1947), **FL.54** (1954)
Breda Ba.19 (1932)
Bücker Bü 131B Jungmann (Doflug) (1936)
CANSA C6b Falchetto (1942)
Caproni Ca.1 (1910), **Ca.6** (1910), **Ca.9** (1911), **Ca.18** (1913), **Ca.20** (1914), **Ca.22** (1913), **Ca.36 (Ca.3 mod)** (1917), **Ca.53** (1917), **Ca.60** (1921), **Ca.100** (1934, 1937), **Ca.100** (floatplane) (1934), **Ca.113** (1938), **Ca.163** (1937), **Ca.193** (1943)
Caproni-Bristol Tipo 153 (1913)
Caproni-Reggiane Re.2000 Falco 1 (1940), **Re.2005 Sagittario** (1943), **Re.2006** (1943)
de Havilland DH 85 Leopard Moth (1934), **DH 104 Dove 6** (1957)
Fairchild F.24C8C (1934)
Fokker D VIII (1920)
Gabardini 2 (1913), **2 Idro** (1913), **1918 Biposto** (1918)
Macchi M.20 (1923), **M.200 Saetta** (1938), **MB.308** (1950)
Mantelli AM.6 (1948)
Manzolini Libellula I (1952), **Libellula II** (1956), **Libellula III** (1962)
North American AT-6 Texan (1952), **F-86K Sabre** (1953)
Partenavia P.53 Aeroscooter (MdB.02) (1961)
Republic RC-3 Seabee (1946)
SAI Ambrosini S.2S (1936)
Saiman 202M (1938)
Savoia-Marchetti SM.80 Bis (1934), **SM.102** (1947)
Siemens-Schuckert D III (1918)
Viberti Musca 1 (1949)
Vizzola II (1938)

The basic airframe of Count Giovanni Caproni's first aircraft, the Ca.1 of 1910, is on show at Venegono. This is the oldest surviving Italian aircraft

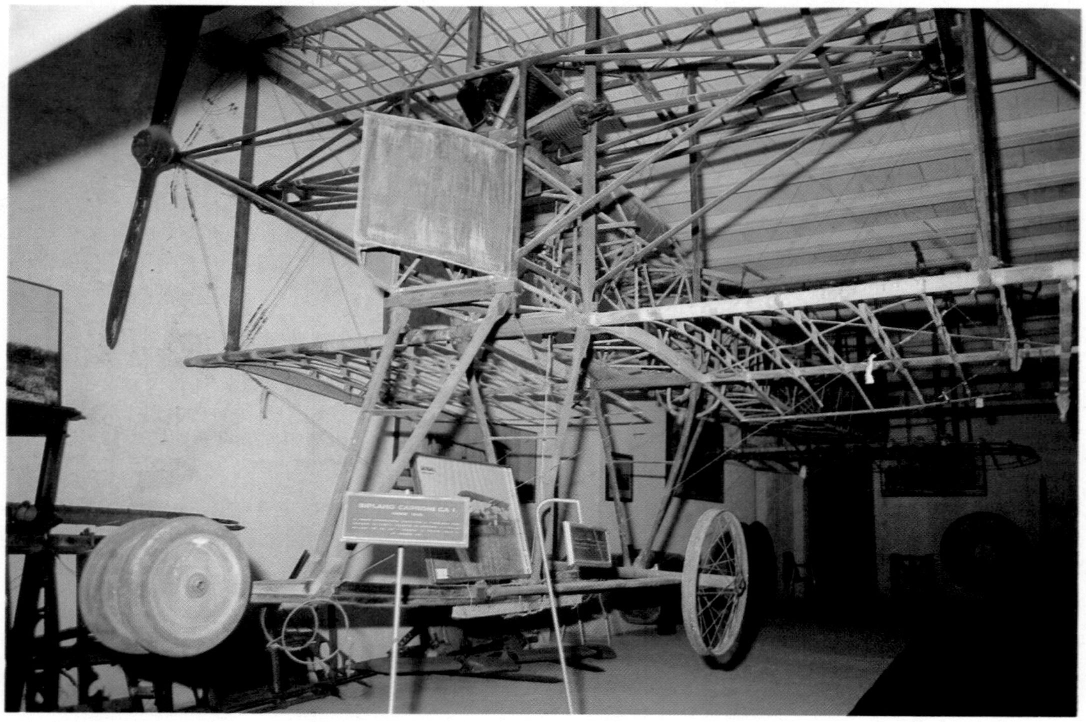

The industrialist Count Gianni Caproni di Taliedo built his first aircraft in 1910 and became head of Italy's oldest and largest aircraft manufacturer in the 1930s. At one time some 20 companies were in the Caproni empire, with factories at many locations. The firm achieved international acclaim with its large biplane and triplane bombers of World War I. The large aircraft theme was carried to excess with the triple triplane Ca. 60, which with its eight engines would have carried over 100 passengers. Unfortunately it never left the ground, but parts still survive in the collection.

The company was interested in the history of its endeavors and established a museum in a small building at its flying school field at Vizzola. The collection moved to the main factory at Ticino in the 1930s and a wide range of aircraft were displayed. These included products of the company, a number of World War I aircraft and other notable Italian machines. The works and museum were bombed in 1944/5 and much was lost, but there was still the nucleus of a collection after the conflict was over.

The aircraft were moved to two locations – the greater number to the Vizzola airfield and others to a former convent in the grounds of the family's summer villa at Venegono Superiore. Little attempt was made to present the collection to the public, and it was not until about 1970 that the Vizzola display was opened on occasions in the summer. Contessa Timina Caproni, widow of Gianni, began the collection of archive material in the 1920s and the family home in Rome houses one of the most significant private archives in the world. The children of the family have been responsible for the survival of the collection, particularly their daughter Maria Fede.

The highlights of the collection are the Caproni aircraft; all of these need some attention, but nevertheless they provide a significant tribute to a great inventor. The original

This Colombo S.63-powered Caproni Ca. 100 is one of five surviving examples of the biplane, which was based on the de Havilland Moth

The first aircraft to fly over Monte Rosa (one of Italy's loftiest peaks) was a Gabardini biplane of 1918; seen here is the sole survivor of this memorable type

Ca. 1 of 1910 is a Venegono, and this is a biplane with the engine driving two propellers mounted between the wings. The Ca. 6 biplane, also from 1910, is shown in an uncovered state, and there are monoplanes such as the Ca. 9 of 1911 and the Ca. 18 of 1913, as well as a triplane, the Ca. 53 of 1917. The Ca. 100 biplane inspired by the de Havilland Moth was produced in great numbers, over 2500 examples being built. The collection has three of these, including one on floats. The Ca. 113 of 1931, when piloted by such notable fliers as Mario de Bernardi and Tito Falconi, won many aerobatic trophies including one at the Cleveland National Air Races. The last example of the type, which was owned by de Bernardi, is preserved. Very little of the extensive World War I collection survived, but the museum does own the fuselage of the only example of the Fokker D VIII monoplane known, two Ansaldo biplanes and three monoplanes from the pioneer Giuseppe Gabardini who flew his first aircraft in 1913.

Maria Caproni has attempted to present a picture of post World War II Italian designs in the collection, and a number of light planes have been added in recent years. The Avia series of low-wing monoplanes, of which over 400 were produced between 1939 and 1947, is represented by a FL.3. The Macchi MB.308, which entered production in 1947, was one of the types responsible for the development of private aviation in the country, and one has been acquired. Three fairly new additions are the small helicopters built by the Manzolini firm between 1952 and the mid 1960s.

Although a lack of finance has prevented the restoration of many of the aircraft, the collection is most significant in tracing the history of an aspect of aviation, and is a memorial to an outstanding designer.

MUSEUM OF THE HISTORY OF ITALIAN MILITARY AVIATION
Museo Storico Dell'Aeronautica Militare Italiana

Aeroporto di Vigna di Valle, Vigna di Valle 00062
Tel: 6-9024-034
Opening times: June-September 9am-6pm Tuesday-Sunday; October-May 9am-4pm Tuesday-Sunday
Location: on the southern shore of Lago di Bracciano, which is about 14 miles (25 km) northwest of Rome

Aerfer Ariete (1958), **Sagittario II** (1956)
Aeritalia G.222 (1970)
Aer Lualdi L.59 (1959)
Agusta-Bell 47G-2 (c.1955), **47J** (c.1958), **102** (1959)
Agusta-d'Ascanio (?)
Ansaldo SVA 5 (1918), **AC 2** (1925)
Avia F.13 (1939)
Beech B18S (C-45H) (1952)
Blériot XI (R) (?), **XI-2** (c.1913)
Bonomi BS.17 Allievo Cantu (?)
Cant Z.501 Gabbiano (c.1936), **Z.506S Airone** (c.1940)
Caproni Ca.33 (Ca.3) (1916)
Caproni-Campini CC1 (?) (1940)
Caproni-Reggiane Re 2002 Ariete (1942)
Caproni-Trento F5 (1951)
Crocco-Ricaldoni Hydroplane (?)
Curtiss A1 (R) (196?)
CVV Canguro (c.1950), **Bonaventura** (?)
de Havilland DH 100 Vampire FB.52A (1952), **DH 113 Vampire NF.54** (1955)
Dornier Do 217 (194?)
Douglas DC-3 (C-47) (1941)
Fairchild F.24R Argus (UC-61K) (1944), **C-119J** (1951)
Fiat C.29 (1930), **CR.32 (Hispano HA.132L)** (c.1932), **G.5 Bis** (1935), **G.46-3B** (1948), **G.46-4A** (1948), **G.46-4** (1948), **G.49-2** (1952), **G.59-2A** (1951), **G.59-4B** (1953), **G.80-3B** (1952), **G.82** (1958), **G.91PAN** (c.1959), **G.91Y** (1962), **G.212CA** (1940)
Garnerin Balloon (?)
Grumman G.64 Albatross (SA-16A) (HU-16A) (1950), **G.89 (S2F-1) Tracker** (1958)
GVI SIAI 3-VI Eolo (?)
Hanriot HD-1 (1916)
IMAM Ro 41/B (1949), **Ro 43** (1940)
Leonardo da Vinci (R) (?)
Lockheed T-33A (1951), **RT-33A** (1953), **F-104G Starfighter** (1962)
Lohner L-1 (1917)
Macchi M.39 (1926), **M.67** (1929), **MC.72** (1933), **MC.200 Saetta** (1939), **MC.202 Folgore** (1942), **MC.205V Veltro (MC.202 ser X)** (1943), **MB.308** (1950), **MB.323** (1951), **M.416 (Fokker S-11)** (c.1954, 1957)
Nardi FN.305 (c.1938)
North American T-6J Texan (CCF) (1951), **P-51D Mustang** (1944), **F-86 Sabre (Canadair CL-13 Sabre 4)** (1953), **F-86K Sabre (Fiat)** (1956), **F-100D Super Sabre** (1954)
Partenavia P.53 Aeroscooter (MdB.01) (1958)
Piaggio D'Ascanio PD.3 (R) (1970)
Piaggio P.108B (1940), **P.136** (1951), **P.136L1** (1956), **P.148** (1951), **P.150** (1952), **P.166M** (1962)
Republic P-47D Thunderbolt (1944), **F-84F Thunderstreak** (1953), **RF-84F Thunderflash** (1952), **F-84G Thunderjet** (1951)
SAAB J-29F (1954)
SAI Ambrosini S.1001 Grifo (1948), **Super S.7** (1950)
Saiman 202M (c.1942)
Savoia-Marchetti SM.56 (1930), **SM.79** (1940), **SM.82PW Marsupiale** (1940)
SPAD VII (1917)
Stinson L-5 Sentinel (1944)
Supermarine 361 Spitfire LF.IX (1944)
Weber A VII Etiopia 1 (1935)
Westland-Sikorsky WS-51 (1949)
Wright Flyer N.4 (R) (?)

The idea of an historical aviation museum in Italy goes back to 1913 when Maj. Giulio Douhet suggested that material from the early days of ballooning and flying should be collected. However, more than 60 years were to pass before the Italian Air Force Museum was to have a permanent home. In 1956 a small historical exhibition was held in the Rome area, and this led to the collection of both aircraft and other items. An International Exhibition at Turin in the early 1960s caused some aircraft to be moved to the city, and when it closed one of the pavilions was taken over as a museum. Around 25 aircraft were on show along with a small amount of historical material. The museum did not prosper, and by the early 1970s it was virtually closed. A restoration center had been set up at Vigna di Valle and this had the task of preparing aircraft for the Turin display. Political decisions were important in the setting up of the museum, which finally opened at Vigna di Valle in May 1977.

The site at Vigna di Valle on Lake Bracciano had been an important seaplane station for many years, and in 1908 the first flight of an Italian airship took place there. Three hangars were still in good condition, and there was a large area of hard standing. The hangars were in themselves historic buildings, and two of them – the large Badoni and the smaller Austro-Hungarian – were restored and connected by a modern prefabricated concrete structure, which in addition to providing extra exhibition space houses the offices. The third hangar is mainly used as a storage and restoration center, and there are plans to extend the exhibition space in the near future. The major restoration work is now carried out at Lecce air force base in the south of the country.

Italy has had a long and varied aeronautical history and over the years many of the big aviation companies have been located there. The country first employed aircraft in a military role in the 1911 conflict against Turkey, when nine aircraft and two airships were sent to Tripolitania. They performed a number of tasks with success and in November 1912 a separate Military Aviation Service was established. The outbreak of World War I caused a rapid expansion of the force, so that when Italy entered the war in May 1915 it had over 100 aircraft. Italy was one of the first countries to use heavy bombers, and the Caproni three-engined aircraft first flew in 1914.

Using mainly home-designed aircraft, in the inter-war period the air force became one of the largest in Europe. In 1935 Italy invaded Ethiopia and the aircraft were tested operationally. Italy also supplied aircraft to General Franco's forces in the Spanish Civil War. When World War II started Italy had vast numbers of aircraft but their fighters were almost all obsolete because of the lack of a suitable high-powered engine with low frontal area. Since the end of this war Italy's combat aircraft have mainly been of American design, although the Fiat G.91 lightweight fighter was used in some numbers. With such a varied history there was ample scope for a museum. Aircraft had been preserved at a number of locations over the years, and the collection now numbers almost 100 aircraft and a similar number of engines. The display has been laid out in chronological order starting in the Austro-Hungarian hangar.

One of the first Italians to investigate flight was Leonardo da Vinci, and a special exhibition is devoted to his work which includes a replica of one of his designs. Italy was also prominent in the field of ballooning and photographs, models and documents highlight this period. Two replica aircraft, a Wright Type 4 and a Curtiss A 1 (two examples), represent the pioneer era. In the Libyan war of 1911-12

The Ansaldo SVA 5 was one of Italy's finest World War I aircraft, and this example took part in the historic 1918 raid on Vienna

the Italians used Blériot monoplanes against Turkish forces, and a replica single-seat XI and a partial replica of an XI-2 can be seen. Dominating this area of the exhibition is a twin-engined Caproni Ca.33 bomber. With a span of some 70 feet (21 meters) this twin-boomed aircraft was built in 1916, and after withdrawal it was bought by an individual who stored it for 38 years before it was acquired by the air force in 1959. Around this bomber can be seen a number of fighters, including the Ansaldo SVA 5 with its distinctively-shaped fuselage.

The inter-war period is often described as the 'golden era' of aviation and in many ways it was for Italy. Aircraft and airships had been developed to such an extent that they were now capable of spectacular long-distance flights and their speeds had increased dramatically, with improvements in the understanding of aerodynamics. The Italian air force was prominent in the making of many of these records, and in the new building some of these are honored. Nobile's polar flights in the airship *Norge* with Amundsen in 1926, and in 1928 in his *Italia*, were spectacular events. The airship *Norge* had covered over 3000 miles (4800 km) across the Arctic ice cap in just over 70 hours. A display commemorating Nobile traces the two historic flights.

The Savoia-Marchetti twin-hulled flying boats achieved world-wide fame when they made a number of formation flights across the Atlantic, and although the sole aircraft of this type is in a Brazilian museum these flights are retold in full detail. The Schneider Trophy Races caused great interest up to the final races in 1931, and fortunately Italy has managed to preserve a number of the contestant machines. The Fiat C.29 was designed for the 1929 race, but one of the two that were built crashed in Lake Garda before the contest. The second, although taken to England, was not flown in the races. In the majority of these races in the 1920s the firm of Macchi supplied aircraft for Italy's challenge.

A Macchi M.9 had won the 1921 contest at Venice in the days when flying boats dominated, and the high-speed floatplanes were not yet even at the peak of their development. The first survivor is the Macchi M.39 in which Maj M de Bernardi won the 1926 contest at Hampton Roads in Virginia in the US. Six M.39s were built, and after winning the Trophy de Bernardi set a World Air Speed record of 257 mph (414.2 km/h). The M.67 was designed for the 1929 race: three were built but only two competed, and both retired when exhaust fumes entered the cockpits; in one

case the engine cooling system failed and the pilot, Monti, was badly scalded. The remains of the pilot Cadringhers's M.67 are under restoration.

The MC.72 represented the ultimate in floatplane design and five were built. In the testing period before the race two were lost in fatal accidents in Italy. The Italians withdrew from the race, but development of the MC.72 continued and in 1933 and 1934 WO Agello raised the World speed record for floatplanes to 417 mph (692.5 km/h) and 438 mph (705.1 km/h). The sight of three of these beautiful aircraft in a line, with a fourth soon to join them, is an evocative reminder of a vanished era.

The large Badoni hangar houses aircraft from 1935 to 1960 and includes a number of unusual and unique aircraft. Biplane fighters such as the classic Fiat CR.32 (although this is a Spanish-built version), monoplane fighters from Macchi, a three engined Savoia-Marchetti SM.79 bomber and a three-engined Cant Z.506 floatplane are rarities, but of most interest is the Caproni-Campini CC.1 which is exhibited in CC.2 configuration. The aircraft had a conventional engine mounted inside its fuselage and was driven by channeling of the exhaust gases and the airflow. It was Italy's first jet aircraft, and the second in the world to fly,

The Macchi M.39 in which Mario de Bernardi won the 1926 Schneider Trophy race at Hampton Roads. Four days later he achieved the World Air Speed record.

although it was not turbine-powered. The first flight was on August 28, 1940 with Schneider Trophy winner Mario de Bernardi at the controls.

The remaining aircraft illustrate the modern Italian air force and types are being added to the collection as they are withdrawn from use. The museum has become one of the largest in Europe, and in all its displays items other than the aircraft are prominent.

Opposite Top
The Caproni company produced some of the largest aircraft of World War I. This Ca. 33 bomber spent 38 years in a private store before the museum acquired it in 1959

Opposite Bottom
The Ansaldo AC 2 was a license-built version of the French Dewoitine D 1: 112 examples were supplied to the Regia Aeronautica

Above
The FIAT G.91 was designed for a NATO requirement and first flew in 1956. The G.91Y shown here is an improved version which entered service in 1971, five years after the flight of its prototype

Netherlands

AVIODOME

Schiphol Centrum, Amsterdam 1118AA
Tel: 020-173640

Opening times: 10am-5pm daily April-October, 10am-5pm Tuesday-Sunday in winter
Location: in the terminal area of the airport which is about 8 miles (13 km) southwest of Amsterdam off route E10

Auster J/1 Autocrat (1946)
Bensen B-6 (1954)
Blériot XI (c.1911)
Cierva C-30A (1934)
de Havilland DH 82A Tiger Moth (1940), **DH 89A Dragon Rapide** (1944), **DH 104 Dove (Sea Devon)** (1955)
Douglas DC-3 (C-47A) (1942)
Fokker Spin (R) (1936), **Dr I (R)** (1978), **S.IV** (1924), **C.VD** (1928), **F.VIIA** (1928), **S.11 Instructor** (1950), **S.12** (1949), **S.14 Mach Trainer** (1951)
Gloster Meteor F.8 (1952)
Grumman G.89 Tracker (S-2N) (1960)
Hawker Sea Fury FB.51 (1951), **Sea Hawk FGA.6** (1954), **Hunter F.51** (1956)
Lilienthal Glider (R) (1959)
Mignet HM-14 Pou-du-Ciel (1936)
NHI H-3 Kolibri (1957)
North American AT-16 Texan (1943)
Piasecki PV-18 Retriever (HUP-2) (1954)
Piper J-3C Cub (L-4J) (1944)
RRG Zogling (R) (1960)
Rienks Gyroglider (1956)
SAAB 91D Safir (1959)
Schleicher Rhonlerche (1959), **Grunau Baby IIB (DFS 108-49)** (1947)
Sikorsky S-55 (HO4S-3) (1953)
Snellen V-20 (1938)
Supermarine 361 Spitfire LF.XIC (1943)
Wright Flyer (R) (c.1958)

This Fokker C VD was acquired by Delft Technical University in World War II, and survived use as an instructional airframe before joining the museum

The origins of a national aviation museum in the Netherlands go back to an article in the magazine *Avia* in 1916 which appealed for items to be donated. This seems to have made little impact on the Dutch public and although Eduard Fuld, a banker, launched another campaign in 1924 it was not until 12 years later that a National Museum Committee was formed. The organization was allotted a building at Schiphol airfield and by 1940 a substantial number of aircraft and exhibits were on view. The German forces invaded the Netherlands on May 10, 1940, and the museum and its contents were damaged. The surviving items were moved to the Fokker factory, and in the following year Hermann Goering assessed the remains and the most interesting were taken to Berlin for the Deutsche Luftfahrtsammlung. The Berlin museum was bombed late in the war and all the aircraft were thought to have been destroyed. About 20 later turned up at Krakow in Poland, including a Fokker Spin III from Schiphol.

The state of the country after World War II meant that an aviation museum was not among the real priorities, but nevertheless enthusiasts began collecting. The re-establishment of a national museum was again put forward with Eduard Fuld to the fore. There were few pre-1939 aircraft left in the country as the escape of two Fokker test pilots to England in 1941 had resulted in the occupiers scouring the country for any other potentially airworthy machines and all they found were scrapped. A meeting between all interested parties was held in 1950 under the auspices of the Royal Aero Club of the Netherlands. The site chosen was again Schiphol, and with the aid of a grant from the City of Amsterdam the museum was in business. Eventually a building was found in a former Fokker test shed and the museum opened on May 17, 1960 with nine aircraft on show.

In the 1960s the airport was completely redeveloped and new terminal areas were constructed on the west or opposite side of the field from the museum. The exhibition was forced to close in 1967, and plans called for a reopening near the new terminal in 1969. Delays and lack of funds meant that the new building, which was completed as a geodetic dome using aluminum cladding, was not ready until 1971. In 1969 three organizations – the Fokker company, KLM (the national airline) and Schiphol Airport – all celebrated their 50th anniversaries and these made funds available for the new building, as did the government.

The museum, now known as the Aviodome, opened on July 10, 1971 and in the subsequent 15 years aircraft were steadily acquired. The name of Anthony Fokker has been associated with aviation in the Netherlands for almost the whole period of powered flight. Fokker went to study in Germany in 1910 and built his first aircraft, a slender monoplane known as the Spin, later in the year. The type was later produced at Fokker's factory near Berlin and the company later made some of the outstanding fighter aircraft in World War I. Fokker returned to his native country in 1919 and the firm is still in existence at Schiphol. In 1936 a flying replica of the Spin III was constructed for the silver jubilee celebrations of the company, and this aircraft has survived and is on view.

Anthony Fokker built this replica of his 1911 Spin in 1935 and flew it at the silver jubilee celebrations of his company

In the inter-war period the firm became well known for its series of high-wing airliners which helped to revolutionize air transport in many countries. After a search for such an aircraft, Fokker and KLM bought a F VIIA in Denmark in 1955, and flew it back to its birthplace the next year. This magnificent machine now carries the markings of the first F VII used by KLM. Other examples of the company's aircraft are on show, including some British military types produced under license.

The museum has an excellent exhibition of associated items including engines ranging from early rotaries to modern jets, propellers, cabin mock ups, wind tunnel models, instruments, documents and other items, which all help to make the exhibition a comprehensive display tracing the story of flight, with particular emphasis on the contribution of the Netherlands.

MUSEUM OF MILITARY AVIATION
Militaire Luchtvaart Museum

Kamp van Zeist, Soesterberg 3769ZK
Tel: 03404-34222
Opening times: April-October 10am-4pm daily
Location: about 6 miles (10 km) northeast of Utrecht just south of route E8

Auster AOP.3 (1942)
Auster AOP.5 (1944)
Avro 652A Anson C.19 (1948)
Beech D.18S (1948)
Consolidated PBY-5A Catalina (c.1942)
de Havilland DH 82A Tiger Moth (1944), **DH 89A Dragon Rapide** (1944), **DHC 2 Beaver (L-20)** (1955)
Douglas DC-3 (C-47A) (1942)
Farman HF.22 (R) (1979)
Fokker D VII (1918), **G I (R)** (1984) **S-11 Instructor** (1951), **S-14 Mach Trainer** (1955)
Gloster Meteor F.4 (1950), **T.7** (1951), **F.8 (Fokker)** (1952)
Grumman S-2N Tracker (S-2A) (1952)
Hawker Hunter F.4 (Fokker) (1956), **F.6 (Fokker)** (1958), **T.7** (1958)
Hiller 360 (OH-23C) (1957)
Lockheed 12A (1939), **T-33A** (1951), **SP-2H Neptune (P2V-7)** (1955, 1961)
North American AT-16 Texan (1942, 1943), **P-51K Mustang** (1944), **B-25J Mitchell** (1944), **F-86F Sabre** (1952, 1953)
Piper PA-18 Super Cub (L-18C) (1953), **PA-18 Super Cub (L-21A)** (1951)
Republic F-84E Thunderjet (1951), **F-84F Thunderstreak** (1953), **F-84G Thunderjet** (1951)
Supermarine 361 Spitfire LF.IXc (1944)

The Dutch navy operated 45 Grumman Trackers like this one during the period 1960-75

Although the Dutch army had set up a balloon unit in 1886, it was only several years later that any real interest in military aviation occurred in the country. In 1911 some officers were sent to Belgium for pilot training and in 1913 the Aviation Division of the Royal Netherlands Army was established; its first base was Soesterberg near Utrecht. The first aircraft were two designed by the Dutch pioneer Marinus van Meel, and to these were added three Farman HF.22 biplanes bought in France. Over the next decades the Dutch air services became established, and a variety of aircraft from several countries were used, many coming from the Fokker factory.

With such a varied and interesting history it was surprising that no attempt was made to set up a specialist military aviation museum. In the days of recovery after World War II, air force officers at some of the bases in the country had managed to preserve aircraft, but there was no real organization.

The situation was remedied in the mid-1960s and the Netherlands Air Force Museum opened in a hangar at the Soesterberg site in 1968. The display in a World War II structure was well presented, with many items tracing the history of the service and about 10 aircraft on view.

Soesterberg developed into a major base for both Dutch and American forces, and this resulted in the hangar being needed for operational purposes. The museum was forced to move the exhibition into storage, although some of the aircraft were temporarily placed on a parade ground at the base. The search for new premises was stepped up and in the early 1980s the museum moved to a former army camp just south of Soesterberg. At the site were a number of buildings, including two large halls and an area of hard standing between them. In a short time work was carried out on the modernization of the buildings, so that an excellent exhibition could be staged. The name was changed to Museum of Military Aviation so that contributions from all three services could be encompassed. The majority of the aircraft on view are from the post-1945 period but attempts are being made to acquire items from the earlier era. A replica of a Farman HF.22 has been constructed, and this is shown with models of personnel in contemporary uniform with a staff car. A Fokker D VII was purchased in Florida at the sale which took place when the Wings and Wheels Museum closed, and this represents the contribution of Fokker to Dutch military aviation. A replica which has recently been presented to the museum by a TV company is of a Fokker G-1 twin-boom fighter.

In the early part of World War II a Dutch Flying School was set up at Jackson Field, Missouri to train crew for service with Dutch forces in exile, and among the equipment used was the Lockheed 12A. One aircraft from this unit had seen service in Sweden, Finland, Norway and Denmark as a civil machine after the end of the conflict, and it ended its days at the Egeskov Museum in Denmark where it had been painted in its Dutch colors. The twin-engined aircraft was returned to the Netherlands in the early 1980s and has just been restored. The North American Mitchell was another type used at Jackson, and also by units of the Netherlands Air Force in Europe and Asia. The Mitchell remained in Dutch service until 1951 and then most were scrapped, but some were transferred to Indonesia when the country gained its independence. Fortunately Indonesia retained the Mitchell in service for a number of years, and the government eventually presented one of the former Dutch aircraft to the museum.

In the immediate post World War II period the Dutch were supplied with ex-RAF aircraft to help them re-establish themselves in their own country and some examples from this period can be seen, including the first Spitfire delivered in 1945. The advent of NATO saw the arrival of American aircraft on the strength of most European air forces, although Fokker produced many British jet fighters under license. The museum has managed to acquire most of the types used by Dutch services since this period, and as types are withdrawn examples now join the museum. One aircraft which was acquired by the collection in 1982 was a Convair Catalina, which had for many years sat at the Bosbad Amusement Park near Hoeven. This classic type, of which over 70 had been used by Dutch forces since the early 1940s, was in fair condition and was exchanged for a Grumman Tracker.

This excellent museum will surely continue to expand and will become an excellent research center for historians of Dutch military aviation.

The S.11 Instructor was the first product of the post-1945 Fokker company. One hundred examples of this trainer were built in the Netherlands, plus 150 in Italy and 100 in Brazil

New Zealand

MUSEUM OF TRANSPORT AND TECHNOLOGY

Great North Road, Western Springs, Auckland 2
Tel: 9-860-198
Opening times: 9am-5pm daily
Location: about 2 miles (4 km) southwest of the city center

Adams MPA (?)
Auster C.4 Antarctic T.7 (1955)
Avro 652A Anson 1 (1941), **683 Lancaster B.VII** (1945)
Beech B18S Kansas (AT-11) (1942)
Bell 15 Airacobra (P-39D) (1941)
Cameron 0-77 (1974)
Cessna 188 Agwagon (1964)
Commonwealth CA-28 Ceres (1959)
Consolidated 28 Catalina (1943)
Curtiss 87 Kittyhawk (P-40E) (1941)
de Havilland DH 82A Tiger Moth (1942), **DH 84 Dragon** (1943), **DH 89 Dragon Rapide** (1938), **DH 98 Mosquito T.43** (1943), **DH 100 Vampire FB.9** (1952), **DH 100 Vampire FB.52** (1953), **DH 115 Vampire T.55** (1955)
Douglas DC-3 (C-47B) (1944)
Fairey Swordfish (R) (198?)
Fletcher FU-24 (1960)
Gere Sport (1932)
Grumman G.40 Avenger (TBF-1C) (1943), **G.44 Widgeon** (1946)
Hawker Hind (1937), **Hurricane (R)** (?)
Lincoln Sport (1935)
Lockheed 10A Electra (1936), **18 Lodestar** (1938), **414 Hudson** (1941), **137 Ventura** (1941)
Mignet HM-14 Pou-du-Ciel (1936)
Miles M.14A Magister (1938), **M.65 Gemini 1A** (1948)
North American AT-6C Texan (1941, 1942)
Pearse Monoplane (R) (1974), **Monoplane** (1930)
Republic P-47D Thunderbolt (1942)
Ryan STM-2 (PT-21) (1938)
Schneider Grunau Baby II (DFS 108-49) (194?)
Short S.25 Sunderland MR.V (1946), **S.45 Solent 4** (1949)
Transavia PL-12 Airtruk (1966)
Vickers 227 Vildebeest III (1936), **266 Vincent** (1936)
Vought FG-1 Corsair (1945)

Since the 1960s this collection has become one of the major tourist attractions in New Zealand. In 1960 a meeting of the Old-Time Preservation League of Matakohe, the Royal Aeronautical Society (NZ Branch) and the Historic Auckland Society was convened with the aim of bringing together various collections. A site at Western Springs near Auckland was chosen and the task of getting the museum ready was underway. The official opening of MOTAT took place in October 1964 and progress has been steady since then. The museum has displays devoted to all forms of

The Lockheed 10A Electra was the first all-metal airliner to fly with Union Airways. This aircraft is painted to represent that machine. The original UA aircraft is shown as a cutaway fuselage

This Short Solent flying boat was operated by Tasman Empire Airways from 1949 to 1960

transport and regular live weekends, when steam engines, cars and aircraft engines are run and trams and buses take tourists around the locality. In addition to the transport items, there is a Pioneer Village with historic buildings, and a Communications Display of photography, computers and music.

The aviation section, with over 30 aircraft, is almost entirely staffed by volunteers although Malcolm Frazer, late of the Shuttleworth Collection, joined MOTAT as Aircraft Engineer in the early 1970s. Early New Zealand aviation is represented by some of the aircraft of Richard Pearse. He built his first aircraft in the early part of the century and it has always been thought that he first flew in the South Island on March 3 1904. His aircraft did not seem to be capable of controlled flight nor was the distance off the ground sufficient. There is some evidence that the first 'flight' may have actually occurred in July 1903, some months before the Wright brothers. The remains of this machine survive at the museum along with a replica built for a television documentary some years ago.

In the 1920s Pearse built a second aircraft which incorporated in a number of innovations. The propeller was of the variable-pitch type, and the whole engine mounting could be tilted to alter the line of thrust. Pearse intended that it could be tilted to an almost vertical position thus enabling the aircraft to hover. For storage, the rear fuselage hinged forward on top of the cabin; another feature was a small tail rotor for hovering flight. The museum acquired this novel design and completely restored the aircraft.

On the main site are shown some of the aircraft and engines in the collection, but the space is restricted. A short distance away is a 20-acre (8 hectare) park connected by a tramway, where the larger aircraft are exhibited. Here a special display shows military aircraft in the context of a World War II airstrip. The museum also has some aircraft in store at Ardmore airfield.

The Meola Road Park is dominated by two flying boats, both built by the UK firm of Shorts. The Sunderland was built at Belfast as a Mark V for the RAF, but was loaned to BOAC for freight flights from 1946-48. In 1952 it returned to the manufacturers and was converted for the RNZAF and served at Hobsonville until 1966. The Solent was developed from the Sunderland, and in 1949 the New Zealand airline TEAL ordered four for their routes across the Pacific. The Solent on show flew the route from New Zealand to Tahiti until 1960.

A varied collection of both civil and military aircraft has been acquired, including one rarity, the remains of a Vickers Vildebeest. This biplane first flew in 1928 and New Zealand bought 27 in the late 1930s and they were used until 1944. The museum has recovered sufficient parts from a filled-in dump to construct a fuselage, and also some wing spars have been found. Reconstruction of the aircraft, which will consist of parts from at least eight machines, was expected to occupy museum workers into the late 1980s.

Crop spraying has played an important part in the agriculture of New Zealand, and three types which served in this role are on view. Many Tiger Moths were converted to have a hopper in their front cockpit, and one is on show along with a Commonwealth Ceres, a design which was based on the Wirraway trainer. A larger top-dresser is a converted Lockheed Lodestar airliner.

The museum has a major aviation library, and its research center is one of the most comprehensive in the country.

Norway

ROYAL NORWEGIAN AIR FORCE COLLECTION
Kongelige Norsk Luftforssvaret Museet

Gardermoen Lufthavn, Gardermoen 2062
Tel: 06-94-10-00
Opening times: 10am-2pm Saturday-Sunday, May-October
Location: about 35 miles (55 km) northwest of Oslo off Route E6

Avro 504K (504A) (1917)
Bell 47D-1 (1953), **204 (UH-1B)** (1962)
de Havilland DH 82A Tiger Moth (1940), **DH 100 Vampire F.3** (1947), **DH 100 Vampire FB.52** (1949), **DH 115 Vampire T.55** (1955)
DFS 108-14 Schulgleiter SG-38 (?)
Douglas DC-3 (C-47A) (1942)
Fairchild M.62 Cornell (PT-19) (1942), **M.62A Cornell (PT-26B)** (1943)
Farman F.46 (1920)
Fieseler Fi 103 (1944)
Focke-Wulf Fw 190F-8 (194?)
Fokker C.VD (1931)
Gloster Gladiator II (1937)
Haerens Flyvemaskinfabrik FF.9 Kaie (1922)
Heinkel He 111P-1 (1939)
Henschel Hs 293 (1944)
Junkers Ju 52/3m g4e (1937), **Ju 88** (194?)
Kjolseth P.K. X-1 (1956)
Lockheed F-104G Starfighter (Canadair CF-104) (1961), **F-104G Starfighter** (1960, 1963), **T-33A** (1951)
Noorduyn Norseman IV (1941)
North American T-6J Texan (1952), **F86K Sabre** (1952-54)
Northrop N-3PB (1941), **F-5A** (1965, 1967), **RF-5A** (1968)
Piper PA-18 Super Cub (L-18C) (1953)
Republic RF-84F Thunderflash (1951, 1952), **F-84G Thunderjet** (1951, 1952)
Royal Aircraft Factory BE.2e (1917)
SAAB S-91B Safir (1956)
Sikorsky S-55 (H-19D) (1956)
Supermarine 361 Spitfire LF.IXe (1942), **365 Spitfire PR.XI** (1945)

In the mid-1980s the efforts of both civilian and service personnel to establish an air force museum in Norway were at last beginning to come together. Over the years, the air force had preserved a number of historic aircraft at its bases, but there was no real coordination between bases. The military authorities now have around 70 historic aircraft on charge, and the last few years has seen around 30 of them placed in a former Luftwaffe hangar at Gardermoen to the north of Oslo. The building is not really suited to the task, and although some work has been carried out on its structure, it gets very damp in the harsh winters. Known as the Flymuseet, the exhibition is open on summer weekends.

A superb restoration has been carried out on this Heinkel He 111P, which was recovered from the Lesja mountains in 1976

Military aviation dates back to 1912, when two aircraft were acquired – one going to the navy and the other to the army. Both services set up training schools and production and repair facilities, which constructed aircraft under license as well as turning out their own designs. Expansion of the services took place in the 1930s, but the invasion of the country meant that many aircraft were abandoned. The pattern of Norwegian military aviation has since followed the path taken by many other European NATO forces. After the liberation of the country, squadrons which had fought in the RAF took their aircraft back to the home country where they were supplemented by other British types. Since then, because of the strategic importance of Norway in the NATO organization, large numbers of American combat aircraft have joined the inventory.

Despite the fact that Norway was occupied for a number of years, several early aircraft survived, and before too long all of these should be restored to original condition. A former air force officer, Captain John Amundsen, who lives near the technical training school at Kjeller, has been responsible for a number of these excellent rebuilds. The first to emerge from his small workshop was a Royal Aircraft Factory BE.2e built by William Denny and Brothers at Dumbarton in Scotland. In all, 18 aircraft were purchased by Norway towards the end of World War I, and they flew until 1925. Amazingly, two survived, and the other is now at the Mosquito Aircraft Museum in England.

The BE.2e was completed in 1981 and its place in the workshop was taken by a Farman F.46 pusher. The army used two F.46s from 1920 to 1929 and parts of both survived, plus a quantity of spares. Meanwhile under restoration at Kjevik is an Avro 504K, orginally built by the parent company as an Avro 504A. One of the most ambitious rebuilds of an early type is taking place at Bødo in the north of the country. The army factory built small numbers of the FF.9 Kaie trainer in the mid-1920s. One Kaie flew into a lake near Vaernes in July 1931, and remained on the bottom until raised in 1974. Members of 331 Squadron have taken on the exciting task of restoring what will be the only complete example of a Norwegian military design to survive.

The Norwegian Air Force collection has gained worldwide acclaim with a number of spectacular recoveries in recent years. The Northrop N-3PB floatplane was ordered in 1939, but by the time the batch of 24 were ready the country had been invaded, and the aircraft were delivered to the 'Little Norway' base in Canada. The aircraft carried out invaluable patrol work, mainly from Icelandic bases, and at the end of the war they were either scrapped or a few were taken back to Norway, where they escaped the torch for a short time. During the action in 1943 one N-3PB landed on a glacier river in Iceland, and subsequently sank. The wreck was located years later by the Icelandic Aviation Historical Society, who contacted its Norwegian counterpart. With the aid of the military the machine was salvaged and taken to California, where it was rebuilt by a volunteer force at Northrop's. The Norwegian contract for the N-3PB was the first obtained by the new Northrop firm, and as part of their 40th anniversary they rebuilt the aircraft to original specification and handed it over to Norway in 1981: thus the N-3PB eventually arrived in the country which had ordered it some 40 years before.

This Gloster Gladiator was restored at Rygge after a long period in store. The aircraft was used by 263 Squadron of the RAF in 1940

The harsh Norwegian terrain, coupled with the climate, has meant that a large number of crashes occurred in World War II, and two German aircraft have been recovered for exhibition at Gardermoen, with others to follow. One of the few genuine Heinkel 111s to be left was brought down from 5000 feet (1500 meters) up in the Lesja mountains in 1976, 36 years after its crash, and in 1983 a Junkers Ju 52/3m was lifted from Lake Hartvigvannet. The Heinkel is now almost completely restored and work should soon start on the Junkers, which is beginning to suffer from corrosion as the air attacks its structure. Projects under way in other parts of the country should see a Focke-Wulf Fw 190 and a Junkers Ju 88 join the collection.

After the Nazi invasion of Norway, the RAF sent 263 Squadron equipped with Gloster Gladiators to try and repel the German forces. Operating from frozen lakes, they found their task too difficult, and within a short time all the aircraft had been destroyed or damaged. A scrap dealer obtained German permission to buy the wrecks, and one was later sold to Ludvig Hope, who stored the Gladiator in a shed. He died in 1954; the aircraft was handed over to the military authorities in September 1977 and taken to Rygge for a rebuild, which was completed in 1980.

The Heinkel He 111 previously mentioned had been involved on raids on 263's bases and was shot down by two Blackburn Skuas from HMS *Ark Royal.* At Gardermoen in 1979 the three surviving members of the crew of the German aircraft met with two of the Skua fliers.

Almost all the modern aircraft used by the Royal Norwegian Air Force have joined the collection, and as types are withdrawn at least one example is allocated. Thus a comprehensive record of recent service history will be built up, and as soon as a purpose-built museum can be obtained some of the valuable historical items will be able to appear in an appropriate standard of display.

Poland

MUSEUM OF AVIATION AND SPACE
Muzeum Lotnictwa I Astronautyki

30-969 Krakow 28
Tel: 44-71-81

Opening times: May-October, 10am-2pm daily
Location: at the disused airfield of Rakowice, which is about 3 miles (5 km) east of the city off Route E22

Aachen FVA 10B Rheinland (1939)
Aero Super 45 (1956), **145** (1959), **L-60 Brigadyr** (1957)
Akaflieg München Mü 13D (1939)
Albatros B IIa (L 30) (1919), **C I (L 6)** (1915), **H I (Siemens-Schuckert D IV mod)** (1926), **L 101** (1932)
Allegemeine Electrizitäts AEG-Wagner E II (1914)
Aviatik C III (1917)
Blériot XI (R) (1967)
Bücker Bü 131B Jungmann (c.1934)
Centrale Studium Samolotow CSS 12 (1950), **CSS 13 (Polikarpov Po-2)** (1949, 1952), **CSS S-13 (Polikarpov Po-2)** (1955)
Cessna T-50 Bobcat (UC-78) (1941)
Curtiss 35 Hawk II (1933)
Deutsche Flugzeugwerke DFW C V (1917)
DFS 108-14 Schulgleiter SG-38 (1938), **108-70 Meise** (1942), **Weihe** (1943)
Douglas DC-3 (Lisunov Li-2T) (c.1942)
Farman F.4 (R) (1957)
Fokker Spin (1913)
Geeste Mowe (1913)
Grigorovitch M.15 (1917)
Halberstadt CL II (1917)
Heinkel He 5e (1928)
Horten Ho II (1935)
HWL Pegaz (1949)
Ilyushin Il-10 (Avia B.33) (1952), **Il-28** (c.1950), **Il-28R** (c.1950)
Institut Lotnictwa BZ-1 Gil (1950), **BZ-4 Zuk** (1956), **TS-8 Bies** (1955, 1958), **TS-11 Iskra** (1961), **JK-1 Trzmiel** (1956)
Instytut Szbownictwa IS-1 Sep (1947), **IS-3 ABC-A** (1957), **IS-4 Jastrzab** (1953), **IS-4 Jastrzab** (1953), **IS-6X Nietoperz** (1950), **Komar 49** (1950)
Jeannin Stahltaube (1913)
Kazan KAI-12 (1958)
Letov LF-107 Lunak (1950)
Levavasseur Antoinette (1909)
Lilienthal Glider (R) (1969)
Lotnicze Warsztaty Doswiadoziane Zuch 1 (1948), **Zuch 2** (1950), **Junak 1** (1948), **Junak 2** (1952), **Junak 3** (1955), **Szpak 2** (1945), **Szpak 3** (1946), **Szpak 4T** (1948), **Zak 3** (1948), **Zuraw** (1950), **LFG Roland D VIB** (1918), **LFG B II** (1913)
Messerschmitt Me 209V1 (1938)
Mikoyan-Gurevich MiG-15 (LIM-1) (c.1952), **MiG-19PM** (c.1957)
Mil Mi-1M (WSK SM-1W) (1957), **Mi-1M (WSK SM-1WS)** (1956), **Mi-1M (WSK SM-1)** (1956)
Podlaska Wytwornia Samolotow PWS.26 (1937)
Panstwowe Zaklady Lotnicze PZL M-4 Tarpan (1964), **PZL MD-12F** (1962), **PZL P.11c** (1935), **PZL S-4 Kania 3** (1958)
Piper J.3 Cub (L-4H) (1943)
Polikarpov Po-2 (1944)
Rogalski, Wigura, Drzewicki RWD 13 (1939), **RWD 21** (1939)
Rumpler R IILC Taube (1932 ?)
Schleicher Rhonsperber (c.1934)
Schneider Motorbaby (1938)
Sopwith F.1 Camel (1917)
Staaken R VI (1917)
Stelmaszyk S-1 Bozena (R) (1975)
Stinson L-5B Sentinel (1942)
Supermarine 361 Spitfire LF.XVI (1944)
Szybowcowy Zaklad Doswiadczalny SZD 8 Jaskolka (1953), **SZD 9 Bocian** (1953), **SZD 10 Czapla** (1955), **SZD 10bis Czapla bis** (1959), **SZD 12 Mucha 100** (1954), **SZD 15 Sroka** (1956, 1957), **SZD 17X Jaskolka L** (1956), **SZD 18 Czajka** (1956), **SZD 19 Zefir 1** (1958), **SZD Zurau (DFS 108-30 Kranich)** (1952, 1953), **SZD 25A Lis** (1961)
Tupolev Tu-2 (modified) (c.1942)
Warsztaty Szybowcowe Wrona bis (1937)
Wojskowe Warsztaty Szybowcowe WWS 1 Salamandra (1946), **WWS 1 Salamandra** (1937), **WWS 2 Zaba** (1938)
WSK SM-2 (Mil Mi-1 modified**)** (1959)
Yakovlev Yak-11 (c.1953), **Yak-12** (1951), **Yak-17UTI** (c.1949), **Yak-18** (1956), **Yak-23** (c.1948)
Zlin Z-26 Trener (1951)

The Polish aircraft industry was one of the most technically advanced in Europe between the World Wars and after a long struggle now has one of the major aircraft collections in Europe. The Muzeum Lotnictwa I Astronautyki was officially set up in 1963 at the disused airfield of Rakowice outside Krakow, taking over one of the old hangars and an area around it.

The spur for setting up the museum was the arrival in Krakow of about 20 survivors from the famous Deutsche Luftfahrtsammlung in Berlin. This great exhibition was bombed and there were thought to be no surviving airframes. In fact the badly battered remnants were taken to a forest in what is now the German Democratic Republic (East Germany) and stored in railway carriages. After a tortuous journey the majority came to Krakow. At the end of the war the Polish forces occupying the area found the aircraft, realized their value and managed to take them back to Poland and keep them hidden for almost 20 years. The clue to the possible whereabouts of Berlin aircraft was provided by the appearance of a fully restored PZL 11c gull-winged fighter of 1931. This aircraft was recognized as the ex-Berlin aircraft by some historians and the collection was discovered in the late 1960s. There are strong, but unconfirmed, rumors current in several Eastern European museums that other aircraft were taken to the Soviet Union.

In the late 1960s all the aircraft were in the main hangar with the Berlin remains stored together but by 1979 a partition separated a formal exhibition from aircraft awaiting restoration stored in racks. The economic climate has resulted in little money being allocated to the museum and ambitious plans for a purpose-built exhibition area and for staff to carry out the extensive restoration seem decades away. One of the historic survivors is the fuselage of the Messerschmitt Me 209 VI in which Fritz Wendel set the then world air speed record of 466 mph (750.75 km/h) on April 26, 1939. Nazi propaganda called this aircraft the Bf 109R to imply that it was a slightly modified version of their standard fighter and this designation appeared on the FAI records.

Unfortunately there are few aircraft from the golden period of Polish aviation when sporting planes carried off many trophies. Two which are on view are the RWD 13

Above
The Blériot XI replica built by Pawel Zolotow. The aircraft was flown in the 1960s before being presented to the museum

Above Left
The Halberstadt CL II: this photograph, taken in 1968, shows how much work was needed to complete restoration of the ex-Berlin aircraft

Left
The gull-winged PZL.11, which was restored in 1957, shows what has been achieved with another ex-Berlin aircraft

high-wing and RWD 21 low-wing monoplanes, which were saved from Romania after World War II when a number were offered back to Poland. They were among a batch of 40 or so light planes which escaped to Romania in 1939 and were then impressed into military service. The RWD 13 with its outstanding STOL performance was a winner of many prizes at international meetings.

Since the formation of the museum a national preservation policy has resulted in at least one example of all noteworthy indigenous designs going to Krakow. If a prototype is not put into production and survives its test period it joins the collection and when production types are becoming rare one is allocated to Krakow. Thus the museum has on its inventory an almost complete record of Polish aircraft and sailplanes of the last three decades and hopefully this foresight will continue. Nowadays Poland's combat aircraft are of Soviet design but so far only a small number have joined the museum, although it is expected that others will soon follow.

One Berlin aircraft has left Krakow, a de Havilland DH 9A which went missing near Kaiserslautern in 1918. After a long period of negotiation its fuselage was exchanged with the RAF Museum for a complete Spitfire and now the fully restored DH 9A is on view in the Bomber Command Museum at Hendon.

This outstanding collection is little known even in the city and the only sign of its existence is a small notice by one of the main roads out of Krakow and then the visitor has to negotiate a typical dilapidated airfield road to the hangar.

Portugal

AIR MUSEUM
Museu Do Ar

Alverca do Ribatejo 2615
Tel: 258-27-22
Opening times: 10am-midday and 1.30pm-6pm Tuesday-Saturday, 10am-midday and 2pm-6pm Sunday
Location: Alverca is about 12 miles (20 km) northeast of Lisbon; the museum is off Route N10. Sintra is about 12 miles (20 km) northwest of Lisbon on Route N9

Auster D5/160 Husky (OGMA) (1963)
Avro 631 Cadet (1934)
Beech AT-11 Kansas (1942), **D-18S (C-45H)** (1947)
Caudron G.3 (R) (1968)
Cid, Varela Hydroplane (1934)
de Havilland DH 82A Tiger Moth (1934, 1938, 1945), **DH 87B Hornet Moth** (1936), **DH 89A Dragon Rapide** (1938), **DH 100 Vampire FB.9** (1950)
Dornier Do 27A-1 (1958)
DFS 108-14 Schulgleiter SG-38 (194?), **108-30 Kranich II** (194?), **Weihe A-3** (194?)
Douglas A-26 Invader (c.1942), **DC-3 (C-47A)** (1943), **DC-4 (C-54A)** (1941), **DC-6B** (1954)
Fairey IIID (R) (1972)
Grumman G.44 Widgeon (1942)
Junkers Ju 52/3mg 3e (1937), **Ju 52/3mg 7e** (1938), **Ju 52/3m (AAC-1)** (1946)
Le Cerf-Aéroplane JV (1912)
Lockheed T-33AN (Canadair) (1948), **PV-2C Harpoon** (1943), **SP-2E Neptune (P2V-5)** (1951)
Maurice Farman MF-4 (R) (1971)
Max Holste MH.1521M Broussard (c.1955)
Nord N.2501D Noratlas (1959), **N.2502A Noratlas** (1958), **N.2502F Noratlas** (1962)
North American AT-6D Texan (1942), **T-6J Texan (CCF)** (1952), **AT-6C Texan** (1942), **F-86F Sabre** (1952, 1953)
Oliveira Nikus Miniplane (1974)
Piper J-3 Cub (1946), **PA-12 Super Cruiser** (1946), **PA-18 Super Cub (L-18C)** (1952), **PA-18 Super Cub (L-21B)** (1954)
Republic F-84G Thunderjet (1951)
RRG Zogling (1936)
Santos Dumont XX Demoiselle (R) (1972)
Schneider Grunau Baby IIB (DFS 108-49) (c.1947)
Sikorsky S-55 (H-19A) (1951), **S-55 (H-19D)** (1958)
Slingsby T.21B (1948)
Sud-Est SE.3130 Alouette II (c.1965)

Portuguese military aviation started in 1912 when funds were allocated for the purchase of aircraft and the formation of a flying school. The school did not open until 1916 but volunteers had been sent abroad for training in 1914. A military airfield was established at Amadora and aircraft were ordered from France in 1917. At the same time the navy established air stations and ordered seaplanes and flying boats. One of the navy's notable achievements was a flight across the South Atlantic from Lisbon to Rio de Janeiro in 1924 by Fairey IIID aircraft. Three aircraft were needed to complete the flight, and a replica of one of them has been constructed for the Air Force Museum. (The original aircraft which completed the flight is in the Navy Museum in Lisbon.) The aircraft used in the inter-war period were mainly French or British although others came from Italy and Germany. A significant development in 1918 was the setting up of PMA official aeronautical workshops (named OGMA from 1928) which has built many aircraft under license over the years.

The Air Force Museum was formally established on February 21, 1968 and opened three years later in a specially converted hangar at Alverca which is the home of OGMA and an important air force base. There was a major reorganization of the display area in the late 1970s but the exhibition space is still limited. From the collection of over 60 aircraft only about a dozen can be shown. The remainder are stored either at Alverca or at other bases. The museum has the use of two hangars at Sintra and here an outside parking area has some of the larger aircraft in store. As types are withdrawn from service some are allocated to the museum and several are duplicated for possible exchange with other museums and organizations. Deals with Belgium and South Africa have added 'missing' types to the collection.

The display at Alverca traces the history of military aviation in Portugal from 1912. Around the walls of the museum are photographs and documents depicting significant advances. There is a large display of engines along with large-scale models of aircraft no longer available in Portugal. Exhibitions of instruments, radios etc. trace the advances in these fields. In addition to the replica of the Fairey IIID three other reproductions. The Brazilian Alberto Santos Dumont made the first powered flight in Europe in 1906 and his Demoiselle of 1907 was hailed as the first practical light aircraft. The Demoiselle replica on show was built in 1972. The Farman MF.4 and Caudron G.3 biplanes were among the first types to serve with the Portuguese forces. The MF.4 was used from 1916 and the G.3 was introduced in the same year and from 1922 was built under license at OGMA.

The air force held a contest for a training aircraft in the early 1930s and single examples of the de Havilland Tiger

The Avro Cadet, which was delivered in 1934 to be evaluated against other trainers. Although the Cadet was unsuccessful in the contest, orders were placed for the larger Avro 626

In store at Sintra is a Lockheed Neptune. Twelve were delivered from the Netherlands in the early 1960s

Moth, the Avro 631 Cadet and the Caproni Ca.100 were ordered. The Tiger Moth was the winner and this aircraft is on show; later OGMA built 91, three of which, including one in airworthy condition, are in store. The Avro Cadet has also survived and is in store, although it was exhibited in the early 1970s.

Ten Junkers Ju 52/3ms were bought from Germany in 1937, two more obtained from Norway in 1950, and 12 French-built models in 1960. Seven are in the collection with one on show. They are the prime attraction for exchanges. Recently one went to Brussels and two helicopters made the reverse journey.

Of the types in store, the Lockheed Harpoon is the rarest: it is the only example of its type in Europe. The Beech Kansas is one of only two in European museums. Forty-two Harpoons and at least six Kansas were used. Two civil machines were brought back from the former colonies in Africa before they achieved independence. A de Havilland Dragon Rapide was used by the air force in Angola and a Hornet Moth came from a flying club in Mozambique.

If sufficient space could be obtained for this interesting collection the Portuguese Air Force Museum could become one of the major displays in Europe.

Spain

AIR MUSEUM
Museo Del Aire

Cuatro Vientos, Madrid
Opening times: 10am-1pm Tuesday-Sunday
Location: on the NV road about 6 miles (10 km) southwest of Madrid

Aerotecnica AC-12 (1959), **AC-14** (1958)
AISA I-11B Peque (1955, 1956), **I-115** (1956)
Avro 504K (R) (1983)
Blériot XI (R) (1973)
Boeing KC-97L (1953)
Bréguet 19 Grand Raid (CASA) (1928)
Bücker Bü 133C Jungmeister (1944)
Cessna 305 Bird Dog (L-19A) (1951)
Cierva C.19IVP (Avro 620) (1932)
CASA C-352L (Ju 52/3m) (1942), **C-1.131E (Bücker Bü 131)** (1944), **C-2.111B (Heinkel He 111)** (1951), **C-207C Azor** (1962)
de Havilland DH 60GIII Moth Major (1931), **DH 89 Dragon Rapide** (1935)
DFS 108-14 Schulgleiter SG-38 (1941), **108-30 Kranich III** (1951), **Weihe** (1950)
Dornier Do 24T-3 (1944), **Do 28D Skyservant** (1959)
Douglas DC-3 (C-47B) (1945), **DC-4 (C-54A)** (1942), **DC-4 (C-54D)** (1942)
Fiat CR.32 (Hispano HA.132L) (1939)
Fieseler Fi 156C Storch (1943)
Grumman G.64 Albatross (SA-16B) (HU-16B) (1951)
Gurripato II (1959)
Heinkel He 111E-1 (1938)
Hispano HA.1112K-1L (Bf 109) (1952, 1954), **HA.200R-1 Saeta** (1955), **HA.220D Saeta** (1968)
Hispano-Suiza HS.34 (1942)
Huarte-Mendicoa HM-1B (1952), **HM-2** (1954)
INTA VC 101 (c.1952)
North American AT-6D Texan (1944)
Lockheed T-33A (1953)
Morane-Saulnier MS.733 Alcyon (1956)
North American F-86F Sabre (1948)
Schneider Grunau Baby II (DFS 108-49) (1942)
Slingsby T.34 Sky (1952)
Vogt LO 100 (1952)
Westland WS-55 Whirlwind 2 (1955)

This collection was officially opened at the Cuatro Vientos airfield just outside Madrid in March 1982. During the long period of General Franco's rule rumors abounded of a number of rare and historic aircraft preserved in a hangar at the military side of the airfield but even if the authorities did grant permission to view, it usually took a very long time. From infrequent reports an idea of what was in the collection could be pieced together but one was never sure if the visitor had been allowed to see all. Cuatro Vientos was the site of the first aviation school of the Aeronautica Militar Española. Opened in March 1911, it has been an active airfield ever since. In addition to military flying many notable

Now floating on a specially constructed lake at the Museo del Aire, this Dornier Do 24T-3 once saved the lives of many airmen of both sides, downed off Spain in World War II

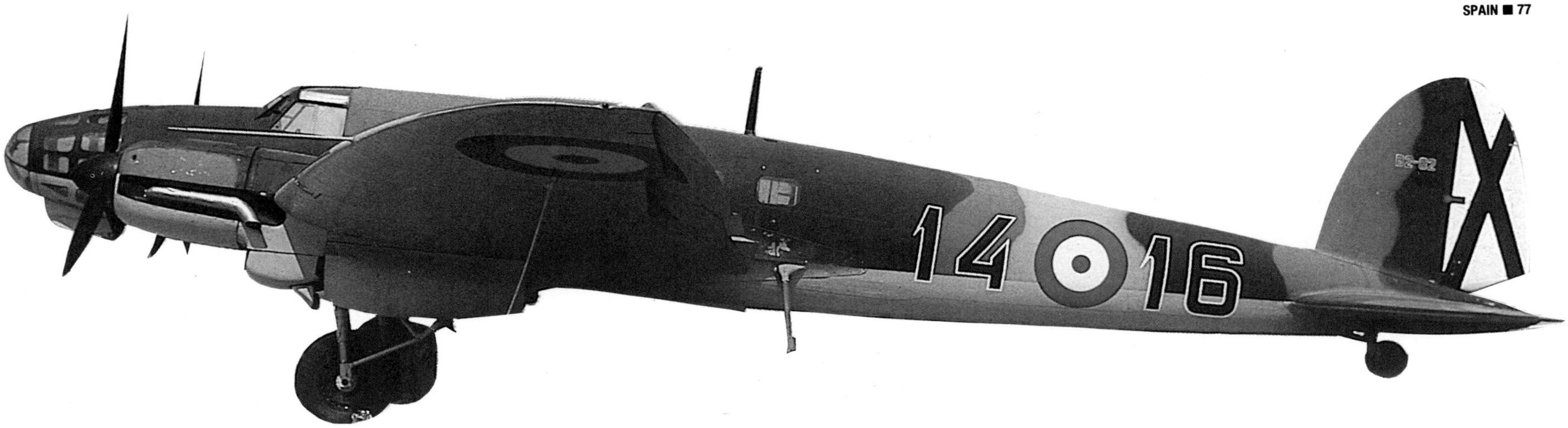

civil flights have taken place from the field.

The pioneer of the autogyro, Juan de la Cierva, was involved with others in producing the first locally designed aircraft, the BCD.1, in 1912 at Cuatro Vientos. When he turned to rotary-wing flight his first experiments were at nearby Getafe and his C.6 made the first cross-country flight by an autogyro – the 7½ miles (12 km) between the two airfields – in December 1924. One example of Cierva's genius has been preserved at Cuatro Vientos, a C.19 built in the UK by Avro. After a brief career in the UK the aircraft left for Spain in December 1932 and later became impressed on the nationalist side in the civil war. Fortunately it survived and flew until the early 1960s before joining the collection.

The aircraft on show are in either a large exhibition hangar or a landscaped park. Two artificial lakes in the parks show the two flying boats in their natural environment, including a Dornier Do 24T of which 12 were bought in 1942 to provide air sea rescue cover for the western Mediterranean and eastern Atlantic. The other aircraft in a lake is a Grumman Albatross amphibian which was bought in the 1960s from the USAF to supplement and replace the Dorniers.

Few aircraft from before the civil war have survived but one is a license-built Bréguet 19 which was used on a number of long-distance flights, including a tour of South America in the inter-war period. When the civil war started both sides acquired a number of aircraft from the splitting of the existing military forces and then were supplied with many others from countries sympathetic to their respective causes. Although some surviving types were used by the new Spanish air force until well into the 1950s the preservation movement had not gathered momentum and what would have by now become unique models were scrapped. The highlight from this period is a rare Heinkel He 111E-1 with a stepped windscreen which was restored to its civil war markings in the late 1970s.

A significant aircraft in the destiny of Spain is a de Havilland Dragon Rapide which was chartered from Olley Air Services of Croydon to fly General Franco from Las Palmas to Tetuan in Spanish Morocco to take charge of the nationalist forces on the death of their leader. After the flight, which finally ended at Seville, the Rapide returned to the UK. When it was withdrawn from service in 1953 it was donated to General Franco and has been restored to pristine condition with a brass plate on its nose commemorating the flight.

The nationalist success in the civil war meant that the air force standardized on German-designed aircraft: the CASA factory built numbers of Bücker Jungmanns and Jungmeisters as well as Heinkel 111s and Junkers 52s which were in use until the late 1960s and have all been saved. Hispano Aviacion built Messerschmitt Bf 109s initially with the Hispano-Suiza HS-12 engine and later with the Rolls-Royce Merlin. Examples of both have been saved.

A Spanish-American Defense Treaty of 1953 gave the Americans bases in Spain in return for training of Spanish air and ground crew and the supply of modern equipment to the Spanish air force. Thus a number of US-built machines are on view along with some of the products of an aircraft industry which was revitalized in the 1950s.

This major collection can now show a wide range of types which in a number of ways show the political influences which have determined the modern history of Spain.

Top
The only surviving Heinkel He 111E-1, with its stepped windscreen, was restored in the late 1970s

Above
The beautifully restored Dragon Rapide in which General Franco returned to Spain at the start of the Civil War, in 1936

Sweden

MALMEN AIR FORCE MUSEUM
Flygvapenmuseum Malmen

Box 13 300, S-580 13 Linköping
Tel: 013-29-92-70
Opening times: midday-3pm Sunday-Friday
Location: about 4 miles (6 km) west of Linköping off Route E4

Albatros 120 (Sk-1) (1925)
Beech B18S (C-45) (1944)
Bréguet U III (B-1) (R) (1983)
Bücker Bü 181B Bestmann (Sk-25) (1942, 1946)
Caproni-Reggiane Re-2000 (J-20) (1942)
CFM 01 Tummelisa (?)
Consolidated PBY-5A Canso (Tp-47) (1943)
de Havilland DH 60T Moth Trainer (1931), **DH 82A Tiger Moth (Sk-11A) (ASJA)** (1936), **DH 100 Vampire F.1 (J-28A)** (1946), **DH 100 Vampire FB.50 (J-28B)** (1951), **DH 112 Venom NF.51 (J-33)** (1953), **DH 115 Vampire T.55 (Sk-28C)** (1955)
DFS 108-14 Schulgleiter SG-38 (194?), **108-30 Kranich (Flygplan)** (1943), **108-70 Meise** (1942), **Weihe** (1943)
Douglas DC-3 (C-47A) (Tp-79) (1944), **AD-4W Skyraider** (1952)
English Electric Canberra T.11 (Tp-52) (1960)
Fairey Firefly TT.1 (1945)
FFVS J-22A (1944), **J-22B** (1945)
Fiat CR-42 (J-11) (1941)
Fieseler Fi 156 Storch (S-14) (1938)
Focke-Wulf Fw 44J Stieglitz (Sk-12) (CVV) (1941)
Fokker C.VE (CVM) (S-6B) (1934)
Gloster Gladiator (J-8A) (1938), **Meteor T.7** (1951)
Hawker Hart (B-4) (ASJA) (1937), **Hunter F.50 (J-34)** (1956)
Hughes 269A (HKP-5A) (c.1965)
Junkers Ju 86K (B-3) (Tp-73) (1938)
Klemm Kl 35D (Sk-15A) (1939)
Macchi M.7 (1919)
Malmö Flygindustri MFI-9B Trainer (1966), **MFI-10B Vipan (Fpl-54)** (1963)
Mignet HM-14 Pou-du-Ciel (c.1935)
Nieuport IVG (1912)
Noorduyn UC-64 Norseman (Tp-78) (1943)
Nord NC.701 Martinet (Si 204) (1950)
North American NA-16 (1939), **AT-16 Texan (Sk-16A)** (1947), **P-51D Mustang (J-26)** (1944)
Percival P.66 Pembroke C.52 (Tp-83) (1955)
Phönix 122 (D III) (J-1) (CFM) (1919)
Piper PA-18A Super Cub (L-21B) (1959)
Powell Racer (1937)
RAAB-Katzenstein RK-26 Tigerschwalbe (1934)
SAAB L-17A (B-17A) (1942), **L-17B (S-17B)** (1942), **18B (B-18B)** (194?), **21A-3 (J-21A-3)** (1947), **21A-3 (J-21A-3)** (1948), **21R (J-21R)** (1948), **29A (J-29A)** (1952), **29B (J-29B)** (1953), **29C (S-29C)** (1955), **29F (J-29F) (29B)** (1955), **32 Lansen (A-32)** (1955), **32 Lansen (S-32)** (1958), **35 Draken** (prototype) (1955), **35A Draken (J-35A)** (1959), **35B Draken (J-35B)** (1960), **35C Draken (S-35C)** (1961), **37 Viggen (AJ-37)** (1967), **91A Safir (Tp-91)** (1946), **105XT** (1963), **210 Lill-Draken** (1951)
SAAB-MFI 15 (1969)
Schneider Grunau Baby II (DFS 108-49) (1943)
Seversky EP-106 (J-9) (1940)
Sparman P 1 (S-1A) (1937)
Supermarine 390 Spitfire PR.XIX (S-31) (1945)
Thulin G (1917)
Vertol V.44 (Hkp-1) (1963)
Vickers 668 Varsity T.1 (Tp-82) (1952)

The neutrality of Sweden has been a dominant factor in the purchase and manufacture of military aircraft since the formation of the first aerial unit of the Swedish navy in 1911. The isolation of the country in World War I resulted in local manufacturers setting up plants for the license production of engines and airframes and also their own products.

The first aviation influence in the country was French, when the navy was presented with a Blériot XI and the army a Nieuport IVG in 1912. The Nieuport was used until 1919 and then placed in store where it survived in excellent condition. It was flown for the last time in 1962 at a display marking the 50th anniversary of Swedish Army flying.

The airfield at Malmslatt was the site of the army aviation workshop and with the formation of an independent air force in 1926 it became one of the major bases in the country. The commander of the base from 1941 to 1951, Overste Hugo Beckhammer, began collecting historic aircraft from bases around the country. He set up a small display of about ten aircraft in an old hangar and although not open to the public many private visitors saw and admired the collection. Discussions about the formal setting up of an official Air Force Museum led to Malmslatt being chosen as the location.

Development at the base resulted in the demolishing of the display hangar and the aircraft were again placed in store. In spite of official backing there was little progress in obtaining new facilities until in the late 1960s the nearby town of Ryd erected a building in which some of the growing collection could be displayed. This exhibition of some 25 aircraft was open to the public on summer weekends until 1983.

After Parliament gave the formal go-ahead in July 1977 building of permanent facilities began and the first stage of the exhibition was opened in March 1984. About 30 aircraft from the large collection were placed on show along with a number of smaller items. Two new exhibition halls and workshops will enable the majority of the aircraft to move to the site from a number of storage areas around the base.

The collection includes several aircraft which are the last survivors of their types. These include the Macchi M.7 flying boat which was in use from 1919-26, the Albatros 120 which served for 14 years from 1915, the RAAB RK-26 designed by Gerhard Fieseler in the early 1930s and the Austrian Phönix 122 of 1919. Of the indigenous aircraft the elegant CFM Tummelisa biplane which flew from 1919 to 1935 and again from 1951 to 1962 and the low-wing Sparman S-1A trainer are unique.

The museum has gone to great lengths to obtain examples

One of two known de Havilland Moth Trainers known to survive. This example was recently restored by Air Force Museum staff

Under construction by a volunteer group at a workshop near Stockholm is this replica of a Bréguet U III, which was the second aircraft operated by the Swedish Army. The engine from the original will be fitted

of aircraft which have served with the air force but were no longer preserved in the country. One of the most spectacular projects is the rebuild of a SAAB 18 bomber. The 18 was the first twin-engined aircraft produced by SAAB and almost 250 were made, of which the last survivors were scrapped in the early 1960s. A wreck of a B 18B which made a forced landing on the frozen sea off Sundsvall in February 1946 was traced and raised in September 1979. A complete rebuild, with the cooperation of local industry, will provide a unique example for the display.

A complicated exchange deal which involved the supply of several SAAB Lansens, a Hunter, some Skyraiders and Dakotas to a Californian collector resulted in a Spitfire from Canada joining the museum. A flyable Tiger Moth bought in the UK was exchanged for one of the two de Havilland DH 60T Moth Trainers surviving in Sweden. Sweden purchased a number of North American NA-16 trainers but none survived. A North American Yale was acquired from Canada and a Commonwealth Wirraway was exchanged with an Australian museum for a Texan and components of the two were mated to produce the NA-16-4M. Also in this workshop a full-size replica of the second Swedish army aircraft, a Bréguet U III, has been built using an original engine.

This enterprising museum is going to great lengths to create a complete record of a unique air force which has never taken an aggressive part in any conflict.

The distinctive SAAB J-29 fighter was a most successful aircraft and the museum has seven on its inventory

Switzerland

SWISS TRANSPORT MUSEUM
Verkehrshaus der Schweiz

Lidostrasse 5, Luzern CH-6006
Tel: 041-31-44-44
Opening times: March-November 9am-6pm daily; December-February 11am-4pm Tuesday-Saturday, 10am-5pm Sunday
Location: on the north side of Lake Lucerne about 1¼ mile (2 km) east of the town center

Bell 47G (1953)
Blériot XI-b (1913)
Bücker Bü 131B Jungmann (Doflug) (1935), **Bü 133C Jungmeister (Doflug)** (1936)
Chanute Hang-glider (R) (?)
Comte AC-4 Gentleman (1930)
Convair CV-990A Coronado (1962)
de Havilland DH 100 Vampire FB.6 (1949), **DH 112 Venom FB.4** (1956)
Dewoitine D-26 (EKW) (1933), **D-27 (EKW)** (1934)
Douglas DC-3 (C-47B) (1945)
Dufaux III (1910)
EKW C-35 (1936), **C-3603-1** (1942), **N-20 Arbalete** (1951), **N-20 Aiguillon** (1952)
Farner WF-7 (1934)
Fieseler Fi 156C-3 Storch (1943)
FFA AS.202/15 Bravo (1975)
Fokker F.VIIA (1927)
Hanriot HD-1 (Nieuport Macchi) (1918)
Hug Spyr IIIB (1933)
Lockheed Orion 9C (Altair) (1931)
Messerschmitt Bf 108B Taifun (1938)
Michel Ikarus Hang-glider (1975)
Mignet/Donat Guignard Pou-du-Ciel (1935)
Mignet/Roland Py Pou-du-Ciel (1969)
Nieuport 28C-1 Bebe (1918)
North American P-51D Mustang (1944)
Piper PA-18 Super Cub (1957)
Rech Monoplane (1912)
RRG Zogling (1943)
Soldenhoff S-5 (1935)
Spalinger S-21H (1942, 1945)
Stierlin Helicopter (1964)
Sud-Est SE.3160 Alouette III (1965)

Restored by the Swissair team at Zürich, this Lockheed Orion is the sole survivor of its type. It is painted in markings used by the airline in the 1930s

This excellent transport museum on the shores of Lake Lucerne is a relative newcomer to the field. Unlike the many European countries which set up transport collections at around the turn of the century, Switzerland did not start planning the museum until 1940, when an advisory group formed. A museum association was set up in Zürich in 1942 but there were no significant developments for a decade. Then construction of the museum eventually started in 1957 and the opening was in July 1959. The next 10 years were a period of consolidation, followed by expansion of the facilities in the 1970s. By 1978 the building additions had made the museum one of the largest in Europe. The first director of the museum, Dr Alfred Waldis, was appointed in 1957 and is still in charge of the collection.

For many years a selection of historic aircraft had been preserved and stored at airfields throughout the country and were occasionally on view at open days. In the early years of the museum only six aircraft were on show with a small display of engines and other equipment. The planning for the new Air and Space Wing took several years and when it opened in July 1972 most of the stored aircraft were exhibited. Since its opening there has been close cooperation with the Air Force Museum and there has been considerable exchange of exhibits between the two collections.

An historic machine owned by the museum is the biplane built by Armand and Henri Dufaux at Geneva in 1910. This was the first really successful Swiss airplane, which in April 1910 flew 41 miles (66 km) in 56 minutes over Lake Geneva

The EKW Arbalete, a 3/5 scale model of the ambitious Aiguillon fighter, which is also in the collection

and set up a record for the longest flight over water. The Dufaux was demonstrated to the Swiss Military Commission in May 1910 but was found to be unsuitable. However, the improved Dufaux 5 was leased by the army for their 1911 autumn maneuvers. Experience with the Dufaux led to the formation of the air force in August 1914 with two Blériot XI-bs as its first aircraft. One of these original aircraft is on view at the museum – it was bought from Oskar Bider and used for border surveillance with a carbine attached to the fuselage side. The Blériot was withdrawn in 1930 but took to the air again in 1940 for a film about Bider.

Neutral Switzerland has often seized stray military aircraft and the testing of these machines by the air force has sometimes led to orders for the foreign manufacturers. Two such types on show are a Hanriot HD-1 and a Nieuport 28. In June 1918 an Italian flier landed his HD-1 at Samedan and after six months of testing by the Swiss it was returned. In 1921 16 of the type were bought from Italy and used until 1930. Later in the same year an American landed his Nieuport 28 at Solothurn and the aircraft was rebuilt, leading to an order for 14 from France.

The range of military aircraft encompasses several Swiss-designed types and others built under license. The most spectacular are two delta jets which were part of the program to produce a combat aircraft in the 1950s. The EKW firm at Emmen built two 3/5ths scale models to test the concept – the first was a glider and the second, the Arbalete, has four small Turboméca Pimene jets. This tiny research aircraft flew in 1951 and completed 91 research missions before being presented to the museum. The full size N-20 started trials in 1952 but the engines were not powerful enough so only a few straight hops were made. Parliamentary approval for the purchase of Armstrong-Siddeley Sapphire engines was refused and this prototype with many technical innovations was presented to the museum in 1965.

One of the highlights of the collection is the exhibition of airliners. Airline operations started in Switzerland in 1919 and two of the historic machines on show have been restored by a group at Swissair at Zürich-Kloten. Balair was founded in 1926 with a Fokker F II and later in the year five ex-KLM Fokker F IIIs were added to the fleet. The first new aircraft ordered was a F VIIa, which was acquired in April 1927 and used until 1950 when it was stored at Berne Airport. With the addition of a new hall to the museum the airliner moved to Zürich for its rebuild to original status. Swissair used two Lockheed Orions from 1932 to 1936 and the museum searched for an example for years, leaving a space for one in the display. In 1976 the museum bought the last survivor of the type from California and flew it aboard a Swissair Boeing 747. It has been restored and painted to represent the first Swissair aircraft.

A feature of the Air and Space Hall is the arrangement of galleries at different levels and the suspension of aircraft from the ceiling which enables the visitor to view the exhibits from a variety of places.

The Dufaux III was demonstrated to the military authorities in 1910 and is the oldest aircraft in the museum

Thailand

ROYAL THAI AIR FORCE MUSEUM

Don Muang Air Force Base, Bangkok
Tel: 2-523-6151
Opening times: 8.30am-midday, 1pm-4.30pm Monday-Friday; 9am-midday, 2pm-5pm first weekend in month, also occasionally other weekends
Location: about 15 miles (24 km) northeast of the city center on the military side of the airport

Beech B18S (C-45F) (1944), **35 Bonanza** (1947)
Bell 47G (H-13H) (1956)
Bréguet 14 (scale replica) (?)
Boeing 100E (1931)
Cessna 305 Bird Dog (1951)
Curtiss 68 Hawk III (1935), **75 Hawk** (1938), **84 Helldiver (SB2C-5)** (1943)
de Havilland DH 82A Tiger Moth (1942 ?), **DHC 1 Chipmunk** (1949)
Douglas A-1H Skyraider (1955)
Fairchild F.24W (UC-61A) (1943)
Fairey Firefly I (1951)
Grumman G.58 Bearcat (F8F-1) (1945), **G.44 Widgeon** (1946)
Helio H.395 Courier (U-10B) (1966)
Hiller UH12B (1951)
Kaman K.600 Huskie (HH-43B) (c.1960)
Nieuport Monoplane (R) (?)
North American AT-6C Texan (1942), **F-86D Sabre** (1953), **F-86F Sabre** (1953)
Percival P.50 Prince (c.1952)
Piper J.3C Cub (L-4H) (1943)
Republic F-84G Thunderjet (1952)
Sikorsky VS.375 Dragonfly (YR-5A) (1943), **S.55** (1957)
Stinson V.76 Sentinel (L-5B) (1942)
Supermarine 379 Spitfire F.XIVE (1945)
Tachikawa Ki 36 (1942)
Vought V-93S Corsair (1934)
Westland WS.51 Dragonfly (1953)
Two primary gliders of unknown type

There are not many major aviation museums in Asia and one of the most significant in the continent is located in Thailand. Military aviation in the country commenced in 1911 when two officers were sent to France for training. With their return home two years later with seven French aircraft, the army was in the aviation age. Don Muang airfield opened in 1914 and has been a military base ever since, and today the airfield is also the international airport for Thailand.

The Royal Thai Air Force was established as a separate entity in 1937. In the inter-war period aircraft from several countries were acquired, and in addition license-built machines and indigenous designs emerged from the Don Muang production facilities. When Japan invaded in 1941, a truce was soon agreed, and although the Thai forces were supposed to assist their occupiers few genuinely offensive missions were undertaken. As a result of this policy a number of types survived, and some are seen in the museum. When World War II ended, aircraft were bought in the UK, US and Canada but since 1950 almost all equipment has been supplied by the US.

The idea of an Air Force Museum was proposed in 1952 and the collection opened formally on March 27, 1959. A permanent building to house the aircraft and other material was ready to be opened on January 24, 1969. Four American designs from the 1930s are the highlight of the impressive display. Two Boeing 100Es were bought in 1931 and one was still in use in 1949. Siam bought twelve Curtiss Hawk III biplanes in 1934, and others were built under license at Don Muang. The name Hawk was also used for a series of monoplane fighters which followed the biplane line. Twelve H75Ns with non-retractable undercarriage were purchased in November 1938 and took part in the futile attempt at repelling the superior Japanese forces. The sole survivor of this small fleet has been preserved along with its biplane ancestor.

The rarest aircraft in the collection is the only known Vought V-93S Corsair. The name of Corsair is familiar to most enthusiasts, as borne by the cranked-wing monoplane which the Vought company first flew in 1940; this was the first fighter to achieve over 400 mph (640 km/h) in level flight. However, the company had used the name before for its two-seat biplane which was first tested in 1926. The type was an instant success, and over the next decade Corsairs set many records and were exported to a number of countries in addition to being used in vast numbers by the US Navy. Siam bought twelve in 1934 and up to another 72 were built in Siam at Bang Sue. They served until 1949: one of the Siamese-built batch is on show and is the oldest Vought aircraft in existence.

The air force also used some Japanese aircraft, and one has survived: a Tachikawa Ki 36 low-wing trainer and army cooperation design. Over 1300 were built in Japan and a small number went to Thailand in 1940. The other exhibits, although not as rare, nevertheless include some impressive aircraft. Thirty Spitfire XIVs were bought in 1948, as were ten Firefly 1s and a number of Tiger Moths from the UK. The large and powerful Grumman Bearcat was selected as the front line fighter at this time, and 100 were supplied along with another 29 which were used for spares. The fighter, designed for ship use, had an impressive short field performance which was of use when operating from fields in the outlying areas of the country. The Bearcats remained in use until 1961, when they were replaced by Sabres. The first jet equipment for the air force arrived in 1957 when Thunderjet fighters and T-33 trainers came from the USAF and one of the former type is on view.

Examples of most of the types supplied by the US have been preserved in the museum, and they present an impressive display tracing the story of an air force which is little known outside its own region. With such an excellent collection it is hoped that as types are withdrawn from service they will be added to the museum. Although most tourists may not visit Thailand to view an aircraft museum, they would be well advised to take it in on their sojourn in the capital of this delightful country.

Right
Twelve Curtiss Hawk 75s with fixed undercarriage were supplied to Siam in 1938/39. This is the only survivor

Below
The Tachikawa Ki 36 was supplied in small numbers to Thailand during World War II

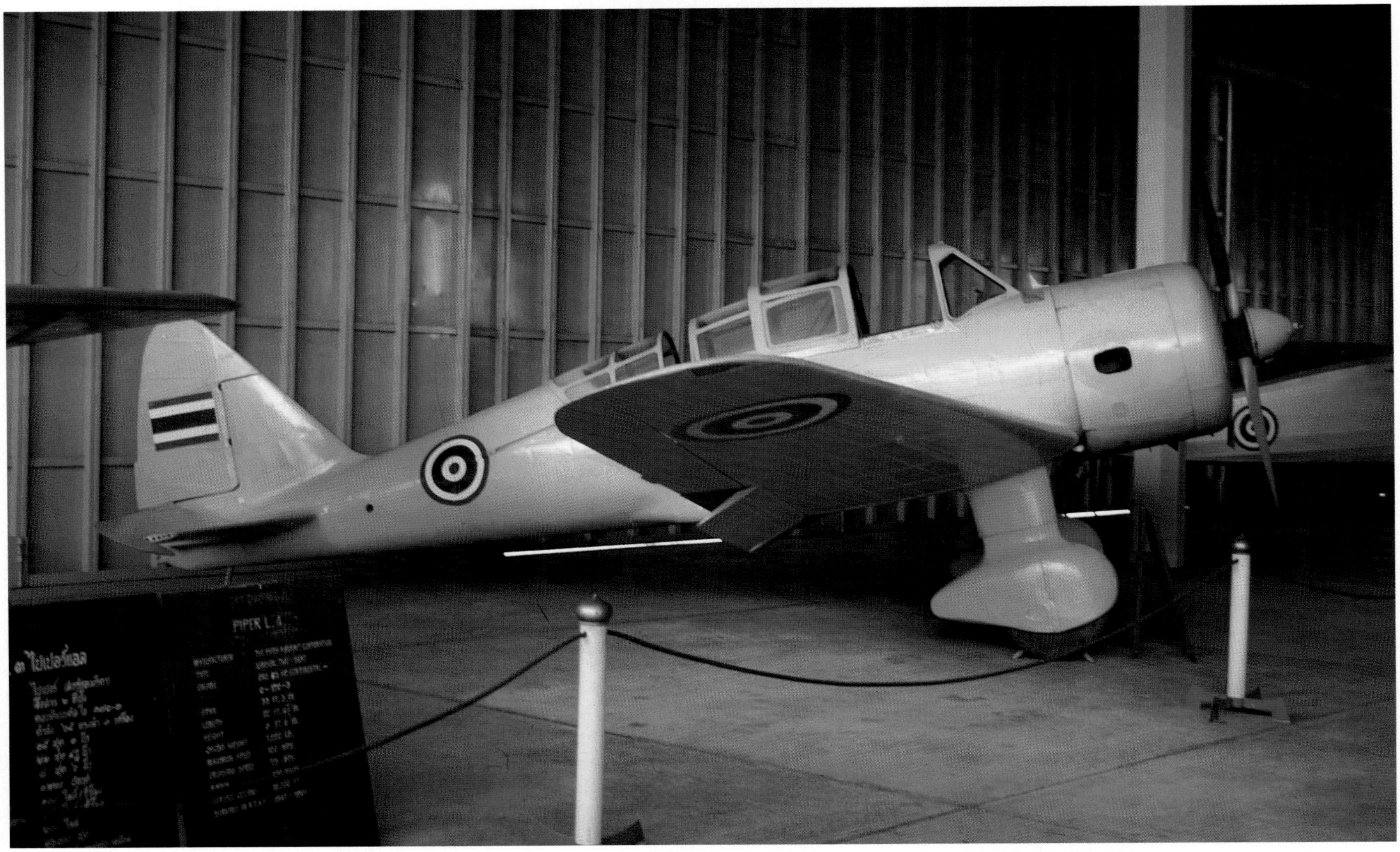

Union of Soviet Socialist Republics

AIR FORCE MUSEUM

141170 Monino, Moscow
Tel: 2445624 ext 2186 or 2225

Opening times: 10am-1pm, 2.30pm-5pm Monday-Thursday; 10am-2.30pm Saturday; but access is restricted
Location: about 56 miles (90 km) east of Moscow

Aero L-29 Delfin (1963)
Antonov An-2 (1950), **An-8** (1956), **An-10A** (1960), **An-12** (1967), **An-13** (1958), **An-14** (1967), **An-22** (1966), **An-24** (1960), **A-11** (1958), **An-15** (1960)
Bereznyak-Isayev B-1 (R) (?)
Beriev Be-12 (1964), **Be-32** (1977)
Burevestnik S-3 (1926)
Farman F.4 (c.1911)
Ilyushin Il-2m3 (1943), **Il-10m** (1951), **Il-12** (1947), **Il-14P** (1953), **Il-18** (1959), **Il-28** (1950), **Il-62** (1968)
Ivensen (1929)
Kamov KA-18 (1959), **Ka-25** (1962)
Kazan KAI-19 (1964)
Lavochkin La-7 (1943), **La-11** (1948), **La-15** (1949), **La-250** (1958)
Lisunov Li-2 (DC-3) (1940)
Mikoyan-Gurevich MiG-3 (R) (?), **MiG-9** (1947), **MiG-15UTI** (1948), **MiG-15bisISh** (1950), **MiG-17** (1952), **MiG-19** (1953), **MiG-19PM** (1957), **MiG-21PFMA** (1965), **MiG-23** (1968), **MiG-25R** (1971), **MiG-29** (1978), **YE-166** (1960)
Mikoyan-Tupolev A-144 Analog (1966)
Mil Mi-1 (1950), **Mi-2** (1961), **Mi-4** (1953), **Mi-6** (1958), **Mi-10** (1975), **V-12** (1968), **Mi-24** (1972)
Myasishchev M-50 (1958)
Petylakov Pe-2FT (1942), **Pe-8** (1938)
Polikarpov I-16 Type 6 (R) (?), **R-5** (c.1930), **Po-2VS** (c.1940)
Rafaelyants Turbolyet (1957)
Sikorsky Ilya Mouromets (R) (?), **S-58** (1958)
Sopwith Triplane (1917)
Sukhanov Diskoplan (?)
Sukhoi Su-7B (1959), **Su-7BK** (1960), **Su-9B** (1959), **Su-17** (1968), **Su-24** (1974), **T-100** (1972)
Tatlin Makholet (1933)
Tupolev ANT-2 (1924), **ANT-25 (R)** (?), **ANT-6** (1931), **ANT-40** (1935), **Tu-2** (1943), **Tu-4** (1948), **Tu-16** (1954), **Tu-20 (Tu-95)** (1955), **Tu-22** (1960), **Tu-28** (1967), **Tu-? (Blackjack)** (1981), **Tu-104A** (1958), **Tu-114** (1957), **Tu-124** (1960), **Tu-144** (1973)
Vertol V.44 (1958)
Voisin L (1914)
WSK M-15 Belphegor (1975)
Yakovlev UT-2 (R) (?), **Yak-3** (1944), **Yak-9U** (1943), **Yak-11** (1947), **Yak-12R** (1951), **Yak-17** (1947), **Yak-18PM** (1965), **Yak-18U** (1955), **Yak-23** (1948), **Yak-24U** (1957), **Yak-25** (1954), **Yak-26 (Yak-25RD) (Yak-RV)** (1959), **Yak-27R** (1960), **Yak-28** (1961), **Yak-36** (1967), **Yak-40** (?), **Yak-50** (1968)

One of the major collections of military aircraft in Europe is located at Monino, which is also the site of the Soviet Air Force Academy. This establishment had collected aircraft and material before the museum was officially set up, in November 1958. The museum first opened in February 1960 but since then access has been, to say the least, rather difficult. Groups from official Soviet organizations are granted access, but visits by foreigners are often the result of long negotiations with the authorities. The Monino region is restricted, although fortunately there are moves afoot to construct a separate entrance to the aircraft collection, thus divorcing it from the Academy grounds. The above times of opening are quoted from a 1983 East German publication, and there has been no official announcement since that time.

The major part of the collection consists of aircraft from the post World War II period and gives an insight into the rapid advance in Soviet technology since 1945. In addition to the aircraft there are displays of engines, armaments, equipment and memorabilia. Altogether, the display tells the story of Soviet aviation from its humble beginnings, including items from the time of the Tsars. The earliest aircraft is a Sopwith Triplane, believed to have been seized during the Allied involvement in the civil war. Some reports have stated that it is a Dux-built copy. From the Dux plant, which was established in 1910, are license-built examples of the French Farman F.IV and Voisin L.

After the revolution, the Soviet Union steadily developed an aircraft industry, but not many aircraft from the pre-1939 period are to be seen. Two of the most influential designers from this period were Andrei Tupolev and Nikolai Polikarpov. Tupolev built his first aircraft, the ANT-1, in 1922, and this was followed two years later by the high-wing ANT-2. This design was the first all-metal aircraft produced in the Soviet Union, and although only one was made it provided valuable data for the larger transports which followed. Great efforts are being made to fill gaps in the collection, and the practice of sending out expeditions to search for wrecks is well established. The Tupolev ANT-6, when it first flew in 1930, was the largest landplane in the world, with a span of 130 feet (42 meters). Currently under restoration is one located in 1982 near Arkhangelsk, where it force-landed in 1943.

Another Tupolev product which is on show is an ANT-40 (SB) twin-engined bomber of 1934. This was found in 1979 and was restored by the Tupolev design bureau and presented to Monino in 1982. Tupolev and Igor Sikorsky featured prominently in a film tracing the early days of Soviet aviation and for this production full-size replicas of the ANT-25 long-range record breaker, and Sikorsky's giant Ilya Mouromets bomber of World War I, were constructed. When filming was over these were passed to the museum.

Nikolai Polikarpov joined the former Dux plant in 1918 and was appointed chief designer. During World War I several examples of the de Havilland DH 9 were captured, and Polikarpov developed from these the R-1, the first mass-

The Beriev Be-12 amphibian first flew in about 1960 and at least 200 examples served in many roles

produced aircraft in the Soviet Union. In 1927 his U-2 or Po-2 appeared, and this classic biplane was in production for over a quarter of a century and became possibly the most prolific type of all time. Estimates of the number constructed vary between 29,000 and 40,000, and a small number, including one in France, are still flying. His R-5 served in a multitude of roles in the 1930s, and over 6000 were produced. One has been preserved, and there is also a replica of his I-16 fighter.

There are strong rumours in Eastern Europe of the existence of many World War II aircraft in the Soviet Union, and if these are true one wonders why some of them are not on show. Certainly in the early 1950s an exhibition at the Central Museum of the Armed Forces featured about 10 such aircraft. They are now believed to be in the store at the Zhukovsky Institute in Moscow, and if this is so hopefully they will one day reappear. Replicas of some types from this period have been constructed, and these include the world's first rocket-powered fighter, the Bereznyak-Isayev BI, which flew in May 1942.

Standing side by side in one of the hangars are two of the classic Soviet types of World War II. The Ilyushin Il-2 Shturmovik, of which over 36,000 were produced, was at one time thought to be extinct in the Soviet Union. Searches have resulted in five being located and restored. The Monino example was forced down in a marsh in 1942, and after 25 years it was taken to the Ilyushin OKB, who restored it to pristine condition. The Yakovlev OKB performed a similar task on the Yak-9U which was obtained from Bulgaria. Awaiting its turn in the restoration queue is a Petlyakov Pe-8 found in 1980. One significant aircraft on show is the Lavochkin La-7 in which the fighter ace Kozhedub shot down 17 of his score of 62.

In the post-1945 period a new range of design bureaux were to the fore, and the collection has aircraft from the factories of Beriev, Ilyushin, Lavochkin, Mikoyan-Gurevich, Sukhoi, Tupolev and Yakovlev. In this period Soviet designers also developed the helicopter, and the names of Kamov and Mil came to be well known.

The first Soviet jet aircraft to fly was the MiG-9, which took to the air on April 24, 1946. Later in the day the Yak-15 also flew, but the Mikoyan-Gurevich aircraft won the honour on the toss of a coin. There are a number of types from this pioneering era of jet flight, showing the different approaches to the problem of getting the best out of this form of propulsion. The fighter line of the MiG types has

become well known since the 1960s and their development is portrayed in examples of most of the designs to emerge. A 1984 arrival at Monino was a MiG-29, which was first observed in about 1977.

There are a number of experimental aircraft on view, including two supersonic bombers, the Sukhoi T-100 and the Myasischev M-50. Although both types made a great contribution to the research programme both were probably too advanced for their time. The MiG Ye-166 was specifically designed for high speed research, and in the early 1960s it set a number of records. A MiG-21 was modified to test the wing plan for the Tupolev Tu-144 supersonic airliner, and this research aircraft is on view, as is a Tu-144.

An important feature of the display is the number of transport aircraft on show, almost all significant types produced in recent years. Also most of the helicopters, including the unsuccessful Yakovlev Yak-24, can be seen.

No doubt with the great enthusiasm shown at the museum and with the assistance of the authorities, more aircraft will be added to this outstanding collection. It can only be hoped that some way will be found of allowing the vast number of enthusiasts who would like to visit Monino to have access to this great museum.

Above
This Mikoyan-Gurevich MiG-21 was fitted with a scaled-down wing of a Tupolev Tu-144 supersonic airliner

Left
The Yakovlev Yak-24 was not a great success; it proved to be the last rotary-wing type from the famous design bureau

Opposite Top
About 500 production examples of the Lavochkin La-15 jet fighter were produced in the late 1940s

Opposite Bottom
The Mikoyan-Gurevich Ye-166 high-speed research aircraft set several records in the early 1960s

United Kingdom

FLEET AIR ARM MUSEUM

Royal Naval Air Station, Yeovilton, Ilchester, Somerset BA22 8HT
Tel: 0935-840551 ext 521
Opening times: 10am–5.30pm or to dusk if earlier, daily
Location: on the B3151 road about 2 miles (3 km) east of Ilchester

Albatros D Va (R) (1977)
Beech T-34C Turbo Mentor (1980)
Bensen B.8M (1971)
Blackburn B-24 Skua I (1937), **B-103 Buccaneer** (1958), **B-103 Buccaneer S.1** (1963)
British Aircraft Corporation BAC.221 (1956)
British Aircraft Corporation/Aérospatiale Concorde 002 (1969)
de Havilland DH 82A Tiger Moth (1940), **DH 100 Sea Vampire I** (1943), **DH 110 Sea Vixen FAW.1** (1958), **DH 110 Sea Vixen FAW.2** (1966), **DH 112 Sea Venom FAW.21** (1955), **DH 115 Sea Vampire T.22** (1954)
Douglas Skyraider AEW.1 (AD-4W) (1951)
Eclipse Super Eagle (powered hang-glider) (?)
Fabrica Militar de Aviones IA.58A Pucara (1980)
Fairey Swordfish II (Blackburn) (1943), **Albacore I** (1939), **Fulmar II** (1939), **Barracuda II (Boulton-Paul)** (1942), **Firefly TT.4 (FR.4)** (1947), **Firefly AS.5** (1948), **Gannet AEW.3** (1960), **Gannet COD.4 (AS.4)** (1957)
Fokker Dr 1 (5/8 scale replica) (1969?)
Gloster Sea Gladiator (1938), **Meteor T.7** (1957), **Meteor TT.20 (NF.11)** (1957)
Grumman Martlet I (F4F Wildcat) (1940), **Hellcat II (F6F)** (1942), **Avenger AS.6 (TBM-3E) (AS.4)** (1945)
Handley Page HP.115 (1961)
Hawker Sea Fury FB.11 (1945), **Sea Fury T.20** (1948), **Sea Hawk FGA.6 (FGA.4)** (1954), **Sea Hawk FGA.6** (1954)
Hiller UH 12 HT.1 (HTE-2) (1953)
Macchi MB.339A (1981)
North American AT-6D Texan (Harvard) (1941)
Percival P.57 Sea Prince T.1 (1951)
Saunders-Roe P.531 (1958)
Short S.27 (R) (1979), **184** (1915)
Sopwith Baby (1915), **Camel (R) (Slingsby T.57)** (1969), **Pup (R)** (1981)
Supermarine 236 Walrus I (1939), **384 Seafire F.XVII** (1945), **398 Attacker F.1** (1951), **544 Scimitar F.1** (1959)
Vought Corsair IV (FG-1A) (1944)
Westland W.34 Wyvern TF.1 (1947), **WS-51 Dragonfly HR.5** (1953), **WS-55 Whirlwind HAR.1** (1953), **WS-55 Whirlwind HAS.3** (1954), **WS-55 Whirlwind HAS.7** (1960), **WS-58 Wessex HAS.1** (1958), **WS-58 Wessex HAS.3 (HAS.1)** (1966), **Wasp HAS.1** (1965)
Westland-Bell 47G-3 Sioux AH.1 (1965)
Yokosuka MXY-7 Ohka (1945)

In just over 20 years the Fleet Air Arm Museum has grown from a few aircraft displayed beside a fence to one of the major service aviation museums in the world. The story starts in the early 1960s when the A303 road, which at that time passed the base, was one of the major tourist routes to the west country. A problem arose when motorists took to stopping at the roadside to watch activities and aircraft on the base, so the navy provided a special off-road viewing enclosure, to which they thoughtfully added three historic aircraft. The display proved to be so popular that the naval authorities decided to go ahead with a permanent museum, and thus the senior service became the first in the United Kingdom to establish an aviation-based collection.

The museum, sited in one hangar, was formally opened by the Duke of Edinburgh in May 1964, and the ceremony almost coincided with the golden jubilee of the formation of the Royal Naval Air Service. The number of aircraft in the collection increased steadily during the 1960s and within 10 years of the opening over 30 were on show. Space in the hangar was at a premium and aircraft were packed in, many with their wings folded. Temporary accommodation was obtained in an adjacent hangar, and other aircraft were stored outside. The Trustees of the museum commissioned a detailed report dealing with the technical problems associated with preventing corrosion, and a fund-raising consultant was asked to advise.

In 1973 an appeal was launched so that the museum could be developed into a major exhibition. The plans called for the display to be built up in stages. The original estimate for the extensions was £500,000 but by the time the work was completed inflation had added another 30 per cent. The foundation stone for the new museum was laid by HRH The Prince of Wales in September 1974 when he was training at Yeovilton to be a helicopter pilot. Funds came in fairly rapidly, and the first phase of the development was ready in late 1975. This in essence joined Hangar 11 to the adjoining Hangar 12, and with the cladding of the now inside walls removed a large exhibition area was available. The building was named the Caspar John Hall after the President of the Appeals Committee, Admiral of the Fleet Sir Caspar John, who holds the distinction of being the first FAA pilot to hold the positions of First Sea Lord and Chief of the Naval Staff.

Development continued and Phase 2, the Queen Elizabeth Silver Jubilee Hall, was opened by Admiral of the Fleet, Earl Mountbatten of Burma in October 1977. This area housed a workshop, library and archive facilities, lecture rooms, offices and a special display area. Earl Mountbatten first flew in 1911 and at the opening ceremony he expressed a wish that a replica of the Short S27 Variant in which he made this flight should be built. Sadly this great man was savagely murdered before he could see his wish fulfilled.

The final phase of the development was completed in

Hanging in the entrance hall of the museum is this partial replica of the Sopwith Baby. Apprentices at Lee-on-Solent constructed it from parts of two genuine aircraft

January 1980 and named the Mountbatten Memorial Hall by the Earl's daughter. This consisted of a new entrance hall and further exhibition space. Since this date the museum has not stood still, and smaller improvements to the exhibition and facilities are always taking place.

Adjacent to the museum is the Concorde Exhibition operated by the Science Museum. The British prototype of the supersonic airliner first flew in April 1969 and after its trials it flew to Yeovilton on March 4, 1976. The building was completed by 1979 and the exhibition traces the story of the project since 1956 right up to the airline operations of the present day. In addition to the Concorde, two aircraft which were important in its development, the BAC 221 and the Handley Page HP.115, are on view.

Suspended in the entrance hall is a Sopwith Baby floatplane. The type was developed from the Tabloid which won the Schneider Trophy at Monaco in 1914 and first entered naval service in late 1915. The Baby was used up until 1917 and the aircraft on show is a partial replica which was rebuilt from the remains of two aircraft by apprentices at Lee-on-Solent.

The special exhibition area is now devoted to an exhibition tracing the role of the Fleet Air Arm in the Falklands conflict. Helicopters made a vital contribution in the operations and a number have been acquired and are on show. In addition some Argentinian aircraft captured in the war have been brought back for exhibition. The display opened as the South Georgia Exhibition in November 1982, and told the story of the territory since it was first sighted in 1675 and explored in the next century by Captain Cook. The full exhibition, expanded to cover the whole conflict, was opened by HRH Prince Andrew on July 11, 1983.

Nearby is a photographic display tracing the life of Lord Mountbatten, showing all aspects of the Admiral's military and diplomatic roles. A further exhibition is devoted to bird control at Yeovilton – an unspectacular but neccesary task which has saved many expensive machines from damage.

In an alcove off the hall are shown the remains of a Blackburn Skua which landed on the ice of Lake Grotli in Norway in April 1940. The crew set fire to the cockpit area according to instructions, causing the ice to melt and sinking the wreck. The Skua was salvaged by a team of divers in 1974, and now it is part of a diorama depicting the event.

Before the visitor reaches the Caspar John Hall, there are a series of smaller exhibitions which may divert his attention. One is entitled 'Ark Royal', a name synonymous with naval carrier operations, and the 1985 launching of the latest ship to bear the proud name adds interest to this display of models of all the Arks. Modern naval operations are also highlighted in 'The Modern Navy'; 'Wings over the Sea' traces the development of the aircraft carrier; and a display traces the life of 'Rex' Warneford who won the Victoria Cross in June 1915 when he attacked Zeppelin LZ 37. Close to these displays is an exhibition of excellently restored aero engines which shows the rapid strides propulsion units have made in 80 years.

The main aircraft display is in the Caspar John Hall, where many of the outstanding types which have seen service from both land and sea bases are on view. Unfortunately few of the inter-war period aircraft have survived, and only the Sea Gladiator and the Swordfish represent the classic biplanes which flew from our carrier fleet. These will soon be joined by a Fairey Albacore which is now being rebuilt by Viv Bellamy at Land's End Airfield. The remains of this aircraft were found at Tongue in Scotland and were in store for many years before moving to Cornwall. The rebuild is now well under way and another type which was thought to be extinct in complete form should take its place in the exhibition before too long. Another Fairey design, a Barracuda which was built at Wolverhampton by Boulton Paul, may go to Land's End when the Albacore is completed.

The Sea Gladiator was bought back from the services by the Gloster company, and after use as an instructional airframe at Ansty it was bought along with a Gladiator by Viv Bellamy, a former FAA pilot. In the 1950s his workshops were at Eastleigh, Southampton and he rebuilt the Gladiator to flying condition and it is now a favored display mount at Old Warden. The Sea Gladiator followed its airworthy brother around and was a feature of the Old Warden sheds before being loaned to the museum, where it has been carefully restored by volunteers.

The Swordfish is one of the best known naval aircraft of all time and the parent company built almost 700 before production was transferred to the Blackburn company, who constructed a new factory at Sherburn in Elmet for the line where another 1700 emerged. The example on show is Yorkshire-built, but its early history is obscure until it appeared at the Royal Naval Engineering College at Manadon near Plymouth. The Swordfish was one of the first aircraft to join the museum and was soon painted in the markings of the aircraft in which Lt Cdr Eugene Esmonde won a posthumous Victoria Cross in leading the heroic but disastrous attack on the battleships *Gneisnau*, *Prinz*

One of the highlights of the display is this Supermarine Walrus, found derelict in the early 1960s and restored by RNAS Arbroath in Scotland

The Fairey Firefly shows its wing folding mechanism

Eugen and *Scharnhorst* as they escaped through the English Channel in February 1942.

Rivaling the Swordfish as the best-loved FAA aircraft is the Supermarine Walrus. The 'Stringbag' and 'Shagbat', as they were affectionately known by generations of naval fliers, were outstanding aircraft which served with distinction in all theaters of war. The Walrus on show saw only limited service with the navy, as soon after delivery it was sold to the Irish Air Corps who flew it from 1939 to 1945. Aer Lingus bought the amphibian in 1945 but never used it, and after a short period of joyriding at Biggin Hill the Walrus moved to Thame in 1949, where it lapsed into dereliction. In the early 1960s the hull and some other components were saved by the Historic Aircraft Preservation Society, who realized that a rebuild was beyond their capabilities. This rare aircraft was restored to pristine condition by RNAS Arbroath and joined the museum in December 1966.

In the remainder of the hall are shown the majority of the types which have served the FAA since 1945. Fixed-wing aircraft were operated by the navy until the late 1970s, when only helicopters were used until the advent of the Sea Harrier. A walk round the display will enable the visitor to see a wide range of both the fixed- and rotary-wing aircraft which have been used by our senior service.

Located on the south side of the field in a restricted area is a small hangar which houses the FAA Historic Flight whose aircraft delight visitors at many air shows in the UK. Despite major problems which have involved rebuilds after crashes, corrosion problems with engines and airframes, this small but dedicated team usually can put two or three aircraft into the air at any time. Pride of place in the flight is taken by a Blackburn-built Swordfish which was used for a brief period in the late 1940s by Faireys as a civil aircraft.

The Swordfish was the sole aircraft of the flight for many years, until in 1972 it was joined by a Hawker Sea Fury, whose powerful lines were in contrast to the elegant biplane. Now in addition to these the flight has a Tiger Moth, a Firefly and its first jet, a Hawker Sea Hawk which was restored at Culdrose in the mid-1970s.

This impressive museum has much to offer for both the aeronautical and military enthusiast, but has also proved popular with the general public, who come in vast numbers to see the well-thought-out displays.

This Fairey Swordfish is painted in the colors of the aircraft in which Lt Cdr Eugene Esmonde won a posthumous Victoria Cross

A recent addition to the flyable museum aircraft is this replica Sopwith Pup, built in Hertfordshire

One of the two TSR-2s completed is preserved at Duxford as a reminder of what might have been

IMPERIAL WAR MUSEUM

Lambeth Road, London, SE1 6HZ
Tel: 01-735-8922
Opening times: 10.00am–5.30pm Monday–Saturday, 2.00pm–5.30pm Sunday; closed Bank Holidays
Location: south of the River Thames close to Waterloo Station and Elephant and Castle Station

Site of the main aircraft collection:
Duxford Airfield, Duxford, Cambridgeshire CB2 4QR
Tel: 0223-833963
Opening times: 10.30am–5.30pm daily March 15–November 2; closed Good Friday and May Bank Holiday
Location: on the A 505 road about 10 miles (16 km) south of Cambridge

Airspeed AS.40 Oxford 1 (1940)
Auster B.5 AOP.9 (1961)
Avro 652A Anson 1 (1938), **652A Anson C.19** (1945), **698 Vulcan B.2** (1960), **716 Shackleton MR.3/3** (1958)
Avro-Canada CF-100 Canuck Mk.4 (1955)
Beech 18 Model 3TM (c.1947)
Boeing 299 Fortress (B-17G) (1944), **A-75N1 (PT-17)** (1941), **345 Superfortress (TB-29A)** (1944), **464 Stratofortress (B-52D)** (1956)
Bristol 96 F.2B (1918), **149 Bolingbroke IVT** (1942), **171 Sycamore III** (1951), **175 Britannia 312** (1958)
British Aircraft Company Drone (1936)
British Aircraft Corporation TSR-2 (1964)
British Aircraft Corporation/Aérospatiale Concorde 01 (1969)
Cierva C-30A (Avro 671) (1934)
Convair 240 (VT-29B) (1951)
Curtiss P-87 Kittyhawk (P-40E) (1941); **(P-40M)** (1943)
Dassault Mystère IVA (1953)
de Havilland DH 2 (R) (1978), **DH 82 Tiger Moth** (1942), **DH 89A Dragon Rapide** (1941, 1945), **DH 98 Mosquito T.III** (1945), **DH 98 Mosquito TT.35 (B.35)** (1945), **DH 104 Dove 6 (2), (2B)** (1948), **DH 106 Comet 2R (C.2)** (1956), **DH 106 Comet 4** (1958), **DH 110 Sea Vixen FAW.2** (1964), **DH 112 Sea Venom FAW.21** (1956), **DH 112 Venom FB.50** (?), **DH 115 Vampire T.11** (1952), **DH 115 Sea Vampire T.22** (1955), **DH 121 Trident 2E** (1967), **DHC 1 Chipmunk 22** (c.1952)
Douglas DC-3 (C-47A) (1943, 1944)
English Electric Canberra B.2 (1954), **Lightning F.1A** (1959)
Fabrica Militar de Aviones IA.58A Pucara (c.1980)
Fairey Swordfish III (1944), **Firefly I** (1944), **Gannet ECM.6 (AS.4)** (1957)
Focke-Achgelis Fa 330A-1 Bachstelze (1942)
Focke-Wulf Fw 190A-8 (c.1943)
Fokker Dr 1 (R) (1965)
Gloster Meteor F.8 (1953), **Meteor NF.11** (modified) (1952), **Javelin FAW.9 (FAW.7)** (1958)
Grumman G.40 Avenger (TBM-3E) (1944), **G.58 Bearcat (F8F-2)** (1945)
Handley Page HP.67 Hastings C.1A (1947), **HP.80 Victor B(K.2P), 1A (BK.1A) (B.1)** (c.1958), **HP.81 Hermes 4** (1950), **HPR.7 Herald 201** (1963)
Hawker Sea Hurricane I (1941), **Sea Hawk FB.5** (1954), **Hunter F.2** (1954)
Heinkel He 111 (c.1943), **He 162A** (1945)
Junkers Ju 52/3mge (AAC.1) (c.1939); **Ju 52/3m (CASA 352L)** (1957)
Lockheed T-33A (1952)
Max Holste MH.1521M Broussard (c.1958)
Messerschmitt Me 163B-1 Komet (1943)
Miles M.14A Magister (1939)
Morane-Saulnier MS.500 (Fi 156) (c.1946)
North American AT-6D Texan (1942), **P-51D Mustang** (1944), **P-51 Mustang (CA-18)** (1947), **B-25J Mitchell** (1944), **F-100D Super Sabre** (1954)
Percival P.34A Proctor III (1944)
Republic P-47D Thunderbolt (1944)
Royal Aircraft Factory BE.2c (1916), **RE.8** (1918)
SAAB 35a Draken (J-35A) (1958)
Saunders-Roe SR.A1 (1946)
Short S.25 Sunderland MR.V (1944), **SB.4 Sherpa** (1953)
Sopwith 2F.1 Camel (1918)
SPAD VII (1917)
Supermarine 300 Spitfire I (1940), **361 Spitfire HF.IXB** (1943)
Vickers 668 Varsity T.1 (1952, 1953), **701 Viscount** (1952), **1151 Super VC-10** (1963), **F4U-7 Corsair** (1945)
Westland WS-51 Dragonfly HR 3 (1952), **WS-55 Whirlwind HAS.7** (1957), **WS-58 Wessex HAS.1** (1965), **Lysander III** (1942)

The main purpose of the Imperial War Museum is to preserve and display items relating to British and Commonwealth military operations since 1914. The museum was formally opened in 1920, and moved to South Kensington in 1924, where space for the exhibitions was restricted. Although no documentary evidence has survived it is likely that a great deal of the collection was lost at this stage. Certainly many of the aircraft from another exhibition at the Agricultural Hall were supposedly donated to the Imperial War Museum but have not survived.

The museum moved to its present home in 1935. During World War II it was bombed and some exhibits lost. A major reconstruction in the mid-1980s will result in almost all of the aircraft from South Lambeth moving to Duxford for about three years.

The development of Duxford airfield in Cambridgeshire as a museum site is one of the most significant events in aircraft preservation in the UK for many years. Duxford was selected as a postwar RAF station in the closing years of World War I and opened in 1919. From 1923 to its closure in 1961 it was primarily a fighter base. Many of the famous squadrons of the Royal Air Force were housed at the field and it played an important part in the Second World War. The airfield was derelict until 1968 and in 1971 the museum obtained permission to use some of its hangars for storing aircraft. Work was started on improving the buildings and soon work started on the restoration of some of the exhibits. The siting of the museum on an active airfield is a bonus since in addition to airshows large aircraft can be flown there. Three of the historic two-bay hangars have been carefully restored to original condition but cannot house all the aircraft at the base. A modern hangar can exhibit some of the larger aircraft but the very largest are still exhibited outdoors. A so-called 'Superhangar' is a great advance in the preservation of some of the large historic bombers and transports.

In the 1960s the museum obtained a North American Mustang from Canada which was among the first aircraft to move to Duxford. It was painted in the colours of a 78th Fighter Group aircraft of the USAAF which had been based at Duxford in World War II. From these modest beginnings the collection grew rapidly in the 1970s. A de Havilland Sea Vixen flew in from Northern Ireland in March 1972 and an Avro Shackleton followed in August. A wide range of recently withdrawn types from both the RAF and Royal Navy were acquired, enabling a comprehensive history of military aircraft of the 1950s onwards to be staged.

The UK has not been the sole source of aircraft and the IWM searches have ranged far and wide to diversify the exhibition. From Canada came a Grumman Avenger which had served with both the US and Canadian navies before ending its active life with the well known Conair company who have a fleet of fire-fighting aircraft. In the same shipment was a Stearman Kaydet training biplane which was originally built for the USAAF. The Kaydet in its many variants is one of the outstanding training aircraft of all time, of which 10,000 were built. Portugal provided a French-built Junkers Ju 52/3m which was restored to represent a Luftwaffe aircraft. A Short Sunderland flying boat, which after being retired by the Aéronavale was used as a café in France, was saved from dereliction by a team from Duxford.

In March 1980 a Boeing B-29 Superfortress flew in from the US. No example of this classic bomber which achieved everlasting fame by dropping the two atomic bombs on Japan existed in Europe. A few were in US museums and others were on the installations at China Lake in California and Aberdeen in Maryland. The B-29 had flown over 100 missions in the Korean War and after a major restoration in the US flew across the Atlantic to Duxford.

Two other famous Boeing bombers are on show. The first to achieve fame for the Seattle firm was the B-17 Fortress, of which two are normally on show at Duxford. Both came to England from France where they were part of the fleet operated by the IGN mapping organization. One is the well known flyable 'Sally B' whereas the other arrived by road and is nearing the end of a long term rebuild. In October 1983 an eight-jet B-52D Stratofortress which was offered to the RAF Museum by the USAF and then taken on by the IWM flew in. This aircraft served with 15 USAF Bomb Wings and was a major force in the Vietnam conflict.

A number of the early aircraft which had been on show at Lambeth have been moved to Duxford for restoration. An RE.8 which had flown for only 30 minutes in 1918 moved in 1974 and is now in pristine condition. Its place in the workshops was taken by a BE.2c and these two biplanes represent a link with Duxford's vintage hangars.

Duxford owes its present healthy state to cooperation between the state-run museum administration and volunteer bodies. The first group to assist was the East Anglian Aviation Society but in 1975 internal politics resulted in the formation of the Duxford Aviation Society. Members of the DAS assist the museum in a number of tasks including the restoration of aircraft. In addition the DAS has over the years acquired a number of aircraft in its own right, particularly airliners which are not strictly within the terms of reference of the exhibition. Nevertheless they are an interesting part of the display and provide a welcome variety from purely military hardware.

The first airliner to arrive was a de Havilland Comet 4 which when delivered to BOAC in 1958 took part in the first transatlantic crossings by the type when one aircraft left London as another departed from New York. The Comet was donated by Dan-Air and flew in in February 1974. Another ex-BOAC aircraft which came from another independent airline was a Bristol Britannia, which flew in from Luton where it was used by Monarch Airlines. 1977 saw the arrival of a pre-production Concorde, 1980 a British Airways Super VC-10 and 1982 a Trident 2E, also from BA. One of the important airliner recoveries took place in 1981 when the fuselage of an ex-BOAC Handley Page Hermes which had ended its days as a cabin trainer at Gatwick was moved to Duxford. The Hermes was an attempt by the famous company to try and break into the postwar airliner market, but only BOAC bought the type and only 28 left the Radlett lines.

A number of privately-owned historic aircraft at Duxford provide further variety. These obviously change from time to time as they are sold but a variety of airworthy machines can always be seen. The whole site has been carefully refurbished and apart from the modern hangars the field is a typical inter-war RAF station. The close cooperation between the IWM and the DAS has resulted in more rapid progress than could have possibly been envisaged when the airfield was originally obtained for storage purposes. In only 14 years Duxford has become one of the most significant collections in the world.

The Saunders-Roe A.1 jet flying-boat fighter was a novel idea, but only three were built and this is the sole survivor

The large delta-wing Avro Vulcan bomber, now displayed in a large new hangar known as the Superhangar at Duxford

This RE.8 was built in 1918 and named 'A Paddy Bird from Ceylon' as it was sponsored by the Ceylon Government. Flown for only 30 minutes, it spent years at Lambeth before going to Duxford in 1975 for restoration

The BE.2c shown in a corner of one of Duxford's historic hangars is another ex-Lambeth aircraft restored at Duxford

MOSQUITO AIRCRAFT MUSEUM

Box 107, Salisbury Hall, London Colney, Near St Albans, Hertfordshire AL2 1BU
Tel: 0727-22051

Opening times: 10.30am–6pm Sunday and Bank Holidays, Easter–October; and 2pm–5.30pm Thursdays July–September
Location: off the A6 road about 5 miles (8 km) south of St Albans

Airspeed AS.58 Horsa II (1943, 1944)
Blériot XI (1909)
Cierva C.24 (1934)
de Havilland DH 82A Tiger Moth (1939, 1940), **DH 87B Hornet Moth** (1935), **DH 98 Mosquito** (1940), **DH 98 Mosquito FB.VI** (1945), **DH 98 Mosquito B.35** (1945), **DH 100 Vampire FB.6** (1948), **DH 103 Sea Hornet NF.21 (1950)**, **DH 104 Dove 6 (2B)** (1953), **DH 106 Comet 1** (1953), **DH 110 Sea Vixen FAW.2** (1960), **DH 112 Sea Venom FAW.22** (1957), **DH 112 Venom NF.3** (1955), **DH 115 Vampire T.11** (1953), **DH 121 Trident 2E** (1970), **DH 125** (1963), **DHC 1 Chipmunk T.10** (1952)
Royal Aircraft Factory BE.2e (1918)

The seventeenth-century moated house of Salisbury Hall to the north of London was the unlikely location for the construction of one of the most famous aircraft of all time and is now a major private aviation museum celebrating that aircraft: the Mosquito.

The Mosquito project was conceived in great secrecy by the de Havilland company in the late 1930s and the team associated with the design moved into the hall in October 1939. A hangar was constructed for the building of the prototype and four more aircraft were started. The first and second Mosquitos were moved by road to nearby Hatfield for their maiden flights but the remaining three were flown out from an adjacent field. In October 1940 the Airspeed design office moved to the hall, and major assemblies of the first two Horsa gliders were built in another hangar on the site.

In 1946 Salisbury Hall became the de Havilland apprentice school for a year, after which it lapsed into dereliction before being bought in the 1950s by Walter Goldsmith. He found some sketches on the wall and set about researching its aviation connection. The prototype Mosquito had been saved, largely due to a de Havilland employee, W J S Baird. He had defied company orders to burn the aircraft and it had been dismantled and stored. Mr Goldsmith convinced the company that the historic prototype should return to its place of origin and it moved back in March 1959. Funds were raised for building a hangar and the aircraft went on show in May 1959 as an added attraction at the hall.

In the winter of 1967/8 a Venom which was saved from the gate at RAF Debden and a Vampire T.11 joined the Mosquito. A second Mosquito arrived in 1971, a Hatfield-built Mk.35 which had never seen war service but had starred in a number of films, donated by Liverpool Corporation.

Real progress was made in 1974 with the adoption of the present name and the formation of a supporters' society. The land on which the hangar stood and the adjoining site where the Mosquitos had been built was bought and plans were made for expanding the collection. The aim was for the collection to include any products of de Havilland companies. The next ten years saw many de Havilland aircraft arrive at the site and the museum gained international recognition. A Vampire FB.6 donated by the Swiss Air Force flew into Hatfield in August 1974, some 26 years after it had

Flown into Hatfield in 1974, this Vampire came as a gift to the museum from the Swiss air force

The prototype Mosquito rests at its birthplace at the historic Salisbury Hall site

been delivered. The Deutsches Museum in Munich has loaned the collection a Dove which flew for many years on airfield calibration work in Germany. A third Mosquito fuselage was obtained from the Netherlands and will be mated to a wing found on a kibbutz in Israel and flown back to the UK by El Al.

Major fund raising drive in the late 1970s paid for a large exhibition hangar; some of the farm buildings were converted with one now a workshop and another an exhibition hall for the famous line of de Havilland engines. The museum has examples of most postwar de Havilland types but the price of the prewar series of light aircraft has put them beyond its financial reach. It was fortunate to obtain a Hornet Moth in 1974 and some derelict Tiger Moth airframes in 1975 before the prices of de Havilland products soared.

The Airspeed connection is maintained by several Horsa fuselage sections which are gradually being restored into a complete exhibit. The Science Museum has loaned the unique Cierva C.24 autogyro which was built by de Havilland. The construction of the front fuselage was similar to that employed on the Puss Moth. This rare machine was restored by Hatfield apprentices in 1973/4 and moved to Salisbury Hall soon afterwards.

On loan from the Deutsches Museum in Munich, this de Havilland Dove served for many years in Germany on airport radio calibration duties

It is most appropriate that a museum devoted to one of the greatest British aviation companies should be at a major site for the development of one of the most versatile designs ever built. Perhaps it is a reflection on industry that this excellent collection has come about by the work and dedication of private individuals.

This Auster AOP.9 is one of the aircraft maintained in flying condition and flown by the Army Air Corps Historic Flight

MUSEUM OF ARMY FLYING

Army Air Corps Centre, Middle Wallop, Stockbridge, Hampshire SO20 8DY
Tel: 0264 62121

Opening times: 10am–4pm daily
Location: about 6 miles (10 km) southwest of Andover off the A343 road

Aérospatiale SA.341 (1970)
AFEE Rotabuggy (R) (1982)
Agusta-Bell 47G-3 Sioux AH.1 (1964)
Airspeed AS.51 Horsa I (1943), **AS.58 Horsa II** (1944)
Auster J AOP.5 (1944), **K AOP.6** (1946), **B.5 AOP.9** (1954/62)
Bell 204 Iroquois (UH-1H) (1973)
Bristol 171 Sycamore HR.14 (1955)
Cessna 305 Bird Dog (L-19A) (1951)
Cody Kite (R) (P) (?)
Cody 1909 Flyer (scale replica) (?)
de Havilland DH C2 Beaver AL.1 (1961/2)
FMA IA.58A Pucara (c.1980)
General Aircraft GAL.49 Hamilcar I (1945)
Hafner R.II (1932), **Rotachute III** (1943)
Lancashire Aircraft EP.9 Prospector (1959)
ML Utility Delta (1955)
Saunders-Roe Skeeter AOP.12 (1958/9)
Sopwith Pup (1916)
Westland WS-55 Whirlwind HAS.7 (1958), **WS-55 Whirlwind HAS.10** (1956), **Scout AH.1** (1962)
Westland-Bell 47G-3 Sioux AH.1 (1966/8), **47G4** (1969)

The origins of army aviation in Britain go back many years, to the ballooning exploits of the last century and to the formation of the Royal Flying Corps in 1912. The establishment of the Royal Air Force as a separate service in 1918 saw a loss of momentum in this aspect of the army's task. A rebirth occurred in World War II, with the formation of the Glider Pilot regiment and of the Parachute Regiment: the two combined in 1942 and were later joined by the Special Air Service. The army also maintained a number of Air Observation Post Squadrons, using RAF aircraft but crewed mainly by army personnel, and these served with distinction in many conflicts up to the mid-1950s. In 1957 all these activities were brought together when the Army Air Corps (AAC) was formed, with headquarters at Middle Wallop near Andover.

The idea of a museum was first put forward in 1960 under

the title Army Air Corps Museum, and the collection of memorabilia was begun. In 1973 premises in a former cinema on the base were obtained, and the display opened to the public in 1974. Space was restricted, but an interesting exhibition tracing the history of army flying from the earliest days was staged. Nevertheless, only a small amount of the museum collection could be shown, and this included three aircraft. Another small display of aircraft was mounted near the main gate.

The collection grew steadily and in 1982 a large air display was held at Middle Wallop to celebrate the 25th anniversary of the AAC. At this event an appeal was launched to raise funds for a new museum building. Funds came in rapidly and the new exhibition hall, with its associated offices and research area, was ready for opening in 1984. Even with this new facility, less than 50 per cent of the aircraft now in the collection are on view. In addition to the aircraft there are several motor vehicles and a number of powered target drones on view. The associated displays cover ballooning, the RFC in World War I, army co-operation between the wars, the work of the Glider Pilot Regiment and post World War II duties in Asia, Africa, Northern Ireland and the Falklands.

Auster aircraft have played a prominent role in army work for decades, and three of this successful range of high-wing monoplanes are on view with others in store. The earliest is a Mark 5 of 1944, and the Mark 9 was the last version from the famous Rearsby factory to be used by the army. The last AOP.9s were withdrawn in 1967, but two are still part of the AAC's Historic Flight.

The Army captured several aircraft in the Falklands conflict, and a Bell Iroquois which was seized by 656 Squadron is on view inside while two Pucaras designed and built in Argentina are outside. Two interesting aircraft on view were designed by the helicopter pioneer Raoul Hafner. The R.II is probably the earliest surviving helicopter in the world. It was built in 1931 in Austria, and its designer brought it to the UK in 1932. Although it did manage to leave the ground, the R.II was not a successful helicopter. The other Hafner aircraft, the Rotachute, was a gyroglider, designed to be towed behind a motor vehicle on the ground.

The museum is gradually acquiring components from the troop-carrying gliders which were used in World War II. At the end of the war, many were sold off to farmers, to whom their fuselages were of great use as storage sheds. Over the years these deteriorated but in the 1960s and 1970s several were still recognizable. On show is the nose and two fuselage sections of the Airspeed Horsa, with more in store. Also in store are two fuselage sections of the massive General Aircraft Hamilcar, but these will require a great deal of work before they can go on show.

One of two Pucara aircraft captured from the Argentinians in the Falklands operation

ROYAL AIR FORCE MUSEUM COLLECTION

A unique aircraft in the Battle of Britain Museum is the sole remaining Boulton-Paul Defiant. It is painted in the colors of No.307 (Polish) Squadron

Plans for the establishment of a military aviation museum date back to before the formation of the Royal Air Force. In 1917 Lord Rothermere, Secretary of State for Air, persuaded the Air Council to decree that an example of every World War I aircraft should be preserved. Discussions were held on the setting up of a national aeronautical museum, but little was done apart from an exhibition at the National Agricultural Hall in Islington. Many aircraft were on show here, but after this they mostly passed to the Imperial War Museum and many faded into obscurity. It was also the intention that after the formation of the Royal Air Force on April 1, 1918, one example of each type should be preserved as they were withdrawn from service. If this dictum had been followed the collection would have been one of the most comprehensive in the world.

Lord Rothermere resigned his posts in 1918, and the idea lapsed, the Imperial War Museum being interested only in aircraft of the war period, and the Science Museum collecting only a few of what it considered the most significant aircraft.

A Royal Air Force Museum and indeed a National Aeronautical Museum remained a dormant idea for decades. In the early 1960s John Tanner, who was on the staff of the Royal Air Force College at Cranwell, published a paper in an attempt to revive the concept. As a result of this the Air Force Board in 1962 formed an advisory committee chaired by Marshall of the Royal Air Force Sir Dermot Boyle, and this group recommended that a museum be established with Dr Tanner as director.

Work commenced from Cranwell, but soon Dr Tanner moved to London to organize the mammoth task. The choice of site fell upon the RAF base at Hendon in the northern suburbs of London. Hendon had been an aerodrome since the early days and the military moved in during 1914. In the inter-war period great crowds had flocked to the site for the RAF pageants. The airfield became part of a major residential area as London expanded and all powered flying ceased there in 1957.

The airfield still possessed many historic buildings, and the site for the museum was to be in two early hangars with Belfast Truss roofs. Dr Tanner wished to retain these as the main exhibition halls, but many of the plans put forward by noted architects had demanded demolition of the hangars. An ex-RAF officer, Dr John Reid, helped to develop a suitable design that still incorporated these hangars, together with a new exhibition hall containing galleries and administrative areas. The museum was opened by Her Majesty the Queen on November 15, 1972. Display space at Hendon is restricted and normally only about 30 aircraft are on show, although the collection now numbers almost 200.

Two more museums were subsequently constructed on the Hendon site, and there are also major collections at the RAF stations at Cosford in the West Midlands and St Athan in South Wales. The museum has restoration and storage facilities at RAF Cardington and RAF Henlow in Bedfordshire, and a number of aircraft are on show in Manchester. There are thus six main components of the RAF Museum Collection, which are presented here in alphabetical order.

AEROSPACE MUSEUM, RAF COSFORD

RAF Cosford, Wolverhampton, West Midlands WV7 3EX
Tel: 090-722-4872

Location: off the A41 road about 8 miles (13 km) northwest of Wolverhampton

Opening times: 10am–4pm daily April–October; 10am–6pm Monday–Friday November–March

Armstrong-Whitworth AW.660 Argosy C.1 (1962)
Avro 652A Anson C.19 (1954), **685 York C.1** (1944), **694 Lincoln B.2** (1945), **696 Shackleton MR.2/3** (1953), **698 Vulcan B.2** (1961), **707C** (1953), **716 Shackleton MR.3** (1954)
Boeing 707-436 (1960)
Boulton-Paul BP.108 Sea Balliol T.21 (1953)
Bristol 171 Sycamore HR.14 (1956), **175 Britannia 312** (1957), **188** (1963)
British Aircraft Corporation TSR-2 (1965)
Britten-Norman BN-1F (1950)
Consolidated Vultee PBY-6A Catalina (1945), **B-24L Liberator** (1945)
de Havilland DH 98 Mosquito TT.35 (B.35) (1945), **DH 104 Devon C.1** (1948), **DH 106 Comet 1A** (1953), **DH 112 Venom FB.4** (1955), **DH 121 Trident 1C** (1964), **DH C.1 Chipmunk T.10** (1953)
Douglas DC-3 (C-47B) (1944)
English Electric Canberra B(I).8 (1958), **Lightning F.1** (1959)
Fabrica Militar de Aviones IA.58A Pucara (1980)
Fairey Jet Gyrodyne (1949)
Fairey FD.2 (1954)
Fieseler Fi 103 (1945)
Focke-Achgelis Fa 330A-1 Bachstelze (1942)
Folland Fo.141 Gnat F.1 (1955)
Gloster F.9/40 Meteor (1942), **Meteor T.7/8** (1949), **Meteor F.8 (Prone pilot)** (1956), **Meteor NF.14** (1953), **Javelin FAW.1** (1955)
Handley Page HP.67 Hastings T.5 (C.1) (1948), **HP.80 Victor B.1A (B.1)** (1958)
Hawker Fury II (R) (1970?), **P.1052** (1948), **Hunter F.1** (1953), **Hunter 3** (?)
Hunting H.126 (1963)
Hunting-Percival P.84 Jet Provost T.1 (1954)
Junkers Ju 52/3m (CASA 352L) (1951)
Lockheed SP-2H (P2V-7B) Neptune (1961)
Lockheed T-33A (1951)
Messerschmitt Me 163B-1a Komet (1945)
Percival P.56 Provost T.1 (1953)
Saunders-Roe Skeeter AOP.12 (1959), **SR.53** (1956)
Scottish Aviation Twin Pioneer CC.1 (1958)
Short SB.5 (1952), **SC.5 Belfast C.1** (1965)
Supermarine 379 Spitfire FR.XIVe (1945), **510** (1948)
Vickers 657 Viking 1 (498 Viking 1A) (1946), **659 Valetta C.2** (1946), **668 Varsity T.1** (1952), **701 Viscount** (1952), **1101 VC-10** (1963)
Westland WS-51 Dragonfly HR.3 (1951), **WS-55 Whirlwind HAR.10** (1961)
Yokosuka MXY-7 Ohka II (1945)

Cosford opened in 1938 as a Technical Training School, and this is still the primary function of the station. The origins of the museum go back to the 1960s when the station housed three aircraft for the Air Historical Branch. In 1973 due largely to the efforts of an instructor, Flt Lt 'Josh' Wort, a museum collection was established. The collection was operated on an informal basis up to 1979 when it came under the auspices of the Hendon museum. Flt Lt Derek Eastwood left the service to become curator, a position which he held until his death in 1983.

The museum has worked hard to establish itself as a major collection and now over 60 aircraft are on show. There has recently been some rationalization of types between Cosford and St Athan, and this has resulted in the Midlands station acquiring more prototypes and research aircraft to add to its already impressive numbers. Highlights in this field are the prototype Meteor, the Fairey Delta 2, the Hunting H.126, the Saunders-Roe SR.53 and two aircraft recovered from the Shoeburyness ranges: a Bristol 188 stainless steel jet and one of the two remaining TSR-2s. A recent development at Cosford has been the expansion of the British Airways Collection, which now includes a range of airliners used since 1945. In addition to the aircraft, Cosford has a number of engines and components on show to round off a most impressive display. One great advantage of the site is that as it is on an active airfield aircraft can be flown in for preservation.

BATTLE OF BRITAIN MUSEUM

Hendon, London NW9 5LL
Tel: 01-205-2266

Opening times: 10am–6pm Monday–Saturday, 2pm–6pm Sunday, closed Bank Holidays
Location: about 9 miles (15 km) northwest of London off the A5 road and close to Exit 2 of the M1 motorway

Boulton Paul P.82 Defiant I (1940)
Bristol 149 Blenheim IV (1942)
Fiat CR-42 (1939)
Gloster Gladiator II (1937)
Hawker Hurricane I (1940)
Heinkel He 111H-23 (1944)
Junkers Ju 87D-3 (1942), **Ju 88R-1** (1942)
Messerschmitt Bf 109E-3/B (1940), **Bf 110G-4/R6** (1942)
Short S.25 Sunderland MR.V (MR.III) (1944)
Supermarine 228 Seagull V (1935), **300 Spitfire F.I** (1939)
Westland Lysander III (1940)

The second museum at Hendon honors both sides in Britain's most traumatic air engagement in World War II. Opened by Her Majesty the Queen Mother on November 28, 1978, this museum traces the story of the battle in vivid detail. There is an accurate reconstruction of the 11 Group Operations Room at RAF Uxbridge as at 10.30 am on September 15, 1940. There are displays of radar stations, gun emplacements, searchlight and spotting stations. Fourteen complete aircraft from three nations are on view. The Spitfire I and Hurricane I were the mainstay of the British defenses and examples of both are shown in sandbagged dispersals with camouflage netting. A unique aircraft is the sole remaining Boulton-Paul Defiant, shown in the colors of 307 Squadron – a Polish unit which helped in the defense of the United Kingdom. Towering over the two lines of British and Axis aircraft is a Short Sunderland flying boat, saved by Peter Thomas who acquired the aircraft from France to put on show at Pembroke Dock in Wales, until it was transferred to Hendon in 1971. The Blenheim on show is actually a Canadian-built Bolingbroke, modified into the

configuration of a Blenheim of the period. The only Italian aircraft on show is a Fiat CR.42 which was forced down in Suffolk in November 1940 during the only major Italian attack on the UK. The German aircraft include the only complete Messerschmitt Bf 110, one of the three genuine Heinkel He 111s and two Junkers types – the classic Ju 87 dive-bomber and a Ju 88 which defected to Britain in 1943.

The Mitsubishi Ki 46, a long-range reconnaissance aircraft. This one at St Athan is believed to be the only survivor out of the 1742 examples built between 1941 and 1944

Top
Enjoying a rare appearance in the open air at Cosford is this ex-Danish Air Force Consolidated Canso

BOMBER COMMAND MUSEUM

Hendon, London NW9 5LL
Tel: 01-205-2266

Opening times: 10am–6pm Monday–Saturday, 2pm–6pm Sunday, closed Bank Holidays
Location: as RAF Museum

Avro 504K (1918), **683 Lancaster I** (1942), **698 Vulcan B.2** (1961)
Boeing 299 Fortress (B-17G) (1944)
de Havilland DH 9A (1918), **DH 98 Mosquito T. III** (1946)
Handley Page HP.61 Halifax II (1940)
Hawker Hart (1931)
North American B-25J Mitchell (1944)
Royal Aircraft Factory BE-2b (1914)
Sopwith Tabloid (R) (1980)
Vickers 619 Wellington T.10 (B.10) (1944), **758 Valiant B(K).1 (B.1)** (1956)

In the later stages of World War II the Allied bomber offensive was a deciding factor in the outcome of the conflict. The bomber museum, which opened at Hendon in April 1983, serves as a memorial to the crews of RAF Bomber Command and the US 8th and 9th Air Forces who made this important contribution. The aim is also to show the development of bombers through some 70 years. The first strategic bomber raid was probably carried out in October 1914 when a Sopwith Tabloid flew from Antwerp to bomb the Zeppelin sheds at Düsseldorf. In the late 1970s Don

Cashmore constructed a replica of the Tabloid, and this is now in the museum. Another World War I bomber is the de Havilland DH 9A, one of the ex-Berlin aircraft held at Krakow in Poland. An exchange deal which took a Spitfire to Poland brought the fuselage of the DH 9A to the UK and a complete rebuild, including construction of the missing parts, was carried out by the Cardington craftsmen.

Two of the classic heavy bombers of World War II can be compared. The famous Avro Lancaster was the mainstay of the British offensive, and the example on show had a substantial operational history, with 137 sorties. The US equivalent was the Boeing Fortress, used in vast numbers on the daylight offensive, and the museum obtained one from the US in 1984. The sole remaining complete Wellington is another prized exhibit, as is a Mosquito. The V bombers were a potent force in the RAF for many years, and the last remaining Valiant and a Vulcan B.2 (the last type to drop bombs in active RAF service, during the Port Stanley raids) complete the spectrum of development of the bomber aircraft.

RAF BATTLE OF BRITAIN MEMORIAL FLIGHT

RAF Coningsby, Lincolnshire LN4 4SY
Tel: 0526-42581

Opening times: by permission of the Station Commander
Location: Coningsby is about 13 miles (20 km) northeast of Sleaford on the A153 road

Avro 683 Lancaster I (1944)
de Havilland DH C1 Chipmunk T.10 (1952)
Hawker Hurricane IIc (1944)
Supermarine 329 Spitfire F.IIa (1940), **349 Spitfire F.VB** (1941), **390 Spitfire PR.XIX** (1945)

The flight was formed at Biggin Hill in 1957 and is now located at Coningsby in Lincolnshire with four Spitfires, one Lancaster and two Hurricanes. Aircraft are regularly flown at displays and there are plans for the unit to be regularly open to the public.

The RAF Museum's Supermarine Stranraer is the only complete example of a British-designed biplane flying boat of the inter-war period

ROYAL AIR FORCE MUSEUM

Hendon, London NW9 5LL
Tel: 01-205-2266

Opening times: 10am–6pm Monday–Saturday, 2pm–6pm Sunday; closed some Bank Holidays
Location: about 9 miles (15 km) northwest of the center of London, off the A5 road and close to Exit 2 of the M1 motorway

AEA Silver Dart (R) (1983)
Avro 504K (1917)
Blackburn B-101 Beverley C.1 (1957)
Blériot XI (1909), **XXVII** (1910)
Bristol 156 Beaufighter TF.10 (1944), **192 Belvedere HC.1** (1962)
Caudron G.III (1916)
Cierva C.30A (Avro 671) (1934)
Clarke TWK Biplane Glider (1910)
Cody Man-lifting Kite (?)
de Havilland DH 82A Tiger Moth (1941), **DH 100 Vampire F.3** (1947)
Dornier Do 24T-3 (1944)
English Electric Canberra PR.3 (1953), **P.1B** (1957)
Folland Fo.144 Gnat T.1 (1955)
Gloster Gladiator II (1937), **Meteor F.8** (1954)
Hanriot HD-1 (1918)
Hawker Cygnet (1924), **Hart Trainer IIA** (1935), **Hind (Afghan)** (1937), **Typhoon IB** (1943), **Tempest V** (1944), **Sea Fury FB.11** (1948), **Hunter F.5** (1955), **P.1127** (1960)
Lockheed 414 Hudson IV (1942)
Morane-Saulnier BB (1916?)
Royal Aircraft Factory SE.5a (1918)
Sikorsky VS-316 Hoverfly I (1944)
Sopwith 1½ Strutter (R) (1980) **Pup** (semi-replica) (1973), **Triplane** (1917), **F.1 Camel** (1917)
Supermarine 304 Stranraer (Canadian) (1940), **300 Spitfire F.I** (1939), **356 Spitfire F.24** (1946)
Vickers FB.5 Gunbus (R) (1966)

The side galleries depict many facets of service life and include a typical workshop in Royal Flying Corps days, a scene inside a Bessoneau hangar, a typical service living-hut and other items leading up to the modern era. The aircraft on show are arranged in almost chronological order and span some six decades of military aviation. Many of the early machines come from a collection gathered in the inter-war period by R G J Nash, most of which went to the Royal Aeronautical Society in 1953 and then to the RAF Museum in July 1963.

One of the earliest aircraft on show is a Blériot XI from the Nash Collection, while another Blériot, the rare XXVII, is in the RFC workshop display. The World War I period is particularly well covered with both genuine aircraft and faithful replicas. The Vintage Aircraft Flying Association (VAFA) at Weybridge, Surrey, built a flyable Vickers Gunbus replica in 1966, and this appeared at several shows before joining the museum. Of similar configuration is the Caudron G.3 which was flown as a civil aircraft in Belgium and England before being bought by Nash.

A line-up of four products of the famous Kingston-on-Thames firm of Sopwith is the highlight of this era. The two genuine machines are a triplane which is believed to be the last completed (built under license by Oakley at Ilford) and a Camel, considered to be one of the outstanding fighters of the period. The other two are a Pup (a partial replica built by Desmond St Cyrien and flown in the late 1970s) and a 1½ Strutter which is a replica built by Viv Bellamy at Land's End.

The center gallery of the museum is named after Sir Sydney Camm who joined the Hawker company in the early 1920s. He was chief designer from 1925 to 1959, and chief engineer until his retirement. In his period at Hawker's many of the outstanding RAF aircraft of all time came from his design staff. On show in the museum are eight aircraft ranging from the Cygnet of 1924 up to the P.1127 prototype of the Harrier. Three of his classic biplanes, the Hart, Hart Trainer and Hind, contrast with the later monoplanes – the Tempest, Typhoon and Sea Fury. Until the opening of the Battle of Britain Museum one of his best-loved aircraft, a Hurricane, was on show here.

Other aircraft in the main museum include two flying boats from an era that has sadly passed. Representing British-designed biplanes is a Supermarine Stranraer (obtained from Canada) and a German monoplane, the Dornier Do 24T, shown in Spanish markings. The latter has been a controversial exhibit for some, but it has to be remembered that the Spanish Do 24s saved many allied airmen in the waters off their coasts during World War II.

The RAF museum is now an excellent record of the traditions and equipment of a world-famous service, and when the other museums are taken into account a comprehensive range of the aircraft used is presented.

Although never operated by BOAC, this Comet 1 has joined the collection of British Airways at Cosford

Painted in Afghan markings, this Hawker Hind is one of a small number retrieved from Kabul for the RAF Museum

RAF MUSEUM RESERVE COLLECTION

(not open to the public)

Airspeed AS.40 Oxford I (1944), **AS.58 Horsa I** (1943), **AS.65 Consul (AS.40)** (1943)
Avro 504K (1917)
Beagle B.206 Basset CC.1 (1965)
Boulton-Paul BP.108 Sea Balliol T.21 (1953)
Bristol 96 F.2B Fighter (1918), **156 Beaufighter TT.10** (1944), **171 Sycamore HR.12** (1949), **173 Series 1** (1951)
Curtiss JN-4 Jenny (1918)
de Havilland DH 89A Dragon Rapide (1944), **DH 98 Mosquito B.35** (1944), **DH 100 Vampire FB.5** (1949), **DH 106 Comet C.2** (1955), **DH 112 Venom NF.3** (1954), **DH 115 Vampire T.11** (1954, 1955)
English Electric M.3 Ayr (1925), **P.6 Kingston** (1925), **Canberra B.2** (1951), **P.1A** (1954)
Fairchild F.24W Argus II (1944)
Fairey Swordfish IV (1942)
Farman F.141 (F.40) (1913)
Fieseler Fi 103 (1944)
Fokker D VII (1918)
General Aircraft GAL.48 Hotspur II (1941), **GAL.49 Hamilcar I** (1943)
Handley Page HP.80 Victor K.1 (B.1) (1958), **HP.115** (1961)
Hawker Tempest V (1944), **P.1121** (1956), **Kestrel FGA.1** (1960)
Lockheed L.37 Ventura II (1942)
Messerschmitt Bf 109G-2 (1944)
Miles M.2H Hawk Major (1935), **M.38 Messenger 4A** (1944)
Percival P.56 Provost T.1 (1953)
Royal Aircraft Factory FE.2b (1916)
Slingsby T.7 Cadet TX.1 (1947), **T.30 Prefect TX.1** (1949)
Sopwith 5F.1 Dolphin (1918)
Supermarine Southampton I (1925), **390 Spitfire PR.XIX** (1944), **390 Spitfire PR.XIX** (1944), **356 Spitfire F.21** (1944), **356 Spitfire F.22** (1944)
Vickers 758 Valiant B.1 (195?)
Westland Wallace (1932), **WS-51 Dragonfly HR.1** (1951)
Wright Flyer (R) (1965?)
Yokosuka MXY-7 Ohka II (1945)

RAF ST ATHAN HISTORIC AIRCRAFT COLLECTION

RAF St Athan, Barry, South Glamorgan CF6 9WA, Wales
Tel: 044-65-3131

Opening times: by prior permission only or 2pm–5pm on the first Sunday in every month
Location: about 12 miles (20 km) west of Cardiff, north of the B4265 road

Auster T.7 Antarctic (Model C.4) (1950), **B.5 AOP.9** (1962)
Avro 504K (R) (?), **698 Vulcan B.2** (1965)
Blériot XI (1909)
Bristol Scout (R) (?)
de Havilland DH 100 Vampire FR.9 (1952)
English Electric Canberra B.2 (1950)
Fairey Battle I (1939)
Fieseler Fi 103 (1945), **Fi 156C-7 Storch** (1944)
Focke-Wulf Fw 190F-8/U1 (1943)
Gloster Meteor F.4 Special (1945), **Meteor F.8** (1952), **Meteor NF.14** (1953)
Heinkel He 162A-2 (1944)
Kawasaki Type 5 Model 1b (1945)
Messerschmitt Me 262A-2 (1944), **Me 410A-1/U2** (1943), **Me 163B-1a** (1944)
Mignet HM-14 Pou-du-Ciel (1936)
Mitsubishi Ki-46-III (c.1943)
Percival P.34A Proctor III (1940), **P.56 Provost T.1** (1953)
Royal Aircraft Factory BE.2c (R) (?)
Saunders-Roe Skeeter AOP.12 (1959)
Slingsby T.45 Swallow TX.1 (1964)
Sopwith F.1 Camel (R) (?)
Supermarine 261 Spitfire LF.IX (1943), **549 Swift FR.5** (1954)
Watkins CHW Monoplane (1908)
Westland WS-55 Whirlwind HCC.12 (1964), **WS-58 Wessex HAS.1** (1959)

St Athan since its opening in 1939 has housed mainly maintainance and technical training units and thus a nucleus of highly skilled craftsmen has always been available. The first historic aircraft was moved to the base in 1960 and since then the numbers have grown steadily. The collection has specialized in rebuilding Axis aircraft, and some of their excellent restorations were moved to Hendon when the Battle of Britain Museum opened. There are still many German and Japanese aircraft on view, including the sole Mitsubishi Ki 46 and the sole Kawasaki Ki 100. From Germany are a two-seat Focke-Wulf Fw 190 and a genuine Fieseler-built Storch in addition to more common types such as the Heinkel He 162 and the Messerschmitt Me 163 and Me 262. Moving from Cosford is one of the few surviving Me 410 twin-engined fighters. Around these captured aircraft are displayed a wide range of RAF aircraft, plus a few civil types. The oldest of these is the Watkins Monoplane of 1909, which was constructed in Cardiff.

SCIENCE MUSEUM

Exhibition Road, South Kensington, London SW7 2DD
Tel: 01-589-3456
Opening times: 10am–6pm Monday–Saturday, 2.30pm–6pm Sunday, closed Bank Holidays
Wroughton is open on selected days – see the press for details. For Yeovilton, see Fleet Air Arm Museum times
Location: the museum is south of Hyde Park and north of the Cromwell Road in west London. Wroughton is about 4 miles (6 km) south of Swindon off the A361 road. Yeovilton is on the B3151 road about 2 miles (3 km) east of Ilchester

Aérospatiale SA 341 (1970)
Avro 504K (1918)
Bensen B.8 Gyroglider (197?)
Birdman Promotions Grasshopper Hang-glider (1976)
Boeing 247D (1933)
British Aircraft Corporation 221 (FD.2) (1956)
British Aircraft Corporation/Aérospatiale Concorde 002 (1969)
Cameron A.150 Hot Air Balloon (1972)
Chargus Midas E Powered Hang-glider (1977)
Cierva C.24 (1934), **C.30A (Avro 671)** (1934)
Clarke Biplane Glider (1910)
Cody Biplane (1912)
de Havilland DH 60G Gipsy Moth (1930), **DH 84 Dragon 1** (1933), **DH 100 Sea Vampire 1** (1943), **DH 104 Dove** (Devon C2) (1949), **DH 106 Comet 4** (1960), **DH 121 Trident 1 E** (1967), **DH 121 Trident 3B** (1970)
Douglas DC-3 (1936)
Fieseler Fi 103 (1944)
Focke-Achgelis Fa 330A-1 Bachstelze (1943)
Fokker E III (1916)
Folland Fo.144 Gnat T.1 (1962)
Gloster E.28/39 (1941)
Goodhart MPA (1966)
Handley Page HP.39 Gugnunc (1929), **HP.115** (1961)
Hawker Hurricane 1 (1938)
Hill Pterodactyl 1A (1925)
Huntair Pathfinder II (1983)
JAP-Harding Monoplane (1910)
Levavasseur Antoinette Developed Type VII (1910)
Lilienthal Standard XI (1895), **Standard XI (R)** (1976)
Lockheed 10A Electra (1935), **L-749A Constellation** (1947)
MacCready Gossamer Albatross (1980?)
Messerschmitt Me 163B-1 Komet (1943)
Mignet HM-14 Pou-du-Ciel (1936)
Piaggio P.166 (1960)
Pilcher Hawk (R) (1930)
Roe Triplane No.1 (1909)
Rolls-Royce Thrust Measuring Rig (1954)
Royal Aircraft Factory SE.5A (1918)
Saunders-Roe Skeeter AOP.12 (1960)
Short S.25 Sandringham IV (Sunderland III) (1944), **SC.1** (1957)
Southampton University Man Powered Aircraft (?)
Supermarine S.6B (1931), **300 Spitfire 1A** (1940)
Vickers FB.27 Vimy (1919)
Wallis WA.120 (1970)
Wright Flyer (R) (1948)
Yokosuka MXY-7 Ohka II (1944)

The Great Exhibition of 1851 spawned the South Kensington Museum which opened in 1857. Industrial expansion and developments in science resulted in this part of the collection growing rapidly and in 1909 the Science Museum became a separate entity.

Aeronautical exhibits were first collected in 1896 when Sir Hiram Maxim donated a model of his gigantic 1894 flying machine, one of its 18-foot (6-meter) propellers and the steam engine from the biplane. A new gallery, designed to represent a hangar with some aircraft suspended from the roof, was begun in 1961 and officially opened in 1963. The centerpiece of the display was the Vickers Vimy which made the first transatlantic flight.

Two replicas which illustrate the pioneer work in hang-gliding are on show. An original Lilienthal monoplane glider, the eleventh built by the famous German in 1895, was donated to the museum in 1920 but its structure is now so weak that a faithful replica built at Uxbridge in 1975 by Shawcraft Ltd has replaced the original in the exhibition. The Lilienthal was imported into the UK by Percy Pilcher who flew his first glider, the Bat, in 1896. This British aviator was killed in 1899 when his Hawk glider crashed. The original machine was repaired and is now on show in Edinburgh. At South Kensington is a 1930 replica copied from the original by Martin and Miller.

Owing to a dispute between Orville Wright and the

The JAP-Harding Monoplane of 1910 was based on the Blériot XI and fitted with a 40 hp JAP engine

The Vickers Vimy in which Alcock and Brown made the first non-stop flight across the Atlantic in June 1919

In the inter-war period Geoffrey Hill designed a series of tailless aircraft: this one is the Pterodactyl I of 1925

Smithsonian Institution in the US, the Science Museum had on loan the original Wright Flyer which made the first ever powered flight, at Kitty Hawk, North Carolina on December 17, 1903. It eventually returned to the US where it is now exhibited in pride of place in the Air and Space Museum in Washington. Before the aircraft returned, a replica was built by apprentices of the de Havilland Aeronautical Technical School from drawings made in London and approved by Orville Wright.

AV Roe, one of the first British aviators, flew his triplane No.1 with a JAP engine from Lea Marshes in 1909. On July 13, 1909 he made the first real flight in an all-British airplane. The aircraft appeared at a number of meetings in 1909 and was later fitted with a 24 hp Antoinette motor. It came to the museum in 1925.

Samuel Cody, an American, built the first aircraft to fly in the UK: his biplane flew on October 16, 1908 for a distance of 1390 feet (424 meters) at a height of 30 feet (9 meters). Cody developed his designs which proved to be outstanding machines for the period. The first aircraft to join the collection was the 1912 biplane which took part in military trials. This sole remaining example of Cody's work was acquired in 1913.

The aim of the collection is to demonstrate technical advances in aeronautics over the years and the rapid strides made in the early years are well illustrated. The pre-World War I aircraft, which also include a classic French Antoinette presented to the museum by Robert Blackburn in 1926 and the JAP-Harding monoplane of 1910, compared with the World War I fighters, highlight the pace of development. Two significant British types are an Avro 504K trainer which joined the collection in 1920 and an SE.5 fighter designed by H P Folland. Built by Wolseley Motors, it was delivered too late to see active service. In the inter-war period it was one of a fleet of skywriters and was presented to the museum in 1939.

The museum's Vickers Vimy is the very one piloted by Alcock and Brown which made the first crossing of the Atlantic Ocean. Leaving St John's, Newfoundland on June 14, 1919 the flight ended 16½ hours later in a bog in Galway in Ireland. The makers of the airframe and Rolls-Royce, who constructed the Eagle engines, rebuilt the Vimy which had been damaged on landing and presented it to the museum.

The exhibition contains many other aircraft which were significant in the development of aviation in the UK. The Schneider Trophy races in the late 1920s and early 1930s captured the imagination of the British public. Reginald Mitchell of the Supermarine company developed a series of beautiful monoplanes powered by Rolls-Royce engines, which secured wins in the 1927, 1929 and 1931 contests to win the trophy outright for Britain. The winner of the 1931 contest was the S.5B flown by Flt Lt John Boothman who set a speed of 340 mph (547 km/h) over a course in the Solent. The Air Ministry presented this machine to the museum in 1932. The S.6B ultimately led to the Spitfire and its Rolls-Royce R engine to the Merlin. Close by is exhibited a Spitfire IA built in 1940.

In the inter-war period aviation became possible for the ordinary citizen and many outstanding long-distance flights were made in almost normal production models. Amy Johnson became a heroine in May 1930 when, in the fourth production de Havilland Gipsy Moth, she flew solo from England to Australia. This epic flight left Croydon on May 5 and arrived at Darwin 19 days later. After the Moth returned to the UK it embarked on a publicity tour and in 1931 Associated Newspapers donated it to the museum.

Another very important aircraft in the museum is the first British jet aircraft to fly. Frank Whittle's long research program into this new form of propulsion was rewarded when

This Boeing 247D was purchased from the defunct Wings and Wheels Museum in Florida and flown across the Atlantic to Wroughton

the Gloster E.28/39 lifted off on May 15, 1941 with P E G Sayer at the controls. Two examples of this small single-seater were built: the first, which is the one on show, last flew in 1944 and joined the collection in 1946.

The design and location of the gallery makes it very difficult to change the exhibits, which include a comprehensive display of engines, propellers, components and memorabilia. Two significant out-stations have been set up by the museum in recent years. The Fleet Air Arm Museum at Yeovilton's exhibition has as its centerpiece the British prototype of the Concorde supersonic airliner. The development of this outstanding achievement is well documented and two of the aircraft designed to test aspects of the design are also on display. These are the BAC 221 (modified from the Fairey Delta 2) which was for high-speed research, and the Handley Page HP.115, which explored the low-speed range.

Airliners have long been neglected by museums because of their size and the hangarage required to keep them in good condition. The former RAF airfield at Wroughton in Wiltshire has a considerable number of hangars from its maintainance unit days. The Science Museum now has use of a number of them, and the airfield site enables aircraft to fly in for exhibition. Although not yet open permanently, the Wroughton collection has proved to be very popular on its annual open days with examples of such famous airliners as the Boeing 247, Douglas DC-3 and Lockheed Electra and Constellation.

The Handley Page Gugnunc of 1929 was designed for the Guggenheim air safety competition. Presented to the museum in 1934, it has spent most of its life in store, but is now assembled at Wroughton

SHUTTLEWORTH COLLECTION

Old Warden Aerodrome, Biggleswade, Bedfordshire SG18 9ER
Tel: 0767-27-288

Opening times: 10.30am–5.30pm daily, check times in winter
Location: the aerodrome is about 3 miles (5 km) west of Biggleswade and is well signposted from the A1 road

Air Navigation and Engineering Company ANEC II (1923)
Arrow Active 2 (1932)
Avro 504K (504N) (1918), **621 Tutor** (1931)
Blackburn D Monoplane (1912)
Blake Blue Tit (1925)
Blériot XI (1909)
Bristol Boxkite (R) (Miles built) (1963), **14 F.2B Fighter** (1918)
British Aerial Transport F.K.23 Bantam (1919)
British Aircraft Swallow 2 (1937)
Cierva C.30A (Avro 671) (1934)
de Havilland DH 51 (1924), **DH 53 Humming Bird** (1923), **DH 60X Moth (DH 60)** (1925), **DH 60G Gipsy Moth** (1930), **DH 80A Puss Moth** (1931), **DH 82A Tiger Moth** (1940), **DH 87B Hornet Moth** (1938), **DH 88 Comet** (1934), **DH 89A Dragon Rapide** (1939), **DHC 1 Chipmunk T.10** (1950)
Deperdussin Monoplane No.13 (1910)
Desoutter I (modified) (1931)
Dixon Ornithopter (R) (1964)
English Electric Wren (1923)
Fieseler Fi 103 (R) (?)
Gloster Gladiator (1937)
Granger Archaeopteryx (1930)
Hawker Tomtit (1930), **Hind (Afghan)** (1937), **Sea Hurricane** (1940)
Hunting Percival P.84 Jet Provost T.1 (1954)
LVG C VI (1918)
Mignet HM-14 Pou-du-Ciel (1935)
Miles M.14A Magister (1939)
Parnall Elf II (1929)
Percival D.3 Gull Six (1935)
Roe Triplane Type IV (R) (1960)
Royal Aircraft Factory SE.5A (1917)
Sopwith Pup (Dove) (1916)
Southern Martlet (1931)
Supermarine 349 Spitfire Vb (1942)
Voisin scale replica (1980)

The sole remaining de Havilland DH 51, 'Miss Kenya', awaits its turn to take part in a flying display at Old Warden

Richard Shuttleworth's first aircraft, this de Havilland DH 60X Moth, has been based at Old Warden for over half a century

The last remaining airworthy Gloster Gladiator, a popular performer at the regular flying days

A visit to the airfield at Old Warden, especially on a flying day, must be one of the most rewarding experiences for the aviation enthusiast and historian. There are few places in the world where genuine aircraft from 1909 can be seen flying in an appropriate setting. The collection covers all facets of aviation from the early days, through World War I to the 'golden' period between the wars; and it also includes a few World War II aircraft.

In the 1930s Richard Shuttleworth had the foresight to acquire a number of veteran cars and aircraft when most people did not value them. He had the money and resources to construct an aerodrome and hangars on the family estate. In 1932 he bought his first aircraft, a four-year-old de Havilland Moth. This aircraft is still based at Old Warden and must have lived on one aerodrome for longer than any other aeroplane. He also established an engineering company at Old Warden which gained a fine reputation.

During World War II the historic aircraft were put in storage; Richard Shuttleworth joined the RAF and was killed in 1940. After 1945 his mother, Dorothy Shuttleworth, set up the Richard Ormonde Shuttleworth Remembrance Trust to run the aeronautical and automobile collection and be responsible for an agricultural college in the former family house on the estate. Two companies Richard Shuttleworth had set up, Warden Aviation Company (which operated charter aircraft) and Warden Engineering Company, were merged into the Warden Aviation and Engineering Company which runs the collection, the workshops and the airfield. During the 20 years following World War II the collection was not open to the public, although genuine enthusiasts were always welcome. Gradually more aircraft were acquired, and the income from the trust became insufficient to maintain the exhibits. The trustees decided to open the airfield and hangars daily, and in 1964 the Shuttleworth Veteran Aeroplane Society was formed to assist in the preservation and restoration of the aircraft and to raise funds.

The unique semi-tailless Granger Archaeopteryx homebuilt: this example was first flown in 1930 and then stored for 30 years, before being donated to the collection

A most popular innovation came in 1965 when a number of Open Days were added to the aviation calendar: aircraft from the collection were flown, and for many people at that time this one of the few places in the UK where they could see some of the types in the air. All sources of income were sought, and the appearance of Shuttleworth aircraft in TV and film sequences was of great assistance. As funds came in many of the stored aircraft were brought into the workshops, and on completion they had to be exhibited. A building program was started, and soon two more hangars were added to the two original structures. The 1970s and 80s have seen further extensions including the de Havilland hangar in which a range of designs from the maestro of the light aeroplane are on view.

The displays, with the exception of the DH hangar, are now arranged in roughly chronological order starting with the veterans. Three genuine machines and two replicas illustrate the pioneer days, and the former may sometimes be seen aloft on the calm summer evenings, when special events are held to display these graceful but slender aircraft. Two aircraft were acquired from AE Grimmer in 1935. He had bought a Blériot XI which used to be one of the original school aircraft at Hendon in 1910. The aircraft crashed in 1912 and was stored under Blackfriars Bridge in London until Grimmer bought it and restored it. Richard Shuttleworth bought it in 1935 and it appeared at three Royal Aeronautical Society garden parties before World War II. Although this historic machine is now restricted to straight hops across the airfield, it is a most popular performer, although unfortunately it has twice been damaged. Grimmer also bought a Deperdussin from Hendon and flew it from a polo ground near Bedford for a time, but when bought by Shuttleworth in 1935 it was in a poor condition; it had to be rebuilt to fly again in 1937.

A prized possession is the oldest genuine flying British aircraft, a Blackburn Monoplane of 1912. This, the last of the seven built, was ordered by Cyril Foggin, who learnt to fly at the Blackburn School at Hendon. Francis Glew bought the aircraft but put it into storage in 1914, and when it was rediscovered in 1937 it was largely hidden under a haystack. A rebuild was started in 1937 but was not completed until 1949, and sadly Richard Shuttleworth did not see this significant aircraft in its natural setting.

The two replicas of a 1910 Roe Triplane and a Bristol Boxkite from the same year were built for the film 'Those Magnificent Men in Their Flying Machines'. These two are powered by modern engines and thus can be flown more often. The acquisition of these two represented a change in policy for the collection, but it was felt that the two types made such a significant contribution to early British aviation that they should be preserved at Old Warden.

Very few actual World War I aircraft are regularly flown, although in recent years the replica builders have been very active on both sides of the Atlantic. At Old Warden five types from the period are maintained in flying condition, although the scarcity of spares has sometimes meant that they have been grounded for long periods. The Avro 504

The last airworthy Bristol Fighter makes a pass over Old Warden airfield

trainer set new standards in instructional techniques when it was transferred to these duties from its original role as a fighting airplane. Many generations of service flyers made there first tentative steps into the air in a 504, and developments of the design were still in use in the 1930s. The aircraft at Old Warden was built in 1918 as a 504K with a rotary engine, but was later converted to a 504N with a radial, in which form it was impressed back into military use for World War II. It survived World War II, and afterwards Avro apprentices converted it back to its original state for the collection.

The three British fighters were among the best that appeared over the Western Front. The Sopwith Pup on view was converted on the Kingston line in 1918 to a two-seat Dove and used as a civil aircraft until 1936, when it was taken to Old Warden and rebuilt to Pup standard. The Bristol Fighter, although constructed too late to see wartime use, served in Turkey in 1923 and was acquired by the well known collector C P B Ogilvie in 1936, who stored it in his Watford premises along with many other aircraft. After World War II the Bristol Aeroplane Company rebuilt the fighter and passed it to the Trust, and in 1980-82 it underwent a major refurbish. The SE.5, designed at Farnborough, which spent some time as one of the famous Savage fleet of sky writers in the 1920s, was found in 1955 hanging from the roof in the Armstrong-Whitworth flight shed at Whitley. Apprentices at Farnborough restored this racy fighter and it flew again in 1959.

German aircraft of World War I in flying condition are almost non-existent, and the sight of the massive LVG VI, with its slow-turning Benz engine, its lozenge camouflage on the wings and its varnished fuselage, brings long-forgotten scenes vividly to life. The aircraft was brought to the UK in 1918 and was stored for many years by the Air Ministry but flew at the 1937 Hendon Pageant. The collection obtained the aircraft on long-term loan in 1966, and it flew again a few years later.

The collection of private aircraft from between the wars gives a picture of the era in which air transport became available to the general public, and many of the British firms became household names. Geoffrey de Havilland had built his first aircraft in 1909, and after a successful career he formed his own company at Stag Lane in 1920. He was convinced that private flying would prosper as the economy improved, and produced a number of designs before the classic Moth flew in 1925. Two of his earlier designs are with the collection – the large DH 51 which was brought back to the UK in 1965 after almost 40 years in Kenya, and the diminutive DH 53 Humming Bird, built for the 1923 light aircraft trials. Three Moths, including Richard Shuttleworth's original aircraft, are on view, and other examples from the famous family are a Puss Moth, a Hornet Moth and a Tiger Moth.

Another de Havilland aircraft at Old Warden is the famous Comet racer which won the 1934 MacRobertson Race from England to Australia. The Comet joined the collection in 1965 and a rebuild was started in the early 1970s, but this was not without problems: fortunately, though at the cost of much time, these were overcome.

Other aircraft from this period include the Parnall Elf biplane, lovingly rebuilt by two of the former apprentices of the collection in the late 1970s, the semi-tailless Granger Archaeopteryx built by two Nottingham brothers in 1930, and a beautiful BA Swallow. The Swallow is on loan to the collection from Tony Dowson, who rebuilt it to pristine condition. Shuttleworth also possesses the Percival Gull used by Jean Batten on her record flights in the 1930s.

A number of military aircraft from the same period also survive, including the sole remaining example of the Hawker Tomtit, the only surviving Avro Tutor trainer. The Tomtit was unfortunately damaged in 1985. Two others which are the only flying examples of their types are the Gloster Gladiator and the Hawker Hind. The former was the last biplane fighter to be ordered by the RAF and found fame in Malta and Norway. The aircraft was rebuilt in 1952 by Viv Bellamy at Eastleigh and was then bought back by Gloster's, who presented it to the trust. The Afghan Air Force ordered a number of Hinds in 1938 and some survivors were discovered in a hangar at Kabul in the late 1960s. The Afghan Government presented one to the collection and a 12,000 mile (19,000 km) round trip by road brought this classic biplane designed by Sydney Camm back to its native shores. In August 1981 it flew for the first time for over 25 years.

A recent change in policy has seen some of the more modern aircraft sold to raise funds, but a flyable Spitfire will soon be joined by a Hurricane so that examples of the pair of fighter types that once saved Britain will be based with the Shuttleworth collection. There are a number of other significant aircraft in store, but funds will have to be raised before they can be seen in the hangars at the delightful Bedfordshire grass airfield.

United States of America

Alabama

UNITED STATES ARMY AVIATION MUSEUM

Fort Rucker, Alabama 36360
Tel: 205-255-4507 or 4516

Opening times: 9am–5pm Monday–Friday, 1pm–5pm Saturday–Sunday
Location: close to the Daleville entrance to the base off Route 85

Aero Commander 520 (YL-26A) (YU-9A) (1952), **560A (L-26A) (U-4A)** (1955), **680 (L-26C) (U-9C)** (1957), **680 (RL-26D) (NRU-9D)** (1957)
Aeronca 65 (0-58A) (L-3A) (1942), **7BC Champion (L-16A)** (1947)
American Helicopter XA-8 (XH-26) (1951)
Auster B.5 AOP.9 (1961)
Beech B18S (SNB-5) (UC-45J) (1942), **B18S (C-45G)** (1943), **45 Mentor (YT-34A)** (1950), **50 Seminole (L-23A) (U-8A)** (1952), **50 Seminole (L-23D) (U-8D)** (1956), **50 Seminole (RL-23D) (RU-8D)** (1956), **50 Seminole (RL-23D) (U-8D) (U-8G)** (1958), **65 Queen Air (NRU-8F) (RU-21A)** (1963)
Bell 47D Sioux (H-13B) (1948), **47D Sioux (H-13B) (H-13C)** (1948), **47D Sioux (H-13E)** (1951), **47G Sioux (TH-13T)** (1967), **200 (XH-33) (XV-3A)** (1954), **204 Iroquois (XH-40)** (1955), **204 Iroquois (UH-1A)** (1959), **204 Iroquois (UH-1B)** (1960, 1962), **204 Iroquois (UH-1C) (UH-1M)** (1965, 1966), **205 Iroquois (UH-1D)** (1960), **206 (OH-4A)** (1962), **206 Kiowa (OH-58A)** (1968), **207 Sioux Scout** (1963), **209 Huey Cobra (AH-1G)** (1966), **309 King Cobra (AH-1J)** (1972), **409 (YAH-63)** (1975)
Boeing 451 Scout (L-15A) (1947)
Boeing-Vertol YUH-61A (1974)
Brantly B2 (YHO-3) (1959)
Cessna R.172E Mescalero (T-41B) (1967), **195 (LC-126C)** (1951), **305 Bird Dog (L-19A) (0-1A)** (1950-52), **305 Bird Dog (TL-19D) (TO-1D)** (1955), **310A Blue Canoe (L-27A) (U-3A)** (1957), **318 (T-37A)** (1956), **CH.1B Seneca (YH-1)** (1956)
Convair L-13A (1946)
Curtiss-Wright VZ-7AP Aerial Jeep (1958)
de Havilland DHC 2 Beaver (YL-20) (YU-6A) (1951), **DHC 2 Beaver (L-20A) (U-6A)** (1952, 1956, 1958), **DHC 3 Otter (U-1A)** (1957, 1959), **DHC 4 Caribou (AC-1) (YC-7A)** (1957)
Del Mar DH1A Whirlymite (1960)
Douglas DC-3 (C-47A) (R4D-5) (C-47H) (1941)
Fairchild-Hiller FH.1100 (OH-5A) (1962)
Firestone 45C (XR-9) (1948)
Goodyear XAO-3GI Inflatoplane (1957)
Grumman G.134 Mohawk (YAO-1F) (YOV-1A) (1957), **G.134 Mohawk (AO-1B) (OV-1B)** (1960, 1962), **G.134 Mohawk (AO-1C) (OV-1C)** (1962, 1963)
Gyrodyne QH-50 (1965)
Hawker P.1127 Kestrel (XV-6A) (1964)
Helio H.391 Courier (YL-24) (1952), **H.395 Courier (L-28A) (U-10A)** (1963)
Hiller UH12 Raven (H-23A) (1951), **UH12 Raven (H-23B) (OH-23B)** (1951), **UH12C Raven (H-23C) (OH-23C)** (1955), **UH12C Raven (H-23D) (OH-23D)** (1955), **UH12E Raven (H-23F) (OH-23F)** (1962), **HJ.1 Rotor Cycle (XROE-1)** (1957), **HJ.1 Rotor Cycle (YH-32)** (1955)
Hughes 269C (TH-55A) (1967), **(369M (YOH-6A)** (1962), **369M (OH-6A)** (1967), **YAH-64A** (1974)
Interstate S1B1 Cadet (0-63) (L-6) (1941)
Kaman K.240 (HTK-1) (1958)
LET L.200A Morava (1961)
Lockheed AP-2E Neptune (P2V-5) (1961), **749 Constellation (VC-121A)** (1948), **XH-51A** (1961, 1964), **Q-Star (YO-3A)** (1969), **X-26B** (1967), **YAH-56A Cheyenne** (1966), **CL-475** (1959)
McCulloch MC.4C (YH-30) (1957)
McDonnell XV-1 (XL-25) (1953)
Mil Mi-4 (1952)
North American P-51D Mustang (1944), **Navion (L-17A)** (1947), **T-28A Trojan** (1951), **T-39A Sabreliner** (1961)
Piasecki PD.18 Retriever (H-25A) (1951)
Piccard AX-6 Balloon (?)
Piper J-3C Cub (0-59A) (L-4A) (1942), **J-3C Cub (0-59B) (L-4B)** (1942), **PA-18 Super Cub (L-18C)** (1952), **PA-18 Super Cub (TL-21A) (U-7A)** (1951)
Raven S-60 Balloon (?)
Rotorway Scorpion 1 (1971)
Ryan Navion A (L-17B) (1948), **VZ-3RY** (1956), **XV-5B Vertifan** (1962)
Sikorsky VS-316 Hoverfly (R-4B) (1943), **S-51 Dragonfly (R-5) (H-5)** (1943), **S-51 Dragonfly (HO3S)** (c.1947), **S-52 (YH-18A)** (1949), **S-55 Chickasaw (UH-19D)** (1955), **S-56 Mojave (CH-37B)** (1955), **S-58 Choctaw (H-34A)** (1956), **S-58 Choctaw (H-34A) (VCH-34A)** (1956), **S-58 Seahorse (HUS-1)** (1955), **S-59 (XH-39)** (1949)
Stinson V.76 Sentinel (0-62) (L-5) (1942), **V.76 Sentinel (0-62G) (L-5G)** (1945)
Taylorcraft D (0-57A) (L-2A) (1942)
Vertol V.43 Shawnee (CH-21C) (1956), **V.114 Chinook (CH-47A)** (1960, 1965)
Vultee V.74 Vigilant (0-49A) (L-1A) (1940)

The sole Soviet helicopter on show at Fort Rucker is this Mil Mi-4, of which about 4500 were built in the USSR and China

in 1955 and were formally recognized in 1963. In the early stages the collection was administered by volunteers, but full-time staff were appointed in 1966. Two years later the museum moved into its present buildings. These consist of three World War II wooden structures, around which are a number of aircraft parks. The collection has grown to such an extent that these premises are now inadequate, and there are plans for a new purpose-built exhibition complex.

Special displays are staged which highlight important facets of the role of the aviation side of the US Army. The Vietnam war stimulated the development of attack aircraft,

Above
Five American Helicopter XA8 lightweight collapsible helicopters were tested in the early 1950s, but no production followed

Right
The Hiller Hornet lightweight helicopter was another design that failed to enter production, even though the army took 14 examples for evaluation

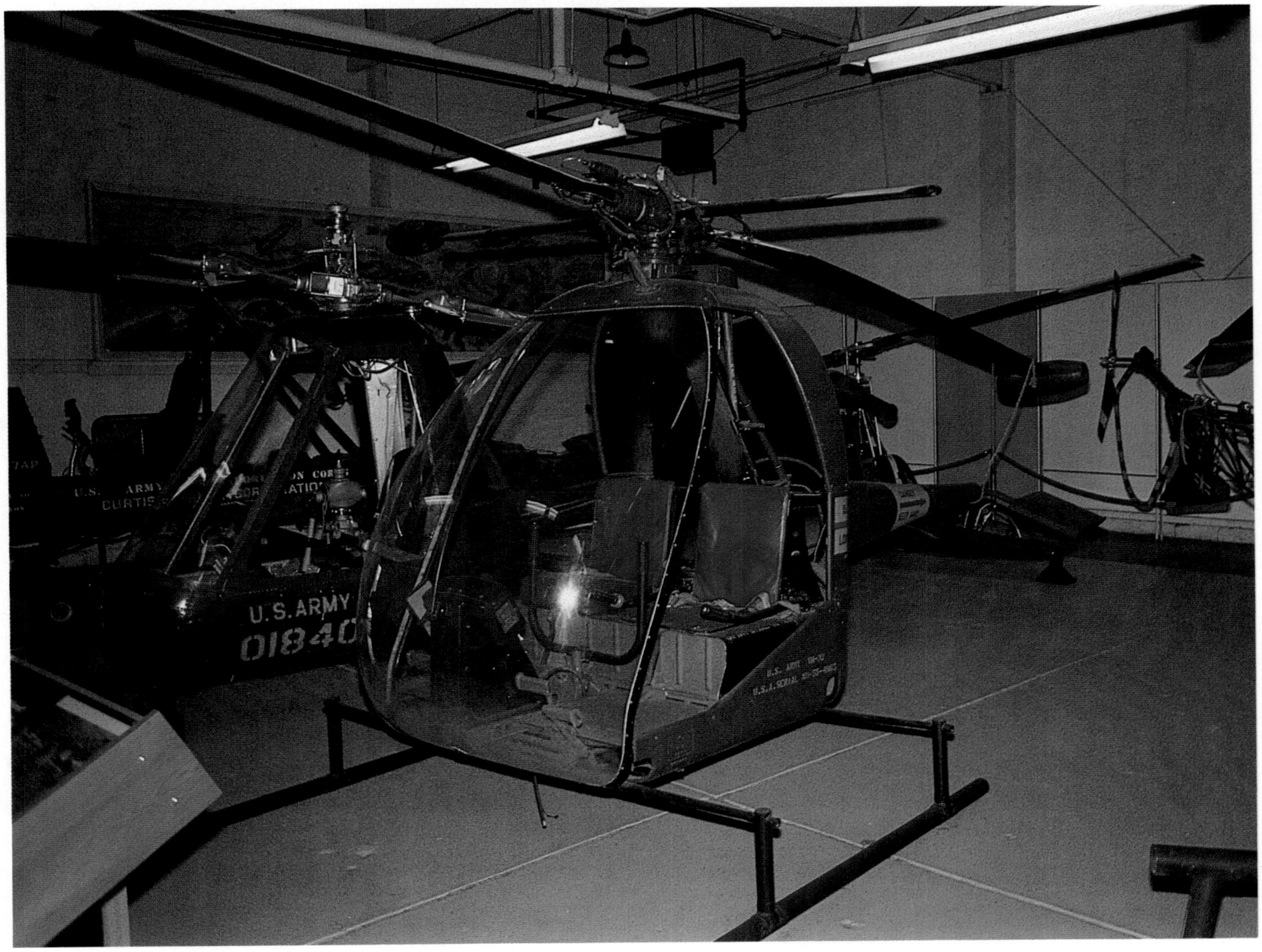

The role of aircraft and helicopters in army tactics has become ever more vital in recent years. The museum at Fort Rucker traces this development with an impressive display of hardware and memorabilia. Fort Rucker has been the home of US Army aviation since 1953. At its vast site helicopters can be seen operating from the three airfields in the complex as well as from a number of unprepared sites. The museum today also has a practical role in the army: units are involved in pilot and combat training, maintenance, air traffic control and aeromedical training.

Plans for the Fort Rucker museum were first put forward particularly the helicopter, a trend that is well highlighted in the displays. Army aviation uniforms over the years are also on show, and there is an art gallery of paintings of military importance.

Fort Rucker has the largest exhibition of helicopters in the world. The first helicopter to enter service with US forces was the Sikorsky R-4B Hoverfly. The prototype of this design first flew in January 1942, and 131 examples were built. The USAAF took delivery in 1943 and their worth was soon proved. Some R-4s were deployed to Southeast Asia, where the world's first helicopter rescue of a downed pilot soon followed. Captain James Green had crashed in Burma and rescue teams took a day and a half to reach him. He was too badly injured to be carried back, so a clearing was made for the R-4 to fly in and transport him to hospital. In jungle fighting the helicopter often meant the difference between life and death for the injured.

The Sikorsky company were among the pioneers of the helicopter in the US, and the display contains almost the whole range of their products. The S-51 was developed from the R-4 and first flew in 1946. Subsequently 220 were built and used by all US services in a variety of roles. A rarity from the firm is the S-52, of which only 95 were built and few survive. This four-seater first flew in 1950, and only four were supplied to the army: the aircraft on show is the first of this batch. Two of the four were converted to the higher powered S-59, and one of these has also been preserved. Other helicopters from the Connecticut firm include examples of the famous S-55 and S-58, which were both produced in substantial numbers, and a massive S-56 Mojave heavy transport helicopter.

The Bell company was another manufacturer that moved into the rotary-wing field in the early days, and their first helicopter, the Model 30 built to the design of Arthur Young, flew in June 1943. The Model 47 was the third version of the 30, and this single-engined helicopter remained in production for three decades. With its bubble canopy it achieved fame in the 'MASH' television series, which showed the excellent work it performed in the Korean War. Several versions of this important type are on view along with a development, the Sioux Scout, which was produced in prototype form only.

The Vietnam war saw the emergence of the Bell Iroquois as a fighting weapon. First flown in 1956, the Model 204 was the winner of an army contest for a utility helicopter. Since then over 11,000 have been delivered to US forces, and many others to foreign air arms, and the type has also been built under licence in Italy, Japan and Taiwan. Included in this total is the fearsome Huey Cobra gunship with a redesigned fuselage.

There are experimental and production helicopters from all the major US manufacturers including some which incorporated advanced ideas for their time. Lockheed pioneered the rigid rotor concept, building the CL-475 in great secrecy and testing it in the Mojave Desert. There were vibration problems but these were solved, and the CL-475 first flew in November 1959. Its success attracted the interest of the US Army and Navy. Two prototypes were ordered as the XH-51A. These were fast helicopters with a top speed of 174 mph (280 km/h) but the rotor had not reached its design limits. Thus the second aircraft was fitted with a jet engine mounted on the side of the fuselage and a stub wing. In this compound form the aircraft set an unofficial speed record for its class of over 300 mph (480 km/h). All three of these helicopters are at the museum along with the sole survivor of the 10 AH-56A Cheyennes built. The Cheyenne suffered a number of problems and the production contract was canceled. The failure of this advanced gunship led to Lockheed withdrawing from helicopter design and manufacture.

Four Lockheed fixed-wing aircraft are on show, the best-known being the Constellation named 'Bataan' which was used by General MacArthur as an aerial command post in the Korean War. This aircraft was later used by NASA in the late 1960s for testing the tracking stations used in the Gemini and Apollo space flights. The museum received this historic aircraft in 1970. The Missile and Space Division of Lockheed became involved in aircraft design when it produced a machine for specialized use in Vietnam. The aircraft was needed in the tracking of Viet Cong units when they faded back into the dense jungle. The Division modified two Schweizer SGS.2-32 sailplanes by fitting an engine with silencers and a slow-turning propeller. The combination proved to be exceptionally quiet. Their effectiveness was demonstrated in Vietnam in 1968, and the sole survivor is on show along with a development, the YO-3A, of which 14 were built and used in Vietnam from 1970 to 1972.

The army has tested ways to make the foot soldier more mobile in the field and a number of one-man devices are on view. The Hiller HJ.1 was a light ram-jet helicopter of which 14 were delivered to the army; two Curtiss-Wright VZ-7AP VTOL platforms were supplied; and the Goodyear XAO-3G was an inflatable aircraft which could be carried in a pack. Examples of all these interesting devices are on show.

The US Army used balloons in the very early days, and there are details of Professor Lowe's observation balloon which was used in the Civil War. The army first used aircraft in the role of airborne artillery spotting in the 1941 maneuvers held in Louisiana, when Piper Cubs were flown in this role. A number of slow-flying light aircraft were employed during World War II, where their ability to fly in and out of short unprepared strips was essential. The evacuation of stretcher-borne casualties was also part of the work of these flights, and many aircraft were modified to accept the load. Liaison and utility transport have also been required by army units, and a range of fixed-wing machines complements the helicopters.

The museum has two aircraft from the Eastern Bloc: a Soviet Mil-4 helicopter which is the only one in the USA, and a Czechoslovak L-200A Morava twin-engined monoplane which was evaluated by the Czechoslovak army.

Opposite Top
Seven Hawker-Siddeley Kestrels were evaluated in the US and a number are now on show at museums around the country

Opposite Bottom
Two Ryan XV-5As were tested in the mid-1960s. The aircraft was a VTOL machine, and the example on show ended its operational days with NASA

U.S. AIR FORCE
18264
4

NASA
705
N705NA
U.S.ARMY

CHAMPLIN FIGHTER MUSEUM

4636 Fighter Aces Drive, Mesa, Arizona 85205
Tel: 602-830-4540

Opening times: 10am–5pm daily (except public holidays)
Location: at Falcon Field Airport Mesa which is about 3 miles (5 km) north of the town. Mesa is 10 miles (16 km) east of Phoenix

Albatros D VA (R) (1979)
Aviatik D I (1918)
Curtiss 87 Warhawk (P-40N) (1941)
Dewoitine D.514 (1939)
Focke-Wulf Fw 190D (1945)
Fokker E III (R) (1981), **D VII (R)** (1979), **D VIII (R)** (1970), **Dr I (R)** (1973)
Great Lakes 2T-1A (1932)
Grumman G.32 (F3F) (1938), **G.36 Wildcat (FM-2)** (1942), **G.50 Hellcat (F6F-3)** (1943), **G.58B Gulfhawk IV (Bearcat)** (1946)
Hispano HA.1112M (Bf 109) (1953)
Lockheed P-38M Lightning (1944)
Mikoyan-Gurevich MiG-17A (c.1954)
Nieuport 27 (R) (1980)
North American F-86F Sabre (1953), **P-51D Mustang** (1943)
Pfalz D XII (1918)
Republic P-47D Thunderbolt (1942)
Rumpler Taube (R) (1982)
Sopwith Pup (R) (1971), **F.1 Camel (R)** (1981), **7F.1 Snipe (R)** (1982), **Triplane (R)** (1983)
SPAD XIII (R) (1983)
Supermarine 509 Spitfire T.IX (1942)
Thomas Morse S-4C (R) (1977)
Vought F2G-1 Corsair (1945)

Doug Champlin is an Oklahoman who began collecting combat aircraft in 1969 at Enid in his home state. In 1981 he moved his collection to Falcon Field Airport on the outskirts of Mesa, Arizona. The building consists of two former World War II hangars joined by an administrative area, with workshops nearby. The museum is unique in specializing in fighters. One hangar is devoted to the pre-1920 period: most of its contents are flying replicas, painted in the colors of famous examples of their types. The museum has commissioned replicas from a number of firms and has also built some of its own. Some have also been bought from private individuals, so that a comprehensive array of most of the significant fighters of World War I have been collected.

One rare original machine is the Austrian Aviatik D I, designed by Julius von Berg. Over 700 examples of this biplane were built, and apart from overheating troubles with the Austro-Daimler engine they were able to give a good account in combat. The aircraft on show survived because the designer modified it into a two-seat tourer and thus saved it from confiscation by the allies. Even so it was felt necessary to hide it in a barn, where it remained until 1976 when it was bought by the German-based American restorer Arthur Williams. He did not realize the rarity of his find until on stripping away the extra structure and fairings he discovered the original airframe. The D I was sold to the Champlin museum in 1978, and has finished an extensive restoration to its original condition. (One other D I is in the Vienna Technical Museum).

The rarest aircraft in the museum is this Focke-Wulf Fw 190D designed by Kurt Tank, who assisted in the restoration of the aircraft in Germany in the mid-1970s

The earliest replica is of a 1914 Rumpler Taube monoplane, which was started in Germany by Arthur Williams. By 1986 this monoplane with its distinctive wing shape was at the Champlin museum awaiting its fabric covering. The hangar, with its lines of Allied aircraft facing their German counterparts, evokes a long-gone era of combat, when skilled fliers in basic machines fought individual battles over the French countryside.

The second hangar shows the vast strides in the development of combat aircraft which took place in the two decades between the two major conflicts. Gone are the fragile-looking biplanes and monoplanes with fabric covering and external bracing. Here are monoplanes of all-metal construction with massive engines of many times the power of their forebears. The German aircraft on show are perhaps the most interesting from this period. The most valuable aircraft in the collection is the Focke-Wulf Fw 190D, which was brought to the US in 1945 for evaluation. Five of these long-nosed 190s were tested, and the survivor was donated to Georgia Technical University. The aircraft was later moved to California, where Champlin bought it in 1972. This classic fighter then returned to its homeland for restoration to its original condition by Arthur Williams, who enlisted the help of its designer Dr Kurt Tank. After thousands of man-hours' work it returned to the US in 1976.

In 1972 the museum started the search for a genuine Messerschmitt Bf 109, and many rumors were followed up but without success. In 1973 a Spanish-built Hispano Ha 1112 with a Rolls-Royce Merlin engine was bought, and an original Daimler-Benz DB 601 engine in its cowlings was acquired. The task of converting the airframe to Bf 109E configuration was given to Williams, and he completed it in 1977. The aircraft is one of two Bf 109s flying with an original engine.

The Focke-Wulf and the Messerschmitt are just the highlights of the display, which holds many US Air Force and Navy fighters, a rebuilt Spitfire IX trainer and a Dewoitine D.514 that still needs a lot of attention.

A recent extension to the periods covered by the collection has seen two classic jet fighters arrive. In December

1983 a Moroccan air force Soviet-built MiG-17 arrived in Arizona, and since very few products of the famous Soviet design bureau of A I Mikoyan and M I Gurevich are on show in Western museums this is a most welcome addition. The other jet, which came in 1984, was a North American F-86F Sabre, one of the outstanding fighters of all time.

The museum is also home of the American Fighter Aces, an organization of pilots who have downed five or more enemy aircraft. A display commemorating and naming these aviators is near the entrance to the museum.

Above
This replica of the Fokker D VIII was built in Illinois by E O Swearingen. It is fitted with a Warner radial engine instead of the original Oberursel rotary

Below
Basking in the Arizona sun, this rare Aviatik D I was built in Austria in 1918

PIMA AIR MUSEUM

6400 South Wilmot Road, Tucson, Arizona 85706
Tel: 602-574-0462 or 0646

Opening times: 9am–5pm daily
Location: about 12 miles (20 km) southeast of Tucson, north of Interstate 10

Aeronca 65 TC (0-58B) (L8) (1943)
American Eagle A-101 (1928)
Bede BD-5 (1978)
Beech B18S Kansas (AT-11) (1941), **B18S (AT-7)** (1943), **B18S (SNB-5) (UC-45J)** (1944), **B18S (SNB-5P) (RC-45J)** (1944), **D18S** (1938), **N35 Bonanza** (1961), **50 Bonanza (U-8D) (L-23D)** (1956)
Bell 33 Kingcobra (P-63E) (1943), **47D (TH-13N)** (1956), **204 Iroquois (UH-1F)** (1963)
Bellanca 14-13 Crusaire (1948)
Boeing 299 Fortress (B-17G) (PB-1G) (1944), **307 Stratoliner** (1939), **345 Superfortress (B-29) (TB-29J)** (1944), **345 Superfortress (KB-50J)** (1949), **367 Stratofreighter (C-97G)** (1952), **367 Stratotanker (KC-97G)** (1953), **450 Stratojet (B-47A)** (1949, 1953), **464 Stratofortress (NB-52A) (B-52A)** (1952), **464 Stratofortress (B-52D)** (1955), **953 (YC-14A)** (1972)
Boeing-Steaman E75 Kaydet (PT-73D) (1941)
Bowers Flybaby 1A (c.1975)
Budd RB-1 Conestoga (1944)
Cessna T-50 (AT-17A) (1942), **T-50 (UC-78B)** (1943), **310 (U-3A) (L-27A)** (1958)
Consolidated 32 Liberator (B-24J) (1944)
Convair B-58A Hustler (1961), **TF-102A** (1955), **F-102A** (1956), **240 (T-29B)** (1951), **240 (T-29D)** (1952)
Culver NR-D Cadet (PQ-14B) (1944)
Curtiss-Wright CW-15 Sedan (1930), **CW-20 Commando (C-46D)** (1944)
de Havilland DHC 1 Chipmunk 22 (c. 1954), **DHC 2 Beaver (L-20A) (U-6A)** (1951, 1955)
Douglas EA-1F Skyraider (AD-5Q) (1951), **YEA-3A Skywarrior (YA3D-1)** (1953), **A-4C Skyhawk (A4D-2N)** (1954), **TA-4B Skyhawk (A4D-2)** (1954), **A-26A Invader (B-26K)** (1964), **A-26C Invader** (1943, 1944), **B-18A Bolo** (1938), **B-23 Dragon** (1939), **WB-66D Destroyer (B-66D)** (1955), **DC-3 (C-47)** (1941), **DC-3 (C-47B)** (1945), **DC-4 (C-54D) Skymaster** (1942), **DC-3 (C-117D) (R4D-8)** (1943), **DC-6 (VC-118A)** (1953), **C-124C Globemaster II** (1952), **C-133B Cargomaster** (1959), **F-6A Skyray (F4D-1)** (1951), **TF-10B Skynight (F3D-2)** (1952)
Easy Rider Ultralight (c.1982)
Fairchild M.62 Cornell (PT-19A) (1941), **M.62A Cornell (PT-23)** (1942), **C-82A Packet** (1944), **C-119C Flying Boxcar** (1949), **C-123B Provider** (1955)
Flaglor Sky Scooter (1967)
Fleet 7 (1932)
Focke-Wulf Fw 44J Stieglitz (1940)
Grumman G.40 Avenger (TBM-3) (1944), **G.50 Hellcat (F6F-3)** (1945), **G.51 Tigercat (F7F-3N)** (1945), **G.64 Albatross (HU-16A) (SA-16A)** (1951), **G.79 Panther (F9F-4)** (1949), **G.89 Tracker (S-2F) (S2F-1)** (1955), **G.93 Cougar (RF-9J) (F8F-8P)** (1954), **G.93 Cougar (TAF-9J) (F9F-8T)** (1954), **G.93 Cougar (TF-9J) (F9F-8T)** (1954), **G.98 Tiger (F-11A) (F11F-1)** (1955), **G.117 Tracer (E-1B) (WF-2)** (1959), **G.134 Mohawk (OV-1B)** (1962), **G.134 Mohawk (OV-1C)** (1961)
Hiller UH12C (1955)
Hughes 269B (TH-55A) (1964, 1967)
Hyperlight Hang-glider (c.1977)
Icarus Hang-glider (c.1980)
Kaman K.600 Huskie (HH-43B) (1959), **K.600 Huskie (OH-43D) (HOK-1)** (1960)
Lockheed 10A Electra (UC-36A) (1942), **18 Lodestar (R50-5)** (1943), **37 Harpoon (PV-2)** (1943), **049 Constellation (C-69)** (1942), **749 Constellation (VC-121A) (C-121A)** (1948), **1049 Super Constellation (EC-121T) (EC-121D)** (1953), **P-38L Lightning (F-5G)** (1944), **P-80B Shooting Star** (1945), **F-94A Starfire** (1949), **F-94C Starfire** (1951), **F-104D Starfighter** (1957), **T-33A** (1953), **T-33B (TV-2)** (1953), **T-1A Seastar (T2V-1)** (1956), **AP-2H Neptune (P2V-7)** (1961), **YO-3A Quiet Star** (1969)
McCulloch MC4A (HUM-1) (1952)
McDonnell F-3B Demon (F3H-2) (1954), **YF-4J Phantom** (1963), **F-101B Voodoo** (1957), **RF-101C Voodoo** (1956), **RF-101H Voodoo (F-101C)** (1956)
McDonnell-Douglas YC-15A (1972)
Martin 162 Mariner (PBM-5A) (1945), **B-57E Canberra** (1955), **EB-57D Canberra** (1953), **WB-57F Canberra (RB-57F)** (1963)
North American NA.64 Yale (BT-14) (1939), **T-6G Texan (AT-6B)** (1941), **AT-6D Texan (SNJ-5B)** (1942), **T-6G Texan (CCF)** (1949), **B-25J Mitchell** (1943), **B-45A Tornado** (1947), **AF-1E Fury (FJ-4B)** (1954), **F-86H Sabre** (1953), **F-86L Sabre (F-86D)** (1953), **F-100C Super Sabre** (1954), **YF-107A** (1955), **T-28A Trojan** (1950), **T-28C Trojan** (1952), **T-39A** (1961), **RA-5C Vigilante (A-3J)** (1963), **X-15A** (mock-up) (?)
Northrop YC-125A Raider (1948), **F-89J Scorpion** (1953), **T-38A Talon** (1961)
Piasecki PV.18 Retriever (HUP-2) (UH-25B) (1950), **PD.18 Retriever (HUP-3) (H-25A)** (1951)
Piper PA-23 Aztec (U-11A) (UO-1) (1960)
Republic F-84B Thunderjet (P-84B) (1949), **F-84C Thunderjet (P-84C)** (1947), **F-84F Thunderstreak** (1952), **RF-84F Thunderflash** (1951), **F-105D Thunderchief** (1961), **F-105G Thunderchief** (1962)
Ryan ST.3KR Recruit (PT-22) (1941)
Scheibe Zugvogel IIIB (?)
Schweizer SGS.2-12 (TG-3A) (1942)
Sikorsky S43 (JRS-1) (1930), **S-51 Dragonfly (R-5G) (H-5G)** (1948), **S-55 (H-19B)** (1952), **S-56 (CH-37B)** (1958), **S-58 (VH-34C)** (1957)
Stinson V.76 Sentinel (L-5G) (1944)
Swallow A (?)
Taylorcraft D (L-2M) (1943)
Vertol V.43 Shawnee (CH-21C) (1956)
Vought F4U-4 Corsair (1945), **F7U-3 Cutlass** (1950), **DF-8F Crusader (F-8A) (F8U-1)** (1955)
Vultee BT-13A Valiant (1942)
Waco ZKS-6 (1937), **CG-4A Hadrian** (1945)
White D-1X Der Jäger (c.1976)
Wright Flyer (R) (?)
Homebuilt aircraft, unknown type (?)

The dry climate of Arizona is ideal for storing and preserving aircraft and over the years this has been made use of by the United States Air Force. The Military Aircraft Storage and Disposal Center (MASDC) at Davis-Monthan Air Force Base on the outskirts of Tucson was set up in 1945, adopting its current name in 1965. In the mid-1960s the army, navy and coast guard also used the site for storing their aircraft. Thousands of aircraft have passed through the base, of which many have been scrapped, others reduced to spares and some stored for possible return to service.

A sample of the aircraft in store, which sometimes numbered over 5000 at any one time, were lined up near the entrance to the base. It was not open to the general public but proved a popular tourist attraction and led to a proposal and agreement for establishing an air museum in the region which would be supplied with aircraft from the vast resources of MASDC. In 1969 MASDC approved the transfer of 35 aircraft to the museum although they were still in store at the unit. The new museum also set about acquiring its own aircraft and the first three were obtained in 1969/70. A damaged Lockheed F-94A Starfighter was found in Patagonia, Arizona, a Vultee BT-13A was presented by a local school district and a Stinson Sentinel was donated by the Arizona Wing of the Civil Air Patrol.

In the early 1970s further work was carried out on the site and the MASDC aircraft were beginning to make the short journey to the museum. By May 1973 almost all had moved and a caretaker was in residence. In 1970 the museum acquired a Consolidated Liberator bomber from the Indian Air Force which had two squadrons of the aircraft rebuilt and refurbished from World War II B24s. When they were finally withdrawn in 1968 museums showed interest in the Liberators and four were made airworthy and flown to new homes in the USA, Canada and the UK, including the Pima Air Museum. It is now displayed with Indian markings on one side of its fuselage and US colours on the other.

The museum officially opened in May 1976 with nearly 100 aircraft on show, a number which has since doubled to make the museum one of the largest in the country. The site has been steadily improved over the years and the first indoor exhibition area was opened in March 1983. This addition has enabled the museum to display some of its lighter fabric-covered aircraft.

A museum within the main exhibition area commemorates the local 390th Bombardment Wing and its successor the 390th Strategic Missile Wing. The Wing was formed in 1943, moved to England after six months, was deactivated in 1945, to be reactivated in 1962 as a missile unit with sites around the Tucson area. A hut transported from its English wartime base is part of the display and has been restored to represent a briefing room of the period. A Fortress bomber has been painted in the markings of the 390th during its spell in England and a Titan missile stands near the aircraft outside the exhibition hall.

Within this large collection there are naturally some rare and unique aircraft, some of which have been restored at the museum. The restoration staff have a large open-sided shelter within the main exhibition area where visitors can see the tasks involved in bringing the aircraft up to exhibition condition. Many of the MASDC machines are merely placed on site and little is done to them.

The sole surviving Martin Mariner is one of the stars of the display. The prototype of this twin-engined flying boat first flew in February 1939 and 1235 were built before the last delivery was made in April 1949. The amphibious version on show is one of the 500-plus Mariners which served in the Korean war. At the end of 1938 America's first pressurized four-engined airliner lifted off from Boeing Field at Seattle. Using the flying surfaces of the B-17 Fortress, the new Stratoliner was ordered by PanAm and TWA. However, only 10 were built and one of the three ex-PanAm aircraft survives in the museum.

Another airliner which is fast becoming a rarity is the sleek Lockheed Constellation. The museum has four of these graceful four-engined airliners on show, two standard models and two military Super Constellations. The oldest 'Connie' surviving has recently been painted in the colors of TWA which it wore in its heyday. Built as a military transport in 1945 it flew for less than a year with the air force before going into storage. TWA bought it in 1948 and it flew almost 38,000 hours in 13 years with the airline. Finally in 1970 it was traded with a Grumman Albatross so that it could be preserved as a reminder of a more gentle age of airline transport.

With such a vast number of aircraft it is almost impossible to highlight more than a few but in the storage compound awaiting their turn are the last Budd Conestoga and one of the (if not the) last Northrop Raider. The stainless steel Conestoga flew in October 1943 but production delays with the new techniques of construction resulted in about only 25 being completed. The three-engined Northrop Raider was conceived as a short take-off transport but only two dozen were completed for the air force and after a short career most ended their days with airlines in Central and South America. The museum's example was used in Mexico before becoming derelict at an Arizona airfield.

The majority of aircraft are obviously military, but the indoor display has acquired some light civil aircraft, to add to the variety of this vast collection.

The Grumman Tracer is an Airborne Early Warning aircraft, mounted with a massive white radome

Above
'Star of Switzerland', a Lockheed Constellation that served with TWA from 1948 to 1961. It is displayed in TWA colors: polished metal finish, with red trim

Below
This Consolidated Liberator carries the markings of the USAAC on its port side and those of the Indian Air Force on the starboard

Right
The last remaining Budd Conestoga, a stainless steel transport aircraft, in the storage area at Pima

Below
A Vought Crusader – just one of the many ex-military aircraft transferred from the nearby Davis-Monthan AFB to Pima

California

THE AIR MUSEUM 'PLANES OF FAME'

7000 Merrill Avenue, Chino Airport, California 91710
Tel: 714-597-3722

Opening times: midday-5pm Monday-Friday, 10am-5pm Saturday-Sunday
Location: at Chino Airport, which is about 7 miles (11 km) south of Ontario on Route 83

Aichi D3A Val (1941)
Bell 26 Airacobra (P-39N) (1943), **27 Airacomet (YP-59A)** (1942)
Bensen B-8 (1968)
Boeing 67 Hawk (1927), **234 (P-12E)** (1932), **248 Pea Shooter (P-26A)** (1933), **299 Fortress (B-17G)** (1944), **345 Superfortress (B-50)** (1946)
Bristol 96 F2B (R) (1984)
Bureau of Standards Bat (?)
Cessna 318 (XT-37) (1954)
Convair L-13A (1947), **F-102A** (1956)
Culver NR-D (PQ-14) (1944)
Curtiss Pusher (R) (?), **87 Warhawk (P-40N)** (1944)
Douglas SBD-5 Dauntless (1943), **A-26C Invader** (1943), **D-558-2 Skyrocket** (1948)
Fairchild M.62A Cornell (PT-26A) (1943)
Fieseler Fi 103 (1944)
Fokker Dr I (R) (1982)
Grumman G.37 (F3F-2) (R) (1983), **G.36 Wildcat (F4F-8) (FM-2)** (1944), **G.40 Avenger (TBM-3)** (1944), **G.50 Hellcat (F6F-5)** (1944), **G.79 Panther (F9F-5K)** (1951), **G.98 Tiger (F-11A) (F11F-1)** (1958)
Hanriot HD-1 (1918)
Heinkel He 162A-1 (1945)
Hispano Ha.1112 (Bf 109) (1954)
Horten Ho IV (1941)
Keith Rider R-4 (1935), **R-6** (1936)
Le Vier Cosmic Wind (1949)
Lilienthal 1895 Glider (R) (?)
Lockheed P-38J Lightning (1942), **P-80A Shooting Star** (1945), **F-80C Shooting Star (T-1)** (1947), **T-33A** (1953)
Messerschmitt Bf 108B Taifun (1942), **Bf 109G-10/U-4** (1943), **Me 262A** (1945)
Mitsubishi A6M5 Zero Sen (1943), **J2M3 Raiden** (1944), **J8M1 Shusui** (1945)
Nieuport 28C1 (R) (?)
North American 0-47A (1938), **T-6D Texan (SNJ-5)** (1944), **P-51A Mustang** (1943), **P-51D Mustang** (1945), **B-25J Mitchell** (1944), **F-86A Sabre** (1948, 1949), **F-86H Sabre** (1952)
Northrop N9MB (1943)
Republic P-47G Thunderbolt (1942), **YP-84A Thunderjet** (1945), **F-84B Thunderjet** (1945), **F-84E Thunderjet** (1950), **RF-84K Thunderflash (RF-84F)** (1952)
Ric Jet 4 (?)
Ryan 28 Fireball (FR-1) (1944)
Seversky 2PA Guardsman (AT-12) (1940)
Stinson V.76 Sentinel (1945), **V.77 Reliant (AT-19)** (1942)
Supermarine 389 Spitfire PR.XIX (1945)
Vertol V.43 (H-21C) (1956)
Vought F4U-1 (WM) Super Corsair (1944), **F4U-1 Corsair** (1944)
Wright Flyer (R) (1982)
Yokosuka MXY-7 Ohka 11 (1945)

Although there is some controversy over whether valuable and unique aircraft should be flown, the fact remains that viewing an aeroplane in its natural element is a bonus for both restorer and general enthusiast. Ed Maloney and his team at Chino have delighted many with their superb workmanship, and the opportunity to see the last examples of many types in the air has caused crowds to flock to Chino on the occasions of the air displays.

The story of the collection goes back to the end of World War II when Ed Maloney began acquiring aeronautical items. As his hobby developed, engines and airframe components joined the growing collection. He acquired his first complete aircraft in 1948 with the purchase of a Mitsubishi Shusui – an almost exact copy of the Messerschmitt Me 163 rocket-powered fighter. After evaluation by the US forces, the aircraft had been sent round the country as an attraction and ended its days at a Californian fairground.

This acquisition led to the idea of setting up an aeronautical museum on the west coast as at the time none existed. Progress was slow, however, and it was not until January 1957 that the collection opened its doors at Claremont. The public were slow to respond and this, coupled with other problems, meant that there was little money available for new aircraft and to tackle major restoration projects. Also the site was not close to a suitable airfield, so new types could not fly in.

In 1965 the entire collection moved to Ontario airport; business improved, and by now almost 50 aircraft were on the museum inventory. Then Ontario was designated as the regional center for air-freight services, and so the museum was forced to look for another home. The new site was Buena Park, which housed the 'Movieland Cars of the Stars' museum and it was hoped that the two collections would complement each other, but after a short period this was found not to be the case. The Buena Park museum opened in 1969 but soon afterwards the collection was taken to Chino airfield, where it is now well established, and the field has become a renowned warbird haven.

Among the highlights of the collection are a number of Japanese aircraft and on April 26, 1984 a special exhibition featuring these was opened. In addition to the five aircraft on show there are model aircraft, World War II uniforms, posters, instruments, swords and other artifacts. The Shusui, of which, only three powered versions were completed before the Japanese surrender, was the first aircraft to join the collection. The first crashed on its maiden flight, the fuel systems of two others were being modified as a result of the crash and four others were tested as gliders. In addition, some 50 pure glider versions were constructed. This rare aircraft is a prominent feature of the display.

Probably the most famous Japanese fighter of World War II was the Mitsubishi Zero, of which almost 11,000 were produced including just over 500 of the two-seat trainer version. The museum has two genuine Zeros, one on view and the other in store. The two aircraft were saved from scrapping and initially placed in store. One was captured at Saipan and the other on Truk. One (61-120) arrived at San Diego in July 1944 and was soon flown to the naval test and evaluation center at Patuxent River, where it flew for around 200 hours. Among the many pilots who sampled its qualities was Charles Lindbergh. The Zero then returned to San Diego for disposal. The history of the other is somewhat obscure but at some stage its wings were cut off.

Ed Maloney acquired both these Zeros and put 61-120 on show as a static exhibit. However, when he visited Japan in 1973 he was inspired to restore it to flying condition. This mammoth task took around four years. The first engine runs of its original Nakajima Sakae radial took place in November 1977 and after internal fitting out the Zero flew on June 28, 1978. In the following month the aircraft returned to its homeland and in the next six months flew over most of the major cities in the country. Over ten million people viewed the first Zero to be seen over Japan since 1945. The second aircraft was rebuilt in 1979/80 as a static exhibit and was then taken to Japan along with the Shusui, the Okha and five other aircraft from the museum for the World Aeroplane exhibition at Kyushu. The other Japanese aircraft in the exhibition are the Ohka rocket-powered suicide machine, one of two Mitsubishi Raiden fighters intact, and an Aichi D3A dive-bomber. This exhibition is an excellent record of the Japanese contribution to the Pacific War.

Two early Boeing fighters, both great rarities, can often be seen in the air. The P-12E of 1932 was generally recognized as one of the most maneuverable biplane fighters ever built. Large numbers were built for the USAAC and as the F4B for the navy. This aircraft is painted in the colors of the personal aircraft of General Hap Arnold when he was commander of March Field in California. The P-12E is the only flying example of the type, as is the other Boeing model, a P-26A which was the first all-metal fighter to enter squadron service with the USAAC in 1933. This monoplane is painted in the markings of the 34th Pursuit Squadron which was based at March Field in the early 1930s. When its US days were over it served with the Panamanian and Guatemalan air forces before being bought by the museum in 1957.

Two other unique fliers are a Seversky AT-12 and a North American O-47A (a second example of the O-47 was being rebuilt at another collection during 1986). The Seversky was originally ordered as a two-seat fighter by the Swedish Air Force, but with the entry of the US into World War II it was commandeered by the USAAC and pressed into service as an advanced trainer. The O-47 was originally designed as the General Aviation GA-15 before the company changed its name to North American Aviation. This rather bulky low-wing monoplane flew in 1935; 164 O-47 As and 74 of the more powerful O-47B were built and used as observation aircraft, but saw little combat duty and were soon relegated to more mundane tasks. The O-47A at Chino is the oldest North American Aviation aircraft still flying.

The museum has rebuilt an early North American P-51A Mustang. The history of this Allison-powered version of the famous fighter is obscure, but it spent some time at a USAF training school at Glendale in California in 1953, from where it was bought by the museum. Restoration commenced in the mid-1970s and the first flight took place in August 1981. Although it never served with the Royal Air Force the aircraft is painted in these colours, as the Mustang was designed to an RAF specification. The P-51A flew in the 1981 Reno Air Races, along with a Rolls-Royce Merlin-powered P-51D which is also owned by the museum. Air racing is an important part of the museum's life and usually at least one warbird will be entered at Reno. Their latest mount is a highly modified Vought Corsair.

A most interesting project is currently taking place in the museum workshops. Northrop produced their first flying-wing design in 1929 but it did have a conventional tail for stability. The aircraft flew well and the first true flying-wing, the N1M, flew in 1940. General Hap Arnold urged the company to investigate the possibilities of a flying-wing bomber. Four 60-foot (18-meter) span N9Ms were built in 1942, the last of which is with the museum. Development of the idea was continued and culminated in the 172-foot (52-meter) span XB-35 and YB-49. These giants were a familiar sight over California in the early 1950s and hopefully it will not be too long before the unconventional shape will again be seen in the air.

In addition to the range of flying aircraft, the museum has many others in static condition, including modern and classic jets. As time passes it may be possible to get some of these back into the air. The museum should be on any Californian tourist's route and in addition there are several other collections at Chino which are worth visiting.

This Mitsubishi Zero is the only authentic example of its type in flying condition. It carries the markings it wore when captured on Saipan

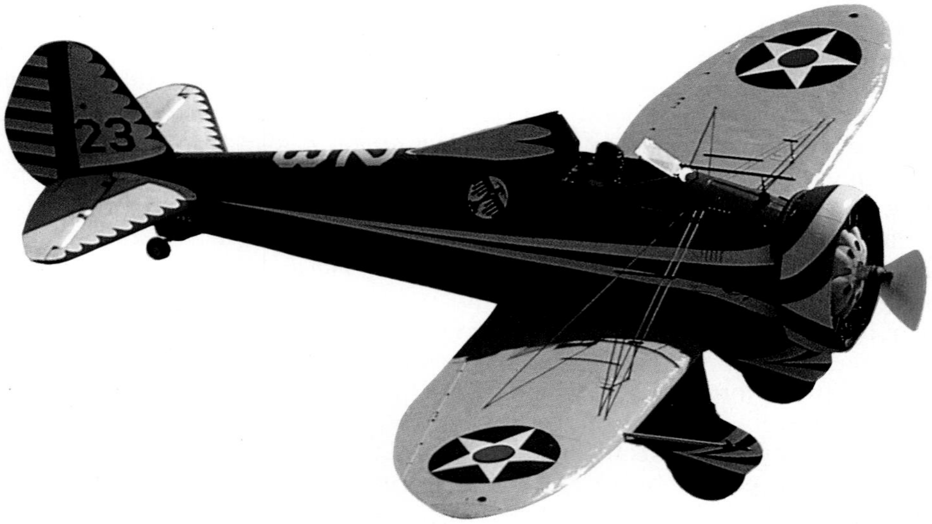

Top
A formation flight by a Curtiss P-40N Warhawk, which flew with the RCAF in World War II, and the only genuine flyable Mitsubishi Zero

Left
Only two Boeing P-26A Peashooters survive, and the Air Museum's is the only one in airworthy condition

A pair of Mustangs in flight: banking away from the P-51A Mustang is the P-51D version

Above
A P-47G Thunderbolt fighter flies in formation with a North American B-25J Mitchell bomber

Right
The Air Museum's Seversky 2PA is a two-seat version of the P35 and is the only flyable example remaining of the Seversky fighters

Below
Two of the classic US Navy types of World War II, seen in formation: flying below the Grumman Avenger torpedo bomber is the Hellcat fighter from the same company

The Boeing Stratofreighter was developed from the Superfortress. The aircraft seen here is the tanker variant of the Stratofreighter, with two jet engines to aid take-off, known as the Stratotanker

CASTLE AIR MUSEUM

Castle Air Force Base, Atwater, California 95342
Tel: 209-726-2011

Opening times: 10am-8pm daily (closes at 4pm in winter months)
Location: on the west side of the AFB which is about 2 miles (3km) north of Highway 99, about 8 miles (13km) northwest of Merced

Avro 698 Vulcan B.2 (1963)
Avro-Canada CF-100 Canuck 5 (1958)
Beech B18S (C-45G) (1951), **45 Mentor (YT-34)** (1950)
Bell 47G Sioux (H-13H) (1956)
Boeing 299 Fortress (B-17G) (1943), **345 Superfortress (B-29A)** (1944), **345 Superfortress (WB-50D) (B-50D)** (1949), **377 Stratotanker (KC-97L) (KC-97G)** (1953), **464 Stratofortress (B-52D)** (1956)
Boeing-Stearman A75 Kaydet (PT-17) (1942)
Cessna T-50 Bobcat (UC-78) (JRC-1) (1943), **310 (L-27A) (U-3A)** (1957), **337 Skymaster (O-2A)** (1967)
Consolidated 32 Liberator (B-24M) (1944)
Convair L-13A (1947), **F-102A** (1956)
Curtiss-Wright CW-20 Commando (C-46D) (1944)
de Havilland DHC 2 Beaver (L-20A) (1954)
Douglas DC-3 (C-47A) (1943), **DC-4 (C-54E)** (1944), **B-18A Bolo** (1937), **B-23 Dragon** (1939), **A-26C Invader** (1944)
Fairchild M.62A Cornell (PT-23A) (1942), **C-123K Provider (C-123B)** (1955)
Kaman 600 Huskie (H-43B) (H-43F) (1962)
Lockheed 18 Lodestar (C-60) (1941)
McDonnell F-101B Voodoo (1957)
Martin 179 Marauder (B-26B) (1941)
North American AT-6A Texan (1941), **T-28C Trojan** (1957), **B-25J Mitchell** (1944), **B-45A Tornado** (1947)
Northrop A-9A (1971)
Piper J-3C Cub (L-4) (1942), **PA-18 Super Cub (L-18C)** (1952), **PA-18 Super Cub (L-21A)** (1951)
Republic F-105B Thunderchief (1957)
Sopwith Pup (R) (?)
Vultee BT-13 Valiant (1942)

Castle Air Force Base opened in September 1941 and was named after Brig-Gen Frederick W Castle who was a noted B-17 Fortress pilot in World War II. Today the base houses the 93rd Bomb Wing of Strategic Air Command, which trains aircrew for bomber and tanker operations in addition to combat duties. The museum was set up a number of years ago and has gradually developed into one of the major air force base collections in the country. The Castle Air Museum Foundation is in charge of fund raising and of maintaining and restoring the aircraft. There is an indoor display in a building on the museum site, including a large collection of Army Air Corps and Air Force uniforms and an example of the famous Norden Bomb Sight, one of the most secret devices of World War II. The history of the base and its units is told in an exhibition of photographs and personal items.

The aircraft, which currently number around 40, are on show in a pleasant park around the building. There are plans to double this number as aircraft become available. Castle has traditionally been a bomber base, and almost every major US type from World War II is on view. The four-engined heavies – the Boeing Fortress and the Consolidated Liberator – can be compared with the twin-engined Douglas Invader, North American Mitchell and the Martin Marauder.

From a slightly earlier era are the Douglas B-18 Bolo and the Douglas B-23 Dragon, both of which are now becoming rarities. The B-18 was a bombing version of the famous DC-3 airliner, and over 300 were built after the type had won the 1936 Air Corps competition. The Dragon was a much cleaner version of the same basic concept; it first flew in July 1939, but was already outdated, such was the pace of aerodynamic development. Only 38 were built, 12 of which were converted to transports; the others saw limited use as patrol aircraft before being used as trainers or glider tugs. The Bolo served as a fire bomber, and the Dragon as an executive aircraft before joining the museum.

The only original aircraft of non-American origin is an Avro Vulcan bomber. The large RAF deltas were frequent visitors to Castle on exchanges or for the bombing competitions in which SAC crews compete against their RAF counterparts. In honor of these visits the Vulcan is on indefinite loan to the museum from the British government, and was the first Vulcan to go on display at a museum outside the United Kingdom.

The North American B-45 Tornado was the first US four-jet bomber to fly, and was the first jet bomber to be put into large-scale production. The prototype flew in March 1947, and 143 were built. The Tornado was based in the UK in the 1950s and became a familiar sight in East Anglia. In its reconnaissance role it flew in the Korean war and the last Tornado in service, on special duties, continued into the 1960s. The Castle aircraft was sent to the China Lake Naval Weapons Center for use as a ground target, but it was not used in this role and after 17 years at the site was dismantled and brought to the museum.

The Canadian Government has donated an Avro Canada CF-100 Canuck fighter to the museum. This twin-jet is the only Canadian-designed combat aircraft to see operational use. In addition to the Canadian squadrons at home, some were operated in Europe by both the RCAF and the Belgian Air Force. The example in the collection was used as an ECM carrier aircraft by 414 Squadron (the Black Knights) to train fighter crews in the techniques of interception.

In addition to the bombers there is a wide range of transport aircraft on show including a Curtiss Commando which has made a round the world journey. After service with the US forces it was supplied to the Japanese Self Defence Force and reached Asia by way of the South Atlantic and Africa. On its return journey to the US it flew to California via Alaska.

This excellent collection has already an impressive range of types on view, and if the ambitious plans materialize the Castle Air Museum could become one of the largest museums on the west coast.

The Douglas B-18 Bolo was a bomber version of the DC-3 transport. Only a handful survive from the original 370 built

MARCH FIELD MUSEUM

March Air Force Base, California 92518
Tel: 714-655-3725

Opening times: 10am-2pm Monday-Friday, midday-4pm Saturday-Sunday
Location: the AFB is on Interstate 215 about 4 miles (6km) southeast of Riverside

Beech B.18S (JRB-4) (UC-45J) (1944)
Bell 27 Airacomet (P-59A) (1944), **205 Iroquois (UH-1F)** (1964)
Boeing 299 Fortress (B-17G) (1944), **345 Superfortress (B-29A) (SB-29)** (1944), **367 Stratotanker (KC-97L) (KC-97G)** (1953), **464 Stratofortress (B-52D)** (1955)
Boeing-Stearman E75 Kaydet (PT-13D) (1942)
Cessna 337 Skymaster (O-2B) (1967)
Consolidated 32 Liberator (B-24J) (1944)
Curtiss 87 Warhawk (P-40E) (1942)
Douglas A-26C Invader (1944)
Fairchild M.62 Cornell (PT-19B) (1943), **C-123K Provider (C-123B)** (1954)
Grumman G.64 Albatross (HU-16E) (UF-2G) (1951)
Lockheed 18 Lodestar (R50) (1942), **U-2D** (1956)
McDonnell F-101B Voodoo (1959), **F-4C Phantom** (1963)
Martin EB-57B Canberra (B-57B) (1952)
North American AT-6C Texan (1942), **B-25J Mitchell** (1944), **F-86H Sabre** (1953), **F-100C Super Sabre** (1954), **T-39 Sabreliner** (?)
Northrop F-89J Scorpion (1952), **A-9A** (1971)
Republic F-84C Thunderjet (1947), **F-84F Thunderstreak** (1951), **F-105B Thunderchief** (1957), **F-105D Thunderchief** (1962)
Stinson V.76 Sentinel (L-5) (1944)
Vultee BT-13 Valiant (1941, 1942)

March Field, activated in 1918, is one of the oldest military airfields in the USA. Over the years it has housed a variety of units and still has air force and air national guard units on site. With a growing interest in the historical aspect of military bases and units it was natural that a field with such a long past should be the site of a museum. The museum was formally opened on December 19, 1979 and has grown into a major collection.

The policy for the base museums being set up is that aircraft which are already on base should be displayed plus new additions which have served at the base or with units housed there. When the March Field museum was founded, however, the then 15th Air Force Commander Gen James Mullins had grand ideas of displaying every type that could be collected. Thus there are a number of aircraft on view which have no connection with March but

An ex-US Navy Lockheed Lodestar, painted in false USAAC colors

they were in place before the current policy was adopted.

A former commissary building houses the indoor display of five aircraft; there are another 28 outdoors. The inside display has engines, model aircraft, vehicles, training devices, uniforms, paintings etc. relating the story of the base, supported by a continuous audio-visual presentation. There are three famous trainers and an equally well known liaison aircraft in this building. The Stearman 75 series, which was produced in vast numbers, was one of the best known biplane trainers and is still much sought after by private owners. The Fairchild Cornell and the Vultee Valiant low-wing monoplanes were the next generation of military trainers. A Bell Airacomet is soon to join this display. The type was the first jet fighter conceived in the USA and flew for the first time at Muroc in the Californian desert on October 2, 1942. Sixty-six Airacomets were built and although they were unsuitable for combat made a valuable contribution in training pilots for the next generation of jets which were ready at the end of World War II.

The outdoor display exhibits a number of World War II aircraft including an ex-Indian Air Force Liberator and a Curtiss P-40 Warhawk which are on loan from a private collector, David Tallichet. Next to these two is the Boeing B-17G Fortress which is believed to have been the personal transport of General Ira Eaker in World War II. In 1957 this aircraft went to Bolivia to be one of the fleet used by the airline Lloyd Aero Bolivia. In the course of this arduous work it crashed at La Paz in 1968 and was rebuilt with parts of another aircraft and used by Frigorifico Reyes for freight work. The rarest aircraft in the collection is, however, a relatively modern design. Two Northrop A-9As were built to compete with the Fairchild A10 in the close support role. The Northrop design was the loser of the contest but both have been preserved; the other is at the Castle Air Museum, also in California.

Plans for a small building to house the contents of the present indoor display plus a few more aircraft and a purpose-built exhibition hall in which almost all the collection would be on view should make the museum one of the largest on the west coast. The total cost of this expansion will not be far short of $10 million. The local community of Riverside supports the plan, which should bring a vast number of tourists into the area.

Two Northrop A-9s were built, but they did not win the contract with the USAF that they were intended for: it went to Fairchild, with their A-10 attack plane

SAN DIEGO AEROSPACE MUSEUM

2001 Pan American Plaza, Balboa Park, San Diego, California 92101
Tel: 619-234-8291

Opening times: 10am-4.30pm daily
Location: in the center of the city just off Interstate 5. The museum has a facility at Gillespie Field about 10 miles (16 km) northeast of the city off Interstate 67

Aeronca C-3 (1933)
Albatros D V (R) (1980)
Albatross Sails ASG-21 (1976)
Aldridge Ornithopter (1970)
American Eagle A-1 (1928)
Beech E17B (1938)
Blériot XI (R) (1966)
Boeing-Stearman B75 Kaydet (N2S-3) (1942)
Brunner Winkle BK Bird (1930)
Chandelle Hang-Glider (1981)
Consolidated PT-1 (1927)
Convair XFY-1 (1953), **XF2Y-1 Sea Dart** (1953)
Coward, Changa, Montijo Wee Bee (R) (1979)
Curtiss A-1 (R) (1983), **JN-4D Jenny** (1918), **JN-4D Jenny B (R)** (1985), **50 Robin B-1** (1930), **Little Looper** (1947)
de Havilland DH 2 (R) (1975), **DH 4 (R)** (1968)
Deperdussin C (1911)
Douglas SBD Dauntless (R) (1977), **A-4B Skyhawk (A4D-2)** (1958)
Eipper MX Quicksilver (?)
Evans VP-2 Volksplane (1971)
Fleet 2 (1930)
Fokker D VII (R) (1978)
Ford 5-AT-B (1928)
Glasflugel 201 Libelle (1966)
Grumman G.15 Duck (J2F-6) (1946), **G.50 Hellcat (F6F-3)** (1944)
Junkers Ju 87B (R) (197?)
K & S Jungster VI (1975)
Kucenich Icarus II (?)
Lilienthal Glider (R) (1968)
McDonnell F-4N Phantom (1962)
Mercury Air Shoestring (1949)
Mikoyan-Gurevich MiG-15 (?)
Mitsubishi A6M7 Zero Sen (1945)
Montgomery Evergreen (1912)
Morane-Saulnier MS.230 (1950)
Nieuport 11 (R) (1972), **28C.1** (1918)
North American F-86 Sabre (Canadair CL-13A Sabre 5) (1953)
North American T-28B Trojan (1953)
Peregrine Owl Hang Glider (?)
Piasecki PV.18 Retriever (HUP-2) (1950)
Piper J-3C Cub (1939)
Pitts S-1S Special (1975)
Quickie Aircraft Quickie 1 (1977)
Rearwin 8135T Cloudster (1940)
Ryan M-1 (R) (1980), **NYP-III (R)** (1979), **B-5 Brougham** (1931), **STA** (1937), **3ST.KR Recruit (PT-22)** (1942), **69 Vertijet (X-13)** (1954)
Seagull V Hang Glider (?)
Smith DSA-1 Miniplane (1956)
SPAD VII (1917)
Standard J-1 (1918)
Staudhammer Ornithopter (1950)
Supermarine 361 Spitfire XVI (1945)
Swallow OX-5 (1928)
Thomas Morse S4C (1918)
Volmer Jensen VJ-11 (?)
Vought F-8J Crusader (1960)
Waco YKS-7 (1937)
Waterman W-5 Aeromobile (1958)
Wright Flyer (R) (1979), **EX Vin Fiz (R)** (1980)

The city of San Diego has been associated with aviation since the pioneer days. Glenn H Curtiss made several flights in the area in 1911 and over the years a number of military bases were established. Industry came to the area with the Consolidated Aircraft Corporation and the Ryan Aeronautical Company among the firms that set up at the airport now named after Charles A Lindbergh, the famous flier who used a Ryan monoplane on his epic flight from New York to Paris.

With such an aeronautical history the city was an obvious location for the aviation museum which was set up in the early 1960s and opened in February 1963. From 1965 the collection was housed in a temporary building which it shared with the Hall of Science Museum, over the next decade the museum building up an impressive range of exhibits. The display covered the entire era of flight and early original machines included a 1909 Chanute glider and a 1911 Montgomery monoplane.

From the Consolidated company there was a PT-3 trainer found in Arkansas and bought for the museum by Reuben Fleet who founded the firm in 1923 from the Gallaudet and Dayton-Wright companies. Consolidated moved to San Diego in 1935 from Buffalo in New York in one of the largest relocations in aeronautical history. In 1969 the PT-3 was flown to San Diego and after a four day trip touched down at Lindbergh Field. A few weeks later at the age of 82 Reuben Fleet took the controls of the PT-3 and flew it over his home. The Ryan company was represented by an original M-1 which was the first monoplane put into production in the USA.

In 1977 disaster struck when the museum was almost completely destroyed by a fire started by a vandal. Most of the historic aircraft were lost as well as the library of books, manuals, photographs etc. A great effort was initiated to try and obtain another collection which would once again be a major museum. The work was rewarded in June 1980 when the new museum opened in a building in Balboa Park originally built in 1935.

The exhibition has been steadily improved since its reopening. The displays have specific themes, including the Pioneer Days with replicas of the Wright Flyer, a Montgomery Glider and a Curtiss Pusher: World War I aviation; Flying the Mail; the Barnstormers; the Golden Age of Flight; World War II training; General Aviation and the Armed Forces. In each of these areas there are aircraft plus relevant memorabilia and vehicles.

Some of the aircraft lost in the 1977 fire have been replaced by other examples of their types and replicas of some which have been impossible to obtain have been made. In recent years a number of home-built aircraft have been added to the collection including some which are scaled down military aircraft. The museum has a large collection of engines, components etc. on view and has recreated a 'Pilots Ready Room' from a typical aircraft carrier in which an audio-visual presentation relives World War II operations.

The local firms are again well represented with a Consolidated PT-1 replacing the lost PT-3. From Ryan there are original aircraft such as a B-5 Broughman and two low-wing monoplanes, the STA and PT-22, and replicas of the M-1 which was lost in 1977 and of Lindbergh's NYP-III.

A rarity in a US museum is a French Morane-Saulnier MS.230 parasol trainer. Used in the film 'The Blue Max', it as bought by the film's star, George Peppard, and taken to the US. The aircraft came to San Diego in 1978 and was completely restored before going on show in 1982 next to a 1925 French Amilcar sports car.

The museum has an extensive restoration center and at Gillespie Field a hangar has been used since 1983. Here a number of aircraft for which there is currently no room at Balboa Park can be seen by appointment.

This replica Ryan M-1 was built to replace the original, lost in the San Diego museum's disastrous fire in 1977

Connecticut

NEW ENGLAND AIR MUSEUM

Bradley International Airport, Windsor Locks, Connecticut 06096
Tel: 203-623-3305

Opening times: 10am-6pm daily
Location: on the north side of the airport off Route 75

Aeronca 65CA Super Chief (1941), **11AC Chief** (1947)
Bell 33 Kingcobra (RP-63C) (1944), **47D Sioux (OH-13E)** (1952), **47D** (1948), **204 Iroquois (UH-1B)** (1962)
Blériot XI (1911)
Boeing 299Z Fortress (B-17G) (1944), **345 Superfortress (B-29A)** (1945), **450 Stratojet (B-47E) (WB-47E)** (1953), **707-120** (1957)
Boeing-Stearman B75 Kaydet (N2S-3) (1942)
Bristol 149 Bolingbroke IVT (1942)
Brooks Balloon (1886)
Bourdon Kittyhawk (1928)
Burnelli CBY-3 Loadmaster (Cancargo) (1945)
Cessna T-50 Bobcat (UC-78B) (1943)
Consolidated 28 Catalina (PBY-5A) (1943)
Convair F-102A (1955), **F-102A** (1956)
Corben E Junior Ace (1976)
Curtiss Pusher (1912), **99 (XF15C)** (1945)
de Havilland DH 115 Vampire T.35 (1958), **DHC 2 Beaver (L-20A) (U-6A)** (1957)
Douglas A-24B Dauntless (1942), **A-26C Invader** (1943), **A-1D Skyraider (AD-4N)** (1952), **A-3B Skywarrior (A3D-2)** (1957), **A-4A Skyhawk (A4D-1)** (1957), **F-6A Skyray (F4D-1)** (1956), **F-6A Skyray (F4D-1)** (1956), **D-558-II** (1948)
Dyndiuk Sport (1934)
Fokker Universal (1928)
Gerath Hang Glider (1926)
Goodyear K-28 Puritan (ZNPK) (1946)
Granville A Gee Bee Sportster (1930)
Grumman G.36 Wildcat (FM-2) (1943), **G.50 Hellcat (F6F-5)** (1945), **G.64 Albatross (HU-16B) (SA-16A)** (1953), **G.64 Albatross (HU-16E) (UF-1G)** (1953), **G.79 Panther (F9F-2)** (1950)
Gyrodyne XRON-1 (1955), **QH-50C (DSN-3)** (1970)
Heath LNB-4 Parasol (1931)
Hiller UH12E (OH-23G) (1962)
Kaman K.16 (Grumman G.38 mod) (1942), **K.225** (1949), **K.240 Huskie (HTK-1) (TH-43E)** (1953), **K.600 Huskie (H-43A)** (1958), **K.600 Huskie (H-43B) (HH-43F)** (1960), **K.600 Huskie (HOK-1) (OH-43D)** (1954), **K.20 (H-2)** (1976)
Kawanishi N1K2-J Shiden-Kai (1944)
Keith Rider R-3 (1934)
Laird LCDW-300 Solution (1930)
Lazor-Rautenstrauch LR-1A (1976)
Lockheed 14 Super Electra (1939), **T-33A** (1952), **TV-2 (T-33A)** (1955), **F-94C Starfire** (1952), **F-104C Starfighter** (1956), **SP-2E Neptune (P2V-5)** (1954)
Macchi MC.200 Saetta (1942)
Martin 210 Mauler (AM-1) (1944), **RB-57A Canberra** (1952)
McDonnell F-4A Phantom (1959)
McMahon Ford Motor Airplane (1918)
Mead Rhon Ranger (1982)
National Ballooning AX-8 (?)
Navy Gas Training Balloon (?)
North American AT-6 Texan (1940), **P-15D Mustang** (mod) (1944), **B-25H Mitchell** (1943), **T-28C Trojan** (1955), **F-86A Sabre** (1948), **F-100A Super Sabre** (1952, 1953), **FJ-1 Fury** (1948)
Northrop F-89J Scorpion (1953)
Piasecki PV.3 Rescuer (HRP-1) (1947), **PV.18 Retriever (HUP-2)** (1952)
Piccard AX-1 (1972)
Piper J-3F Cub (1946), **J-3L Cub** (1946), **PA-18 Super Cub (L-18C)** (1952), **PA-38 Tomahawk** (1978)
Pratt-Read LNE-1 (1944)
Quickie Aircraft Quickie 1 (1982)
Raven S-40 Vulcoon (1963)
Rearwin 8135 Cloudster (1940)
Republic P-47D Thunderbolt (1945), **RF-84F Thunderflash** (1953), **F-105B Thunderchief** (1957)
Short SA.6 Sealand (1948)
Sikorsky S-39B (1930), **VS-44A (XPBS-1)** (1942), **VS-316 Hoverfly (R-4B)** (1943, 1944), **VS-316B Hoverfly II (R-6A)** (1944), **VS-316B Hoverfly II (R-6A)** (Doman mod) (1944), **S-51 Dragonfly (R-5)** (1952), **S-51 Dragonfly (H-5H)** (1952), **S-55 Chickasaw (UH-19D)** (1957), **S-58 Seabat (HUS-1L) (LH-34D)** (1958), **S-59** (1955), **S-60 Skycrane** (1959)
Stinson SM-1DX Detroiter (1928), **SR.5 Reliant** (1934), **10A Voyager** (1944)
Sud-East SE.210 Caravelle VIR (1961)
Ultralite 166 Mosquito (1980)
Vought XF4U-4 Corsair (1944), **F-8K Crusader (F8U-2)** (1960)
Vultee BT-13 Valiant (1940)
Zephyr ZAL (?)

The New England area has a rich aviation heritage and several notable manufacturers have had factories in the region. In 1959 the Connecticut Aeronautical Historical Association (CAHA) was formed and soon decided that a museum was the best way of preserving the material they had available. Work on a site at Bradley International Airport was soon under way and the Bradley Air Museum opened in May 1968.

The four-acre site initially had no buildings apart from the entrance office, so special displays were put on in some of the larger transport aircraft. These covered various aspects of the history of flight, often with particular reference to the region. A number of light aircraft, balloons etc had been collected and were placed in store pending the

The Corben Junior Ace first flew in the 1930s until a Federal ruling virtually killed the amateur-built aircraft movement of that time. This example was constructed in 1976 from original drawings

construction of a permanent exhibition hall. In the 1970s buildings were constructed and an indoor exhibition was staged.

Whatever the plans were for the museum, a few minutes in October 1979 changed everything. A tornado blew through the site and over a dozen aircraft were completely destroyed, many were seriously damaged and little escaped the force of the wind. The roof of the exhibition hall was lifted off and the outdoor area devastated. A giant transport – the four-engined Douglas C-133 weighing over 50 tons – was completely broken up, a rare Douglas Skyray delta wing naval fighter was lost for ever and a Boeing Fortress with a fifth engine mounted in the nose for test purposes was badly damaged.

Despite the devastation the CAHA was determined to open again. A temporary site was obtained and about 25 relatively undamaged aircraft were moved there. In June 1980 this new exhibition was opened full time. In addition much work was going on behind the scenes to acquire new aircraft for the museum. Airframes were collected from around the country and spares were sought to repair the less damaged aircraft. A new site on the other side of the airport was obtained and there are plans for its development.

Top
Only nine Gee Bee A biplanes were built before the Granville brothers turned their attention to air racing. This is the sole survivor, and dates from 1930

Above
The Burnelli CBY-3, with its lifting fuselage, rests in one of the storage compounds awaiting attention

The first stage, a large exhibition hall with room for about 40 aircraft and a shop and offices, opened in October 1981. The next stage will involve the restoration and assembly of a World War II hangar which is owned by the museum. A large workshop area will be constructed and a reconstruction made of an old time flying field. A display of the amphibious aircraft and the flying boats will be staged near a lake. A hangar typical of the inter-war period will be erected to house sporting aircraft from this golden era. When complete the museum, which adopted its present name in 1984, should be one of the most impressive anywhere. Only about 10 of the 56 acres (4 of the 23 ha) are developed and behind the main building is a line of aircraft awaiting their turn for restoration. A few of the larger aircraft are stored on the airfield itself and the museum has the use of several small storage buildings around the field. In the open air compounds the damage from the tornado can still be seen on some of the airframes.

The Russian Igor Sikorsky who emigrated to the US after World War I set up his company at Bridgeport in Connecticut and a special display honors his work. In Russia he built an unsuccessful helicopter in 1909 and during World War I became well known for his large four-engined aircraft. The 1920s and 30s saw the firm established as one of the leading suppliers of amphibians and flying boats to both civil and military customers. The museum has a number of products from the company on show and in store. The earliest is a 1930 S-39B. This distinctive amphibian, with its wing and single engine mounted on struts above the hull, was built in comparatively small numbers.

Undergoing restoration at the Sikorsky factory is a VS-44A flying boat. Three examples of this four-engined giant designed by Michael Gluhareff were built and were intended for the New York-Lisbon run. However, they were operated by American Overseas Airlines under a navy contract for the duration of the war. Post-war service included an abortive delivery flight to Peru. The boat was recovered by Dick Probert of Avalon Air Transport in 1957 and for several seasons flew to and from Catalina Island off the Californian coast. In 1968 the famous pilot Charles Blair bought it for use on his Virgin Island services operated by Antilles Air Boats. On his death in a flying accident the VS-44A was saved and taken temporarily to the Naval Aviation Museum at Pensacola in Florida. In 1982 it made the journey back to its birthplace and will be a most prestigious exhibit when completed. In 1939 Sikorsky flew his first successful helicopter and the company has turned exclusively to this form of aircraft. Nine helicopters including one modified by the Doman company are in the collection.

The Kaman Aircraft Corporation was founded in 1945 with headquarters in Bloomfield, Connecticut. The company developed the intermeshing rotor system which was first tried in Germany by Anton Flettner in 1939 on his Fl 265. This novel idea eliminated the need for a tail rotor to counteract torque. The K-125A appeared in 1947 and in the 1950s developments were delivered in quantity to all the branches of the services. The museum has five variants of this basic design plus the unique K-16B. The fuselage of a Grumman Goose was fitted with a short-span tilt wing on which were mounted two turboprop engines. The K-16B underwent tethered tests in the early 1960s but was never flown. In addition, the mock-up of the Sealite helicopter is on view.

The museum has a number of other interesting aircraft on its inventory. In one of the storage compounds is the Burnelli CBY-3 built in 1945 by the Canadian Car and Foundry Company. Vincent Burnelli conceived the idea of using a lifting fuselage on transport aircraft. His first aircraft using this concept flew in 1920 and several prototypes were built by a number of firms over the next 20 years. In 1936 the CCF obtained manufacturing rights to the CB-14 but never built the type and turned its attention to a larger variant, the CB-34. War work stopped this project and in 1943 an agreement between CCF and the Central American Airline TACA was drawn up for the construction of 20 CBY 3s. The prototype flew in July 1945 but the TACA contract had been canceled before this. This unique aircraft spent much of its life on trials and was chartered to a polar expedition in 1955 which was abandoned. The last flight of the CBY-3 took place in 1959 when it made the short hop from Beacon Field near Washington to Friendship Airport, Baltimore. The engineless hulk was saved by the museum in 1973.

The oldest surviving balloon in the US is in store: this is the 'Jupiter' built in 1886 by Silas Brooks. The Granville Brothers became well known for their odd-looking Gee Bee racers but before this they built a small number of sporting biplanes. Only nine were constructed and the sole survivor is the Sortster on view. Two classic racers from the 1930s are on view: Keith Rider's low-wing R-3 monoplane of 1934, the 'Marcoux-Bromberg Special', and the Laird Solution biplane which took part in the Cleveland 1930 races, winning the Thompson Trophy.

These are just a few of the highlights of this extensive collection of aircraft which spans a century of flight and has gathered types which have served in all roles. The CAHA has also shown what can be achieved by a voluntary organization in spite of a major disaster.

District of Columbia

NATIONAL AIR AND SPACE MUSEUM

Smithsonian Institution, Washington, DC 20560
Tel: 202-357-3133

Opening times: 10am-5pm daily; admission to the Garber facility is by appointment only
Location: in Washington Mall in the center of the city

Abrams Explorer (1937)
Aeronca C-2 (1928)
Aichi B7A1 Ryusei (1944), M6A1 Seiran (1943)
Akerman 1-1936 Tailless (c.1936)
Albatros D VA (1917)
Antonov An-2 (c.1952)
Applebay Zuni II (?)
Arado Ar 196A (1941), Ar 234B (1944)
Arlington Sisu 1A (1963)
Avro-Canada VZ-9V (1958)
Bachem Ba 349B-1 Natter (BP-20) (1945)
Baldwin Red Devil (1911)
Beck-Mahoney Sorceress
Bede BD-5 (c.1980)
Beech C17L Traveller (1938), D18S (1949), A35 Bonanza (1948)
Bell 26 Airacobra (P-39Q) (1944), 27 Airacomet (XP-59A) (1942), 30 (1944), 33 King Cobra (P-63A) (1942), 47J (VH-13J) (1957), 204 Iroquois (UH-1B) (1962), 206L Long Ranger (c.1980), Rocket Belt (c.1960), X-1 (1946), ATV (1954)
Bellanca CF (1924), 14-13 Crusaire Senior (1948)
Benoïst XII (1913)
Bensen B-6 (1954), B-8M (1967)
Berliner Helicopter (1923)
Blériot XI (1911)
Blohm & Voss Bv 155B (1945)
Boeing 67 Hawk (FB-5) (1926)
Boeing 235 (F4B-4) (1937), 247D (1933), 266 Pea Shooter (P-26A) (1933), 299 Fortress (B-17D) (1940), 299 Fortress (B-17G) (1944), 307 Stratoliner (1940), 345 Super Fortress (B-29) (1944), 367-80 (707) (1954)
Boeing-Stearman E75 Kaydet (N2S-5) (PT-130) (1944)
Bowlus Baby Albatross (1932)
Bowlus-Dupont 1-S-2100 Falcon (1934)
Bücker Bü 133C Jungmeister (c.1936), Bü 181B Bestmann (1940)
Burgess-Curtiss D (1909)
Caudron G-4 (1917)
Cessna 180 (c.1960), 305 Bird Dog (O-1A) (L-19A) (1951), 337 Skymaster (O-2A) (1967)
Cierva C.8L (Avro 617) (1928)
Consolidated 28 Catalina (PBY-5) (1943)
Convair XFY-1 (1954), XF2Y-1 Sea Dart (1953), 240 (1948)
Crowley Hydro Air Vehicles (?)
Culver TD2C-1 (1944)
Curtiss D (1912), E (1914), E A-1 (R) (1961), JN-4D Jenny (1917), N-9H (1917), NC-4 (1919), 28 (TS-1) (1921), 34C Gulfhawk 1 (F6C-1) (1934), 42A (R3C-2) (1925), 50 Robin J-1 (1935), 58 Sparrowhawk (F9C-2) (1932), 84 Helldiver (SB2C-5) (1944), 87 Warhawk (P-40E) (1941)
Curtiss-Wright CW-1 Junior (1931), CW-24 Ascender (XP-55) (1942), X-100 (1959)
Custer CCW-1 (1942)
Dassault Falcon 20 (1970)
de Havilland DH 4 (1918), DH 4 (R) (1968), DH 98 Mosquito B.35 (1945)
Delta Wing Mariah M-9 (c.1980), 162 (c.1980), Phoenix 6 (c.1980), Phoenix 6B (c.1980), Phoenix Streak 130 (c.1980), Phoenix Viper (c.1980)
DFS 108-14 Schulgleiter SG-38 (c.1942)
Dornier Do 335A-1 (1945)
Douglas DWC-2 (1924), M-2 (1927), DC-3 (1936), DC-3 (C-47A), (R4D-5) (1942), DC-7 (1956), SBD-6 Dauntless (1945), A-1E Skyraider (AD-5) (1951), A-4C Skyhawk (A4D-3) (1960), A-26B Invader (B-26B) (1944), XB-42A (1943), XB-43 (1944), D558-II Skyrocket (1950)
Ecker Flying Boat (1913)
Eipper-Formance Cumulus 20 (c.1982)
Ercoupe 415 (1941)
Fairchild 71 (1931), FC-2 (1929), M-62 Cornell (PT-19) (1943),
C-82A Packet (1944)
Farman Sport L (1923)
Felixstowe F.5L (1918)
Fieseler Fi 156 Storch (MS.500) (1944)
Fisher P-75A Eagle (1944)
Focke-Achgelis Fa 330A-1 Bachstelze (1942)
Focke-Wulf Fw 190D-9 (1944), Fw 190F-8 (1944), Ta 152H (?)
Fokker D VII (1918), F IV (T-2) (1921)
Ford 5-AT-B (1929)
Fowler Gage Tractor (1912)
Frankfort TG-1A (1942)
Franklin PS-2 Eaglet (1930)
Fulton FA-3 (1946)
Gallaudet Hydro Kite (1921)
Gates Learjet 23 (1965)
Goodyear GA-468 Inflatoplane (1956)
Gotha Go 229 (Horton Ho IX) (1945)
Granville Gee Bee Z (R) (?)
Grumman G.21 Goose (1938), G.22 Gulfhawk II (1936), G.36 Wildcat (FM-1) (1942), G.40 Avenger (TBF-1) (1943), G.50 Hellcat (F6F-3) (1944), G.58 Bearcat (F8F-2) (1946), G.89 Tracker (S2F-1) (US-2B) (1953), G.93 Cougar (F9F-6) (1952)
Halberstadt CL IV (1918)
Hawker Hurricane IIC (1944), P.1127 Kestrel FGA.1 (XV-6A) (1965)
Heinkel He 162A (1945), He 219A (1944)
Helio No.1 (1949)
Herrick HV2A Convertoplane (1935)
Hiller XH-44 (1944), Flying Platform (c.1952), HJ.1 (HOE-1) (1955), HJ.1 (YROE-1) (1955)
Hispano HA-200 Saeta (1962)
Horten Ho II (1934), Ho IIIF (1938), Ho IIIH (1938), Ho VI (1940), Ho IX (see Gotha Go 229) (1945)
Huff-Daland Duster (1925)
Hughes H-1 (1937)
Junkers Ju 388L (1944)
Kaman K.225 (XHOK-1) (1949)
Kawanishi N1K1 Kyofu (1943), N1K-2J Shiden Kai (1943)
Kawasaki Ki 45 Torvu (1944)
Kellett XO-60 (1942), XR-8 (1944)
Kyushu J7W1 Shinden (1944)
Langley Aerodrome A (1903), Aerodrome 5 (1896)
Lilienthal Standard (1894)
Lippisch DM 1 (1945)
Lockheed 5B Vega (1928), 5C Vega (1930), 8 Sirius (1929), 10E Electra (XC-35) (1936), 18-56 Lodestar (R50-5) (1940), P-38J Lightning (1942), XP-80 Shooting Star (1944), F-104A Starfighter (1955), XP2V-1 Neptune (1946), SP-2H Neptune (P2V-7) (c.1958), CL-475 (1959), U-2C (1956)
Loening OA-1A (1927)
Macchi MC.202 Folgore (1944)
McCready Gossamer Albatross (1978), Gossamer Condor (1976), Solar Challenger (c.1980)
McDonnell FH-1 Phantom (1946), F-4A Phantom II (1960), XHJH-1 Whirlaway (1947), XV-1 Convertiplane (XH-35) (1953), RF-101C Voodoo (1956)
Manta Pterodactyl (1979)
Martin 162A (⅜ scale test model) (1940), 162 Mariner (PBM-5A) (1945), 179 Marauder (B-26B) (1941), B-57B Canberra (1952), JV K-III Kitten (1920) WM Glider (1908)
Maupin Lanteri Black Diamond (1910)
Messerschmitt Bf 109G-6 (1944), Me 163 Komet (1945), Me 262A (1945), Me 410A-1 (1943)
Mignet HM-14 Pou-du-Ciel (1935)
Mitsubishi A6M5 Zero-Sen (1944), A6M7 Zero-Sen (1945), G4M3 (1944)
Monocoupe 70 (1929), 110 (1931)
Montgomery Santa Clara (1905), Evergreen (1911)
Mooney M.18 Mite (1946)
Nagler-Rolz 54 (1943)
Nakajima B6N2 Tenzan (1943), C6N-1S Saiun (1943), Kikka (1944), J1N1-S Gekko (1943), Ki 43-2 Hayabusha (1943), Ki 115 Tsurugi (1945)
NACA Rotorcraft (?)
NASA Paresev (?)
Naval Aircraft Factory TS-1 (1923), N3N-3 (1943)
Nelson BB-1 Dragonfly (c.1935)
Nieuport 12 (1915)
Noorduyn YC-64 Norseman (1941)
North American O-47A (1937), AT-6C Texan (SNJ-4) (1943), P-51C Mustang (1944), P-51D Mustang (1944), F-86A Sabre (1948), F-100D Super Sabre (1956), X-15A (1956), FJ-1 Fury (1948)
Northrop Alpha (1930), Gamma (1933), XP-56 (1942), P-61C Black Widow (1943), M2-F1 (1963), M2-F3 (1970), HL-10 (1966), N-1M (1940)
Olmstead Amphibian (1912)
Pentecost E III Hoppicopter (1945)
Pfalz D XII (1918)
Piasecki PV.2 (1943), PV.3 (XHRP-1) (1945)
Piper J-2 Cub (1938), J-3C Cub (1945), J-3C Cub (L-4B) (1942), PA-12 Super Cruiser (1947), PA-18 Super Cub (1955)
Pitcairn PA-5 Mailwing (1930), PCA-1 (1930), AC-35 (1940)
Pitts S-1S (1969)
Platt-LePage XR-1 (1942)
Princeton Air Scooter (?)
Quickie Aircraft Quickie (1983)
Republic P-47D Thunderbolt (1944), RC-3 Seabee (1947), XP-84 Thunderjet (1945), F-105D Thunderchief (1960)
Ryan NYP-III (1927), X-13 (1954), XV-5B (1962)
SAAB 29E (29B) (1954)
Schneider Grunau Baby II (DFS 108-49) (1940)
Schweizer SGS.2-22 (1960)
Shoemaker Biplane (1910)
Sikorsky S-43 (JRS-1) (1931), VS-316 Hoverfly (XR-4) (1941), VS-327 Dragonfly (S-51) (XR-5) (1943), S-58 Choctaw (CH-34C) (1955), S-58 Choctaw (VH-34C) (1957), S-58 Seahorse (UH-34D) (1961)
SPAD VII (?), XIII (1918), XVI (1917)
Sperry-Verville M-1 Messenger (1922)
Standard J-1 (1917)
Stanley Nomad (c.1930)
Stearman-Hammond Y (1935)
Stinson SR.10F Reliant (1939), V.76 Sentinel (L-5) (1942)
Stits SA-2 Skybaby (1952)
Stout Skycar (1931)
Supermarine 359 Spitfire VIII (1941)
Turner RT-14 (1936)
Vertol VZ-2 (1956)
Verville Sportsman (1931)
Voisin (1908), 8 (1916)
Vought V-173 (1942), OS2U-3 Kingfisher (1941), F4U-1D Corsair (1941), XF8U-1 Crusader (1955)
Vultee BT-13A Valiant (1941)
Waco Glider (1922), 9 (1927), UIC (1933), CG-4A Hadrian (1945)
Waterman Whatsit (1948), Aerobile (1958)
Weedhopper Ultralight (1982)
Westland Lysander III (1942)
Wiseman-Cooke (1911)
Wittman Buster (1930)
Wright Flyer (1903), Military Flyer (1909), EX Vin Fiz (1911)
Yakovlev Yak-18 (1940)
Yokosuka MXY7 Ohka 11 (1944), MXY7-K2 Ohka (1944), P1Y2 Ginga (1944)

Lindbergh's heroic aircraft, 'Spirit of St Louis' in its resting place at the National Air and Space Museum.

Above
A Fairchild FC-2, in the markings of the first aircraft to serve with Pan American-Grace Airways

Right
'Winnie Mae', the Lockheed Vega that Wiley Post used on many of his record-breaking flights

The impressive National Air and Space Museum (NASM), administered by the Smithsonian Institution, is the most visited museum in the USA. It is one of the three major aircraft collections in the world, yet only about a quarter of the museum's aircraft can be seen there: the others are at the Paul E. Garber Facility in the Maryland suburbs of the city or on loan to other museums.

The Smithsonian started to collect aeronautical material in 1876 when a group of Chinese kites was acquired by the then Secretary, Samuel P. Langley, who from 1887 to 1903 flew a number of unmanned 'aerodromes'. In 1920 a temporary World War I building was erected to add to the space in the Arts and Industries Building. Aircraft were gathered steadily but the space was limited and the vast majority of the collection remained in store. Congress officially established the National Air Museum in 1946 and the Space part was added 20 years later. Such a major museum badly needed a prestigious home and the dream was realized when in July 1976 the new NASM building was opened.

The aircraft are shown in 15 major galleries, each devoted to a particular theme. On entering the museum the visitor is immediately confronted by the aeroplane that started it all. The original Wright Flyer with its fragile construction

Right
The fuselage of 'Enola Gay', the Boeing B-29 Superfortress which dropped the first atomic bomb on Hiroshima, awaits assembly at Silver Hill

Below
Volunteers at TWA restored this superb Northrop Alpha. The Alpha used to serve the airline in the early 1930s

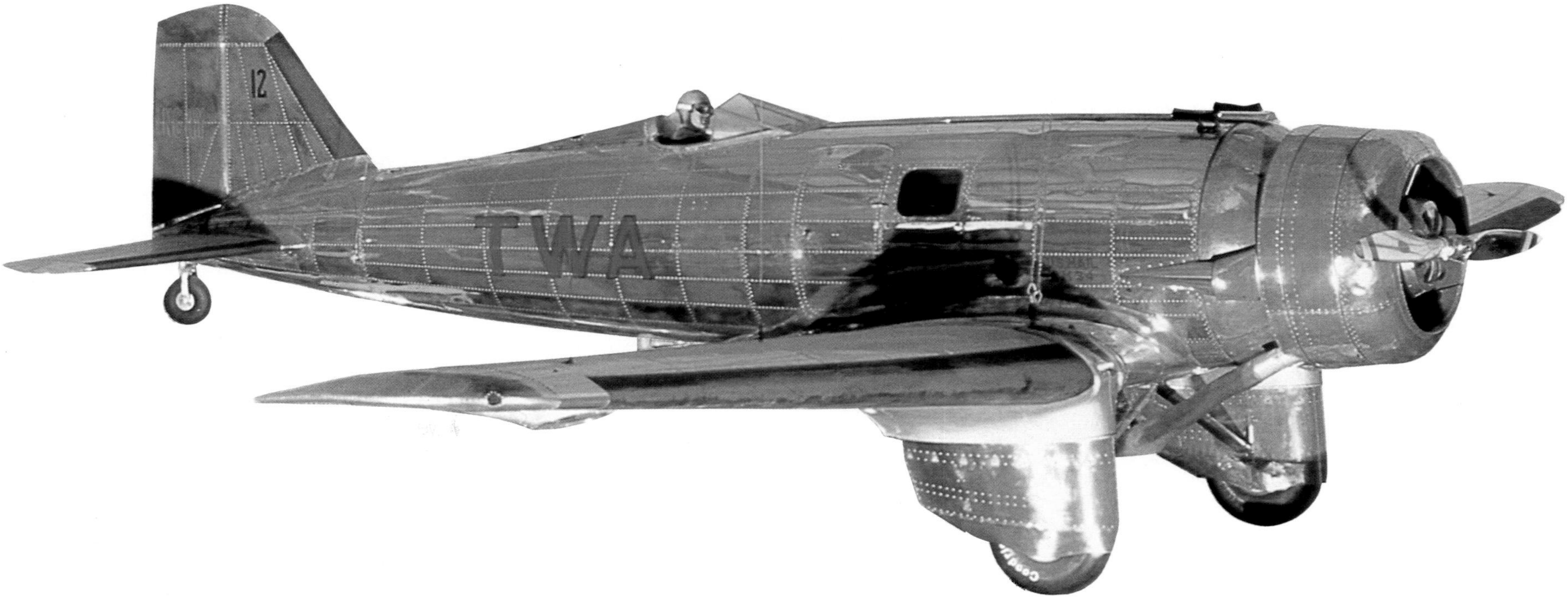

occupies the place of honor. This biplane made its first tentative leap into the air on December 17, 1903 when Orville Wright flew for a distance of 100 feet (30 meters) and was aloft for 12 seconds. Later in the day his brother Wilbur flew 852 feet (260 meters) in 59 seconds. From these modest beginnings have evolved the military and civil aircraft of today. Later on this historic day the Flyer was damaged and taken to Dayton, Ohio where it remained until 1916. It was repaired and placed on exhibition at the Massachusetts Institute of Technology. In 1928 the Wright was loaned to the Science Museum in London where it remained for 20 years, spending World War II stored in a London subway. Other aircraft in this place of honor include the Ryan NYP III in which Charles Lindbergh made the first solo transatlantic crossing. The Ryan company modified the airframe of an M-2 monoplane for the epic flight from New York to Paris which was accomplished in 33½ hours in May 1927. The 'Spirit of St Louis' was shipped home and then went on a triumphal tour of the US and later on another through Central America. It made its last flight from St Louis to Washington in April 1928 when Lindbergh presented it to the Smithsonian. The three other aircraft here are Langley's

This 1927 Waco 9 is on show in the Paul Garber Facility at Silver Hill. The aircraft was acquired for the museum in the mid-1960s

fifth aerodrome which in May 1896 made the first successful flight of any engine-driven heavier-than-air machine, the Bell X 1 in which in October 1947 Captain Charles E Yeager became the first to exceed the speed of sound and the North American X-15A which became the first manned aircraft to exceed Mach 6. The X-15A has flown higher and faster than any other aircraft, heights of 354,000 feet (108,000 meters) and speeds over 4500 mph (7200 km/h) having been reached.

One of the most impressive galleries is the Air Transportation Hall where eight complete aircraft span 60 years of passenger and freight flying. From the pioneering days of flying the mail across the USA are a Douglas M-2 used by Western Air Express in the 1920s and a Pitcairn PA-5 which was once the personal mount of Eddie Rickenbacker. The fast Northrop Alpha which in 1930 provided a comfortable cabin for the passengers but had the pilot in an open cockpit in some ways represented a transition in airliner design. The magnificent example on show was restored by TWA in the 1970s.

Two types which revolutionized travel in the 1930s can be seen in the colors of two of America's most famous airlines. The Boeing 247 was flown to third place in the 1934 MacRobertson air race from England to Australia and has its racing colors on one side and the markings of United Air Lines on the other. The Douglas DC-3 is one of the all-time favorite transports and many remain in service after almost half a century. The aircraft on show was delivered to Eastern Air Lines in late 1937 and in the next 25 years flew over 56,000 hours.

The development of the helicopter and autogyro is portrayed in the Vertical Flight Gallery and there are others devoted to the two world wars, all with a variety of aircraft on show. The Pioneers of Flight area contains several notable machines. One of the Douglas World Cruisers which made the first round-the-world flight in 1924, the Curtiss R3C-2 in which James Doolittle won the 1925 Schneider Trophy and the Lockheed Vega in which Amelia Earhart was the first woman to make a non-stop solo flight across the Atlantic are three of the seven aircraft here. There is also the Wright EX 'Vin Fiz' in which C P Rogers made the first flight across the US continent in 1911. At the end of the 12-week journey the only original parts remaining were the rudder and two wing struts, everything else having been replaced at least once.

There is just one aircraft in the Flight Technology Gallery, the Hughes H-1 racer. In 1935 the eccentric Howard Hughes set a world speed record of 352.322 mph (566.991 km/h) in it and two years later a non-stop transcontinental record from Los Angeles to New York at 332 mph (534 km/h). The H-1 was then stored in the Hughes factory at Culver City before being installed in the museum by Hughes' staff.

These are just a few of the highlights of a truly magnificent exhibition. A high standard of restoration is evident on all the exhibits, the majority of which received attention at the Garber facility at Silver Hill. In recent years much work has been put in at Silver Hill and it is now almost a museum in its own right.

Paul E Garber joined the Smithsonian Institution in 1920 and was ultimately responsible for acquiring a large portion of the aircraft now in the collection. It was Garber who suggested to the Institution that they should ask Lindbergh for his 'Spirit of St Louis'. After World War II General Hap Arnold was determined to preserve an example of every wartime aircraft from both sides for a national air museum. Hundreds of aircraft were earmarked for this impossibly ambitious scheme. Many were stored in a former aircraft factory at Park Ridge in Chicago where they remained until the Korean War when the plant was needed for aircraft production. The Smithsonian had to move its stock around the airfield resulting in loss and damage. Garber and his staff worked frantically to find a new home for their treasures. A portion of swamp land at Silver Hill was acquired and the job of moving the aircraft began. Some were crated and others dismantled and moved on flat trucks. A few had to be scrapped as there was a shortage of time, space and money. The whole move took about three years and in the meantime a few temporary buildings and some roads appeared on the Silver Hill site.

A large number of aircraft were left exposed to the elements and in the late 1960s a series of press articles took the NASM and the US Government to task for allowing these historic aircraft to molder in what was little more than a glorified junk yard. Plans for a purpose-built museum in Washington were passed and more buildings were put up at Silver Hill and a major restoration program started to get the aircraft ready for the new building. As aircraft moved to Washington more space became available and aircraft could be removed from their crates and taken indoors. When the Washington exhibition was ready the then Director of the NASM, astronaut Mike Collins, issued the directive 'Clean up Silver Hill'. Within three months this had been achieved – all the aircraft bar two were inside and the old crates had been removed. Many of the aircraft in store would never go to the main museum so it was decided to open Silver Hill as a 'no frills' museum and in less than six months in January 1977 the first building was ready. In 1980 the complex was named after Paul Garber who had done so much to ensure that the NASM had a great collection of aircraft. Now six buildings at Silver Hill are open to the public

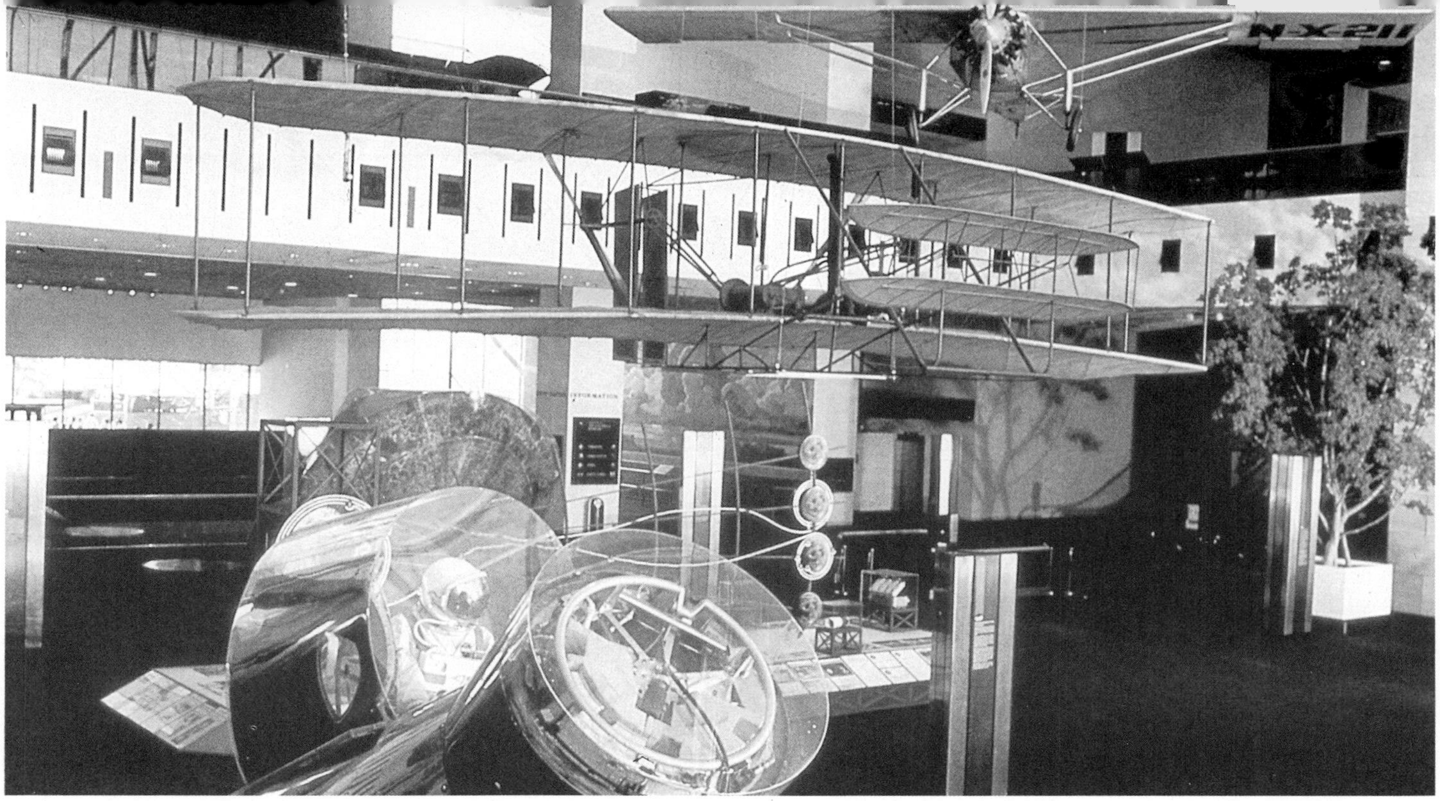

The aircraft that started it all: the famous Wright Flyer of 1903, occupying pride of place at the entrance to the museum

A view of the transport hall, showing an ex-Eastern Airlines Douglas DC-3 and the ex-United Airlines Boeing 247D, which was third in the 1934 MacRobertson Race

with 140 aircraft on show. Only about 40 remain in store – some 60 aircraft are still out on loan but many have recently returned as the facilities improve.

A highlight of the Garber tour is a visit to the restoration area. Usually about half a dozen aircraft are here in various stages of rebuild. Any new parts are clearly marked as such so that future historians and restorers will know exactly what is original. Much research goes into finding out the original color scheme or one representative of the period. Commendably it is the policy of the museum not to paint aircraft to represent an example flown by a famous aviator, which can be misleading.

There are no themes in the Garber displays – as aircraft are restored or assembled they are found a space and exhibited. Nevertheless this has enabled many historic aircraft to be seen. The famous Boeing B-29 Superfortress 'Enola Gay' which dropped the first atom bomb on Japan is close to a Japanese Ohka suicide aircraft. In the same building is a German Arado 234 jet bomber, the experiemental Berliner Helicopter of 1924, a SPAD XIII fighter from World War I contrasting with a World War II Focke-Wulf 190. The whole period of aviation history is covered in this fascinating display. Probably the most comprehensive exhibition of Japanese World War II aircraft anywhere in the world is gathered in the buildings. Six aircraft are currently on show with another eight in the storage buildings, many the only remaining examples of their type. A sad reminder of the 1950s move is the forward fuselage of a Mitsubishi G4M3 'Betty' bomber, which is all that is left of this twin-engined aircraft: the rest, sadly, was cut up for scrap in Chicago. Perhaps one day an expedition could be mounted to the Pacific Islands to recover the missing parts from the many wrecks still in the inhospitable jungles.

The collection of unconventional aircraft is also impressive with such machines as the Custer Channel Wing, the Vought V-173 affectionately known as the Flying Pancake, the tiny Martin Kitten biplane of 1917 and many others.

There are also long-term plans to construct a new museum building at Dulles Airport to the west of Washington. The NASM has emerged as one of the major exhibitors of aircraft in the world with now the vast majority of its aircraft on show. In addition to the aircraft the main museum has many historical and technical displays and is also a major research center for the historian.

Florida

NAVAL AVIATION MUSEUM

Naval Air Station, Pensacola, Florida 32508
Tel: 904-452-3543

Opening times: 9am-5pm daily
Location: in the southwestern suburbs of the city off Route 292

Beech D17S (GB-2) (UC-43) (?), **C18S (RC-45J) (JRB-1)** (1940), **45 Mentor (T-34B)** (1954), **45 Mentor (YT-34C) (T-34B)** (1954)
Bell 47G Sioux (HTL-6) (TH-13M) (1955), **206 (TH-57A) (HUH-57A)** (1968)
Boeing-Stearman A75 Kaydet (PT-17) (1941)
Cessna 180F (1955), **305 Bird Dog (L-19A) (O-1A)** (1951)
Consolidated N2Y-1 (Fleet 1) (1921), **28 Catalina (PBY-5)** (1943), **29 Coronado (PB2Y-3) (PB2Y-5)** (1943), **32 Privateer (PB4Y-2)** (1944)
Convair 340 (R4Y-1) (1953)
Curtiss E A-1 (R) (?), **N-9H** (1917), **JN-4D Jenny** (1916), **25 Seagull (MF)** (1918), **12 (NC-4)** (1918), **48 Fledgling (N2C-2)** (1929), **84 Helldiver (SB2C-5)** (1944)
Curtiss-Wright CW-22 Falcon (SNC-1) (1942)
Douglas DC-3 (C-47A) (R4D-5) (1941), **DC-3 (C-117D) (R4D-8)** (1942), **DC-4 (R5D-3) (C-54D)** (1941), **DC-6A (R6D-1)** (1952), **A-24A Dauntless** (1941), **EA-1F Skyraider (AD-5Q)** (1951), **A-1H Skyraider (AD-6)** (1952), **A-3A Skywarrior (A3D-1)** (1956), **A-4A Skyhawk (A4D-1)** (1954), **A-4B Skyhawk (A4D-2)** (1954), **A-4C Skyhawk (A4D-2N)** (1954), **A-4L Skyhawk (A4D-2N) (A-4C)** (1954), **F-10A Skynight (XF3D-1)** (1951), **F-6A Skyray (F4D-1)** (1951), **D-558-I Skystreak** (1945)
Fairchild F.24W (GK-1) (1941)
Ford 4-AT-B (1926)
Grumman G.15 Duck (J2F-6) (1943), **G.23** (1931), **G.36 Wildcat (FM-2)** (1944), **G.40 Avenger (TBM-3E)** (1944), **G.50 Hellcat (F6F-5)** (1944), **G.44 Widgeon (J4F-1)** (1943), **G.51 Tigercat (F7F-3)** (1945), **G.58 Bearcat (F8F-2)** (1944), **G.64 Albatross (SA-16E) (HU-16E) (UF-2G)** (1947), **G.79 Panther (F9F-2)** (1947), **G.82 Guardian (AF-2S)** (1949), **G.93 Cougar (F9F-8) (F-9J)** (1947), **G.93 Cougar (F9F-8T) (TF-9J)** (1947), **G.96 Trader (TF-1) (C-1A)** (1955), **G.98 Tiger (F11F-1) (F-11A)** (1958), **G.117 Tracer (WF-2) (E-1B)** (1952), **G.121 Tracker (S2F-3) (S-2E)** (1952)
Gyrodyne YRON-1 (1959)
Hiller UH12A (HTE-1) (1952)
Howard DGA.15 (GH-3) (1943)
Kaman K.600 Huskie (HOK-1) (1951)
Lockheed 37 Ventura (PV-1) (1943), **37 Ventura (PV-2)** (1944), **TO-1 Shooting Star (F-80C)** (1948), **TV-2 (T-33A)** (1948), **XP2V-1 Neptune** (1946), **SP-2H Neptune (P2V-7)** (1956), **1049 Super Constellation (EC-121K) (WV-2)** (1952)
McDonnell FH-1 Phantom (1946), **F2H-2 Banshee** (1947), **F-2D Banshee (F2H-4)** (1954), **F-3B Demon (F3H-2)** (1954), **F-4N Phantom (F-4B)** (1961)
Martin 210 Mauler (AM-1) (1946), **235 Marlin (P5M-2S) (SP-5B)** (1948)
Naval Aircraft Factory TS-1 (1921), **N3N-3** (1940), **N3N-3** (1941)
New Standard D-29 (NT-1) (1931)
North American AT-6D Texan (SNJ-5) (1942), **AT-6F Texan (SNJ-6)** (1949), **T-28C Trojan** (1952), **T-2B Buckeye** (1966), **FJ-1 Fury** (1948), **FJ-2 Fury** (1950), **FJ-4 Fury** (1954), **AJ-2 Savage** (1953), **RA-5C Vigilante** (1963)
Northrop YF-17A (1972)
Piasecki PV.3 Rescuer (HRP-1) (1947), **PV.14 (XHJP-1)** (1948), **PV.17 Rescuer (HRP-2)** (1948), **PV.18 Retriever (HUP-3)** (1948)
Piper J-3C Cub (1942)
Pratt-Read LNE-1 (1942)
Ryan ST.3KR Recruit (PT-22) (1942)
Schweizer SGS.2-8 (LNS-1) (1942)
Sikorsky VS-316 Hoverfly (R-4B) (HNS-1) (1945), **S-51 Dragonfly (HO3S-1)** (1946), **S-55 Chickasaw (CH-19)** (1951), **S-55 Chickasaw (HRS-3) (CH-19E)** (1953), **S-56 Mojave (HR2S-1) (CH-37C)** (1957), **S-58 Seahorse (HUS-1) (UH-34D)** (1954)
Stinson V.76 Sentinel (L-5) (OY-1) (1945)
Thomas Morse S-4C (1918)
Timm PT.175K Tutor (N2T-1) (1943)
Vought OS2U-3 Kingfisher (1941), **FG-1D Corsair** (1943), **F-8A Crusader (F8U-1)** (1955), **RF-8G Crusader (F8U-1P)** (1958)
Vultee SNV-1 Valiant (1941)

The Martin Marlin was the last flying boat to be used operationally by the US Navy

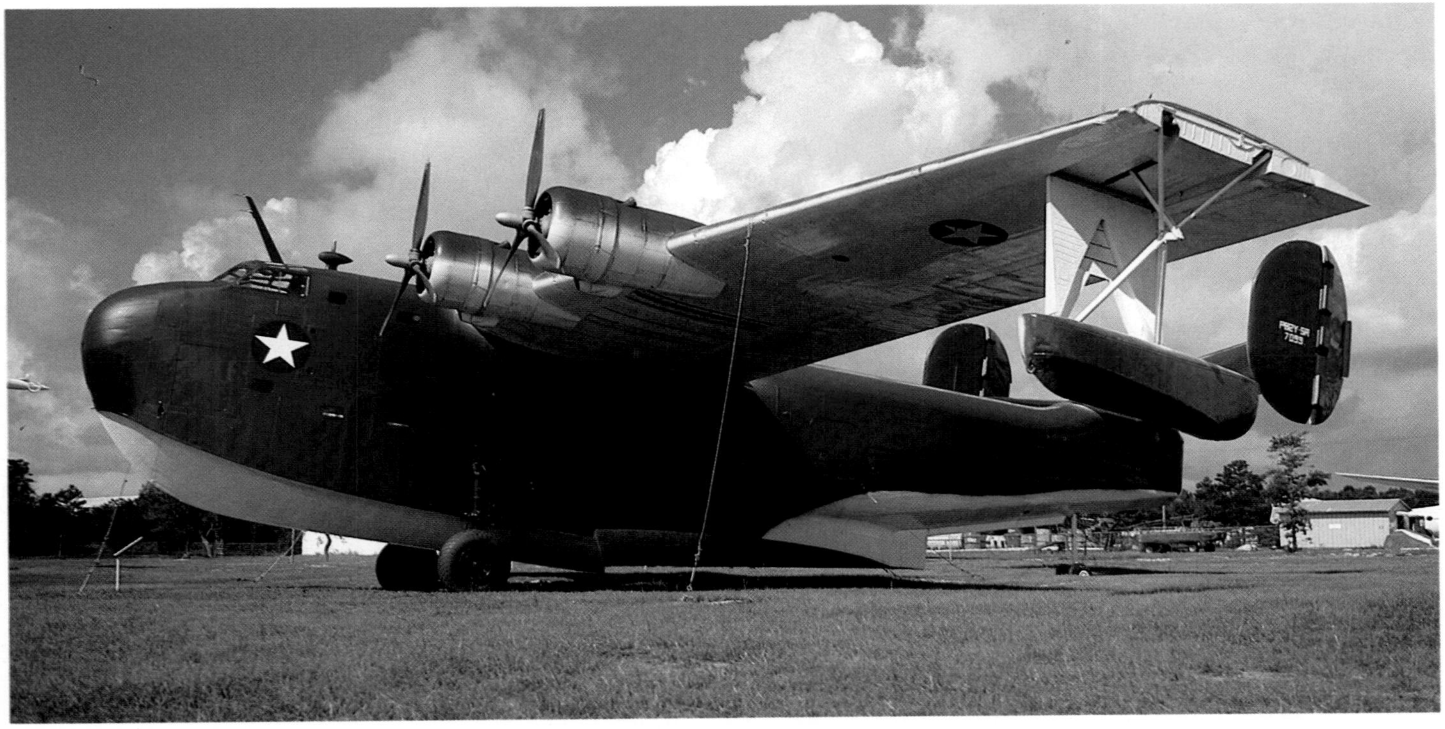

Fifty-five of the large Sikorsky HR2S helicopters were used by the US Navy

The last surviving Consolidated Coronado flying boat is parked behind the main museum building

The Douglas Dauntless dive bomber, designed by Ed Heinemann, proved itself to be an outstanding aircraft and sank more tonnage than any other weapon in the Pacific War

The United States Navy has a long tradition in aviation, having operated its first aircraft in 1911. Since then with both shore- and carrier-based aircraft the navy has been involved in all the United States' major conflicts.

Plans for a naval aviation museum first came about in 1961 when a small building was made available at the Pensacola naval air station. The museum opened in December 1962 with a small number of aircraft and items on view. The collection grew rapidly so that within five years only about a quarter of the aircraft could be displayed and in December 1966 the Naval Aviation Museum Association was set up to raise funds for a new museum building. The initial plans for a 150,000 square foot (14,000 square metre) exhibition area to be surrounded by offices were modified in the economic climate of the late 1960s. Ground was broken for the first stage of the building in November 1972 and with 60,000 square feet (5,500 square metres) of display space it opened on April 13, 1975. The building has been designed so that it can easily be extended to bring it up to the original proposal.

In addition to the 100 or so aircraft in the collection the museum has displays which trace the development of the US Navy and its aircraft as a fighting force. All the naval and marine fliers who have been awarded the Congressional Medal of Honor and all prisoners of war expatriated from Vietnam are mentioned. In World War II one of the outstanding actions by navy aircraft was the attack by Torpedo Squadron 8 on the Japanese fleet at Midway without fighter support, in which the Japanese lost four carriers and 375 aircraft. There is a large-scale, detailed, clear perspex model of a World War II carrier and models, engines, components, paintings, uniforms etc. commemorating this famous force.

The building has about 25 aircraft on show and about double that number in the large park behind the building. At the rear of this is a small workshop where a team of craftsmen are preparing new exhibits. The remainder of the aircraft are stored around the base and are not normally accessible to the public.

A faithful replica of the first aircraft to be operated by the navy, a Curtiss A-1 in which Glenn Curtiss himself taught Lt Theodore G Ellyson to fly, is on display. The Curtiss company was one of the major suppliers of navy aircraft in the early days and it is well represented in the display. The JN series of biplanes, better known as the Jenny, was one of the outstanding trainers of the time and was later the mount of many of the ex-military fliers who tried to earn their living barnstorming around the country in the 1920s. The JN came about by merging the better features of the Model J and the Model N. The first JN flew in 1914 and over 5000 were built in the US with another 1200-plus in Canada. The Jenny on show was acquired from private enthusiasts in New Orleans. The popularity of the JN meant that the J series was dropped but development of the N continued, and the only known survivor, an N-9H built by the Burgess Company at Marblehead, Massachusetts, is also on show. This, like a number of other aircraft, is on loan from the National Air and Space Museum (NASM) in Washington.

Curtiss was one of the first producers of flying boats and two examples of his designs may be seen. The superb skills of the woodworkers who made the hulls is evident and should be admired by all. The MF was a two-seat training boat of which 22 were built by Curtiss at Garden City and another 80 by the Naval Aircraft Factory at Philadelphia. Only three are known to survive and the example on show is an NAF-built aircraft which saw some civil use after World War I.

Dominating the indoor exhibition is a giant NC-4 flying boat. The NC was designed as a joint navy/Curtiss venture as a boat which could be delivered by air from the US to

This Airborne Early Warning version of the Lockheed Super Constellation, complete with giant radomes, joined the museum in 1971

France. There was concern about the number of aircraft lost as ships were sunk on the Atlantic run and many aircraft went down with them. The aircraft were not ready by the time of the Armistice but for prestige the navy decided to make a transatlantic flight. Three NCs were prepared and left Rockaway in New Jersey on May 8, 1919. Two were forced down with engine problems but NC-4 completed the flight when it landed off Plymouth on May 31. This epic journey via Newfoundland, the Azores, Ponta Delgada, Lisbon, and Ferrol was the first flight across the Atlantic.

The hull of this aircraft was on show for years in the Smithsonian Institution in Washington and the boat was completely rebuilt for the fiftieth anniversary of its epic flight. The NC-4 was loaned to the museum by the NASM in the mid-1970s. Around the boat is an exhibition telling the story of the crossing. The TS-1 fighter was designed by the navy around the then new Lawrence J-1 radical and Curtiss won the contract to build the production model. Only 28 were built and the last survivor is in the workshops nearing the end of a complete rebuild.

Another manufacturer whose name is synonymous with naval aircraft is Grumman. The Long Island company has supplied fighters to the US Navy since 1931. The XFF-1 was the first fighter with a retractable undercarriage (landing gear) to be put into production. The basic design of this chubby biplane was developed steadily and the Canadian Car Foundry built the FF-1 for export. One was supplied to Nicaragua and was scrapped at Managua in 1942. J R Sirmons of Tulsa found the airframe 20 years later, rebuilt it to flying condition and it made the journey to the US in 1966. Improvisations in the reconstruction included fitting a Pratt and Whitney engine in place of the original Wright and making a new tailplane spar from a Piper Cub wing spar. Grumman bought this historic machine and painted it in the colors of an FF-1 from the famous VF-5B 'The Red Rippers' Squadron which was based on the USS *Lexington* from 1933-5.

Examples of other famous Grumman types such as the amphibious Duck, the classic Wildcat and Hellcat piston fighters which were so effective in World War II, the mighty Bearcat and twin-engined Tigercat, jet fighters such as the Panther, Cougar and Tiger and twin-piston types including the Albatross, Widgeon, Trader, Tracer and Tracker complete the collection from this famous firm.

The sight of large flying boats is always evocative and in addition to the Curtiss types there are several other examples of this now almost extinct breed. A Catalina on loan from the NASM is inside and outside are the last known examples of a Consolidated Coronado and a Martin Marlin. The prototype Coronado first flew in 1937 and over 200 were built. The Marlin which appeared in 1948 was the last flying boat type to serve with the US navy and was finally withdrawn in November 1967 when one landed in San Diego Bay, where 55 years previously Glenn Curtiss had lifted his first flying boat off the water.

This excellent collection has many other significant aircraft including the Douglas Skystreak which set a world speed record in 1947 and the whole range of modern types is being acquired. By a successful trading policy the museum has managed to obtain from private owners types missing from its listings and also a number of aircraft have been acquired on loan. It is to be hoped that the display space can be extended so that these rare machines can emerge from storage.

WEEKS AIR MUSEUM

14710 SW 128th Street, Miami, Florida 33186

Opening times: 10am-5pm Saturday-Sunday
Location: the airfield is in the southwestern suburbs of the city

Beech B18S (SNB-5) (TC-45J) (1942)
Blériot XI (R) (1967)
Boeing 100 (1934), **299 Fortress (B-17G)** (1944), **345 Super Fortress (B-29)** (1945)
CASA 2.111 (He 111H) (1951)
Curtiss Pusher (R) (1976), **17 Oriole** (1920), **87 Warhawk (P-40N)** (1944)
Curtiss-Wright CW-1 Junior (1930)
de Havilland DH 4 (c.1921), **DH 82C Tiger Moth** (1941), **DH 98 Mosquito TT.35 (B.35)** (1944)
Douglas B-23 Dragon (1939)
Fokker Dr I (R) (1958)
Grumman G.15 Duck (J2F-6) (1943, 1945), **G.40 Avenger (TBM-3E)** (1944), **G.50 Hellcat (F6F-3)** (1944)
Hawker Tempest II (1943), **Sea Fury T.20** (1948)
Lockheed P-38L Lightning (1944)
McCulloch J-2 (1971)
Messerschmitt Bf 108 Taifun (1942)
Morane-Saulnier A1 (1917)
North American B-25N Mitchell (1944), **T-6J Texan (Harvard 4)** (1945), **AT-6D Texan (SNJ-5)** (1943), **AT-6F Texan** (1944), **P-51A Mustang** (1943), **P-51B Mustang** (1943), **P-51K Mustang** (1944)
Orenco F (1917)
Sopwith F.1 Camel (R) (1974)
SPAD VII (1916)
Stampe SV.4C (1945)
Standard J-1 (1917)
Stephens Super Akro (?)
Travel Air 2000 (1927)
Vought F4U-1 Corsair (FG-1D) (1943)
Vultee V.74 Vigilant (0-49) (L-1) (1941)
Weeks S-1W (?), **SW-1S Solution** (?)
Yakovlev Yak-11 (LET C-11) (1952)

The year 1986 saw the opening in March of a major private collection, initially based at Tamiami airport. Assembled by aerobatic pilot Kermit Weeks, the museum will display a wide range of types. Seemingly no expense has been spared to gather aircraft from all over the US, and also three from the UK. Kermit has steadily been collecting warbirds in the last few years and several rare types were acquired. His collection now contains some 50 aircraft.

A star of the collection is one of the few Grumman Ducks left in flying condition, which has been a regular visitor to shows in the region. Now the museum has three of these ungainly amphibians, one of which achieved star status in the film 'Murphy's War'. The other two Ducks came from the now defunct Movieland of the Air museum in California. This collection, set up by Paul Mantz and Frank Tallman, supplied aircraft for many Hollywood epics, and the whole collection was offered for sale in early 1985. Kermit bought around 20 aircraft from Frank Tallman and these include some genuine aircraft and some replicas from the early period.

One now rare biplane is a Boeing 100 which was used by the company as a demonstrator before it went to their technical school. Paul Mantz bought the aircraft and at one time he had two on his movie fleet – the other is now flying at its home of Seattle.

The collection has one of the widest ranges of World War II aircraft in private hands, including a number of multi-engined bombers. One of the two Boeing Superfortresses in flying order will soon make the journey to Florida from northern California to join its older brother, a B-17 Fortress. One of the small number of Douglas Dragons surviving from the 38 built will soon be joined by another twin-engined bomber, a Spanish-built Heinkel He 111 which was purchased in the UK. Fighters include three versions of the great North American Mustang and a Hawker Tempest bought at one of the Duxford auctions. A de Havilland Mosquito bought in the famous Strathallan auction in 1981 has undergone a long rebuild in the hands of the expert Booker-based restorers Personal Plane Services, and in 1986 it made the long journey to Florida.

One of three Grumman Ducks owned by the Weeks Air Museum: this example of the amphibian craft is in flying condition

Georgia

ROBINS AIR FORCE BASE MUSEUM OF AVIATION

PO Box 2469, Warner Robins, Georgia 31099
Tel: 912-926-6870

Opening times: 10am-5pm Tuesday-Sunday
Location: at the southern side of the base on Highway 247 about 17 miles (27 km) south of Macon

Beech E18s (1957), **45 Mentor (T-34B)** (1952)
Bell 47J (UH-13P) (HUL-1) (1957)
Bensen B-8M (c.1965)
Boeing 345 Superfortress (B-29A) (1944), **464 Stratofortress (B-52D)** (1955)
Boeing-Stearman A75 Kaydet (PT-17) (1942)
Cessna 310M (L-27B) (1960)
Convair 240 (T-29A) (1949), **F-102A** (1957)
Douglas DC-3 (C-47B) (R4D-6) (1943), **DC3 (C-47B) (C-47J) (R4D-6)** (1943), **DC-4 (C-54G)** (1945), **DC-6A (DC-6B)** (1956), **C-124C Globemaster** (1951), **WB-66D Destroyer** (1955)
Fairchild C-119C Flying Boxcar (1951), **C-123K Provider (C-123B)** (1954)
Grumman G.64 Albatross (HU-16B) (SA-16B) (1951)
Gyrodyne QH-50 (1971)
Lockheed F-80C Shooting Star (1945), **T-33A** (1952), **P-2H Neptune (P2V-7)** (1957), **1329 Jet Star (VC-140B)** (1961)
McDonnell F-101F Voodoo (1958)
Martin RB-57A Canberra (1952)
North American T-6G Texan (1949), **T-28C Trojan** (1952), **F-86H Sabre** (1953), **F-100C Super Sabre** (1954), **T-39A Sabreliner** (1962), **T-39B Sabreliner** (1963)
Northrop F-89D Scorpion (1953)
Republic F-84E Thunderjet (1951), **RF-84F Thunderflash** (1952), **F-105G Thunderchief (F-105F)** (1962)
Sikorsky S.55 Chickasaw (H-19) (1955), **S.58 Seabat (HH-34J) (HSS-1N)** (1958)
Vertol V.42 Shawnee (CH-21B) (1952)

The classic North American Texan trainer: this one served at air force training schools in five US states

Describing itself as the 'fastest growing aviation museum in the southeastern US', the Robins Air Force Museum of Aviation is an excellent example of what can be achieved with careful planning and a dedicated group of volunteers. The first phase of the exhibition opened on November 9, 1984 with a well-thought out display covering a number of topics beginning with the local history and construction of the base, which opened in 1942. Also featured are the work of women in repairing and modifying aircraft during World War II, the work of Strategic Air Command and the various roles of modern transport aircraft and avionics. Visitors can try their hand at operating the first bombing/navigation computer used by the air force. This vast piece of equipment which takes up almost one room of the display also shows how much electronics has developed in the last few years. A display of armaments also shows the vast strides made in this field.

The only Georgian 'Ace' of both World Wars I and II was Frank 'Monk' Hunter who rose to the rank of General. His personal mementos and details of his career are displayed in a special exhibition. Memorabilia from the Luftwaffe also figure prominently.

A Boeing B-29 Superfortress, recovered and restored at the Robins museum after lying unused for many years at the Aberdeen Proving Grounds in Maryland

The indoor display is housed in single story buildings that have been arranged in rectangular form. Phase Two, scheduled for 1987, consists of a vast increase in the exhibition area, a research centre and a restaurant. By 1992 it is hoped that 70,000 square feet (6500 square meters) of hangarage will have been constructed to house the rapidly increasing number of aircraft which are arriving at the musuem. The aircraft are now shown in a pleasantly landscaped area behind the museum building. Around 20 from the collection are on view in a restored condition, while in the adjoining area many others await their turn. With an active airfield nearby, aircraft can be flown in for display. One of the units based at Robins has as its task the recovery of crashed and battle-damaged aircraft. The members of the unit always need training exercises and they have helped in the move of many aircraft for the museum. The museum has scoured the US for its aircraft, acquiring a number from the former static display at the Confederate Air Force base at Harlingen.

The star of the aircraft exhibit is probably a Boeing B-29 Superfortress. This four-engined bomber was recovered from the Aberdeen Proving Grounds in Maryland after many years on the ranges. The museum has restored it to immaculate condition. Another aircraft from Aberdeen was a Northrop Scorpion fighter. The type was the first to be specifically designed for the all-weather role and this massive twin-jet first flew in 1948. The Scorpions bears the colors of its last unit, the famous 'Happy Hooligans' – the 119th Fighter Group of the North Dakota Air National Guard, who used it from 1958 to 1966.

The museum displays mainly aircraft from the period after World War II, and these include fighters, bombers, transports, trainers, helicopters and rescue types. The display presents both air force and navy aircraft of the modern period.

Judging by the progress made since its formation this museum should develop into one of the most significant in the US.

Iowa

AIRPOWER MUSEUM

Antique Airfield, Route 2, Box 172, Ottumwa, Iowa 52501
Tel: 515-938-2773

Opening times: 9am-5pm Monday-Friday, 10am-5pm Saturday, 1pm-5pm Sunday
Location: about 12 miles (19 km) west of Ottumwa on Route 2

Aeronca C-2 (1930), **C-3** (1933), **K** (1937), **LC** (1937), **65 (L-3B) (0-58B)** (1943)
American Eagle Eaglet B-31 (1935)
Anderson Z (1925)
Arrow F Sport (1937)
Culver LCA Cadet (LFA) (1940), **NR-D Cadet (PQ-14B)** (1944)
Fairchild 22 (1932), **71** (1929)
Fleet 7 (2) (1930)
Great Lakes 2T-1A (1934)
Johnson Rocket (1946)
Kari-Keen Coupe (1928)
Kinner Sportster (1933)
Luscombe 8F Silvaire (1946)
Meyers OTW (1938)
Monoprep (1930)
Monocoupe 90 (1930)
Pietenpol Sky Scout (1932)
Porterfield CP-40 (1938)
Rearwin 7000 Sportster (1935), **8135 Cloudster** (1940), **8135T Cloudster** (1942)
Rose Parakeet A-1 (1935)
Ryan ST.3KR Recruit (PT-22) (1941), **Navion A** (1947)
Smith DSA Miniplane (1957)
Standard J-1 (1917)
Stearman 4-E Junior Speedmail (1930)
Stinson S Junior (1931)
Storms Flying Flivver (1930)
Taylor-Young A (1937)
Taylorcraft D (L-2A) (1941)
Tipton Monoplane (c.1933)
Van Dellen LH-2 (1958)
Volmer Jensen VJ-23 (c.1975)
Vultee BT-13A Valiant (1943)
Welch OW-8 (1937)

Built in 1932 by Bernard Pietenpol, this is the only genuine Sky Scout constructed. The two-seat model, the Aircamper, is still a relatively common aircraft today

This Arrow Sport F, dating from the mid 1930s, has been fitted with an enclosed cockpit; it was one of the last examples built

Situated in rolling country to the west of Ottumwa is the 'Antique Airfield', home of the Antique Airplane Association (AAA). Every August scores of enthusiasts go to Iowa to enjoy the annual gathering of antique and classic aircraft. In the relaxed atmosphere monoplanes and biplanes from a bygone era may be seen flying from dawn to dusk in the hands of their proud owners. Aircraft over half a century old will often make the long pilgrimage to this delightful setting.

In association with the AAA, the Airpower Museum was founded in 1964 and was first housed in a former navy building at Ottumwa Industrial Airport. The conversion of farm land to the antique airfield was started in the early 1970s and the museum made the short journey at that time.

The collection of aircraft, largely from the inter-war period, is housed in two hangars, and a third holds airframes and engines awaiting restoration. A number of the museum aircraft are maintained in flying condition and perform at the annual fly-in, and at other smaller meetings which take place throughout the summer months.

In the large entrance hall to the museum is an impressive display of memorabilia and models. The library contains many books autographed by prominent pilots who were deeply involved with the development of flying in the inter-war period.

The aircraft collection contains several rare types, and when these are all restored a most impressive array of the golden era will be staged. The sole Anderson Z of 1925 is a biplane built by a Minnesota farmer, Andrew Anderson. Though the type was never licensed, it was registered in 1931. Powered by the famous Curtiss OX-5 engine, this two-seater was an early acquisition by the museum. In store are the remains of the Tipton Monoplane, which was built in the Kansas City area by the late Billy Tipton. His widow donated the fuselage and blueprints of the Warner-powered high-wing cabin monoplane to the museum in 1983, and they were moved to await restoration in early 1984. Also in store are the airframes of a 1929 Kari-Keen Coupe designed by Swen Swanson. Only 35 examples of this delightful two-seater were made before the Depression closed the factory.

The major manufacturers are also well represented, notably the Aeronca company. The pre-World War II C-2 and C-3, with their distinctive configuration, were most popular, with over 100 examples of the former and some 500 of the latter being made. With the two-cylinder Aeronca engine of 26 hp uprated to 36 hp in the C-3, these monoplanes gave outstanding service for decades. The low-wing L model appeared in 1935 but was not a commercial success and only 65 were built before the company discontinued production. The company returned to the high-wing format with the K of 1937, which was an improved and refined design based on the C-3. Almost 500 were built and it was the forerunner for the Chief and Champions, which were dominant in the private market in the late 1930s and 1940s. In addition, many were supplied to the USAAC for liaison work.

Of similar configuration to the Aeronca C-3 is one of the last three Welch aircraft surviving. This was donated to the museum by the late John Schildberg of Greenfield in Iowa, whose collection of vintage aircraft is still in existence.

Kansas

COMBAT AIR MUSEUM

PO Box 19142, Topeka, Kansas 66619
Tel: 913-862-9649

Opening times: 9.30am-4.30pm Monday-Saturday, 12.30pm-4.30pm Sunday; closed Monday-Friday from November to March
Location: at Forbes Field, which is about 4 miles (6 km) south of the town on Route 75

Beech B18S Kansas (AT-11) (1942), **B18S (SNB-5) (TC-45J)** (1940), **50 Seminole (RL-23D) (RU-8D)** (1958)
CASA 2.111E (He 111) (1954)
Consolidated 28 Catalina (PBY-5A) (1942), **32 Liberator (B-24J)** (1942)
de Havilland DHC 2 Beaver (L-20A) (U-6A) (1958)
Douglas A-26B Invader (1944), **A-26C Invader** (1944), **DC-3 (C-47B)** (1943), **DC-3 (C-47B)** (1944)
Grumman G.79 Panther (F9F-?) (1949), **G.89 Tracker (S2F-1) (S-2A)** (1949), **G.98 Tiger (F11F-1) (F-11A)** (1955)
Lockheed T-33A (1952), **1049 Super Constellation (RC-121D) (EC-121D)** (1952)
McDonnell F-101B Voodoo (1956)
Messerschmitt Bf 109E (R) (?)
North American O-47B (1939), **T-6G Texan** (1949), **T-6 Texan** (?), **T-6H Texan** (1952), **T-28C Trojan** (1952), **B-25J Mitchell** (1944), **B-25N Mitchell** (1944), **F-86H Sabre** (1952)
Republic F-84F Thunderstreak (1951)
Ryan Navion A (1947)
Stinson V.76 Sentinel (L-5) (1941)
Taylorcraft D (L-2) (1938)
Vultee BT-13A Valiant (1940), **BT-13A Valiant** (1940)

The Combat Air Museum was founded in the mid-1970s and has two hangars at Forbes Field, containing a varied and interesting collection of aircraft and memorabilia. The aim of the museum is to find, collect and restore aircraft and artifacts associated with all wars in which the US has taken part. At the rear of one of the hangars are a number of rooms, each devoted to a theme. The War Room has items from the Spanish-American War onwards, and presents a fascinating story of the conflicts in which the country has been involved. Many Americans were captured in the service of their country, and in the POW Room there are many poignant reminders of the hardships they must have endured. A Command Post of World War II has been recreated in one of these rooms, and this shows clearly the state of development of military affairs at the time. In the main hangar can also be seen bombs, engines, uniforms and

One of the few surviving North American O-47s. Although still under restoration, the aircraft is mounted in the display hangar of the museum as an example of the restorer's craft

A North American Mitchell, one of the Combat Air Museum's steadily growing fleet of flyable aircraft

a number of military vehicles.

The museum is entirely run by volunteers and the membership of the CAM is now over 500. These dedicated persons put their skills to a number of tasks, including keeping a large proportion of the aircraft fleet in flying order. The third weekend each September is the date for the annual CAM Airshow, at which many of the museum aircraft are flown, along with a number of visiting warbirds.

The rarest aircraft in the collection is a North American O-47B observation aircraft dating from 1938. Seventy-four O-47Bs came off the Inglewood lines, with 24 going to Air National Guard units. The O-47B had a 1060 hp Wright Cyclone in place of the 975 hp of the earlier O-47A. This aircraft, of which only a handful now exist, is undergoing a complete rebuild. The O-47B was one of the first aircraft operated by the Kansas Air National Guard in the early 1940s. The North American company is well represented in the collection with two Texans and two Mitchells in flying condition, and a Sabre on static display.

The museum holds a range of multi-engined aircraft in flying order. The largest currently airworthy machine is a Lockheed Super Constellation, which was delivered to the air force in 1954. The aircraft was built for reconnaissance and airborne early warning duties and was thus fitted with large ventral and dorsal radomes. Over its life its electronics were updated and in its final modification to EC-121T the dorsal radome was removed. The Connie's last unit was the 79th AEW of the Air Force Reserve, and it flew out of Homestead in Florida until withdrawn in 1976. The museum bought the aircraft in 1981 and it flew from storage in Arizona to Kansas. The museum has recently acquired a Convair Liberator four-engined bomber and hopefully this will be restored to fly in the future.

In addition to the Mitchells, there are two Douglas Invader attack bombers, a Consolidated Catalina amphibian, two Douglas C-47 transports, a Beech C-45 and a Beech RU-8D twins in flying condition. A Spanish-built Heinkel He 111 was also expected to join this fleet, and a very recent arrival is a Grumman Tracker. For such a small organization this multi-engined fleet requires a considerable amount of planning to keep it in flying order.

Although the primary interest is acquiring aircraft of the World War II period, the museum is now adding jets to its fleet. For the time being these are displayed statically, but in addition to the Sabre a number of others flyable jets have been acquired. Grumman has supplied the navy with fighters for many years, and two of their later models, a Panther of 1949 and a Tiger of 1953, are on view. The Tiger was the mount of the famous 'Blue Angels' aerobatic team, and is displayed in their colors.

This enthusiastic organization has made a major contribution to the aircraft preservation movement in a comparatively short time, in a part of the US where there are few other museums.

Michigan

HENRY FORD MUSEUM AND GREENFIELD VILLAGE

The Edison Institute, 20900 Oakwood Boulevard, Dearborn, Michigan 48121
Tel: 313-271-1620

Opening times: 9am-5pm daily
Location: about 12 miles (19 km) west of Detroit off Highway 12

Blériot XI (1909)
Boeing 40B-4 (1927)
Curtiss MF Seagull (mod) (1916)
Curtiss JN-4D Jenny (1917)
Dayton-Wright RB 1 Racer (1920)
Douglas DC-3 (1939)
Fokker F VII/3m (1926)
Ford 1 Flivver (1928), **4-AT-B Tri-Motor** (1928)
Junkers W 33 (1928)
Laird Biplane (1916)
Lockheed 5B Vega (1929)
Piper J-3C Cub (1946)
Pitcairn PCA-2 (1931)
Ryan B-1 Brougham (modified as Ryan NVP.III) (1930/1960)
Sikorsky VS-300 (1939)
Standard J-1 (1916)
Stinson SM-1 Detroiter (1928)
Waco UPF-7 (1937)

The name of Ford is in most people's minds associated with the manufacture of automobiles, but the company also made a significant contribution in the field of aviation. During World War I the company produced the famous Liberty engines, most of which went to power the almost 5000 de Havilland DH 4s built in the US. In 1923 Edsel Ford, son of Henry, received a request for money from William Stout to develop an all-metal transport aircraft. The initial trials were promising, as Ford set up a factory and airfield at Dearborn for the Stout company. In 1925 there were differences between the two men and Ford bought out Stout. The famous Ford 4-AT trimotor flew in June 1926 and production was soon under way. The Ford Airport was one of the most modern in the US: portions of two of its runways were of concrete, making them the first hard runways in the US.

Ford was keen to enter the private flying market and the prototype of the Flivver low-wing monoplane flew in 1926, and a second aircraft with a 36 hp Ford engine flew two years later. No real development of the Flivver occurred, but in the early 1930s Ford's friend Henry Brooks was killed in Florida in a Flivver while attempting a record flight: Ford pulled out of aviation and closed the factory after almost 200 Trimotors had been built. The Ford Motor Company still uses the factory, and the airfield is part of the test track for its ground vehicles.

In the early 1920s Henry Ford became an avid collector of early American artifacts. One of his first purchases was the historic Red Horse Tavern between Boston and Waterford, which was immortalized in Longfellow's Tales. The site was restored, and he envisaged a museum consisting of an early New England village. His collectors were sent out with the order to acquire at least one example of every tool, utensil and machine used in America. After a change of plan, a new project at Dearborn was announced in 1928: construction started in 1929 and finally opened in 1933. This was Greenfield Village.

Today there are two distinct parts to the exhibition: Greenfield Village, consisting of over 100 historic buildings, and the Henry Ford Museum which is a vast structure housing many transport and scientific exhibits. In the village are the Wright brothers' original cycle shop and family home, transported from Dayton in 1938. The museum collection of aircraft, although not large, contains many significant machines. On show are the first aircraft to fly over the two poles. The north pole was finally conquered by an expedition led by Richard Byrd, using a Fokker F.VIIa piloted by Floyd Bennett. The F.VIIa trimotor came to the US in 1925 to take part in the Ford Reliability Tour, which it won. The epic flight over the pole was in 1926, and in 1929 Byrd was again leader of the expedition to the Antarctic. The aircraft used was the 15th Trimotor to emerge from the Dearborn line and this, with the support of a Fokker Universal and a Fairchild FC-2, were taken to the base at 'Little America' on the Ross Sea. The flight to the pole involved passing over mountains more than 10500 feet (3200 meters)

In the Greenfield Village part of the museum, the original cycle shop of the Wright brothers is displayed. The building was moved from Dayton in 1938.

Above
This Ford Trimotor was the first aircraft to fly over the South Pole. A more powerful engine, a 525 hp Wright Cyclone, was fitted in the nose for its epic flight

Left
The *Detroit News* owned this Pitcairn PCA-2 autogyro between 1931 and 1934, and it made 730 flights for the paper before it was presented to the museum

high, so the 220 hp nose-mounted Wright Whirlwind engine was replaced by a 525 hp Wright Cyclone. Floyd Bennett had died of pneumonia so the Ford was flown by Berndt Balcher, on November 28, 1929.

Another pioneering aircraft is the Junkers W 33 'Bremen' which made the first non-stop east-west crossing of the Atlantic. The crew of Koelly, von Huenefeld and Fitzmaurice took of from Baldonnel in Ireland on April 12, 1928 and 37 hours later their aircraft was forced to land in Labrador. Their original plan had been to fly on to New York, but strong winds had slowed their progress.

The first practical helicopter in the US was the Sikorsky VS-300, which hopped in 1939 and eventually flew successfully. This historic machine made its last flight in 1943, when Igor Sikorsky landed on the lawn in front of the museum. These aircraft are just a few of the aeronautical highlights in a magnificent museum.

Minnesota

THE AIR MUSEUM 'PLANES OF FAME' EAST

14771 Pioneer Trail, Eden Prairie, Minnesota 55344
Tel: 612-941-2633 or 612-293-0075

Opening times: 11am-5pm Saturday-Sunday during May-September, other times by appointment
Location: at Flying Cloud Airport which is about 12 miles (19 km) southeast of Minneapolis on County Road 1

Beech D17S (UC-43) (1944)
Boeing-Stearman B751N1 Kaydet (N2S-3) (1942)
Curtiss 87 Warhawk (P-40N) (1944)
Grumman G.36 Wildcat (FM-2) (1942), **G.40 Avenger (TBM-3)** (1944), **G.50 Hellcat (F6F-5)** (1944), **G.58 Bearcat (F8F-2)** (1944)
North American B-25J Mitchell (1944), **P-51D Mustang** (1944), **AT-6D Texan** (1943)
Piper J-3C Cub (1942)
Republic P-47D Thunderbolt (1944)
Vought FG-1D Corsair (1944)
Yakovlev Yak-11 (c.1952)

Painted in Royal Navy colors is this Grumman Avenger Torpedo bomber. The letters of the code RP are the initials of the owner of the collection – Bob Pond

The appearance of a museum of only 14 aircraft might seem surprising in a book of this nature, but the Planes of Fame-East has set itself such high standards that its inclusion is well justified. All the aircraft are owned by Bob Pond, an ex-naval aviator, and the museum first opened for the summer season in 1984. Two hangars have been converted for museum use, and a third was due to be available around 1986. There are impressive collections of memorabilia and photographs. The permanent staff maintain an extremely high standard, and it is difficult to believe that the immaculate aircraft on display are regularly flown.

The naval theme is evident as soon as one enters the main exhibition hall. One wall is dominated by a painting showing a Corsair making an approach to a carrier at sea, while next to this can be seen a real Corsair in the same markings. Close by are two other classic naval fighters from the Grumman company – the aggressive-looking Wildcat and Hellcat, all in pristine condition. Grumman also produced the best carrier-borne torpedo bomber of World War II, the Avenger, which first flew in 1941 and made its operational debut in the Battle of Midway. The Avenger on show is one of the 7546 built by Eastern Aircraft to supplement the 2293 built by the parent firm. The Avenger is painted in the markings of a Royal Navy aircraft, with Invasion Stripes.

The US Air Force has not been forgotten, with a Mustang and a Warhawk on view. There are three light aircraft: a beautiful Stearman Kaydet in naval training colors, a Piper Cub in the famous yellow factory scheme and a Beech Staggerwing in naval communications gray.

Due for delivery from France in early 1986 was an ex-Egyptian Air Force Yakovlev 11 trainer which was purchased from the Salis Collection, and a North American Mitchell bomber was also expected to join the collection in 1986.

This impressive collection should become a major force in aircraft preservation, and the standards it has set should be emulated by others.

An immaculate Vought Corsair of World War II

Nebraska

HAROLD WARP PIONEER VILLAGE

Minden, Nebraska 68959
Tel: 309-832-1181

Opening times: 8am-sunset daily
Location: in the center of the town at the intersection of Routes 10 and 6/34

Bell 27 Airacomet (P-59B) (1942)
Bensen B-6 (1955), **B-7M** (1957)
Cessna AW (1929)
Curtiss D Pusher (1912), **JN-4D Jenny** (1917)
de Havilland DH 60GM Moth (1929)
Ercoupe 415C (1942)
Hartman Monoplane (1910)
Lincoln-Page LP-3 (1928)
Piper PA-23 Apache (1954)
Pitcairn PAA-1 Autogyro (1930)
Sikorsky VS-316 Hoverfly (YR-4B) (HNS-1) (1944)
Standard J-1 (1918)
Stinson SM-1 Detroiter (1930)
Swallow 3POLB (1926)
Taylor J-2 Cub (1937)
Wright Flyer (R) (?)

Nebraska may not be on the route of many aeronautical enthusiasts in the US but within its boundaries are two excellent, if contrasting, museums. In 1924 Harold Warp left the small country town of Minden for Chicago where he made his fortune in the manufacture of plastics. In 1948 he started collecting items relating to the early days of the Minden region. The Pioneer Village was opened in 1953 and now occupies a large site at the crossroads in the center of the town. On the site are over 20 buildings with more than 30,000 items on show. Original buildings from the surrounding area have been brought to the village, including Harold Warp's one-room school from Grom. There are vast displays of agricultural and domestic life representing the history of a region which has only been settled in the last century and a half.

Harold Warp has always been interested in aviation and he has owned a number of aircraft for his personal use. Two of these are on show, including an Ercoupe 415C which he bought new in 1941 and repurchased for the museum in 1979 after it had been used by five other owners. The aircraft are on show in two halls of the main museum building, and most are mounted on poles. Pioneering is the theme of the museum, so it is appropriate that a 1962 replica of the Wright Flyer is on show. This was constructed by H P Boen in Kobe in Japan, and allegedly incorporates some original parts. A replica of a Curtiss Pusher is also on view, believed to be modeled on the version which flew at the famous 1909 meeting at Rheims in France.

The Hartman monoplane of 1910 is claimed to be the first aircraft to fly in Iowa when it took to the air at Burlington Golf Course on May 10, 1910. This low-wing monoplane was used by Art Hartman until 1920 when it was put in store. In 1955 the aircraft was restored and, according to the museum, flown at Clinton, Iowa with Hartman at the controls, after which it was acquired by the museum. The information board by the aircraft shows photographs of both the 1910 and 1955 events and there are several differences between the two aircraft. The 1910 model has a wooden fuselage with wire bracing, whereas the aircraft on show has one of welded steel tubes. The wings on the later version are in a higher position, and the rudder is of a different shape. It would appear that the 1955 aircraft was an almost new machine.

The period between the two World Wars is particularly well represented. The Swallow 3POLB biplane built in 1926 at Wichita, Kansas was used by Walter Varney in April 1926 to fly mail from Elko, Nevada to Pasco, Washington and made the inaugural flight in the reverse direction with Leon Cuddleback at the controls. Clyde Cessna was one of the founders of the Travel Air Company at Wichita, but he left to form his own firm in 1927 after a disagreement with Walter Beech, who wanted to continue building biplanes. Cessna favored the cantilever high-wing monoplane, and the AW sold well until the Depression closed the factory in 1930. Another high-wing monoplane from the period is a Stinson Detroiter which was a great success for the famous firm.

Two rotary-wing aircraft are interesting exhibits, these being a Pitcairn PAA-1 autogyro and a Sikorsky Hoverfly helicopter. The Pitcairn company built a series of biplanes designed by Agnew E Larsen before purchasing the production rights for the autogyro from the originator Juan de la Cierva. The PAA-1 was built in 1930 and last flew at Fort Lauderdale in Florida in 1954. The Hoverfly was the first US helicopter to enter production, and the Minden aircraft was used by the army and the navy for trials. Another pioneering aircraft is one of the first US jets, the Bell Airacomet.

Forerunner of the famous line of Cessna high-wing monoplanes, the AW of 1928 sold well until the following year, when economic recession set in

The Hartman monoplane first flew in 1910, and this example – in substantially modified form – took to the air again in 1955

Walter Varney used this 1926 Swallow biplane on his mail contract flights between Elko, Nevada and Pasco, Washington

STRATEGIC AIR COMMAND MUSEUM

2510 Clay Street, Belleville, Nebraska 68005
Tel: 402-292-2001

Opening times: 8am-5pm daily
Location: about 10 miles (16 km) south of Omaha just off Interstate 80

Avro 698 Vulcan B.2 (1963)
Boeing 299 Fortress (B-17G) (DB-17P) (1944)
Boeing 345 Superfortress (B-29B) (TB-29B) (1944)
Boeing 367 Stratotanker (KC-97G) (1953), **450 Stratojet (B-47F)** (1952), **464 Stratofortress (B-52B)** (1952)
Convair B-36J (1952), **F-102A** (1954), **B-58A Hustler** (1961), **240 (T-29A)** (1950)
Douglas VB-26B Invader (A26B) (1944), **DC-3 (C-47A)** (1943), **DC-4 (C-54D)** (1942), **C-124A Globemaster** (1949), **C-133B Cargomaster** (1959)
Fairchild C-119C (C-119F) (1951)
Grumman G.64 Albatross (SA-16B) (HU-16B) (1951)
Lockheed T-33A (1958), **U-2C** (1956)
McDonnell XF-85 Goblin (1946), **F-101B Voodoo** (1959)
Martin B-57E Canberra (1955)
North American TB-25J Mitchell (B-25J) (1944), **RB-45C Tornado** (1948), **F-86H Sabre** (1953), **T-39A Sabreliner** (1962)
Republic F-84F Thunderstreak (1951)
Sikorsky S-55 (H-19B) (1953)
Vertol V.42 Shawnee (H-21B) (1952)

The North American B-45 Tornado was the first American four-jet bomber to fly. A photo reconnaissance version, with five cameras in the nose, is displayed at the SAC Museum

Strategic Air Command (SAC) is a name associated with the heavy bombers which have reinforced the power of the USAF for decades. SAC moved its headquarters to Offutt Air Force Base on the outskirts of Omaha in 1948. The field had been an active site since the US Air Mail operated de Havilland DH 4s in the 1920s and during World War I the Glenn Martin company built a factory at Offutt which produced some 1200 B-26 Marauders and over 500 Boeing B-29 Superfortresses. The idea of a museum was first mooted in the 1950s and the first aircraft arrived at the end of the decade. Progress was, however, very slow and it was six years before any more exhibits arrived. Armed Forces Day in 1966 saw the official opening of the museum and at this time negotiations were started with the State of Nebraska, who took over the running in 1971. The majority of the exhibits are on loan from the USAF Museum in Ohio and SAC still maintains an interest in the collection.

An indoor display traces the role of the command since

The Lockheed U-2, a secret high-flying reconnaissance machine, first flew in 1955 but did not become public knowledge for several years

The diminutive McDonnell Goblin was designed to operate from a trapeze under heavy long-range bombers. Only two were built, and they were not successful

its inception, and also the development of strategic bombing and the bomber.

The majority of the aircraft are displayed in the open air on a disused runway; a number of missiles are on show on a hillock behind the museum building. The first aircraft to arrive at the museum was a giant Convair B-36J. The design was conceived in 1941 but the pressure of the war effort meant that this giant aircraft, which had a six-piston engine and a span of 240 feet (73 meters), a length of 163 feet (50 meters) and a height of almost 47 feet (14 meters) did not fly until August 1946. The six 3000 hp Pratt and Whitney Wasp Majors drove pusher propellers, and after 96 aircraft had been built the B-36D, with an additional four jet engines, appeared in 1949. The aircraft on show is a late production B-36J with increased tankage; it spent most of its operational life with the 28th Bomb Wing at Rapid City, South Dakota before joining the museum. From the sublime to the ridiculous is perhaps an apt phrase for moving on to the tiny McDonnell Goblin parasite fighter. With a span of 21 feet (6.4 meters) and a length of 16 feet 3 inches (4.9 meters) this tiny jet was designed to be suspended from a cradle under SAC bombers. Originally conceived for the B-36, the Goblin was tested under a Boeing B-29 in 1948, and although it left the trapeze successfully, attempts to re-engage were thwarted by the air cushion between the two aircraft. After less than a year the program was canceled.

Almost all the range of Boeing bombers from the B-17 Fortress to the B-52 Stratofortress are on view, the exception being a B-50 version of the Superfortress. The development from the four-engined B-17 to the eight-jet B-52 is a reminder of the massive strides which took place in design and power-plant development in less than 30 years.

The Consolidated Vultee B-58 Hustler heralded a new era in bombing as this four-jet delta with its top speed of almost 1400 mph (2250 km/h) brought the bomber into the supersonic range. The first B-58 flew in November 1956 and the type served in the operational role from 1960 to 1970. Although only 116 were built, they were used in many record flights. The aircraft on show, with the appropriate name of 'Greased Lightning', comes from the 305th Bomb Wing and in October 1963 it flew from Bunker Hill, Indiana to London, England via Tokyo. The other large delta on show is a British Avro Vulcan, an ex-9 Squadron aircraft which was donated to the museum by the Royal Air Force.

The first jet bomber to serve with the SAC was the North American B-45 Tornado and the example on show was the last of its type to fly when, after use as an engine test-bed with Pratt and Whitney, it flew into Offutt in 1972.

SAC used fighters in its early days until, with the advent of the fast bomber, they became obsolete; and the command also has a fleet of transport aircraft. The display is completed by a range of aircraft which have served in these essential roles.

New York

CRADLE OF AVIATION MUSEUM

Mitchel Field, Garden City, New York 11530
Tel: 516-222-1191

Opening times: midday-5pm Friday-Sunday, April-October
Location: about 30 miles (48 km) east of Manhattan on Long Island. Off Meadowbrook Parkway between the Northern and Southern State Parkways

Aeronca 7AC Champion (1947)
Bell 47D Sioux (H-13E) (1952), **47G Sioux (H-13G)** (1952)
Blériot XI (R) (c.1982)
Breese Penguin (1916)
Brock Gyroglider (?)
Convertawings Quadrotor (1954)
Curtiss JN-4 Jenny (1918), **JN-4D Jenny** (1918), **87 Hawk (P-40B) (R)** (?)
Curtiss-Sperry Aerial Torpedo (1918)
de Havilland DH C 2 Beaver (2-20A) (U-6A) (1951)
Evans VP-2 (c.1980)
Fairchild 71 (1929), **M.62A Cornell (PT-26)** (1942)
Grumman G.50 Hellcat (F6F-5) (1944), **G.93 Cougar (F9F-7)** (1954), **G.98 Tiger (F-11A) (F11F-1)** (1955)
Herring-Curtiss 1 (R) (?)
Kohm Human Power Vehicle (?)
Lockheed T-33B (TV-2) (T-33A) (1955)
Maniatis MPA (c.1981)
North American F-86H Sabre (1952)
Republic RC-3 Seabee (1947), **P-47N Thunderbolt** (1944), **F-84F Thunderstreak** (1951), **F-105B Thunderchief** (1957)
Rogallo Hang Glider (c.1980)
Roloff RLU-1 Breezy (c.1970)
Rotec Rally 2B (c.1980)
Rotorway Scorpion (1976)
Ryan B-1 Brougham (1930)
Sperry Aerial Torpedo (R) (?), **Messenger (R)** (?)
Stinson 108-1 Voyager (1947)
Stits SA-3B Playboy (1953)
Thomas Morse S4C (1918)
Wizard Ultralight (c.1982)
Wright Flyer (R) (1980), **EX Vin Fiz (R)** (1983)

Long Island has been the scene of many developments in aviation. The first flight in the region occurred in 1909 when the celebrated aviator Glenn Curtiss flew from Hempstead Plains. Two famous airfields, Roosevelt and Mitchel, were located on the island, and were the scenes of many epic flights. It was from the former that Lindbergh took off on his solo flight to Paris in 1927. Many aircraft and engine manufacturers set up plants here, including such famous names as Grumman, Fairchild, Seversky, Republic and Sperry. The historic airfields are now part of a vast housing complex, but at Mitchel part of the line of hangars and some other buildings still survive. Nassau County has allocated two of the hangars (3 and 4) for museum use, and some other rooms are used for offices and restoration.

The museum was set up in the early 1980s and the enthusiastic staff under the direction of Bill Kaiser have in a short time gathered a varied amount of exhibition material. The local industry and other museums have assisted in this venture.

The Grumman company of Bethpage has achieved fame with its navy fighters dating from the XFF-1 of 1931. Three of these classic combat aircraft are in the collection. The oldest is a Hellcat – the type first flew in 1942 and was in action in August 1943. With the arrival of this aircraft in the Pacific the navy had a fighter that was superior to the Japanese Zero in every way. At the end of World War II the Hellcat had shot down 5156 of the 6477 Japanese planes downed by USN fliers. The Cougar, which was derived from the straight-wing Panther, was the first operational carrier fighter with a swept wing, and in the 1950s vast numbers served in a variety of roles. The Tiger was a slight disappointment as a fighter, but for years it was the mount of the famous 'Blue Angels' aerobatic team.

The Seversky company was formed in 1931 and reorganized into the Republic Aviation Corporation in 1939. The bulky Thunderbolt fighter, derived from an earlier

This immaculately restored Thomas Morse S4C saw use as a civil aircraft after its military days were over

The US Army bought 301 examples of the Breese Penguin ground trainer in 1918, but they saw little use

Seversky product, became one of the outstanding combat aircraft of its era and over 15,000 were produced. The firm continued to produce excellent fighters after World War II, and two of its jets – the F-84F Thunderstreak, and the giant F-105 Thunderchief which was so successful in Vietnam – represent this period. There is also a Seabee amphibian which first flew in 1944. In a little over a year 1060 Seabees had been produced when the company moved entirely to military work in October 1947. Exported to many countries, a number of the type are still giving excellent service.

A Curtiss Jenny which was Lindbergh's first aircraft is one of the highlights of the exhibition. Another famous aircraft is the Fairchild 71 'Stars and Stripes', used by Admiral Byrd on his Antarctic Expedition. The aircraft is under a slow restoration program by a team of volunteers.

Replicas of famous aircraft have been built to add to the range of exhibits. The Wright 1903 Flyer has to feature in any collection of early aircraft and running it a close second is the Wright EX 'Vin Fiz'. These two reproductions are from a similar era to the Herring-Curtiss 1 in which Curtiss set a closed circuit record at the 1909 Rheims meeting in France. Representing the Sperry firm are replicas of the Aerial Torpedo and the 1921 Messenger biplane. From a later era, a fiberglass Curtiss Warhawk, made for a film, has been acquired.

This new collection is gradually working towards the day when it can be fully open, but the visitor can see the amount of work which has already gone into this exciting project.

INTREPID SEA-AIR-SPACE MUSEUM

Intrepid Square, West 46th Street and 12th Avenue, New York 10036
Tel: 212-245-2533

Opening times: 10am-5pm Wednesday-Sunday
Location: on the west side of Manhattan at Pier 86

Bell 47G Sioux (OH-13S) (1964), **204 Iroquois (UH-1M) (UH-1C)** (1966)
Curtiss D Pusher (R) (1958)
Douglas XA-3 Skywarrior (XA3D-1) (1952), **A-4B Skyhawk (A4D-2)** (1958)
Grumman G.64 Albatross (HU-16E) (UF-2G) (1951), **G.89 Tracker (TS-2A) (S2F-1)** (1953), **G.98 Tiger (F11F-1) (F-11A)** (1955), **G.98 Tiger (F-1A) (F11F-1)** (1955), **G.117 Tracer (E-1B) (WF-2)** (1958), **G.121 Tracker (S-2E) (S2F-3)** (1956), **G.128 Intruder (IA-6A) (YA2F-1)** (1964)
Lockheed SP-2E Neptune (P2V-5) (1953)
McDonnell F-3B Demon (F3H-2N) (1956), **F-4N Phantom (F-4B)** (1963)
Nieuport 28C.1 (1917)
North American FJ-3 Fury (1953), **RA-5C Vigilant** (1963)
Northrop YF-17A (mock up) (c.1970)
Phoenix M-7 Hang Glider (c.1982)
Republic F-84F Thunderstreak (1951)
Royal Aircraft Factory SE.5A (R) (c.1980)
Santos-Dumont Demoiselle (R) (1965)
Sikorsky S-58 Choctaw (H-34A) (1955)
Waco 9 (1927)

A museum exhibiting complete military aircraft needs both considerable space and to be accessible to a major centre of population. These needs are met in a novel way in the centre of New York: the famous aircraft carrier USS *Intrepid*, berthed at the end of 46th Street in Manhattan, displays the first major aircraft collection in a large city.

The *Intrepid* was built as one of the 24 'Essex' class carriers, and work started on the ship six days before the Japanese attack on Pearl Harbor. It served with distinction in the Pacific during World War II and other highlights from her career include the recovery of astronauts in the early 1960s and three tours in the Vietnam war. Finally withdrawn in 1974, the *Intrepid* was placed in store before being donated to the Intrepid Museum Foundation in December 1980. The ship was towed to Bayonne for the Bethlehem Steel Company to start the conversion to museum use, and in June 1982 it took its place at Pier 86.

Most of the aircraft on show have a naval connection.

Part of the Manhattan skyline is recognizable behind this Grumman Tracker, which carries the colors of the aircraft that served with VS-72 when aboard the USS *Intrepid*

One part of the hangar deck called the 'United States Navy Hall' has three aircraft on view and a film show illustrating famous naval operations. Two of the aircraft are original and the third is an engineering mock-up of the Northrop YF-17 which was unsuccessful in a USAF light fighter competition and was later transferred to the navy for development work. Another section at the same level is the 'Intrepid Hall' where the ship's history is portrayed with photographs, models, documents and an audio presentation of reminiscences by former crew members.

The first-ever take-off and landing from a ship are commemorated in the 'Pioneer Hall'. On November 14, 1910 Eugene Ely flew a Curtiss Pusher off a special platform on the cruiser *Birmingham* which was moored off Hampton Roads, Virginia. Ely had to dive to gain flying speed, and his wheels touched the water but the flight was a success. Ely also made the first landing on a ship in another Curtiss on January 18, 1911. These historic feats are well recorded in a photo display, and a replica Curtiss Pusher is mounted on a reconstruction of part of the deck.

The vast rear hangar is fitted out as the 'Technologies Hall'. Pride of place goes to an Apollo lunar module and there are also several rocket engines, missiles, space technology and a USAF display on milestones in their history.

From the vast flight deck there are impressive views of the Manhattan and New Jersey skylines as well as the growing collection of aircraft. The majority have been painted in the bright colors carried by US Navy machines, but there are some from other branches of the services. One of the most striking schemes is carried by an amphibious Grumman Albatross which was used by the coast guards.

This important museum is now a major attraction in the city of New York and will surely continue to expand the range of its exhibits.

The delta-winged Douglas Skyhawk has had a production life longer than that of any other combat aircraft. The first prototype flew in 1954

OLD RHINEBECK AERODROME

PO Box 89, Rhinebeck, New York 12572
Tel: 914-758-8610

Opening times: 10am-5pm daily mid-May to October; air shows Sundays 2.30pm, Saturdays July-October 2.30pm
Location: north of Rhinebeck at the intersection of Norton and Stone Church Roads off Route 9

Aeromarine 39B (1918)
Aeromarine-Klemm AKL-26A (1930)
Aeronca C-3 (1933)
Albatross D VA (R) (1972)
Albree Pigeon Fraser (1917)
American Eagle A-129 (1929)
Avro 504K (R) (1966)
Blériot XI (1910, 1911)
Bréguet Biplane (1911)
Brunner-Winkle CK Bird (1931)
Caudron G-3 (R) (1983)
Chanute Glider (R) (1980)
Curtiss D Pusher (R) (1958, 1976), **JN-4H Jenny** (1918), **51 Fledgling** (1929)
Curtiss-Wright CW-1 Junior (1931)
Davis D-1W (1929)
de Havilland DH 80A Puss Moth (1931)
Deperdussin Monoplane (R) (1974)
Dickson Primary Glider (R) (1969)
Fairchild F.24C (1937)
Fleet 16B Finch (1942)
Fokker D VII (1918), **Dr I (R)** (1965, 1968, c.1972)
Gazelle HO-2 (1969)
Great Lakes 2T-1 (1929)
Hanriot Monoplane (R) (1974)
Monocoupe 90 (1932), **113** (1929)
Morane-Saulnier MS.130Et2 (1927), **A1 (R)** (1982), **N (R)** (1985)
New Standard D-25 (1929)
Nicholas-Beazley NB-8G (c.1933)
Nieuport 2N (R) (1978), **28C.1** (1917)
Passett Ornithopter (R) (1910?)
Pitcairn PA-6 Mailwing (1928)
Raab-Katzenstein Glider (1921)
Royal Aircraft Factory BE.2C (R) (c.1983), **FE.8 (R)** (1970)
Santos-Dumont Demoiselle (R) (1965, c.1970)
Short S.29 (R) (c.1972)
Siemens-Schuckert D IV (R) (1969)
Sopwith Pup (R) (1966), **F.1 Camel (R)** (1969), **5F.1 Dolphin (R)** (1976), **7F.1 Snipe** (1918)
SPAD XIII (1917)
Spartan C-3 (1929)
Standard J-1 (1918)
Stinson 10A Voyager (?)
Taylor J-2 Cub (1936)
Taylorcraft BC-65 (1940)
Thomas B Pusher (R) (1911), **E Pusher** (1912)
Thomas Morse S-4B (1917)
Voisin 8 (R) (c.1975)
Waco 9 (1927), **10** (1928)
Wright Glider (R) (?), **EX Vin Fiz (R)** (1980)

For the crowds who flock each summer weekend to the tiny undulating airstrip cut out of a wood, the air show put on by Cole Palen and his team tells little about the efforts put into making Old Rhinebeck one of the absolute musts for the aviation enthusiast touring the US. The show is merely the culmination of 35 years' dedication to old aircraft. The story starts in 1951 when Cole was on a mechanics course at Roosevelt Field on Long Island. The airfield was closed in 1948 as housing encroached, and parts of the airport were becoming a shopping centre. There was an aircraft museum at the field and this, too, was faced with closure. By 1951 the six remaining types, a Sopwith Snipe, an Avro 504K, a Curtiss Jenny, a Standard J-1, an Aeromarine Klemm and a SPAD XIII, had been pushed into the corner of a hangar. Each day Cole Palen used to eat his lunch in the cockpit of the SPAD and perhaps this is where the dream was born. He offered $1500 for the six aircraft and was given a month to remove them.

The Jenny was exchanged for a Nieuport 28 and work started on the SPAD which took to the air again in 1956. It is still in the collection and was last flown in 1970. In 1958 the abandoned farm at old Rhinebeck was bought and by 1959 a 1500-foot (460 meter) runway had been cleared. Some private owners moved their aircraft into the farm and small displays were staged throughout 1960. In the early 1960s some of the aircraft were taken around the country and to Canada to help keep the operation solvent. A 13-week tour helped promote the film 'Those Magnificent Men in their Flying Machines'. Heavy snow in the winter of 1963/4 caused a hangar roof to collapse, cutting a Fokker D VII and an Avro 504K in two and damaging the Blériot XI. In the winter of 1964/5 a new venture was tried: most of the airworthy aircraft were taken to Kissimmee in Florida for a series of week-end shows, but this proved a financial disaster, and to pay the debts at the end of the season the Avro 504K was sold to the Canadian National Collection.

In the summer of 1966 Dick King's Sopwith Pup replica was ready, and was soon joined by a Fokker Dr I triplane built by Cole Palen. These two took over the weekend dog-fights, and allowed the genuine World War I aircraft to take part in more sedate maneuvers. During this season the Sopwith Snipe was also damaged following an engine failure, and was completely rebuilt by Gordon Bainbridge in about 12 months. Replica building gathered momentum, and in Florida Cole Palen has used the winters to good effect. World War I types from both sides have been joined by aircraft from before 1914, and together with the genuine machines from the 1920s and 30s the fleet add up to a comprehensive display.

Each Saturday afternoon in the summer the 'golden age' is recaptured, with some of the antics made famous by the barnstormers of those times. There is streamer-bursting, flour-bombing, wing-walking, aerobatics and balloon-bursting. Throughout the show volunteers in period costume roam about the airfield in appropriate vehicles.

Sunday afternoon is World War I day, and dog-fights are the order of the day. All is presented with a tongue-in-the cheek humor. The dastardly 'Black Baron' comes from 'Der Badz Boyz Cafe' on the far side of the field and there is the bold British hero Sir Percy Goodfellow and his girl Trudy Truelove. Against this music hall setting, flying is of a high degree of skill, in aircraft some of which are difficult to handle.

There are a number of hangars on the field where the airworthy machines reside, and on the opposite side of the lane is the museum. Here in three large buildings are the remainder of the fleet. Some are potentially airworthy but have not flown for some time, and the others are waiting their turn in the workshops. Around one third of the fleet of about 60 aircraft are airworthy for any one season, and these may be supplemented by aircraft of Cole's friends.

The early aircraft often make short straight hops down the field when conditions permit, and a 1909 Blériot XI can be joined by replicas of a 1910 Hanriot, a 1911 Curtiss Pusher, a 1911 Nieuport 2N and a 1913 Deperdussin Racer. These replicas, mostly with modern engines, are still a

The Curtiss-Wright Junior first flew in 1930 and this example, which last flew in 1977, retains the troublesome Szekely engine

handful to fly, and they only venture into the air in very calm conditions. None of the genuine World War I aircraft have flown for some time, although it is not the intention that they should be permanently grounded.

From the inter-war period are a number of now extremely rare types. The Nicholas Beazley NB-8G high-wing monoplane with folding wings was designed by Tom A Kirkup and 57 were built between 1931 and 1935. Only about two remain active – the power unit was the 80 hp British-designed Genet radial. The David D-1W parasol-wing monoplane was first flown in 1929 and only 18 examples – 11 with Kinner radials and seven with Warner radials – came out of the Richmond, Indiana factory before the Depression hit. This classic design is very impressive in the air. The Monocoupe series of high-wing aircraft, designed by Clayton Folkerts and Don Luscombe, were an instant success after the appearance of the first Velie-powered model in 1927. The type dominated the market and over 350 were sold. One example of this model is in the museum, with a Monocoupe 90 in flying condition. An early Monocoupe was raced by the factory test pilot Vern Roberts, and this incorporated a number of refinements. These were put into effect on the 90, of which about 100 were built.

Joyrides are available in two New Standard D-25s, and there are more of this model awaiting their turn in the workshops. These large five-seat biplanes were designed by Charles H Day who was responsible for the famous J-1 trainer of World War I. Around 65 D-25s were produced at Paterson, New Jersey between 1928 and 1930 and perhaps another 10 were made from 1933 to 1937. With their vast front cockpit which could seat four, their rugged construction and the power of the 220 hp Wright engine, many ended their days as crop dusters. Cole Palen found this fleet derelict at a strip just to the northwest of Phoenix in Arizona. These aircraft, which are ideal for the job at Old Rhinebeck, were trucked to the workshops, and now with a 220 hp Continental radial the first joined the circus for the 1983 season, and the second the following year.

The Aeromarine company was one of the earliest manufacturers in the US and was founded in Keyport, New Jersey before World War I. In 1917 it received the then largest single order placed by the US Navy, which was for 50 Model 39As and 150 39Bs. For many years the last surviving 39B has been stored at Old Rhinebeck, and this is undergoing restoration. In 1928 the Aeromarine-Klemm Corporation was formed to build under license the most

The Pitcairn PA-6 Mailwing of 1929 was designed by Agnew Larsen and served on east coast routes in the 1930s

successful Klemm series of monoplanes, over 1000 of which were sold in Europe. Ten were imported into the US, and the company built another 85. The AKL-26, with its 70 hp Le Blond engine, is again the last of its type.

Although the display put on is typically 'American showmanship', it must be remembered that the vast majority of the audience are not enthusiasts. They merely want entertainment, and this they get in abundance. The flying shows have meant that historic aircraft are preserved and maintained in flying order. Also, replicas of now extinct types are seen in the air. Replica building is still going on and two more, a Caudron G.3 and a Morane-Saulnier N were due to be ready for the 1986 season.

A general view of the runway at Old Rhinebeck, with the performers lined up. The founder, Cole Palen, is in the center front

This New Standard D-25 is one of a batch purchased in Arizona. Two are now airworthy, and these are frequently used for joyriding

Ohio

UNITED STATES AIR FORCE MUSEUM

Wright Patterson Air Force Base, Ohio 45433
Tel: 513-255-3284

Opening hours: 9am-5pm Monday-Friday, 10am-6pm Saturday-Sunday; annex hours: 9.30am-3pm Monday-Friday, 10.30am-5pm Saturday-Sunday
Location: about 4 miles (6 km) northeast of Dayton off Highway 4

Aeronca 65TC (0-59B) (L-3B) (1942)

American Helicopter XA-8 Jet Jeep (XH-26)

Beech: D17S Traveller (JB-2) (UC-43) (1944), **B18S (C-45H)** (1941), **AT-10** (1941), **18 Kansas (AT-11)** (1942), **45 Mentor (T-34A)** (1955), **90 King Air (VC-6A)** (?)

Bell 26 Airacobra (P-39Q) (1944), **27 Airacomet (P-59B)** (1944), **33 King Cobra (P-63E)** (1943), **47J (UH-13J)** (1957), **X-1B** (1948), **X-5** (1950), **204 Iroquois (UH-1P)** (1964)

Bensen B-8M (X-25A) (1968)

Blériot XI (c.1911)

Boeing 102 (P-12E) (1931), **299 Fortress (B-17G)** (1944), **345 Superfortress (B-29)** (1944), **345 Superfortress (B-50D)** (1949), **345 Superfortress (KB-50J) (B-50D)** (1949), **367 Stratotanker (KC-97L)** (1952), **450 Stratojet (B-47E)** (1953), **464 Stratofortress (B-52D)** (1956)

Boeing-Stearman E75 Kaydet (PT-13D) (1942)

Cessna T-50 Bobcat (UC-78B) (1942), **305 Bird Dog (0-1E) (L-19E)** (1951), **310 (L-27A) (U-3A)** (1957), **318 (T-37B)** (1954), **318D (YA-37A)** (1963), **337M Skymaster (0-2A)** (1967)

Consolidated PT-1 Trusty (1926), **28 Catalina (PBY-5A)** (c.1945), **32 Liberator (B-24D)** (1942)

Convair B-36J (1952), **B-58A Hustler** (1959), **XF-92A** (1946), **F-102A** (1956), **F-106A** (1956)

CASA 352L (Ju 52/3m) (1942), **2.111H (He 111H)** (1954)

Culver NR-D Cadet (PQ-14B) (1944)

Curtiss JN-4D Jenny (1917), **35 Hawk (P-6E)** (1932), **75 Hawk (P-36A)** (1938), **85 Owl (0-52)** (1940), **87A Kittyhawk (P-40E)** (1939)

Curtiss-Wright CW-20 Commando (C-46D) (1944), **CW-25 (AT-9)** (1941)

de Havilland DH 4 (1918), **DH 89A Dragon Rapide** (1944), **DH 98 Mosquito B.35** (1945), **DH C.2 Beaver (L-20A) (U-6A)** (1951), **DHC 4 Caribou (C-7A)** (1962)

Douglas DWC (1922), **0-38F** (1933), **0-46A** (1935), **DC-2 (C-39A)** (1939), **DC-3 (C-47B)** (1943), **DC-3 (C-53)** (1943), **DC-4 (C-54C)** (1942), **DC-6 (VC-118)** (1947), **A-1E Skyraider (AD-5)** (1952), **A-20G Havoc** (1943), **A-26C Invader** (1944), **A-26A Counter Invader** (1964), **B-18A Bolo** (1937), **B-23 Dragon** (1939), **RB-66B Destroyer** (1953), **X-3** (1950), **C-124A Globemaster** (1952), **C-133A Cargomaster** (1956)

Fairchild 100 Pilgrim (C-24) (1931), **F.24R (XUC-86A)** (1939), **M.62 Cornell (PT-19)** (1941), **M.62A Cornell (PT-26)** (1942), **C-119J Flying Boxcar** (1951), **C-123K Provider (C-123B)** (1956)

Fairchild-Republic YA-10A (1971)

Fieseler Fi 156 Storch (1942)

Fisher P-75A Eagle (1944)

Focke-Achgelis Fa 330A-1 Bachstelze (1942)

Focke-Wulf Fw 190D-9 (1945)

General Dynamics F-111A (1963)

Grumman G-15 Duck (J2F-6) (1945), **G.64 Albatross (HU-16B) (SA-16B)** (1951)

Halberstadt CL IV (C-5) (1918), **CL IV** (1918), **CLS I** (1918)

Hawker P.1127 Kestrel (XV-6A) (1964)

Helio H.395 Courier (U-10D), (L-28A) (1966)

Hispano HA.1112K (Messerschmitt Bf 109) (1952)

Interstate S1B1 Cadet (L-6) (1943)

Junkers Ju 88D-1 (1940)

Kaman K.600 Huskie (HH-43F) (1960)

Kawanishi N1K2-J Shinden Kai (1945)

Laister-Kaufmann LK.10 (TG-4A) (1942)

Ling-Temco-Vought XC-142A (1964)

Lockheed 18 Lodestar (C-60) (1943), **P-38L Lightning** (1944), **P-80R Shooting Star (P-80B)** (1944), **P-80C Shooting Star** (1949), **F-94A Starfire** (1949), **F-94C Starfire** (1950), **T-33A** (1953), **F-104A Starfighter** (1956), **F-104C Starfighter** (1956), **YF-12A** (1960), **049 Constellation (R7V-1) (VC-121E)** (1953), **1049 Super Constellation (RC-121D) (EC-121D)** (1953), **AC-130A Hercules (C-130A)** (1954), **U-2A** (1956)

Loening OA-1A (1926)

Martin B-10 (1934), **179 Marauder (B-26G)** (1943), **RB-57A Canberra** (1954), **EB-57B Canberra (B-57B)** (1952), **X-23A (SV-5D)** (1965), **SV-5J** (1967), **X-24B (X-24A)** (1966)

McDonnell YF-4E Phantom (1962), **F-4C Phantom** (1964), **XF-85 Goblin** (1948), **RF-101C Voodoo** (1956), **F-101B Voodoo** (1956), **M-38 (XH-20)** (1947), **F-15A Eagle** (1972)

Messerschmitt Me 163B Komet (1945), **Me 262A** (1944)

Mikoyan-Gurevich MiG-15 (1949)

Mitsubishi A6M2 Zero Sen (1940)

Nieuport 28C.1 (1918)

Noorduyn Norseman VI (UC-64A) (1944)

North American 0-47B (1939), **BT-9C** (1938), **T-6G Texan** (1950), **P-51D Mustang** (1944), **A-36A Mustang** (1942), **F-82B Twin Mustang** (1944), **B-25D Mitchell** (1943), **T-28A Trojan** (1950), **F-86A Sabre** (1949), **F-86D Sabre** (1950), **F-86H Sabre (F-86D)** (1953), **F-100C Super Sabre** (1954), **F-100D Super Sabre** (1955), **F-107A** (1955), **B-45C Tornado** (1948), **XB-70 Valkyrie** (1964), **X-15A** (1956), **T-39A Sabreliner** (1962)

Northrop A-17A (1936), **XP-56** (1942), **P-61C Black Widow** (1943), **F-89J Scorpion** (1952), **YF-5A** (1964?), **X-4** (1946)

Piper J-3C Cub (L-4) (0-59D) (1942)

Republic P-47D Thunderbolt (1942, 1945), **F-84E Thunderjet** (1950), **F-84F Thunderstreak** (1953), **YRF-84F Thunderflash** (1949), **XF-91 Thunderceptor** (1946), **F-105B Thunderchief** (1957), **F-105G Thunderchief** (1963)

Royal Aircraft Factory SE.5E (1922)

Ryan ST.3KR Recruit (PT-22) (1941), **69 Vertijet (X-13)** (1957)

Schweizer SGS.2-12 (TG-3A) (1942)

Seversky P-35 (1936), **P-35A (EP-106)** (1940)

Sikorsky VS-316 Hoverfly (R-4B) (1943), **VS-316 Hoverfly II (R-6A)** (1943), **VS-327 Dragonfly (YR-5A)** (1943), **S-55 Chickasaw (UH-19B)** (1952), **S-58 Seabat (HH-34J)** (1958)

Sopwith Camel (R) (1974)

SPAD VII (1916)

Sperry-Verville M-1 Messenger (1920)

Standard E-1 (1918), **J-1** (1918)

Stinson V.76 Sentinel (0-62) (L-5) (1942)

Supermarine 361 Spitfire XI (1943), **361 Spitfire XVI** (1942)

Taylorcraft D Grasshopper (L-2M) (1942)

Thomas Morse S4C (1917)

Vertol V.42 Shawnee (CH-21A) (1951)

Vultee BT-13B Valiant (1941), **V.74 Vigilant (0-44A) (L-1A)** (1941)

Waco CG-4A Hadrian (1945)

Westland Lysander III (1942)

Wright Military Flyer (R) (?), **B** modified (1909)

Yokosuka MXY-7 Ohka 11 (1945)

The United States Air Force Museum is one of the largest in the world, both in terms of numbers of aircraft on show and in the number of visitors which pass through its doors each year. In addition, the museum is also responsible for the loan of aircraft to other museums, military bases and organizations. Its total inventory now numbers over 1000 aircraft.

The origins of the museum go back to 1923 when the Aeronautical Engineering Center, at McCook Field near Dayton, set up a small display in a corner of one of its hangars. This was known as the Engineering Division Museum and its aim was to show the technology of both US and foreign aircraft of World War I. In 1927 the collection moved to Wright Field and had 1500 square feet (140 square meters) of a laboratory building for its display. Space was so limited that most of the aircraft were shown without wings and the fuselages were placed so tightly together that it was almost impossible to obtain a clear view. Things improved in the mid-1930s when the collection was given a new building which opened in 1936.

After the end of World War II the first director of the 'new' museum was Mark Sloan, who began the search for items for both his collection and the Smithsonian Institution. A former engine overhaul shop at Patterson Field was obtained in 1948. This collection was opened to the public in 1954; however, at first no complete aircraft were on show. Soon aircraft did begin to arrive, and a final name change occurred when in 1956 the United States Air Force Museum was officially established. The USAFM remained in this temporary home until 1971, but the inside structure with many pillars was not ideal for the display of large aircraft. The outdoor display area was overcrowded by the early 1960s and new exhibits were still being collected. In 1960 a group of civilians under the leadership of Eugene W Kettering set up the Air Force Museum Foundation, which launched a fund raising drive in 1964 and eventually raised over $6 million.

Thus financed, work on the present museum commenced in April 1970 and it was opened in August 1971. The building consists of two large hangars with a total length of almost 800 feet (240 meters) and a width of 240 feet (72 meters). In 1976 these were joined by a two-story administration and research building. Around 80 aircraft are on view in the main museum, which can now only house around 45 per cent of the aircraft at Dayton. Outside the museum there is usually a line-up of around 30 aircraft for which

The Boeing B-50 Superfortress was the last propeller-driven bomber delivered to the USAF. This KB-50J tanker version has two additional jet engines to assist take-off with a full load of fuel

there is no space. In 1985 work started on an extension of this main building, doubling the display area.

The harsh climate is no help in preventing corrosion, so an annex display has been set up in two of the old hangars at the now closed Wright Field. A shuttle bus makes regular trips to this facility. Here some 40 to 50 aircraft are on view, the vast majority being unrestored. Also on this side of the field is the restoration center where, in three former World War II hangars, a team of skilled craftsmen carry out their numerous and varied tasks. The site of Wright Field is most appropriate: from its opening in 1927 to its closure for flying when it became too small for modern jets, it was a test and development field for the air force. Between the annex and the restoration center can be seen part of the old runway which goes up a hill. The slope was incorporated to assist the take-off of heavily-laden machines. The hill between the two bases is known as Huffman Prairie and here in 1904/5 those famous Dayton residents the Wright brothers perfected their flying machines.

The indoor display shows the development of military aviation, with particular reference to the USAF and its forebears. Famous personalities such as Octave Chanute, Eddie Rickenbacker and Glenn Miller are honored in special exhibits, and other features include clothing of air aces of both World Wars, prisoner of war exhibits and early space capsules. There is a section on flight before the Wright Brothers with models, photographs, drawings and documents. The next section houses a replica of the first US military aeroplane, purchased from the Wrights in 1909. In 1908 Orville Wright had conducted tests for the army with Lt Thomas E Selfridge as his passenger. The aircraft crashed, and the unlucky Selfridge died from his injuries: he was the first man to die in the crash of a powered aircraft, and (in an earlier flight) the first military pilot to fly solo.

America entered World War I in 1917 and there are many interesting items on view from this period. Fighters and trainers from both sides can be seen, due to be joined in 1986 by at least one example of a Halberstadt biplane. In 1984 the museum acquired a stock of airframe and engine components. Just after World War I former German fighter pilot Paul Strahle bought several Halberstadts for use with a small airline he set up to fly between Stuttgart and other towns in Germany. Some were never converted and others remained in use up to 1939, when the whole stock was stored in the village of Schorndorf. Strahle refused to sell his Halberstadts for years but in 1982 he relented and released three complete aircraft, many airframe components and a number of Mercedes D IIIa engines. There is also a brand new unused CL IV fuselage.

The inter-war period saw a change in the role of all military forces and a vast reduction in their strengths. The US Army Air Corps was no exception and the early 1920s saw little in new aircraft. Thus in order to gain recognition they indulged in spectacular feats to bring their skills to the notice of politicians. Five Douglas World Cruisers (DWCs) were built in 1923-24 for the first flight around the world. This epic started on April 4, 1924 when four aircraft left Seattle and headed west. The route would take them through Canada, Alaska and down the Aleutians to Japan, avoiding the Soviet Union which would not let them fly over its territory. The flight continued across Asia, the Middle East and Europe.

One aircraft was lost in Alaska, and during the Atlantic crossing another force-landed off the Faroe Islands and capsized while being towed. The two surviving DWCs were joined by their prototype at Picton in Nova Scotia, and then flew across the US to Seattle. Both wheel and float undercarriages were used on the trip, which finished on September 28. One of the two which completed the flight, owned by the Los Angeles County Museum, is on loan for

A North American Texan is displayed in a color scheme worn by many trainers in the early 1940s

The Thomas Morse S4C was designed as a fighter. However, hundreds of US fighter pilots during World War I knew it only as a trainer

Above
This Boeing P-12E fighter served in pursuit squadrons from 1929 to 1935

Left
Very few examples of the Martin Marauder medium bomber now survive, though over 5000 were constructed

The Northrop Black Widow was the first American fighter to be specifically designed for night interception. It first flew in 1942, and over 700 were delivered to the USAF

display at the AFM.

Other interesting aircraft in this area include a Verville-Sperry Messenger which was designed and tested at McCook Field. The tiny biplane was fitted with a hook above the upper wing and on September 18, 1923, with Lt Rex Stonor as pilot, made the first successful link-up with an airship in flight. This event took place at Langley Field, Virginia, with the D-3 airship.

The odd-looking Loening OA-1A amphibian, with its long central float merged into the fuselage, was flown by Ira Eaker and Muir Fairchild on a 22,000 mile (35,000 km) goodwill tour of 25 Central and South American countries in 1926-27. Nearby is a Consolidated PT-1 which was the first type to be bought in large numbers since the end of World War I. Around 200 of this rugged biplane were ordered and used for almost a decade. This historic aircraft was found at Ohio State University in 1957.

One of the first military aircraft to be used in Alaska was the Douglas O-38 biplane. The aircraft on show was based near Fairbanks in October 1940. The following June it force-landed away from base and remained where it was until June 1968, when it was lifted out by helicopter. A rarity is one of the few remaining Curtiss Hawk biplane fighters. Considered by many to be among the most graceful biplanes ever built, and with an excellent performance, only a few were built because of the Depression. The only known Martin B-10 was presented to the museum in 1971 by Argentina. The B-10 was the first all-metal monoplane bomber to be produced in quantity. The identity of the aircraft has been lost, and it has been painted to represent one of the 10 that flew from Washington DC to Alaska and back in 1934. This period saw military aircraft in bright colors for both training and operational machines, and the display shows them in typical 1930s plumage.

The larger hangar is dominated by the first aircraft to move into the museum – the giant B-36 bomber. With a span of 230 feet (70 meters) it just fits inside, dwarfing all around including three 'heavies' from World War II. Most of the famous types from this conflict are on view, but there are also some unusual aircraft, including the sole remaining Fisher P-75A. Only 14 of this single-engined fighter, which drove a contra-rotating propeller, were completed. The Boeing B-29 Superfortress on view is the one which dropped the second atomic bomb on Japan on August 9, 1945.

The display then moves on to the jet age, with a wide variety of aircraft including many of the innovative X series of

A defecting North Korean pilot flew this MiG-15 fighter to South Korea in 1953. He was reported to have received a reward of $100,000 for this exploit

research aircraft. The most exotic aircraft is probably the XB-70 Valkyrie bomber that can be seen just outside the main entrance. Two of these six-engined giants were built by North American, and the first flew in September 1964. One was lost in a mid-air collision, but the other flew on the test program until it was delivered to Patterson AFB in February 1969. The last journey made by this futuristic aircraft, which had exceeded Mach 3 in flight, was the slow road journey of 7 miles (11 km) to Wright Field.

The USAF Museum is one of the most comprehensive air force museums in existence, and with the planned extensions one of the largest aircraft collections anywhere in the world will be on view to all.

WALTER SOPLATA COLLECTION

PO Box 65, Newbury, Ohio 44065
Tel: 216-564-5326

Admission by prior arrangement only
Location: just north of the town, which is about 18 miles (26 km) east of Cleveland on Route 87

Avro-Canada CF-100 Canuck 5 (1958)
Beech B18S 3TM (C-45G) (1952), **B18S (C-45G)** (1951), **B18S (SNB-2) (UC-45J)** (1943), **B18S Kansas (AT-11)** (1941)
Bell 26 Airacobra (P-39) (c.1942), **33 King Cobra (P-63A)** (1942)
Boeing 367 Stratotanker (KC-97F) (1951)
Cessna T-50 Bobcat (1943)
Convair YB-36E (1942)
Curtiss 85 Owl (0-52) (1940)
Douglas DC-7B (1956), **XBT2D Skyraider** (1945), **AD-6 Skyraider (A-1H)** (c.1953), **A-26B Invader** (1944), **C-124A Globemaster** (1951)
Fairchild M.62 Cornell (PT-19) (1942), **C-82A Packet** (1944)
Fleetwings XBT-12 (1939)
Grumman G.40 Avenger (TBM-?) (c.1944), **G.98 Tiger (F-11A) (F11F-1)** (1953)
Howard DGA-15P (1941)
Lockheed F-80A Shooting Star (P-80A) (1944), **T-33A** (1951), **SP-2H Neptune (P2V-7)** (1958)
Martin B-57A Canberra (1952)
McDonnell F2H- Banshee (c.1951)
North American AT-6D Texan (c.1942), **T-6G Texan** (1949), **P-51K Mustang** (1944), **XP-82 Twin Mustang** (1944), **F-82E Twin Mustang (P-82E)** (1946), **B-25J Mitchell** (1944), **T-28A Trojan** (1950), **F-86E Sabre** (1951), **F-86L Sabre (F-86D)** (1953)
Republic P-47N Thunderbolt (1944), **F-84E Thunderjet** (1950), **F-84F Thunderstreak** (1952), **RF-84F Thunderflash** (1952)
Sikorsky S-55 Chickasaw (UH-19D) (1954), **S-58 Seabat (HSS-1)** (1958)
Vought FG-1D Corsair (1944), **F2G-1 Corsair** (1945), **F7U-3 Cutlass** (1950)
Vultee BT-13A Valiant (1941), **BT-15 Valiant** (1942)

Not many people have around 50 aircraft in their back garden, but in the small town of Newbury not far from Cleveland there is such a place. Driving up the dirt road by a pleasant lake, everything seems normal until a corner is rounded and a North American Texan is seen sitting on the front lawn of one of the typical wooden houses of the area. On a closer look, more can be seen: a Sikorsky S-55 helicopter on the other side of the drive and, at the rear through a gap in the hedge, more airframes come into view. Then one knows that this is the famed collection of Walter Soplata.

Soplata learned to fly at Chagin Falls in Ohio in 1944, and two years later became a licensed airframe and engine fitter. He acquired his first aircraft in 1947 when he bought a Vultee BT-13 without engines or instruments for $145. Since then he has traveled thousands of miles and spent vast sums of money in adding to his collection.

The aircraft that have arrived at Newbury are not all small, and the work that goes in is typified by the move of a giant Convair YB 36. The second example of this giant bomber was offered for scrap at Wright-Patterson after it had been converted and used as an RB-36E. The giant was dismantled, and 50 journeys were needed to get all the parts to Newbury. There are still parts missing, but the fuselage has been reassembled, and inside it are stored the fuselages of other aircraft.

One of the batch of 25 Douglas Destroyer IIs, from which the highly successful Skyraider was later developed, rests in Walter Soplata's paddock

The unconventional tailless Vought Cutlass shows its elongated nose-wheel leg, incorporated on production aircraft to improve carrier catapult launches

There are some real rarities on show, including the only known Fleetwings BT-12 basic trainer. The aircraft at Newbury is the first example built of this stainless steel low-wing monoplane. It was followed by 24 production models but 176 were canceled. The North American Twin Mustang, which used two standard Mustang fuselages side by side, joined by a common wing and tail plane, was evolved for long-range escort duties. They were too late to see use in World War II but later were used in Korea. The Twin Mustang, of which fewer than 300 were built, is now a rarity but here are two – the incomplete second prototype and the production F-82E.

A number of sheds have been constructed around the site, and in one of these buildings is the Goodyear-built F2G Corsair in which Cook Cleland won the 1947 Thompson Trophy race at Cleveland. This powerful beast is still carrying its racing colors. The F2G can be compared with the standard FG-1 from which it was developed, as one of these is in the collection.

Vought, who designed the Corsair, were also responsible for the tailless F7U Cutlass jet fighter. Based on the ideas of Dr Alexander Lippisch, who had experimented with flying wings in Germany since the late 1920s, the striking-looking Cutlass was a major innovation for the US Navy, and around 300 were eventually built. The Curtiss Owl observation aircraft, of which just over 200 were built, is now almost extinct, but here is one. One of the development Douglas XBT2D torpedo bombers which led to the famous Skyraider is in the collection.

As time permits, restoration is slowly carried out, and some have been assembled in the field. Although not a proper museum, this fabulous collection is well known and visited by enthusiasts from all over the world.

Oklahoma

ADA AIRCRAFT MUSEUM

Frederick Municipal Airport, Frederick, Oklahoma 73542
Correspondence to Mid-America Air Group, PO Box 935, Frederick, Oklahoma 73542
Tel: 405-335-7208 or 2421

Opening times: midday to sunset, Thursday-Sunday
Location: at the northwest side of the airport. Frederick is about 100 miles (160 km) southwest of Oklahoma City

Aero Commander 520 (1952, 1953), **Commander 690B** (1977)
Aeronca K (1937), **65C** (1939), **65TC (0-58B)** (1943), **7AC Champion** (1946), **7BCM (L-16)** (1951)
Beech C18S (1942), **35 Bonanza** (1947), **50 Twin Bonanza** (1956)
Bellanca 14-13 Crusaire (1948), **260** (1960)
Boeing-Stearman B 75N1 Kaydet (N25-3) (1942)
Bushby-Long Midget Mustang (1969), **Mustang II** (1971)
Cessna T-50 Bobcat (UC-78) (1943), **120** (1946), **175** (1958), **195A** (1950), **310** (1955)
Culver V (1946)
Curtiss-Wright CW-1 Junior (1931)
Douglas DC-3 (C-47) (1944), **A-26B Invader** (1944)
Ercoupe 415C (1947)
EAA P-9 Pober Pixie (1982)
Fairchild F.24H (1936), **F.24W (UC-61)** (1946), **M.62 Cornell (PT-19)** (1942), **M.62A Cornell (PT-26)** (1942), **M.62C Cornell (PT-23)** (1942)
Funk B (1940)
Globe GC-1B Swift (1946)
Grumman G.40 Avenger (TBM-3) (1944), **G.89 Tracker (S2F-1) (S-2A)** (1954), **G.111 Albatross (G.64) (SA-16A)** (1951)
Interstate S-1A Cadet (L-6) (1942)
K & S SA-102-5 Cavalier (1982)
Leak Avid Flyer (1978)
Lockheed 5 Vega 1 (1933)
Luscombe 8 Silvaire (1947), **T-8F** (1948)
McCullogh J-2 (1971)
Mooney M.18C Mite (1954), **M.20B** (1954)
North American AT-6F Texan (SNJ-6) (1944), **T-28A Trojan** (1951), **B-25J Mitchell** (1944)
Pietenpol B4A Air Camper (1929)
Piper J-3C Cub (1940), **J-3C Cub (L-4J)** (1943), **J-4A Cub Coupe** (1940), **J-4F Cub Coupe** (1940), **PA-22 Tri-Pacer** (1962), **PA-23 Apache** (1954), **PA-23 Aztec** (1961)
Porterfield CP-65 (1940)
Rand KR-1 (1982)
Rearwin 7000 Sportsster (1937)
Roloff RLU-1 Breezy (1981)
Rutan Vari-Eze (1983)
Ryan ST.3KR Recruit (PT-22) (1941), **Navion A** (1945), **Twin Navion** (1948)
Shober Willie II (1975)
Smith Termite H1 (1966)
Stinson V.76 Sentinel (L-5E) (194?), **V.77 Reliant (AT-19)** (1943), **108-3** (1947), **10A Voyager** (1941)
Taylorcraft D (0-57) (L-2) (1944)
Thorp T-18 (1970)
Viking Dragonfly (1984)
Vultee BT-13A Valiant (1942)

To assemble a collection of over 70 aircraft in less than two years is a major achievement by any standards, and the Mid-America Air Group have done just this. This interesting collection is housed in two hangars at the Municipal Airport of Frederick, Oklahoma, which provides facilities to the museum at no cost. In addition there are office and club rooms, and a vast concrete ramp, outside the hangars. When fully developed the museum will have excellent premises. The person behind the museum is Tom A Thomas, a retired USAF officer who owns all the aircraft in a private trust, which will pass the collection over to the group when it becomes financially self-sufficient. The museum started at the town of Ada, also in Oklahoma, and still uses this name in its title.

The museum held its first major air show at Frederick in June 1985, and one of the highlights was 'Colonel Tom's Last Hurrah': Tom Thomas flew 65 different types of aircraft to celebrate his 65th birthday. Starting at 7.22 in the morning, with breaks at mid-morning and lunch time, this epic was completed at 4.17 in the afternoon. The total flying time was 7 hours 46 minutes. The aircraft used spanned over half a century, from a 1929 Pietenpol Air Camper to a 1984 Viking Dragonfly. About the only thing these two types have in common is that they were both available to

D-Day Invasion Stripes decorate a Stinson Sentinel observation aircraft

This 1937 Aeronca K was the first aircraft to be owned by the founder of the museum, Tom A Thomas

the home builder. In addition to endurance, the skills he displayed in piloting these vastly different aircraft – ranging from ultralights to twin-engined military machines and including one rotary-wing autogyro – are much to be admired.

Included in this total, and in the collection, are two aircraft of particular interest to Tom Thomas. In January 1940 he made his first solo in a Piper J-3 Cub at Ada, and the first aircraft he owned was a 1937 Aeronca K. Both these aircraft have been bought back, to take pride of place in the museum. The majority of exhibits are light aircraft which have been the backbone of the club and sporting movement in the US over the last half century. A walk through the hangars provides a vivid picture of the development of the single-engined aircraft.

From the golden era of the 1930s are a few well-known types from the Rearwin, Piper, Fairchild and Aeronca factories, and in the next period many sporting aircraft which were hastily adapted for military use. The Fairchild F.24 was built in considerable numbers as a utility transport for both American and Commonwealth forces, and examples of variants from before, during and after World War II can be seen. The beautiful Stinson Reliant first flew in 1933, and many private versions appeared in the next few years. These high-wing monoplanes with excellent performance and a high standard of interior comfort were much sought after. Several were impressed when the US entered the war, and then 500 were ordered by the US for delivery to the Royal Navy. Two of this batch are in the collection, one painted in RN colors and the other in Royal Canadian Air Force markings.

The rarest aircraft in the collection is undoubtedly the last Lockheed Vega in flying order. The Vega achieved immortal fame in the hands of such pilots as Amelia Earhart and Wiley Post, but many other famous aviators used the model on record-setting flights. This Vega differs from the standard model in that it has a duralumin fuselage, built in Detroit and fitted to a wooden wing made in California. The Vega gave good service in Alaska before returning to the US. Tom Thomas bought the aircraft from Bob Taylor, founder of the Antique Airplane Association, in 1984 and it flew to Oklahoma from the Antique Airfield at Blakesburg in Iowa.

The collection has obtained a number of fairly modern homebuilt designs and some warbirds, which add to the variety on view. It is to be hoped that this brave venture goes from strength to strength, as it possesses facilities for expansion that are not available to many museums.

OKLAHOMA AVIATION AND SPACE HALL OF FAME AND MUSEUM

2100 North East 52nd Street, Oklahoma City, Oklahoma 73111
Tel: 405-424-1443

Opening times: 10am-5pm Monday-Saturday, 1pm-5pm Sunday
Location: in the northeastern suburbs of the city

American Eagle A-101 (1927)
Bücker Bü 133C Jungmeister (1935)
Cirrus 3 Hang-glider (?)
Cofferman Monoplane (c.1932)
Colomban MC.10 Cri-Cri (c.1980)
Curtiss D (R) (?)
Fokker Dr I (R) (?)
Kaminskas RK.III Jungster (1975)
Mitchell Wing B-10 (c.1980)
Mong MS-2K (1965)
Nieuport 11 (R) (?)
Parker Pusher (?)
Pierce-Sawyer JP-51 (?)
Schweizer SGS.2-12 (1942)
Stinson 108-2 (1948)
Wiley Post A (1935)
Wright Flyer (R) (?)

The opening of a new museum is always of interest and the Oklahoma area has been the site of new developments in recent years. On November 5, 1982 in the Kirkpatrick Center the Oklahoma Air Space Museum, directed by veteran aviator Clarence E Page, was formally dedicated. The museum prides itself on the vast 'hands-on' exhibit area. There are five Link Trainers on which most American World War II military pilots trained, the cockpit of an F-101 Voodoo and an F-111 ejection model simulator. There are also weapons systems to try, and other simulators. The display of memorabilia is particularly impressive, covering flight from the Wright brothers to the space era.

The aircraft display contains some rarities. The highlight of those on display is the last surviving Wiley Post A biplane, originally known as the Straughan A and then renamed after Wiley Post, the famous aviator. The Straughan firm ran into financial difficulties in 1934 and was taken over by Mark Kleedon, who moved the operation to Oklahoma City. Only 13 were built before the company finally closed. This delightful biplane was powered by a converted Ford Model A car engine and with its side by side seating would have surely been a success with proper support from the manufacturers. It is appropriate that this aircraft should be preserved not far from its birthplace, Wiley Post Airport, which is on the outskirts of the city.

An interesting relic that arrived in the summer of 1985 was the framework of what is believed to be one of the two or three Cofferman monoplanes produced in the 1930s. The museum restoration staff had to tackle the problem of unearthing information on the design before they could even attempt the rebuild.

A number of homebuilt designs have been acquired by the museum, including a Mong Sports which was designed in Tulsa, Oklahoma by Ralph Mong and was one of the most popular single-seat biplanes in the early 1960s.

For a collection of unusual aircraft, carefully presented and backed up with impressive side displays, this new museum is well worth a visit.

The Oklahoma-built Wiley Post A occupies a position of pride in Oklahoma's newest air museum

South Carolina

FLORENCE AIR AND MISSILE MUSEUM

PO Box 1326, Florence, South Carolina 29503
Tel: 803-665-5118

Opening times: 9am-dusk daily
Location: about 3 miles (5 km) east of the city off Route 501 at the airport

Bell 47G Sioux (HTL-6) (TH-13M) (?), **206A Kiowa (OH-58C)** (1969)
Boeing 345 Superfortress (B-29) (1944), **367 Stratotanker (KC-97G)** (1952), **450 Stratojet (B-47B)** (1950)
Convair YF-102A (1953)
Douglas A-26K Counter Invader (1964), **BTD-1 Destroyer** (1944), **RB-66B Destroyer** (1953), **C-124C Globemaster** (1952)
Fairchild C-119C Flying Boxcar (1950)
Grumman G.64 Albatross (HU-16B) (SA-16B) (1951), **G.98 Tiger (F-11A) (F11F-1)** (1955)
Gyrodyne QH-50 (1970)
Hiller UH-12C (OH-23C) (1956)
Kaman K.600 Huskie (H-43A) (1958)
Lockheed 1049 Super Constellation (WV-2) (EC-121K) (1951), **T-33A** (1953), **F-104B Starfighter** (1957)
McDonnell TF-101F Voodoo (F-101B) (1956)
Martin RB-57A Canberra (1952)
North American F-86H Sabre (1952)
Northrop F-89J Scorpion (1953)
Republic F-84F Thunderstreak (1952)
Sikorsky S-55 (HO4S-1) (1951), **S-58 Choctaw (CH-34C)** (1955)
Vertol V.42 Shawnee (CH-21B) (1954)

The airfield at Florence was a training base during World War II and has since been developed into the Municipal Airport for the city. The idea for a museum was conceived by the local Chamber of Commerce in the latter part of 1963, and by 1965 aircraft had begun to arrive on a site donated by the city. The museum aims to serve as a memorial to the air corps and air force personnel who lost their lives during World War I, World War II, Korean and Vietnam. Originally just an open-air display of aircraft and missiles, the museum has now a large indoor display area and there are plans to enlarge this still further in the next few years.

The space section is particularly impressive with a Gemini capsule, the suit worn by Alan Shepherd on his Apollo mission, instruments and engines from Saturn rockets and an Apollo launch computer. Another display tells the story of the American pilots who flew for the Escadrille Lafayette in World War I, and there are also sections devoted to Jimmy Doolittle's famous raid on Tokyo. A vast amount of material has been gathered, and the exhibition is steadily being improved as funds become available.

The majority of the aircraft on show are on loan from the USAF Museum at Dayton, and many of them have been acquired with the help of local politicians Senator Thurmond and Congressman McMillan. This has resulted in an emphasis in the display on recently withdrawn military aircraft, although the range is still wide. The first three aircraft acquired were a Douglas RB-66B Destroyer from Shaw AFB (only a short distance away), a North American F-86H Sabre which flew in from McGuire AFB in New Jersey, and a Lockheed T-33A from Langley AFB in Virginia. The T-33 arrived in December 1964, and the other two the following March. Despite over 20 years in the open air, the museum staff have ensured that these and the other aircraft are kept in good condition.

The rarest aircraft is a Douglas BTD-1 Destroyer torpedo bomber, on loan from the navy. This type was designed as a single-seat version of the XSB2D-1 but only 28 were com-

The sole surviving Douglas Destroyer out of the 28 examples of this naval type that were built

Flown in from nearby Shaw Air Force Base in 1965, this Douglas B-66 Destroyer was the museum's second acquisition

pleted before the contract was canceled. The example on show was the last built, even though it carries the earliest serial number of the batch. When it was decided that the SB2D-1 program was not to proceed, the two-seaters were to be modified to single seat BTD-1s on the line, but the first aircraft was too advanced to be converted, so it was scrapped and its serial number used on the last Destroyer.

In the outdoor display there are so many large aircraft that overcrowding is a problem, and two of the giants, a Super Constellation and a Globemaster, have been moved to a separate compound nearby. The Globemaster was formerly used by the 165th MAG of the Georgia Air National Guard, based at Savannah. They used the massive Globemaster from 1967, and when the last two were retired in September 1974 they were the last of the type in USAF service. The Super Constellation was last used by VAQ-33 Squadron of the navy at Key West; it became the last Warning Star Constellation in use, and was withdrawn in July 1982.

One poignant notice beside the Boeing B-47 Stratojet states that on March 1958 an aircraft of this type accidentally dropped an atomic bomb on Florence – fortunately without detonating it.

The proximity of the museum to the airport has meant that many of the aircraft have flown in and then 'demilitarized' on site, which has cut down costs considerably. Although slightly off the beaten track for aircraft enthusiasts, this excellent museum is a major attraction for tourists in the region.

Texas

CONFEDERATE AIR FORCE FLYING MUSEUM

PO Box CAF, Harlingen, Texas 78551
Tel: 512-425-1057

Opening times: 9am-5pm Monday-Saturday, 1300-1800 Sunday
Location: at Valley International Airport which is about 3 miles (5 km) west of Harlingen

Aeronca 65TC (L-3B) (O-58B) (1942), **65TA (L-3E)** (1942)
Beagle B.206S (1966)
Beech B18S Kansas (AT-11) (1942), **B18S Kansas (AT-11) (SNB-2C)** (1942), **B18S (C-45)** (1943), **B18S (C-45H)** (1952), **D18S** (c.1950)
Bell 26 Airacobra (P-39Q) (1943), **33 King Cobra (P-63)** (1943), **33 King Cobra (P-63A)** (1942)
Boeing 299 Fortress (B-17G) (1944), **299 Fortress (B-17G) (PB-1W)** (1944), **345 Superfortress (B-29A)** (1944)
Boeing-Stearman A75 Kaydet (PT-17) (1941), **B75 Kaydet (N2S-3)** (1942)
Cessna C.165 Airmaster (1940), **C.195** (1948), **T-50 Bobcat (Crane)** (1943), **T-50 Bobcat (UC-78B)** (1943)
Consolidated 28 Catalina (PBY-5A) (1942), **RLB-30 Liberator (C-87)** (1941)
CASA 2-111 (He 111) (1954), **C.352L (Ju 52/3m)** (c.1946)
Curtiss 84 Helldiver (SB2C-5) (1943), **87 Warhawk (P-40N)** (1942)
Curtiss-Wright CW-20 Commando (C-46F) (1944)
de Havilland DH 94 Moth Minor (1939)
Douglas DC-3 (1937), **DC-3 (C-47B) (R4D-6)** (1943), **DC-3 (C-47B)** (1944), **DC-3 (C-117D) (R4D-8)** (1943), **DC-4 (C-54D)** (1942), **SBD-5 Dauntless** (1943), **B-23 Dragon** (1939), **A-20G Havoc** (1943), **A-26B Invader** (1941), **A-26C Invader** (1944), **A-1E Skyraider (AD-5)** (1951)
Ercoupe 415C (1941)
Fairchild M.62A Cornell (PT-26) (1943), **M.62 Cornell (PT-19)** (1942), **M.62A Cornell (PT-23)** (1942), **M.62A Cornell (PT-26)** (1942, 1943)
Fleet 16B Finch (1940)
Focke-Wulf Fw 44J Stieglitz (1940)
Grumman G.36 Wildcat (FM-2) (1942), **G.40 Avenger (TBM-3E)** (1944), **G.50 Hellcat (F6F-5)** (1944), **G.58 Bearcat (F8F-2P)** (1945)
Hispano Ha.1112M (Bf 109) (1953, 1954)
Interstate S1B1 Cadet (L-6) (1943)
Lockheed 18 Lodestar (C-60) (1942, 1943), **P-38L Lightning** (1943)
Martin 179 Marauder (B-26C) (1943), **210 Mauler (AM-1)** (1946)
Maule M.5 210C Strata Rocket (c.1972)
Messerschmitt Bf 108D (1942)
Naval Aircraft Factory N3N-3 (1941)
North American NA.64 Yale (1940), **AT-6A Texan** (1940), **AT-6B Texan** (1941), **AT-6C Texan (SNJ-4)** (1941, 1942), **AT-6D Texan (SNJ-5)** (1942, 1944), **AT-6F Texan (SNJ-6)** (1944), **T-6G Texan** (1949), **T-6J Texan (Harvard 4)** (1951), **P-51C Mustang** (1942), **P-51D Mustang** (1944), **F-82B Twin Mustang** (1944), **B-25J Mitchell** (1943, 1944), **(Ryan) L-17B Navion** (1947)
Northrop C-125A Raider (1948)
Piaggio P.166C (1965)
Piper J-5A Cub Cruiser (1940)
Republic P-47N Thunderbolt (1944)
Ryan ST.3KR Recruit (PT-22) (1941)
Schweizer SGS.2-12 (TG-3A) (1942)
Sikorsky VS-316 Hoverfly (R-4B) (1943)
Stinson 108-1 Voyager (1946), **V.76 Sentinel (L-5)** (1942), **V.77 Reliant (AT-19)** (1943)
Supermarine 361 Spitfire IX (1942), **388 Seafire FR.47** (1946)
Taylorcraft D (L-2) (1943)
Vought FG-1D Corsair (1945)
Vultee BT-13 Valiant (1940), **BT-13A Valiant** (1941), **BT-15 Valiant** (1942)
Waco CG-4A Hadrian (c.1943)

The Confederate Air Force is probably the best known collection of flyable World War II aircraft. As with many museums, its beginnings were humble. A small group of pilots in Texas bought a North American Mustang in 1957 and it was ferried from El Paso to a small crop dusting strip at Mercedes. Later in the year the name 'Confederate Air Force' appeared painted on the fuselage, and in this unofficial way the organization was born. Interest grew, and soon two Grumman Bearcats were bought and ferried back from the US Navy at Litchfield Park near Phoenix in Arizona.

In 1960 the objectives of the CAF were formally stated. The first was 'to preserve in flying condition a complete collection of combat aircraft of all military services of the United States in World War II'. A search was initiated to try and fulfill this. Visits were made to the navy at Litchfield Park and to the air force at Davis-Monthan, where they found aircraft being scrapped by the thousands. All members of the CAF were given the rank of 'Colonel' and the mythical Jethro E. Culpeper was made leader. By 1963 examples of 10 types of air force and navy fighters had been acquired, including two from outside the US – a Bell Kingcobra was found in Honduras, and a Republic Thunderbolt in Nicaragua. With the exception of a Bell Airacobra all were airworthy.

The first annual air show was held at Mercedes on March 10, 1963 and this was to be an important event in the development of the CAF. A decision was taken to expand the aims to include all combat aircraft of American origin. Six RCAF Texans had been bought in Canada in 1961, and a North American Mitchell bomber was also acquired that year, in advance of the change of aims. These aircraft began to participate in air shows around Texas, and the collection became known to a wider audience.

The Mitchell was joined by an Invader in 1964 and the CAF 'First Bomb Wing' was organized. With the same enthusiasm as had been shown in the quest for fighters, the search for bombers was under way. By 1967 examples of the Fortress, Liberator, Havoc and Marauder were in flying condition. The facilities at Mercedes were fairly basic but a real step forward occurred in 1965 when a start was made on a permanent museum hangar. The building was dedicated in March 1966, and the CAF had a real home.

Expansion followed steadily, with members joining from all over the world. Many of these new Colonels owned aircraft, and the fleet grew. Sponsorship was obtained for many of the aircraft and permanent staff were appointed. Foreign aircraft were added: a Spitfire came from England, a Mosquito from Canada, and a fleet of five Spanish-built Messerschmitt Bf 109s were purchased from the Spanish Air Force. The 109s spent some time flying in the 'Battle of Britain' film in the UK before making their journey to Texas.

Even with the new hangar, the field at Mercedes was by now becoming too small, and in 1968 the CAF accepted an invitation from the city of Harlingen to move to their new International Airport. Three hangars – one each for the fighter and bomber wings and one for maintenance – were allocated to the museum. A World War II Army Air Corps office building was put into use as the offices, an Officers' Club and the indoor museum. The indoor display contained an exhibition of World War II memorabilia, photographs, maps and guns, and three sections were devoted to the Army Air Corps, the US Navy and the CAF.

The early 1970s saw the setting up of CAF wings elsewhere in the US, and these are now numerous. Many have their own hangars, and aircraft are permanently attached to these units. The CAF fleet now numbers almost 150, about a

EII-142

Opposite
One of the North American Texans that were restyled to represent Zero fighters for the film 'Tora, Tora, Tora'

Right
The only flying North American Twin Mustang is shown in its night-fighting black

Below
The Boeing B-29 Superfortress is the largest bomber in the Confederate Air Force fleet

The Curtiss Commando transport was a vital component in the USAAC efforts in World War II

third of which are at Harlingen. The annual show, now held each October, will see many of the aircraft of the outlying wings make the journey to their HQ.

The fleet has changed from time to time as owners remove their aircraft from the CAF, and there have also been a few crashes over the years. The move to Harlingen also saw the start of the practice of painting the aircraft in typical World War II colors.

Some spectacular recoveries have enhanced the reputation of the CAF. In 1969 Ed Jurist found six Thunderbolts in Lima in Peru, and after negotiations with the Peruvian authorities the aircraft and tons of spares were on their way to Texas. The Thunderbolts had been used in South America from 1957 to 1967 and all were stored in good condition at Piura. All were restored to flying condition by early 1974, and in February that year the five were joined in the air by the first CAF P-47. The CAF could not possibly sustain such a number of any one type, so they have subsequently been offered for sale.

The massive Boeing B-29 Superfortress achieved fame when it delivered the two atomic bombs that ended World War II. The numbers of this bomber had declined sharply until none were in flying condition. A few were in museums, but most of the survivors were on ranges in California or Maryland. After two years of negotiations with the USAF one was acquired. The B-29 had spent 17 years in the California desert; its restoration was completed and it flew to Harlingen in August 1971. The B-29 is one of two now in flying condition, and often has appeared at air shows all around the USA.

Another rare aircraft in flying condition is a North American Twin Mustang. This, the only example to remain airworthy, arrived at Harlingen in 1969. Three years later the epic ferry flight of a de Havilland Mosquito brought one of the most famous and versatile World War II aircraft to Harlingen. The Mosquito had been flown in the films '633 Squadron' and 'Mosquito Squadron' and after maintenance at Booker airfield the vintage aircraft undertook the 6000 mile (9600 km) flight to Texas. The crew of two had to carry out all the maintenance on the flight, which was routed via Spain, the Azores and Newfoundland.

The film 'Tora! Tora! Tora!' which told the story of the attack on Pearl Harbor posed problems for the film makers. There was virtually no Japanese aircraft in existence. Inventive conversions of North American Texans and Vultee Valiants were mocked up to represent Zero fighters, Val dive bombers and Kate torpedo bombers. In 1971 the CAF was able to acquire four of the Zero replicas and one each of the other two. Although not authentic, these have made their contribution to the annual air show – a re-enactment of the Pearl Harbor attack.

The air show specializes in this type of re-enactment and the famous aircraft, carrying the markings of famous units, brings back memories of events which saved the Allies in World War II. There are moves afoot which may lead to a relocation of the CAF from its remote site in southern Texas, and news is awaited.

TEXAS MUSEUM OF MILITARY HISTORY

96 BMW, Dyess Air Force Base, Texas 79607
Tel: 915-696-2121

Opening times: Museum Building (7407) is open 8am-4pm Monday-Friday; the aircraft in the open may be viewed in daylight hours, but a pass must be obtained from the security police
Location: about 3 miles (5 km) southwest of Abilene off Interstate 20

Beech 45 Mentor (T-34B) (1953)
Boeing 299 Fortress (B-17G) (DB-17P) (1944), **367 Stratotanker (KC-97L) (KC-97G)** (1953), **450 Stratojet (B-47E) (EB-47E)** (1954), **464 Stratofortress (B-52D)** (1956)
Cessna T-50 (UC-78B) (1942), **337 Skymaster (0-2A)** (1967)
Convair 240 (T-29C) (1952)
Douglas DC-3 (C-47) (R4D-5) (1942), **A-26C Invader** (1944)
Fairchild C-123K Provider (C-123B) (1954)
Grumman G.64 Albatross (UF-2G) (HU-16E) (1951)
Lockheed T-33A (1951), **F-104A Starfighter** (1956)
McDonnell F-101F Voodoo (1957)
Martin FB-57B Canberra (B-57B) (1952)
North American F-86L Sabre (F-86D) (1953), **F-100C Super Sabre** (1954)
Northrop F-89H Scorpion (1954)
Republic F-84F Thunderstreak (1951), **RF-84F Thunderflash** (1951), **F-105D Thunderchief** (1959)

Texas has a long military tradition and has in the last few years established a museum to cover this aspect of its history. On Alamo Day (March 6) 1980 the Texas Museum of Military History came into being, and funds are now being raised to construct a large purpose-built museum. The present and future site of the museum is at Dyess Air Force Base on the outskirts of Abilene where 70 acres (28 hectares) of land have been donated for the purpose.

The first phase of the exhibition covers the period from 1902 to the present. There are over 20 aircraft parked alongside the main road from the gate to the flight line, and these are to be moved to the site around the museum, to be displayed among military vehicles, ships and weapons used by Texas based units of the armed forces. There are also plans for a major library and research center.

There has been a military presence in the Abilene area since 1852 when Fort Phantom was constructed. During World War II a vast training camp was built at Camp Barkeley on the outskirts of the city. Part of this site was used as a training ground for National Guardsmen, but with the onset of the Korean War the city raised money to purchase more land, and lobbied the authorities in Washington to build a permanent military installation. Ground was broken in 1953 and the new base was ready in April 1956. Since that date the base, named after Lt-Col William Dyess, has been the home of Strategic Air Command units. Dyess was a Texan who was killed in a P-38 when it crashed in California in December 1943.

Dyess is a bomber base, and this is clearly reflected in the display. The earliest is a Boeing B-17 Fortress which was a

Designed by the Chase company and developed from their G-20 glider, the Fairchild C-123 Provider was the first American transport to land in Vietnam during the conflict

This Boeing B-17G Fortress is painted in the World War II colors of the 96th Bomb Group, which is now based at Dyess AFB

type used by the home unit, the 96th Bomb Wing, during World War II. The Boeing company later produced two jet bombers which have given and are still giving excellent service to SAC. The six-jet B-47 Stratojet first flew in 1947 and was innovative in several ways. Its 'bicycle' undercarriage was the first employed on a production aircraft, and its six jets were mounted in pods suspended below the swept wing. The B-47 was the backbone of SAC for many years and the type was based at Dyess in the late 1950s and early 1960s. The eight-jet B-52 was developed from the B-47 and first flew in August 1954. These giants are still the main force of SAC although the later models, which are still in use, are beginning to be phased out as the new B-1s are being delivered. The B-52D on show is an ex-96th aircraft and made the short journey from the flight line to its parking area.

The collection possesses a wide range of the jet fighters which have served the USAF with distinction from the late 1940s. Also, SAC have operated flying tankers for a number of years, and on view is a Boeing KC-97 whose last user was a Texas Air National Guard unit based at Dallas. The KC-97 was standard equipment at Dyess from 1957 to 1960. The Fairchild Provider transport was the forerunner of the famous Hercules, and it became the first US transport to land on Vietnamese soil in the recent conflict.

Although still in the early stages of its development, this museum has the potential to become one of the major military museums in the US. Material is being acquired steadily, and some aircraft have been obtained unrestored.

UNITED STATES AIR FORCE HISTORY AND TRADITIONS MUSEUM

AFMTC, Lackland Air Force Base, Texas 78236
Tel: 512-671-3444

Opening times: 9am-4pm Monday-Friday, 9am-6pm Saturday-Sunday
Location: about 8 miles (13 km) southwest of San Antonio off Highway 90

Beech B18S (C-45J) (SNB-2) (1942), **45 Mentor (T-34A)** (1955)
Bell 33 Kingcobra (RP-63G) (1945), **204 Iroquois (UH-1B)** (1960)
Boeing 299 Fortress (B-17G) (TB-17G) (1944), **464 Stratofortress (B-52D)** (1955)
Cessna 318 (XT-37) (1954), **337 Skymaster (0-2A)** (1963)
Consolidated 32 Liberator (B-24M) (1944)
Convair 240 (T-29B) (VT-29B) (1951), **F-102A** (1953, 1956), **TF-102A** (1956)
Curtiss JN-4D (1918)
Douglas A-26C Invader (1944), **DC-3 (C-47D) (C-47B)** (1944), **DC-6 (C-118A) (R6D-1)** (1951), **WB-66D Destroyer** (1955)
Fairchild C-119C Flying Boxcar (1951), **C-123K Provider (C-123B)** (1954)
Grumman G.64 Albatross (HU-16B) (SA-16B) (1951)
Lockheed T-33A (1951, 1952), **1049 Super Constellation (EC-121S) (C-121C)** (1954), **F-80A Shooting Star (P-80A)** (1944), **EF-80A Shooting Star (P-80A)** (1944), **YF-94A Starfire** (1948), **F-104C Starfighter** (1956, 1957)
McDonnell TF-101F Voodoo (F-101B) (1956, 1958), **F-4B Phantom** (1962)
Martin RB-57A Canberra (1954)
North American AT-6C Texan (SNJ-4) (1942), **B-25N Mitchell** (1943), **T-28A Trojan** (1949), **P-51H Mustang** (1944), **F-82E Twin Mustang (P-82E)** (1946), **EF-86A Sabre (F-86A)** (1947), **F-100A Super Sabre** (1952, 1953), **F-100C Super Sabre** (1953)
Northrop F-89A Scorpion (EF-89A) (1949), **F-5B** (c.1967), **T-38A** (1959)
Republic P-47N Thunderbolt (1944), **F-84B Thunderjet (P-84B)** (1946), **F-84C Thunderjet (P-84C)** (1947), **F-84F Thunderstreak** (1952), **F-105B Thunderchief** (1954), **F-105D Thunderchief** (1961, 1962)

Established in 1941, Lackland has provided basic military training, officer training and instruction in special tasks since 1945. In the 1950s it was decided to set up a museum which would help the airmen and officers in understanding their role in the air force.

The museum opened in October 1956 and is a major tourist attraction in the San Antonio area. Inside the museum building are a number of dioramas depicting aviation scenes from the past. These include Civil War and World War I balloon operations, some of the major battles of World War II and operations in Korea and Vietnam. There are displays of engines, instruments, models and weapons. The engine display covers the period from 1909 up to jets of the modern era. Some of the most famous power units ever built can be seen, including a Curtiss OX-5 which was installed in the famous Jenny, a 12-cylinder Liberty which was fitted in the American-built DH 4, a Wright Cyclone as used on the Boeing Fortress and an Allison V-1710 which powered models of the P-38 Lightning, P-39 Airacobra, P-40 Warhawk and P-51 Mustang. The only aircraft in the building is the uncovered airframe of a Curtiss Jenny, which clearly shows the constructional methods

This famous Consolidated Liberator bomber is shown in the World War II colors of the 93rd Bomb Group

The graceful Lockheed Super Constellation – a shape now disappearing rapidly from the skies

employed. Along one wall of the building are a number of life-size scenes from service life in the past.

The museum has about 70 aircraft on show in the open air around the camp. There are also a number of missiles on view. Immediately around the museum, eight aircraft – all jet fighters and trainers – are parked on the lawns, but by far the most interesting open-air area is the grass parade-ground on the other part of the camp, where aircraft have been arranged round the four sides according to their role. Four classic bombers repose on the southern side, two resplendent in the colorful markings that were employed during World War II. The B-17 Fortress has the black tail bars of a 388th Bomb Group aircraft which flew from Knettishall base in Suffolk, England from June 1943 to August 1945.

The Consolidated Liberator is even brighter, being adorned with yellow vertical surfaces with a black band down the center. These are the markings of the 93rd Bomb Wing which was known as 'The Traveling Circus'. The unit went to England in September 1942. The 93rd has the distinction of being the only wartime unit in the USAF which has not been deactivated since its formation. Today it flies B-52s from Castle AFB in California.

Along the rostrum side can be seen the large transport aircraft, including a Lockheed Super Constellation. Four World War II fighters, all recently restored, face the bombers. The Thunderbolt and Mustang are examples known to all enthusiasts, since both were outstanding aircraft of the conflict. In its night-flying black is a Twin Mustang. This oddity was developed as an ingenious way of producing a very long-range escort fighter at short notice. Two standard Mustang fuselages, with one standard outer wing panel on each, were joined by a new center section and tailplane. The prototype flew in April 1945, and the type was the last piston-engined fighter ordered in quantity by the USAF.

The Bell Kingcobra is another comparative rarity as a large proportion of those built in World War I were supplied to the Soviet Union. This development of the Airacobra, with its mid-mounted engine driving a propeller by means of a long shaft, was an excellent ground-attack aircraft. The fourth side of the ground has three training aircraft, including a bright yellow Texan, standing in line.

The remaining aircraft, mainly jets with a sprinkling of transports and one helicopter, are spread throughout the camp.

Virginia

MARINE CORPS AIR-GROUND MUSEUM

Quantico, Virginia 22134
Tel: 703-640-2606

Opening times: 10am-5pm Tuesday-Sunday, April-November
Location: about 25 miles (40 km) south of Washington DC just to the east of Highway 1

Beech B.18S (JRB-4) (C-45F) (1944), **B18S (C-45G)** (1953), **45 Mentor (T-34B)** (1964)
Bell 47D Sioux (HTL-2) (1950), **47D Sioux (HTL-4) (TH-13L)** (1952), **47G Sioux (HTL-6) (TH-13M)** (1956), **204 Iroquois (UH-1E)** (1967)
Boeing 67 Hawk (FB-5) (1926), **235 (F4B-3) (R?)** (1933)
Cessna 305 Bird Dog (L-19A) (0-1A) (1951)
Curtiss E-1 (R) (1975)
de Havilland DH 4 (1962)
Douglas DC-3 (C-47B) (R4D-6) (1944), **Super DC-3 (R4D-8)** (1944), **A-24B Dauntless** (1943), **XBT2D-1 Skyraider** (1946), **AD-4B Skyraider** (1951), **A-1E Skyraider (AD-5)** (1951), **A-4A Skyhawk (A4D-1)** (1952), **F-6A Skyray (F4D-1)** (1958), **EF-10B Skynight (F3D-2Q)** (1952), **D-558-I Skystreak** (?)
Grumman G.36 Wildcat (F4F-4) (1942), **G.40 Avenger (TBM-3)** (1945), **G.50 Hellcat (F6F-3)** (1945), **G.50 Hellcat (F6F-5K)** (1945), **G.51 Tigercat (F7F-3)** (1945), **G.51 Tigercat (F7F-3N)** (1945), **G.58 Bearcat (F8F-2)** (1948), **G.79 Panther (F9F-2)** (1950), **G.98 Tiger (F-11A) (F11F-1)** (1955)
Gyrodyne YRON-1 (1954)
Howard DGA.15 (GH-2) (c.1943)
Lockheed 37 Ventura (PV-1) (1942), **TV-2 (T-33A) (T-33B)** (1951), **T-1A Sea Star (T2V-1)** (1956)
McDonnell FH-1 Phantom (1947), **F2H-2P Banshee** (1949), **F-2D Banshee (F2H-4)** (1953), **F-4A Phantom** (1958), **F-4B Phantom** (1961)
Mitsubishi A6M2 Zero Sen (1943)
North American 0-47A (1938), **AT-6 Texan** (1940), **AT-6D Texan (SNJ-5)** (1944), **B-25J Mitchell** (1944), **T-28C Trojan** (1956), **FJ-3 Fury** (1953)
Pereira X-28A Osprey I (1970)
Piasecki PV.18 Retriever (HUP-2) (1953)
Sikorsky S-43 (JRS-1) (1931), **S-51 Dragonfly (HO3S-1)** (1949), **S-52 (HO5S-1)** (1952), **S-55 Chickasaw (HRS-3)** (1953), **S-58 Seahorse (HUS-1Z) (VH-34)** (1960), **S-58 Seahorse (HUS-1) (CH-34)** (1961)
Stinson V 76 Sentinel (OY-1) (1945)
Thomas Morse S4B/C (1917)
Vought FG-1D Corsair (1944), **FG-1D Corsair (FG-1D)** (1944), **F4U-4 Corsair** (1945), **F4U-5N Corsair** (1946), **F-8D Crusader (F8U-3)** (1960), **F-8K Crusader (F8U-2)** (1960)
Vultee BT-13A Valiant (1940)
Yokosuka MXY-7 Ohka 11 (1945)

The first US Marine Corps pilots started their training in 1912 and ever since then there has been a strong aviation tradition in the service. The first Marine pilot to gain his license was Alfred A Cunningham, honored in the Aviation Hall of the museum. The First Marine Aviation Force served in France in World War I flying de Havilland DH 4s and DH 9s, while another group was in the Azores flying Curtiss R-6 seaplanes. Marine aviators flew with US units in many places in the inter-war period, and served with distinction in the major conflicts since the outbreak of World War II.

Thus with a strong aviation heritage, it is no surprise that an excellent aviation museum has been set up. The site for the museum is at the Quantico base, which has been in use since World War I. The first museum, which opened at Quantico in 1940, was a collection of trophies and unit mementos. The main displays are in two hangars which were originally erected in the early 1920s on what was then Brown Field 1 at Quantico. These buildings have quite a history themselves, as in the late twenties three of the original four were moved to Managua in Nicaragua. In July 1927 Sandinistas attacked Government forces, and US Marines were soon in action. At the end of the crisis the hangars were returned to the US and now they are sited on the other side of the railway which passes through the base. The location is the former Brown Field 2, which is now the Officer School.

The early aircraft are all housed in a hangar which opened in 1979. The early days are well portrayed, with both replicas and genuine aircraft on view. The Curtiss E Pusher was the first aircraft to be purchased by the US Navy and a faithful reproduction has been constructed. Two members of the museum staff built a replica DH 4 to commemorate the work done in France by Cunningham's unit.

The Thomas Morse S-4C was a successful US Army aircraft in World War I, and some redesigned models were the first type specially built for the Marines. With a Hispano-Suiza engine instead of the original Le Rhone rotary, these MB-3s were little used. An immaculate S-4B which was the prototype of the series is on view in a typical period scene. A superbly restored Boeing FB-5 biplane fighter is on loan from the NASM. This type was first flown in 1926, and 27 were built and delivered to the US Navy. The Marines used other versions of the famous Boeing biplane fighters, including the FB-1 which served in the Expeditionary Force which went to China in 1925. A later F4B-3 with a complex history has recently been added to the display.

World War II aircraft are shown in a separate hangar, which opened in 1977. The operations in which the Marines took part are told in some detail. Some of the significant aircraft of the period are on view both inside and outside the building. Outside, a Texan is displayed in the colors of the sole example on Ewa airfield in Hawaii at the time of the 1941 Japanese attack. The Beech 18 (JRB-4) is painted to represent the personal aircraft of General William Rupertus when he was in charge of the 1st Marine Division in 1943.

The Japanese forces are honored in a special display in which the pride of place is taken by a Mitsubishi Zero fighter. This aircraft actually took part in the Pearl Harbor attack and is the only survivor of this raid. The Zero was recovered from Ballale by Bob Diemert, a Canadian aviation expert, and restored to flying condition. Also on show is a Yokosuka Ohka 11 rocket-powered suicide aircraft. The Marine aircraft are represented by the Grumman Avenger torpedo bomber, the only surviving F4F-4 model of the famous Grumman Wildcat fighter, its successor the F6F Hellcat and one of the few surviving Douglas SDB-5 Dauntless dive bombers. All these aircraft have been restored to the high standards which have been set by the museum. Examples of communications and transport aircraft of the period, and two of the famous Vought Corsair fighters with their distinctive cranked wings, complete this display.

The Marines were prominent in the Korean War, and work is going ahead to open this part of the display by 1987. Future expansion should cover the Vietnam War, but this may be restricted by lack of space. The aircraft collection now numbers over 70 and most of the types used since the 1950s have been collected. These are in store around the

museum grounds and in other hangars on the base. There is thus the basis for a complete range of aircraft depicting the modern work of the force. The museum took up its current name in 1985; this name reflects the role of the Marines more accurately, and more military vehicles and weapons are being added to complement the aircraft.

Left
Just over 700 examples of the North American Mitchell were delivered to the Marines in 1943 and 1944

Below
On loan from the NASM in nearby Washington is this Boeing FB-5 fighter

UNITED STATES ARMY TRANSPORTATION MUSEUM

Fort Eustis, Virginia 23604
Tel: 804-878-3603

Opening times: 8am-5pm Monday-Friday, 10am-5pm Saturday, midday-5pm Sunday
Location: about 11 miles (18 km) east of Williamsburg off Interstate 64

Aero Commander 520 (YL-26B) (U-9B) (1952)
Avro-Canada VZ-9V (1958)
Beech 50 Seminole (L-23D) (U-8D) (1958), **50 Seminole (RL-23D) (RU-8D)** (1959)
Bell 47A Sioux (YH-13) (1946), **47D Sioux (OH-13E)** (1951), **204 Iroquois (UH-1B)** (1961)
Cessna 305 Bird Dog (L-19E) (O-1E) (1963), **310 (L-27A) (U-3A)** (1957)
Curtiss-Wright Gem (1959)
de Havilland DHC 2 Beaver (L-20A) (U-6A) (1958), **DHC 3 Otter (U-1A)** (1955)
Doak 16 (VZ-4) (1956)
Hiller UH-12 (H-23B) (1951)
Lockheed AH-56A Cheyenne (1966)
Piasecki PV.18 Retriever (HUP-2) (H-25A) (1953), **59K Aerial Jeep (VZ-8P)** (1958)
Piper J-3C Cub (L-4) (1942), **PA-18 Super Cub (L-21)** (1952)
Sikorsky S-55 Chickasaw (UH-19C) (1951), **S-56 Mojave (CH-37B)** (1957), **S-58 Choctaw (VH-34C)** (1957), **S-60 Skycrane (YCH-54A)** (1964)
Vertol V.43 Shawnee (CH-21C) (1956)

The Doak 16 VTOL research aircraft was an experiment with ducted fan propellers, mounted at its wing tips. The pilot could adjust the angle of the propellers for vertical or horizontal flight

The slogan 'Nothing Happens Until Something Moves' is displayed prominently in this museum and is even printed on the brochure. The museum was established in 1960 in an old warehouse, and moved several times before finding a permanent and purpose-built home. The money for the building was raised by donations and handed over to the army in August 1975. The 9000 square feet (836 square meters) of exhibition space were formally opened on July 9th 1976.

Outside is a large park in which most of the aircraft are displayed, but a new aviation pavilion is now under construction. The display opens with a film tracing the history and development of transportation in the US Army, and then one can wander around the excellently presented displays which cover the last two centuries. From the horse and wagon of 1776 all modes of transport used by the army are depicted, with dioramas on the Mexican war of 1848, the Civil war, the Spanish-American war, the two World Wars, Korea and Vietnam.

Army Aviation in the US dates from 1942 when liason aircraft were used in military exercises, and from that date fixed-wing aircraft and helicopters were major tactical vehicles. In the indoor display are a number of components, engines and models of types used. The visitors can sit in a helicopter cockpit and view a slide show of operations in Vietnam.

The army has tried many ways of giving the soldier more mobility in the field and two experimental vehicles are on view. The De Lackner Aerocycle was tested in 1956 and had contra-rotating propellers. The Bell Rocket Belt was strapped round the brave soldier, who upon ignition was projected into the air, hopefully to fly over and past any obstacles in his way.

Outside are a number of fixed-wing and rotary-wing types, but there are also several interesting experimental vehicles. The Doak 16 VTOL research aircraft, which flew in 1958, featured ducted propellers at the wing tips which could be rotated through 90 degrees. Only one example was built, and this was tested at Fort Eustis. Even more futuristic is the Avro Canada VZ-9P. Looking like a flying saucer, this VTOL platform was powered by three small jets providing fan lift. The device proved uncontrollable and never rose above three feet. More successful were the two flying jeeps built by the Piasecki company. The VZ-8P-1 was tested in 1958/9 and the VZ-8P-2 in 1961/2. The aim was to produce a general utility vehicle which could carry up to 1000 lb

In the foreground is the Piasecki CH-21C tandem-rotor helicopter, with its distinctive 'banana-shaped' fuselage. Behind is the smaller Piasecki H-25, which was the forerunner of the large helicopters of today

(450 kg) of cargo at 50 mph (80 km/h) over any terrain. The two prototypes were fitted with ducted rotors, and the crew of two were seated between the two fans. Although the designs showed some promise, they were not developed further.

Among the helicopters on show is the Bell UH-1B which was the lead aircraft in a flight of three which made the first rotary-wing flight to the South Pole. The three landed there on February 2, 1963, in support of a military operation known appropriately as 'Deep Freeze'. The Sikorsky VH-34C on view is an executive model developed for carrying the US President and members of his staff. The one on show is known to have been used by John F Kennedy on his Bermuda trip in 1962.

Washington

MUSEUM OF FLIGHT

9404 East Marginal Way South, Seattle, Washington 98108
Tel: 206-767-7373

Opening times: June-September 10am-5pm daily; October-May 10am-5pm Tuesday-Saturday, midday-5pm Sunday.
Location: on the east side of Boeing Field which is about 8 miles (13 km) south of Seattle off Interstate 5

Aero Sport Scamp (c.1976)
Bede BD-5 (c.1975)
Beech B18S (C-45G) (1952)
Boeing 1 B&W (R) (1966), **40A (R)** (c.1980), **80A** (1928), **247D** (1933), **299 Fortress (B-17F)** (1942), **450 Stratojet (B-47E) (WB-47E)** (1951)
Boeing-Stearman 75 Kaydet (PT-13A) (1937)
Bowlus Baby Albatross (1940)
Convair L-13A (1946), **L-13A** (1946), **XF2Y-1 Sea Dart** (1953)
Curtiss JN-4D Jenny (1918), **JN-4C Canuck** (1917), **50 Robin**
C- 1 (1929)
Darmstadt 'Yamaha Clipper' Glider (?)
de Havilland DH 115 Vampire T.35 (1955)
Fairchild M.62 Cornell (PT-19) (1942), **M.62A Cornell (PT-26)** (1943)
Fournier RF-4D (1968)
Grumman G.36 Wildcat (FM-2) (1942), **G.93 Cougar (F9F-8)** (1954)
Gyrodyne YH-50A (1970)
Heath Parasol (1927)
Laister-Kaufmann LK.10B (TG-4A) (1943)
Lockheed TO-1 Shooting Star (F-80C) (1947)
Northrop YF-5A (1959)
Rutan Vari-Eze (c.1980)
Sorrell Parasol (1956), **SNS-7 Hiperbipe** (1975)
Taylorcraft A (1938)
Vought FG-1D Corsair (1945)
Wright Glider (R) (1902?)

The Seattle area has been the home of the Boeing company since it was founded in 1916, and the activities of William Boeing in the region's industry date back further still. Seattle's Museum of Flight was established in 1964, and acquired its first aircraft the following year when a Boeing 80A was rescued from a dump at Anchorage in Alaska and taken back to Seattle. In its first decade, the museum put on small exhibitions at the Seattle Center, also acquiring a Boeing B-47 Stratojet which was flown to Boeing Field.

Here, in 1975, the museum set up the 'Red Barn,' William Boeing's 1910 purchase in which he housed the Boeing Company in 1917. The Red Barn, a wooden building, had been derelict for years and the museum had it moved from its original location to Boeing Field. When its doors opened for an 'open house' in 1975 it drew a crowd of 20,000, ample evidence of the demand for a museum at Boeing Field. The display at the Seattle Center closed in 1979.

In the same year the local authority donated a five-acre (2 hectare) site on the east side of Boeing Field, and this is the present-day location of the Museum of Flight. After a fund-raising drive the Red Barn was fully restored and this, the first phase of the museum's development, opened on September 1, 1983. Inside the historic building is a display comprising some of the aircraft in the ever-growing collection, together with engines, models and other items.

A Boeing 80A, restored at the museum after becoming derelict in Alaska. It is the sole survivor out of the 15 examples of the three-engined airliner

The second and final phase of the current development, due to open in late 1986, is the Great Gallery, a steel-framed structure housing 20 aircraft. The Gallery stands alongside the Red Barn and also contains workshops, a library and offices.

Boeing aircraft naturally occupy a prominent place in the exhibition. In 1966, to mark the 50th anniversary of the company, a replica of the first Boeing aircraft, the B&W floatplane, was built. This flyable biplane was built by the Jobmaster Corporation, whose owner Clayton Scott was a former company test pilot. The replica had a modern engine and some minor structural differences. The Boeing 40 was designed to fulfill a Post Office requirement for a mail carrier, and the company won the right to fly on the San Francisco-Chicago route. Twenty-five 40s were built for this service, and in all 81 were constructed from 1927. The museum has built a replica fuselage of a 40A.

The Boeing 80 trimotor biplane appeared in 1928 and 16 were built. The original 80, of which four were built, was followed by 10 80As, one 80B and one 226 executive for the Standard Oil Company. The museum's aircraft is the second 80A, which was used by Boeing Air Transport and then in World War II found itself in Alaska where a large cargo door was installed in the starboard side of the fuselage. This sole remaining example of its type has been restored to static condition.

The centerpiece of the Great Gallery is a B-17 Fortress suspended from the ceiling. In the summer of 1985 an immaculate example flew in to Seattle from Arizona, where it had been in private ownership.

The Boeing 247D airliner set new standards when it was revealed in 1933. It was some 50 mph (80 km/h) faster than the types in service, and the cabin for 10 was of a degree of comfort not usually obtainable. Only four of the 75 built remain, and the museum's 247 was delivered to Pacific Air Transport in 1933. It then had a varied career with United Air Lines, the Royal Canadian Air Force and airlines in

Above
This view of a Curtiss Jenny clearly shows the constructional details. It is exhibited in the historic Red Barn

Right
In the foreground is the Curtiss Robin with its Curtiss Challenger radial engine; behind it is the Boeing-Stearman Kaydet, in the yellow-and-blue color scheme adopted by USAAC trainers in the early 1940s

Canada, Colombia and Costa Rica. In the 1950s it was a Cloud seeder and firefighter, first in Florida and then in California. The museum bought the aircraft in 1967 and it is being restored to flying condition in its passenger configuration at Paine Field.

In addition to the Boeing aircraft the museum has acquired a selection of other types and, with its latest stage of development, it is becoming one of the major collections on the west coast.

Wisconsin

EXPERIMENTAL AIRCRAFT ASSOCIATION MUSEUM

3000 Poberezny Road, Wittman Field, Oshkosh, Wisconsin 54903
Tel: 414-426-4818
Opening times: 8.30am-5pm Monday-Saturday, 11am-5pm Sunday
Location: the airfield is about 2 miles (5 km) south of the city

Aerocar I (1950)
Aeronca C-2N (1933), **C-3** (1936), **K** (1937)
American Flea Tri-Wing TC-1 (1953)
Baker Special (?)
Bates Tractor (1912)
Baumann B-290 Brigadier (1952)
Bede XBD-2 (1961), **BD-5** (1971), **BD-6** (1973)
Bee Honey Bee (1952)
Beech B17L (1934), **C18S** (1946)
Bensen B-11 (1960)
Boeing 299 Fortress (B-17G) (1944)
Brock KB-2 Gyroplane (1970)
Bücker Bü 133C Jungmeister (1935), **133C Jungmeister (R)** (1967)
Buhl LA-1 Pup (1931)
Cessna AW (1929), **CG-2** (1930), **150H** (1968), **182K** (1967)
Chanute Hang Glider (R) (?)
Chase Church JC-1 Midwing (1928)
Chester Special Jeep (1932)
Clancy Skybaby (R) (?)
Cleave EPB-1C Plank (1963)
Collins X-112 (1963)
Colomban MC-12 Cri-Cri (1983)
Corben C-1 Baby Ace (1954), **D Baby Ace Seaplane** (1958), **E Super Ace** (?)
Culver LFA Cadet (1941)
Curtiss E A-1 (1911)
Curtiss-Thompson A-1 (1911)
Curtiss JN-4D Jenny (1918), **50 Robin B-2** (1929)
Cvjetkovic CA-61 Mini-Ace (1962)
de Havilland DH 82A Tiger Moth (1942), **DH 89A Dragon Rapide** (1944)
Double Eagle V (1981)
Douglas A-26C Invader (1944), **A-1 Skyraider (AD-3)** (1949), **A-1E Skyraider (AD-5)** (1951)
Driggers L-A Sunshine Girl (1930)
Easy Rider Ultralight (c.1980)
Eipper MX Quicksilver (c.1982), **Ultralight** (c.1980)
Ercoupe 415C (1941, 1949)
Estupian-Hovey WD-II Whing-Ding (1971)
Evans VP-1 Volksplane (1970)
Experimental Aircraft Association P-2 EAA Biplane (1960), **P-5 Pober Sport** (1959), **P-8 Acrosport** (1971), **P-8A Super Acrosport** (1973), **P-9 Pober Pixie** (1974), **P-12 Acrosport II** (c.1979), **P-12 Acrosport S-1** (c.1980)
Explorer PG-1 Aqua Glider (1959)
Fairchild FC-2W (1927), **F.24-C8** (1932)
Falck Racer (1937)
Fike C (1933)
Fokker Dr I (R) (1956, 1964)
Folkert Homebuilt (?)
Folkerts Gullwing (1923)
Folkerts-Henderson Highwing (1928)
Ford 4-AT-E (1929)
Goodyear GA-22 Drake (1953), **GA-400R Gizmo** (1955)
Great Lakes 2T-1A-E (R) (1969)
Grumman G.15 Duck (J2F-6) (1944), **G.58 Bearcat (F8F-2)** (1949), **G.82 Guardian (AF-2S)** (1949)
Gunderson Burke Penguin (1971)
Halberstadt D IV (R) (c.1980)
Harlow PJC-2 (1940)
Haufe Dale 2 Hawk (1939)
Heath Feather (?), **Parasol** (?), **Super Parasol** (?)
Hegy RCHA El Chuparosa (1952)
Helisoar HP-10 (1963)
Hendershott Monoplane (1929)
Hispano HA-1112K (Bf 109G) (1954)
Hugo Hu-Go Craft VPS (1965)
Icarus Hang-glider (c.1980)
Jurca MJ.5J2 Scirroco (c.1975)
Kaminskas RK-3 Jungster III (1968)
Keith Rider R-5 Jackrabbit (1936)
Laird LCDW-500 Super Solution (R) (1980)
Langley Aerodrome (R) (?)
Lincoln PT-K (1930)
Lobet Ganagobie (1980)
Lockheed Vega 5B (1929), **12A** (1937), **P-38L Lightning** (1944), **F-80C Shooting Star (P-80C)** (1948), **T-33A** (1951, 1953)
Long LA-1 Midget Mustang (c.1950)
Lovings WR-1 Love (1950)
Luscombe 1 Phantom (1936)
Marinac Flying Mercury (1930)
Mercury BT-120 Aerobat (?)
Meyers OTW (1944), **Little Toot** (1968)
Mignet HM-360 Pou-du-Ciel (1963)
Miles M.2W Hawk Major (1935)
Mitchell Wing A-10 (c.1982)
Monnett Monnett II (c.1982), **Monex** (c.1984), **Soneral II** (1971)
Monocoupe 90A (1935), **110** (1932), **110 Special** (1932), **113** (1929)
Morane-Saulnier MS.181 (1926)
Myers PM-1 Special (?)
Nakajima Ki 43 (1942)
NASA Parasev 1A (?)
Nieuport 24 (R) (?)
Nord N.1002 Pingouin (Bf 108) (1946)
North American P-64 (1940), **AT-6D Texan** (1942), **T-6J Texan (Harvard IV)** (1952), **T-28A Trojan** (1950), **XP-51 Mustang** (1941, 1944), **P-51H Mustang** (1944), **B-25H Mitchell** (1943)
Northrop F-89J Scorpion (1953)
Oldfield Baby Great Lakes Special (1966)
Parker JP.001 (?)
Pereira Osprey II (1982)
Pfalz D XII (1918)
Pheasant H-10 (1929)
Pietenpol B4-A Camper (1933), **P-9 Scout** (1973)
Piper J-4A Cub Coupe (1940), **PA-28 Cherokee** (?), **PA-29 Papoose** (1962)
Pitts S-1S Special (c.1965), **P-6 Special** (c.1965), **SC-1 Special** (1968), **S-1S Special** (c.1970), **S-2 Special** (1966)
Player Special (1941)
Pretty Prairie Special (?)
Quickie Aircraft Quickie 1 (1979), **Quickie 2** (1982)
Rand KR-1 (1972)
Ransor 21 Balloon (?)
Rearwin 7000 Sportster (1935), **8135 Cloudster** (1940)
Republic F-84C Thunderjet (1947), **F-84F Thunderstreak** (1951)
Rotorway Scorpion I (1980)
Rutan 50-160 Vari-Viggen (1972), **Vari-Eze** (1975)
Ryan NYP-II (R) (1977), **SCW-145** (1937)
Schempp-Hirth HS-3 Nimbus (1976)
Schreder HP-18 (?)
Schweizer Glider (?)
Sikorsky S-38 (R) (?)
Smith DSA-1 Miniplane (1956)
Solar Riser (c.1982)
Sopwith Pup (R) (?)
SPAD XIII (1917)
Spartan 7W Executive (1938)
Spencer S.14 (c.1977)
Spezio Sport (c.1965)
Spinks Acromaster (1968)
Stinson SM-8A Junior (1932), **V.76 Sentinel (L-5E)** (1944), **108-3** (1949)
Stits SA-3A Playboy (1953), **SA-8 Skeeto** (1956), **SA-11 Playmate** (1963)
Stolp SA-300 Starduster Too (c.1970), **SA-500L Starlet** (c.1973)
Swallow OX-5 (1927)
Taylor E-2 Cub (1933), **JT-1 Monoplane** (c.1975)
Tessier Biplane (1965)
Thorp T-18 (1968)
Travel Air 1000 (1924), **E4000** (1929), **R (R)** (1974)
Vector 610 (?)
Volmer Jensen VJ-24W (?)
Vought F4U-4 Corsair (1944)
Waco 10 (1928), **CTO** (1929)
Warwick W-4 Hot Canary (1969)
White D-IX Der Jager (1974)
Whittaker Center Wing (?)
Wittman Bonzo (1934), **W-8 Tailwind** (1953)
Woods Woody Pusher (1967)
Wright Flyer (R) (1978)

In just over 30 years the Experimental Aircraft Association (EAA) has grown into the largest organisation of its kind in the World. In 1953 Paul H Poberezny, a retired air force colonel who took up homebuilt aircraft as a hobby, developed the practice of holding informal gatherings of friends who had built their own aircraft, for mutual exchange of ideas and advice. From these events it was realized that there was no organization in the US for the homebuilder, and the EAA was born. Later in 1953 a fly-in was held at Timmerman Field in Milwaukee and around 40 aircraft attended.

From an initial membership of eight, the EAA grew into an international organization with thousands of members. The annual fly-in became the focus for the vast membership, and the facilities (at first at Timmerman and later at Rockford) could not cope with the crowds of aircraft and people attending. In 1970 the airfield at Oshkosh in Wisconsin was selected as the permanent site for the fly-in, which had become the world's largest aviation event. At the 1985 convention an estimated million people attended and some 14,000 aircraft were present on the field. In addition to serving the homebuilt movement, the EAA has divisions for antiques and classics, warbirds and aerobatic aircraft.

The decision to establish a museum was taken in 1964 and aircraft began to gather at Hales Corner in the suburbs of Milwaukee. By the mid-1970s the collection numbered about 150, and some 75 per cent of these were on view. At this time a fund-raising drive was launched in order to expand the facilities. The headquarters of the EAA were sited at Hales Corner, and in addition the Flight Test Center was established at Burlington Airport. Several of the museum's aircraft were in flying condition, and these were kept in the two hangars at Burlington. As attendances at Oshkosh grew it was decided to move both the headquarters and the museum to Oshkosh. The ground for the new Aviation Center was broken in 1981 and for the 31st Convention, held in 1983, the magnificent building was formally dedicated. For the Convention the museum staged an impressive indoor display of about 60 aircraft, while a number of other machines from the collection were on show in the workshops and displayed around the site. Hales Corner museum remained open until the end of 1983, while aircraft were gradually moved to Oshkosh. Including aircraft on loan, around 200 machines are in the collection, and the museum has room to display only about one-third of them. The Burlington facility has been run down, with currently only two aircraft remaining.

On the other side of the field at Oshkosh is the Kermit Weeks Flight Research Center, in which over 20 of the museum's aircraft normally live. To cope with the demands of the convention, many permanent buildings have been erected around the site, and for most of the year museum aircraft are kept in these.

A new development began in 1984 on a site close to the Aviation Center. The ever-increasing number of antique and classic aircraft could not be displayed in the museum and in any case many of these were in flyable condition. Paul Poberezny decided to construct a 'Pioneer Airport' at Oshkosh. The first stage, which opened in 1985, consists of one hangar, typical of many built around America in the inter-war period; this contains about 30 aircraft from the golden era of aviation. Further hangars and a Pioneer Airport Village are planned, and the whole site is to develop into a period airfield.

On entering the museum the first aircraft one encounters are three Pitts Special biplanes, mounted in a 'bomb burst' configuration – a reminder of the excitement these aerobatic machines have created at many airshows. In the Hilton Aviation Theater, films on the background of the EAA and the museum give the visitor an insight into what may be seen, as well as the hard work which has gone into the organization.

Homebuilt aircraft are the central theme of the exhibition, and one of the first aircraft viewed is a replica of the most famous 'homebuilt' ever constructed. This is a faithful copy of the 1903 Wright Flyer which made powered flight a reality.

The aircraft most closely associated with the start of the EAA is the Baby Ace of 1954. The original Ace series of aircraft, designed by OG Corben, appeared in the 1930s and from his modest factory at Madison, Wisconsin, both complete aircraft and kits were offered for sale. In 1954 Paul Poberezny redesigned and updated the plans, and *Mechanix Illustrated* published full details in three parts. On the cover was the slogan 'Build this plane for under $800 including engine'. This immediately brought worldwide interest and changed the course of the EAA and the homebuilding movement in general. Since that date many other original designs have come from the EAA team, and plans have been supplied to would-be constructors.

Another homebuilt exhibit is the prototype EAA P-2 biplane, constructed over a three-year period from 1957 by students of St Rita's High School, Chicago. Paul Poberezny and Jim Stewart had designed the P-2 so that it could be built by students with little prior knowledge of aircraft construction. Also on view is a low-wing EAA P-5 Pober Sport which in 1960 made a 13,500 mile (21,700 km) tour of the US. Flown by Anders Ljunberg of Sweden, the P-5 visited all the local EAA Chapters in a 30-day flight. The P-5 design consisted of a modified Corben Baby Ace fuselage, shortened wings from a Luscombe 8A and an undercarriage adapted from a Piper Cub.

The homebuilt aircraft on display clearly demonstrate the vast strides in design occurring over the last few decades. The transition from wood and fabric to modern composite materials is aptly demonstrated by the Baby Ace and the Vari-Eze. The latter, designed by Burt Rutan, was the outstanding design at the 1975 Convention. With its canard (tail first) configuration and outstanding performance, the Vari-Eze attracted such interest that plans of a slightly larger version were made available. In 1975 the prototype set a closed course distance record, flying 1638 miles (2636 km) in just over 13 hours on 40 gallons (151.4 liters) of fuel. A larger, longer-range version, the Long-EZ, is now offered and almost 5000 have been built or are under construction. The Vari-Eze has been one of the most influential designs in the last decade, and many aircraft of similar concept and construction are now appearing.

The Warbird section contains some high-powered machines that contrast with most of the rest of the display. Pride of place is occupied by the fourth North American Mustang produced, which was also the first to see service with the USAAC. The Mustang was designed to a British requirement for an advanced fighter. North American came up with a proposal and were given 120 days by the British to deliver. The airframe was completed three days before the deadline, but it was almost two months later before the engine was available. The fourth and tenth Mustangs were supplied to the USAAC for evaluation. Over 15,000 Mustangs were produced over the next few years, and the type was probably the most versatile fighter of World War II. This historic aircraft was stored at the National Air and Space Museum (NASM) for a period before it was acquired by the EAA Foundation. Darrell Skurich restored the Mustang in Colorado and it was flown regularly until, in August 1982, Paul Poberezny took it aloft for the last time.

Aircraft from Germany and Japan can also be seen in this section. A Spanish-built Messerschmitt Bf 109 which flew in the 'Battle of Britain' film was donated to the museum, and a Nakajima Ki 43 is on loan from the NASM. The Ki 43, known as 'Oscar' by the Allies, was the prime fighter of the Japanese Army Air Force, and over 6000 were built. The example on show was restored to its former glory by volunteers from the Wisconsin Air National Guard and EAA members.

The museum also has an Antique and Classic section. This contains a Curtiss Jenny trainer from World War I, restored in 1967 by Daniel and Vona Neuman to such a high standard and to original state that at the 1981 Convention it was the Pioneer Age champion. A genuine World War I fighter on show is a Pfalz D XII which appeared in the film 'Dawn Patrol' in the 1930s and other Hollywood epics, and is one of four survivors of the type.

A Lockheed Vega, painted in the exact colours of the famous 'Winnie Mae' used by Wiley Post on his round-the-world, inter city speed and high altitude flights, is on loan from David Jameson of Oshkosh. (The genuine Winnie Mae is in the NASM in Washington.) Nearby, a beautiful red biplane is the oldest Beech aircraft surviving. This B17L 'Staggerwing' was the third of its type to fly, and the first with a retractable undercarriage and automatic engine starting. The aircraft was neglected after 1951 but in 1980 Richard Perry and Richard Hansen acquired it and it appeared at the 1983 convention in the condition in which it had left the Wichita factory half a century before.

The International Aerobatic Club is a special division of the EAA and some of the outstanding types used in this sport are shown. In addition there are models and a Frasca Flight Simulator to enable visitors to appreciate the art. The German Bücker Jungmeister, which first flew in 1935, was one of the best aircraft ever designed for aerobatics, and in the hands of many noted pilots it was still winning contests some quarter of a century after its first flight. This graceful biplane is mounted in a flying attitude to show its lines to the best effect.

The Pitts Special dominated contests in the 1960s and 1970s, and besides the three single-seaters in the entrance hall, the two-seater version is shown in the main museum. This first appeared in public at the 1966 Convention at Rockford.

In the late 1960s 'Pappy' Spinks was President of the Aerobatic Club of America, and a driving force behind the sport. He designed the Spinks Acromaster, which was the first US monoplane specifically made for aerobatics, and in the hands of Charlie Hillard the Acromaster was in the US team that won the 1970 and 1972 World Team Championship.

Air racing exhibits occupy a special corner of the museum. Three aircraft are mounted around a pylon, simulating a turn in a contest, while three more are on the ground. Steve Wittman of Oshkosh started racing in 1926 and won many honours, competing in every Cleveland National Air Race from 1928 to 1949. The small 'Bonzo' monoplane of 1934, with its 435 hp Curtiss D-12 engine, had a speed of over 325 mph (520 km/h) and was the very first aircraft to be donated to the EAA foundation.

The 'Air Challengers' gallery shows innovative aircraft, some of which have set records, such as the Thorp T-18 which in 1976 became the first homebuilt to fly around the world. After completing this epic voyage, the builder and pilot, Don Taylor, flew the T-18 to Australia and New Zealand in 1980, and in 1983 he flew it over the North Pole, arriving back on the last day of the Convention to retire his aircraft to the museum.

'Homebuilder's Corner' shows the tools and techniques needed for the construction of an aircraft, and the Stits Overlook (named after Ray Stits who has designed many aircraft) allows the visitor to view the restoration work going on in the workshops. Other displays of art, publishing, engines and models make this exhibition a superb experience.

A short walk to the Pioneer Airport will enable some of the greatest sporting aircraft of the 1920s and 1930s to be seen in their true environment. Some of the greatest names of American aviation appear here: Monocoupe, Stinson, Spartan, Waco, Rearwin, Ryan and Aeronca are just a few. With such a vast range of exhibits, Oshkosh is very much on the map for the aviation enthusiast, and a visit there is an unforgettable experience.

An aerial view of the first hangar to be constructed at the Pioneer Airport. Only the modern cars show that this is not a 1930s scene

Above
This rare Wright-powered Waco CTO is an example of the famous 'taperwing' biplanes from Waco's Ohio factory

Left
The famous Oshkosh aviator Steve Wittman designed the powerful Bonzo in 1934, and it raced successfully until 1939

The Spartan Executive was the first four-place all-metal monoplane to be sold in the US. Thirty-four were built between 1936 and 1940

Right
In the entrance hall to the EAA Aviation Center, these three Pitts Specials are mounted in a typical aerobatic pose

Below
The prototype EAA P-2 Biplane, built in 1957 by students at Chicago, heralded a new era in the homebuilding movement

Index to Collections

166
E